THE LUCK OF O'REILLY

BY IVAN FALLON

A Biography of Tony O'Reilly

WARNER BOOKS

A Time Warner Company

Warner Books, Inc., 1271 Avenue of the Americas, New York, NY 10020

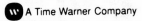 A Time Warner Company

Printed in the United States of America
First U.S. Printing: November 1994
10 9 8 7 6 5 4 3 2 1

Library of Congress Cataloging-in-Publication Data

Fallon, Ivan.
    The luck of O'Reilly : a biography of Tony O'Reilly / Ivan Fallon.
        p.   cm.
    ISBN 0-446-51782-8
    1. O'Reilly, Tony.   2. Businessmen—United States—Biography.
3. Businessmen—Ireland—Biography.   4. Chief executive officers—
United States—Biography.   5. H.J. Heinz Company—History.
I. Title.
HC102.5.O74F35   1994
338.7'664'0092—dc20   94-27469
    [B]   CIP

Book design by Giorgetta Bell McRee

Contents

List of Illustrations

A Wagner; The young Heinz executive in England, *Thomson Newspapers*; Gookin made O'Reilly president of Heinz, *H J Heinz Co. Ltd*; The key management team, *Associated Photographers Inc*; Annual General Meetings in two countries, *Lensmen*; In 1979, O'Reilly succeeded Gookin to become cheif executive, *H J Heinz Company*.

Castlemartin, on the banks of the Liffey; *Dr O'Reilly private collection*; The entrance hall has seen many parties, *Susan Fallon*; Key men in O'Reilly's life . . ., *Frank Farrell*; Different places, different places. *The Irish Times, H J Heinz Company*; Henry Kissinger . . . a renaissance man, *H J Heinz Company*; The Ireland Fund, *Press Association*; Family Business in Australia, *Susan O'Reilly*; Three O'Reilly boys, *family collection*; Oldest friend, Jim McCarthy, *Lensmen*.

Marriage to Chryss Goulandris, On her wedding day in the Bahamas, Watching the local rugby in County Cork, in Sydney . . . Newspaper Publishing; *Dr and Mrs O'Reilly*; Founders of Weight-watchers, *Peter T Kane 1981*; Olive Deasy, *H J Heinz Company*; Key men at Heinz, *Associated Photographers*; The player, a drawing in oils, *Derek Hill*.

Acknowledgments

I first saw Tony O'Reilly at Lansdowne Road in January 1956, when he played for a combined Ireland–Scotland team against England–Wales. I was an 11-year-old schoolboy, but I can still remember vividly his red auburn hair contrasting so startlingly against the green of the immaculate turf as he trotted out on to the pitch. He was superb that day, scoring two classic tries, rounding the Welsh fullback at such blistering speed that, as one commentator wrote the next day, one shuddered at the very thought of trying to stop him. Not yet twenty, he was already our schoolboy hero, the man who in South Africa the summer before had set a try-scoring record for the British Lions which has never been beaten (sixteen tries in fifteen matches); in full flight, his long legs pumping and his fourteen stone headed at Olympic pace for the line, he was one of the great sights of the sporting world.

I first actually met him in London twenty years later, by which stage he was an Irish legend for other reasons: he was now the man who had launched Kerrygold butter, bailed out the Irish Sugar Company and rocketed to the top of H J Heinz in Pittsburgh. He also had business and newspaper interests in Ireland which were bringing him his share of problems and controversy. There were rumours at the time he was about to return home for a career in Irish politics, but he remained in the business world, probably wisely—today he is Ireland's richest man, and probably its best-known personality.

The idea of writing a biography of him came not from me or from him but from Eric Major of Hodder & Stoughton who had known O'Reilly for some time. I was keen to do it, particularly as O'Reilly's early background, and the influences and education he was subjected to—with some notable exceptions—was very similar to my own. My father knew O'Reilly's father; they were not friends but they were born within a year of each other, joined the Irish Customs service in the early 1920s at almost the same time, and would occasionally see each other, sometimes in a professional capacity, over the next forty years. My father saw the job as a useful sinecure which allowed him time to write his poetry and plays, but Jack O'Reilly, ambitious and energetic, rose to the top. To both men, the 1916 Rising, the creation of the Irish Free State and the civil war that followed it were not just history, but events they actually lived through. Tony grew up, as I did, steeped in his country's culture and history, from the ruthlessly efficient massacres carried out by Cromwell through Catholic Emancipation, Redmond, the Treaty and the creation of Northern Ireland. An understanding of this heritage is essential to an understanding of what has shaped—and still drives—Tony O'Reilly, and I have dwelt on it for that reason.

This is not O'Reilly's 'approved' book; it is *my* book, written with his co-operation but not necessarily his full agreement. He read it in manuscript and if he 'approved' parts, he equally 'disapproved' of others. I interviewed him over many hours in his two houses in Ireland, Castlemartin and Glandore, in the Bahamas, in Pittsburgh and in London where I live. He allowed me free and unfettered access to his family: to his wife Chryss who patiently put up with the many times I interrupted what should have been their private weekends together; to his former wife Susan; to his children; and of course to his friends and colleagues. But we had agreed in advance that he would have no control over what I put in the book, other than the most private details of his personal life which affect only him and those closest to him. Otherwise, he could comment—and he has, at times forcibly—but he could not change. He dislikes my interpretation of some of the events described in here, notably some aspects of his Irish business interests. I have made alterations where I have accepted I was factually inaccurate, but otherwise the material has stayed, and having made his protest he has accepted with good grace. He is not a man who sulks. For legal reasons I cannot dwell, as I would like to have done, on the battle for Fairfax in Australia, which is becoming, at the time of going to the printers, one of the biggest court battles in Australian legal history. It will have to await a later edition of the book.

The early history of his father in this book was as much a revelation to O'Reilly as it was to me—he knew only the bare outline of it, none of the detail. Even today, Jack O'Reilly's life would have been an occasion for comment, but in the context of 1930s Catholic Ireland it was many times more dramatic. It was also desperately poignant, and I am grateful to Jack's first family for making available his letters, photographs and other material, and for talking about events which are still painful for them, and which I suspect they would much rather had stayed buried. O'Reilly's first cousin and close friend, Fr John Geary, also provided some helpful insights into the family.

This book is the work of over three years and about 120 interviews. One of the joys of writing about O'Reilly is that he was, even as a small boy, already memorable, and there was a wealth of material available on him from the earliest days. Childhood friends such as John McKone, Joe McAleese, Paddy Masterson, Sam Stephenson, Kevin McGoran, Dr Karl Mullen and Tony Twomey have all talked about his childhood years, and the *Belvederean* was an invaluable source of information on his school career. Jim McCarthy, Niall Brophy, Cecil Pedlow, Ronnie Dawson, Andy Mulligan and others were prepared to talk almost indefinitely about his rugby, although in the end I came to rely more on contemporaneous match reports and the books written on the Lions tours of 1955 and 1959 than I did on faded—and sometimes exaggerated—memories. The story of the Ben Hur episode, which I believe is the definitive one, is taken from a tape of an interview the actor Noel Purcell gave before he died. Joe McGough was a fount of knowledge on Bord Bainne and the launch of Kerrygold, and Vincent Ferguson and Nicholas Leonard recalled in great detail the early story of Fitzwilton; Liam Healy, David McGrath and others did the same on the Independent.

In Pittsburgh and the United States I interviewed too many people to mention individually, but I am particularly grateful to David Sculley, Don Wiley, William P Snyder III, Al Lippert, Luigi Ribolla, Dave Williams, Dr Richard Cyert, Jay Connolly, George Greer, Dick Wamhoff, Ned Churchill, Dick Beattie, Ralph Johnson and of course Ted Smyth who has taken the keenest interest in this project all the way through. I am also immensely grateful to Olive Deasy, who first joined O'Reilly in Cork in 1961 as his secretary and probably knows more about him than anyone alive; and to Arthur Whelan, O'Reilly's driver.

I was also fortunate in the fact that since the age of eighteen there has scarcely been a year without a major interview or profile of him in one or another magazine or newspaper, and as the years went on they became more and more frequent. I am grateful to those who put them together for me, and to Marion Fitzgerald, Julia Bright, Arwen Burrett, Jonathan Davis, Sue Wilgoss and my daughter, Lara Fallon, for helping with research and the tedious work of transcription. I have also freely dipped into Eleanor Foa Dienstag's excellent new history of Heinz, *In Good Company*.

I could not have written this book without the help and support of Sue Fallon who, as she has done with all my books, did most of the hard work, managing the research and organizing files, interviews and the team of transcribers for the numerous taped interviews. Credit is also due to Sue for much of the photographic research and for some of the originals of Castlemartin. My brother Brian read and corrected my own rusty Irish history. Finally a special note of thanks to Richard Cohen who started off with me on this venture, and to Rowena Webb with whom I finished it.

IVAN FALLON
LONDON, JUNE 1994.

1

Double Life

BY THE STANDARDS OF HIS GENERATION, AND OF HIS NATIVE IRELAND, Tony O'Reilly's father led a remarkable double life. He was christened John Patrick, but worked all his life for the Irish government under the name Patrick John. His family name was Reilly rather than O'Reilly, and he was born in the town of Drogheda on 14 March 1906, rather than 1903, which was what he put on his application form when he joined the Irish civil service in 1925. Patrick John (or Paddy) was his older brother, born three years before him. John Patrick (or Jack as he was usually known) was too young at the time to be accepted by the civil service, so he adopted his elder brother's name and age. For reasons which are obscure, he later added an 'O' to the family name. So, in his early twenties, John Patrick Reilly became Patrick John O'Reilly, aged twenty-one rather than eighteen. For over forty years, as he rose to the top of the Irish Customs and Excise service, Jack never disturbed the official records. He even retired, on full pension, when he was sixty-two rather than sixty-five—at a time when early retirement was almost unknown.

It was a relatively harmless subterfuge, employed by Reilly (as he still was) to land one of the precious civil service jobs in the fledgling Irish Free State. In the Ireland of the mid-1920s there were not many careers open to a nineteen-year-old boy with an indifferent education. He had no hope of going to university because he could never afford it, even if he passed the entrance examinations. The civil service offered security, respectability and, for a young man

stranded on a farm which he detested, even excitement. So Jack went
for it, applying under the name of his brother; he turned up for an
interview, sat an examination for which he had studied night and
day, and was offered the post of trainee Customs officer. He would
not move—except upwards—for the rest of his working life.

Jack O'Reilly was not cut out to work on a farm. His family were
townspeople, an ordinary enough Irish Catholic family who had
moved up the social ladder by dint of hard work and modest entrepreneurial flair. When his father, John Reilly, married Margaret
McIver on 3 September 1899, he listed his profession as 'carman'.
He probably plied his trade with a horse and cart in Drogheda,
operating in what was then a busy little port on the estuary of the
Boyne, straddling the main Dublin-to-Belfast road and railway line.
Margaret—or Maggie—gave her profession as 'servant' and that of
her father as 'carpenter'; Jack's grandfather also put down 'carman'
against his profession.

The Reillys seem to have been both hard-working and ambitious,
and certainly quick to grasp new opportunities. In 1899 'carman'
implied a horse-drawn vehicle, but within a few years it was to mean
something else. By the time Jack, his fifth child and third son, was
born seven years later, John Reilly had become, according to the
birth certificate, a 'car-owner'. In fact the car he bought was used as
a taxi, and for every other purpose he could find for it, from funerals
to weddings. Several years after that he had become a 'garage-owner'
with 'John Reilly & Sons' above the door, owner of one of the petrol
pumps in the town. He had also expanded his taxi business to include
a funeral parlour, and owned several cars at a time when a motor
vehicle on the Irish roads was so rare as to be a cause of some wonder.
In addition he bought and sold cars, and when the British company
Vauxhall (later owned by General Motors) moved into Ireland, John
Reilly acquired the agency for the county of Louth.

Drogheda was a large town by Irish standards. In Reilly's day it had
a population of about twenty thousand, with a harbour, breweries,
ironworks and a large cement factory. All around Jack O'Reilly as
he grew up were the scars of its turbulent history, which was also
Ireland's history, and which was drilled into him at school, told to
him by the priests, his parents, uncles and townspeople, and which
he in turn would pass on to his son. Some of it was almost fable: St
Patrick was said to have landed at nearby Colp on his way up the
Boyne valley to Tara, where he began Ireland's 'golden age', con-

verting the whole island to Christianity in a generation and establishing it for several centuries as the 'land of saints and scholars'. In the tenth century Drogheda was first a Danish stronghold and then Anglo-Norman. Later, it was the northern edge of the Pale, which was the area around Dublin subject to English law. In the seventeenth century it was used by the English armies as an assembly point as they marched into Ulster to subdue the rebellious Irish chieftains, the O'Neills and O'Donnells. The remains of the old walls, which had withstood several notable sieges, were young Jack's playground, but they were also a stark reminder of one of the grimmest events in Ireland's grim history. Jack grew up with the emotive story of how Oliver Cromwell selected Drogheda for his most barbarous slaughter in all of Ireland, when he killed two thousand of the three thousand defenders. Afterwards, so Jack learned at school, Cromwell offered up thanks to the Almighty for his mercies, and then shipped the survivors off to Barbados.

He also learned of some of the other epoch-making events which had taken place in the town. Thirty years after Cromwell, Drogheda was taken again, this time by King William of Orange on the day after his fateful battle of the Boyne which was to set the stage for so much that would happen—and indeed is still happening—in Ireland. Its defender that day was Lord Iveagh of the Guinness family, whose successor many generations later would feature in Tony O'Reilly's life. Of the town that Jack knew as a boy, the only remnant of the original fortifications was St Lawrence's Gate on the east side, with its two lofty drum-towers and loopholed connecting wall, but these were enough to enable him to visualize how it had once been. In the main church, with its massive tower and spire, there was another grisly memory, which every schoolboy was taken to see: the embalmed head of the Blessed Oliver Plunket, Archbishop of Armagh (since St Patrick's time, the head of the Catholic Church in Ireland), who had been taken to London and hanged at Tyburn in 1681 for his part in what was known as the 'Popish Plot'.

That was the dead history of the place, but there was plenty of living history too. Jack's childhood was a time of great change in Ireland, when the days of British rule were coming to an end amid a rising tide of civil and military resistance. After six hundred years of English rule Ireland was on the cusp of becoming a nation again— but a nation divided by religion and class, and, by the time Jack was in his teens, by a formal line on the map as well. In 1912, when he was six, the House of Commons finally passed a Home Rule Bill under which Ireland, including Ulster, would be self-governing while remaining part of the British Empire. It was what many Catholic families such as the Reillys had dreamed of, but their elation was subdued: forty years earlier Gladstone had introduced the first Home Rule Bill, which had failed, as had another one since. No one underestimated the power of the Conservatives, and the threat of the Ulster Protestants led by Sir Edward Carson, to wreck this one. Home rule in any case fell short of the fully fledged republic which an increasing number of Catholics now sought. In the event the bill was defeated in the House of Lords, preventing it becoming law for two years. Jack was seven when the framework for what was intended as a temporary division of Ireland was put in place in bitter circumstances: in January 1913, under Carson's influence, an Ulster Volunteer Force was formed which threatened the British government with civil war, and a year later the bill was amended to allow six Ulster counties to opt out. And he was eight when the force was formed which was to grow, with many splits and changes of direction, into the IRA: the Irish Volunteers, Dublin's response to the Ulster Volunteers. By then Britain was at war with Germany and all around Jack young Irishmen, Catholic and Protestant, went off to fight, as they had done for centuries, in a British army. The Home Rule Bill received Royal Assent in September 1914, but its implementation was suspended until the end of hostilities.

In 1916, when Jack O'Reilly was ten, an event occurred which changed the history of the country forever, finally dashing the hopes of the moderate Irish Parliamentary party—and of the British government—that Ireland might achieve a peaceful evolution into a Canadian or Australian type of Commonwealth status. The Easter Rising in Dublin, and the execution of its leaders afterwards, marked a turning point in British rule. What was intended as a nationwide rising went off at half-cock and became instead a relatively small insurrection in Dublin alone. But a thousand men seized the General Post Office building in O'Connell Street, raised the flag of the Irish Republic, and held out for a week against twenty thousand British troops. At first greeted with dismay and apathy by the Catholic population, the rising soon raised the spirit of Irish nationalism in a way that made it unstoppable. 'The tale was told gradually, and gradually Ireland . . . found Irish heroism to admire, and started back towards its heroic past,' wrote P. S. O'Hegarty (*A History of Ireland Under the*

Union, 1801 to 1922—Methuen & Co.). The poet W. B. Yeats was inspired to write perhaps his most memorable poem;

> *All changed, changed utterly:*
> *A terrible beauty is born.*

Even in 1916, Drogheda was near enough to Dublin for the events of that fateful week to overshadow everything else in the Reilly household and at school. Jack lived with the sight of British troops travelling through the town on the Belfast train. He would also have seen the artillery and other heavy weapons being brought up, and could not have escaped the increased level of military activity in the town. Republican and anti-British slogans were daubed on walls and railway arches, and newspapers and posters provided an hour-by-hour account of events in Dublin. After the rising, the Reilly family felt the same lift in republican fervour as did large tracts of the Catholic population, demanding as never before the urgent end of British occupation.

The events of 1916 meant that, even though the Home Rule Act had become law, home rule was no longer an option. The opposition from the Northern Protestants, and the growing level of resistance in the South, killed it. The Sinn Fein party, led by the man who was to dominate Irish politics throughout much of Jack's life, Eamon de Valera, wanted full independence and sought it through political means, while the Irish Volunteers, now known as the Irish Republican Army, sought it militarily. The Ulster Protestants resisted it in every way they could, while in London the government of the day could not decide what to do.

The years between the end of World War I and the formal acceptance of the Irish Free State in 1922 would always be known as 'the Troubles', a phrase that Tony O'Reilly's father often used. It was a formative time for a lad in his early teens. Jack Reilly grew up aware of the near-adulation felt for Michael Collins, an exuberant and clever militant who had played a major role in setting up the Irish Volunteers before the war, and was now the leading figure in the IRA. From June 1919 Collins, who had fought in the Easter Rising and been jailed afterwards, was the IRA's highly effective director of intelligence, dominating the guerrilla effort against a British army which was growing desperate. Britain's immediate objective was to win the guerrilla war and then get out, imposing a political solution which would still keep Ireland within the empire, and would set the pattern for other countries, notably India, which were militating for independence at this time.

This was also the time of the notorious Black and Tans, eye-witness accounts of whose brutal excesses were legion when Tony O'Reilly was growing up. Winston Churchill had overall responsibility for the provision of troops in Ireland during the 1916 rising, and after the war, as Home Secretary, he despatched not only more regular troops but also irregulars, war veterans who were hastily recruited and sent in as half police/half soldier, with a uniform which reflected the ambivalence—hence their nickname, the Black and Tans. Essentially they were poorly disciplined but well-armed thugs, let loose in the hope that they would accomplish what the more disciplined regular troops could not. In the absence of any clear political policy for a situation which seemed insoluble, the British government tried to fight violence with violence. But despite the Black and Tans it was half-hearted: the government sanctioned martial law but denied its own forces the powers to implement it. The Black and Tan experiment rebounded savagely: they were neither numerous nor clever enough to win the war, but they were visible and brutal enough for their atrocities to turn the weight of Irish opinion in favour of the nationalists. More importantly, they also outraged British liberal opinion, and their exploits were reported and exaggerated around the world where colonialism, particularly British colonialism, had gone hugely out of fashion. In America and elsewhere there was a growing clamour for the British to get out and leave Ireland for the Irish. De Valera spent eighteen months in the United States where he raised large sums of money from communities indignant about the tales he related. The British were both losing the propaganda war and failing utterly to crush the rebellion.

The aftermath of World War I and the events leading up to Ireland's independence were, however, by no means a period of glorious nationalism. In February 1920 Lloyd George finally passed the Government of Ireland Act, but it was a total surrender to the Ulster Protestants, formally establishing a six-county Northern Ireland. Partition now existed on a map, the lines drawn between the Protestant North and the Catholic South just 35 miles north of Drogheda. Louth, where old John Reilly sold his Vauxhall cars and Bedford vans, was in the South. The activities of the IRA, as active in Drogheda as anywhere in the whole country, were largely confined to ambushes and raids, usually directed against the Royal Irish Constabulary rather than the British army. They were also increasingly directed at the Protestants in the North. The Protestants retaliated by excluding Catholics from their places of work in Belfast; and in Dublin Sinn Fein ('Ourselves Alone'), led by de Valera, further increased the tension by starting a boycott against Belfast goods, with the avowed intention of bringing Northern business to its knees. The boycott, rigidly enforced, must have made John Reilly's business life difficult: its effects were considerable, further widening the division between North and South, Catholic and Protestant. 'It was merely a blind and suicidal contribution to the general hate,' said O'Hegarty, one of Sinn Fein's idealistic thinkers. It killed, possibly forever, any chance of a union between the two sides.

So Tony O'Reilly's father grew up in a period of general hate and violence, of a war of terror and revenge throughout a country which was in the twilight of British rule, and whose successful fight for independence would mark the beginning of the long decline of the power of the British Empire. O'Hegarty called the period 'the last days of captivity', and the young Jack, like the vast majority of Irish Catholics, must have seen it that way too. There were bombs, murders and skirmishes all around Drogheda—and atrocities on both sides. Collins ruthlessly weeded out informers in the IRA and executed them. Considerable damage was also caused to property and business: during the Troubles the IRA burned down some of the finest houses of the Anglo-Irish Protestant minority, and the British forces hit back with martial law, executions and mass jailings. Jack grew to manhood resenting the British, probably hating the Protestants in the North, and knowing many friends and neighbours involved in the fighting— though there is no evidence that any of the Reilly family were themselves active militarily.

In 1921, unable to find a political solution, the British government stepped up its military campaign to bring the IRA to its knees, but finally accepted the inevitable. In July, with the South African Prime Minister Jan Smuts acting as mediator, Lloyd George negotiated a truce with Collins. Talks on a political solution now began in earnest, with Lloyd George insisting that the Irish must accept membership of the British Empire and the nationalist Sinn Fein rejecting it. The divisions within the Irish ranks were almost as great as those with Britain and the Ulster Protestants. Arthur Griffith, probably the leading Irish statesman of the day, and Michael Collins, who was a political pragmatist as well as a charismatic military leader, were prepared to accept dominion status on the Canadian principle, but de Valera and Sinn Fein insisted on full control of the whole country's foreign and tax policy, including that of the Protestant North.

On 6 December 1921 Griffiths and Collins signed a formal treaty which gave Ireland its dominion status; the Northern Irish Presbyterians, however, were not a party to it, and were allowed to petition the Crown to leave. The Irish Free State was to be a Catholic state for a Catholic people, the North a Protestant state for a Protestant people. Even in the South there was bitter division which, with the British gone, would rise to fresh heights in a civil war. When Jack Reilly was sixteen, the Free State held its first election; the fight was essentially between those who accepted the Free State controlling just twenty-six counties with dominion status, led by Collins and Griffith, and the anti-treatyists, led by de Valera, who would accept nothing less than a republic for the whole thirty-two counties, run from Dublin. The pro-treaty candidates won and their party took its first momentous decision: it would move against the anti-Treaty IRA.

The year which followed the birth of the new state was as bloody as anything in Ireland's recent history, with both sides committing atrocities as appalling as anything perpetrated by the Black and Tans. Collins rooted the IRA out of Dublin and drove them down into the south-west, but by August 1922 he was dead, killed in an ambush in his native west Cork. Griffith was dead, too—of a cerebral haemorrhage; the two founders of the Free State went within ten days of each other. But de Valera was forced to accept defeat for his republican ideal 'for the moment', and at last there was an uneasy peace; however the two sides of Ireland were now permanently divided and the conditions had been created for many decades of tension.

No family in Ireland could stand aside or be unaffected by the enormous upheaval that formed the backdrop to Jack Reilly's first seventeen years. Until 1914 life in Drogheda was calm enough, with the move towards home rule essentially a political rather than a guerrilla process. John Reilly's business had ups and downs, but the ups were in the majority and the house and business premises occupied a large part of Mayoralty Street. Jack's mother is remembered as the brains and driving force of the business, taking more control, with her son Paddy, as the year passed. 'I remember being struck by her as being a very intelligent woman,' says one member of the family. 'She was very well presented and well spoken, with beautiful features and beautiful bone structure—much better-looking than her son Jack, who had a heavy nose.' The family now lived in a large house near the centre of the town, increasingly middle-class in a time of major social as well as political change in Ireland. Trade unions and socialism in the years before World War I gained considerable support among urban workers and agricultural labourers. In 1907 Belfast was caught up in the longest industrial dispute Ireland had ever seen; led by the carters, it resulted in a lock-out. The young Jack may well have stood on the edge of one of the gatherings held by the Irish trade union leader James Connolly as he set up branches of his National Union of Dock Labourers in all the ports along the east coast, including Drogheda. Then in 1913 Connolly and James Larkin led a strike of the Irish Transport and General Workers' Union in Dublin, which was more prolonged and bitter even than the Belfast dispute. The spokesman for the Dublin employers was William Martin Murphy, a prominent home ruler and owner of the *Irish Independent* newspaper, which would later feature centrally in the life of Tony O'Reilly.

The Easter Rising in 1916, when he was ten, must inevitably have raised Jack's political and nationalist awareness. The Troubles touched Drogheda in much the same way that they touched other parts of Ireland, but were magnified there because of the town's halfway position between Dublin and what was to become the North.

Jack Reilly was of the generation of Irish men and women who probably lived through more change than any other, before or since. Every Catholic Irishman of his age, born under British rule—therefore technically a British citizen—and reaching adulthood as the new nation came into being, would be moulded by it for life. Each man would have a curious love–hate relationship with the British, but also a lingering feeling of inferiority to a country which had once been its master. Jack would later reminisce with his son about the Troubles, the Black and Tans, and the activities of the guerrillas, a number of whom would become almost fabled heroes to the local populace. Jack might not have held a gun, but he, like everyone of his age, was a part of it.

Jack had other problems in his adolescent years. For one thing, he did not get on well with his father, who had different ambitions for his restless, and probably rebellious, son. Jack's eldest sister, Mary, married another customs man and the second eldest, Cathleen or

Kitty, studied social science at Trinity College, Dublin before becoming a nun; she went to India in 1936, and did not return until 1970. Of the boys, young Jack was probably the brightest academically in a family not very interested in education. His elder brother Michael married an English girl and returned to Dublin where he and his wife Sybil ran a small store and would later be a major part of young Tony O'Reilly's growing up. The second son, Paddy, would eventually take over the garage which he ran for years with his mother after John died; there was a younger brother, Dermot, who became a successful small-town businessman, with betting shops, the Brown Derby pub and the Bonbon café in Dublin, plus what his family called 'upmarket catering services' at race meetings.

When Jack and his father had a major quarrel, Maggie Reilly decided to get him out of the home with a traditional Irish solution: she sent him to live with an old uncle who was a farmer and had no children. Her son, she reasoned, would work and learn from him, and would eventually inherit the land. Jack, who was a town boy and knew nothing about farming, went reluctantly and hated every second of it, developing a lifelong abhorrence for cows and the smell of dung. He must have thought about emigrating to America, common among Irishmen since the Great Famine eighty years before, or even to Britain—anything to get out.

But there was another opportunity closer to home. In 1922, when Jack was sixteen, Michael Hayes, the new Speaker of the Dáil (the lower house of Parliament), announced that the new state was seeking bright young men to join the civil service. Britain had left behind an efficient and well-trained civil service, with many of the top positions filled by Irishmen. No one thought to change it, or to design a new model, as would many other countries emerging into independence later. 'Britain appeared to be the greatest power in the world, still the biggest empire, recent victor in a clash of titans,' wrote Professor Joseph Lee (*Ireland, 1912–1985*, Cambridge University Press). 'Was it not great good fortune that circumstances permitted one to model oneself on not only the most familiar, but the most successful, example?' Ireland's civil servants were well educated, the product of a society which traditionally placed education high on its priority list, very much encouraged by the Catholic Church which saw the schools as an opportunity to tighten its grip on the country. To Jack, it must have been a heaven-sent chance. His employment options were limited: for an aspiring professional with limited education there were the banks, which were taking on people, and there was the civil service—and not much else.

Jack set about the task determinedly and systematically. He had to catch up on the studies he had neglected, and began working late into the night and rising early. To his pleasure, Jack discovered in himself a considerable ability to concentrate and absorb knowledge, plus plenty of energy. To get into the civil service he needed Latin, and although most Irish schools taught it, Jack had missed out. So he befriended a Christian Brother, a member of a lay order which provided free education for the poorer classes in Ireland. This man seems to have been the driving force behind Jack's interest in educating himself which would last for the rest of his days. He certainly taught him Latin, and in later years Jack often talked of this Brother and how he had helped change his life. Jack developed an almost mystical respect for any Latin scholar, regarding the language as the high point in anyone's education.

In 1925, after sitting the stiff and highly competitive examination, using his elder brother's name and age, Jack found himself in the Customs and Excise, probably the fastest-growing department in the new state. Before independence Ireland barely needed a Customs service except to collect excise taxes and stamp out the illegal distilling of poteen in the west. But now it had a fully fledged border with the North, and Britain had become a foreign country. Curiously, it was not until the protectionist Fianna Fail party under de Valera came to power in the 1930s that Ireland put up high tariff walls to protect its industry, and in these early years of the new state it followed a brave course of free trade (rightly so: industrial employment rose). None the less, there were border posts to be manned, ports to be watched and an ever-rising tide of duties to be collected. Because Ireland was essentially a rural country, with over half the population dependent on farming, no more than 20 per cent of government revenue came from income tax; the rest came from Customs and Excise duties and a variety of indirect taxes.

Jack, now officially aged twenty-two rather than his actual nineteen, happily bade goodbye to his uncle, left farming forever, and went to Dublin for training. A few years before—and indeed a few years later—he would have been based in the Custom House, which, at least on the outside, was one of the finest buildings in the city. But like most of the other great buildings of Ireland it had suffered during the Troubles—it was burned by republicans in 1921. As a much older man Jack would be in charge of that building and all who worked in it.

He spent some months in Dublin before being sent to the town of Clones in County Monaghan, just a few miles inside the Irish Free State. The border between North and South was still very new and virtually uncontrollable, with cattle and pigs going north and manufactured goods of every kind coming south, almost at will. Many of the farms were divided by the border, which in several cases ran through the centre of barns and houses, and every lane and road crossed and recrossed the border.

By contrast with Dublin, Jack must have found Clones quiet and boring. He spent a year there before being transferred again, this time to the then busy port of Wicklow, 35 miles south of Dublin. It was a bigger town, and Jack was earning more by now, so he was able to buy himself a good suit and probably take a decent lodging. In reality he was still only twenty-one, a red-haired, smart young man of five foot ten, restless and ambitious to move on to better things. He was still studying hard, intent not only on winning promotion in the civil service, but also on equipping himself with some outside qualifications. He applied to Trinity College, Dublin for details of their law courses. Curiously, he never developed much interest in literature or the arts, confining his reading and study to subjects which would promote his career—including Latin, which he would need for the law. He had long ago shed all trace of both Drogheda and of his uncle's farm. It was around this time that he added a further slight, legitimate enough, embellishment to his name: by the time he arrived in Wicklow, John Patrick Reilly had become John Patrick O'Reilly, or plain Jack O'Reilly, a name he would live under for the rest of his life.

His time in Wicklow, although short, was to prove the most tumultuous and tragic period of his life. Given his strict Catholic background he was quite probably still innocent of women when he arrived there, but soon he was in love. Judith Clarke—Juie to her family and friends—was a tall, auburn-haired, fine-boned nineteen-year-old. Pictures of her show a delicate neck and shoulders and an elegant figure. She came from one of the more established, relatively well-to-do families in the town, living in a house in Church Street behind which stood their large, rambling builder's yard. The family firm had thrived on the back of the building boom in the second half of the nineteenth century, following some years after Catholic

Emancipation which was only delivered by Britain in 1829. The Clarkes had been coopers in the time of Cromwell, but William was the third-generation builder and had built churches, cathedrals, schools and convents all over the area. Like most builders he was also something of a speculator and owned a number of properties, including a large house called Mount Carmel in the Wicklow Hills to the south of the town—one of the prettiest places in Ireland, with a magnificent view out over the sea. Long before William bought it, Mount Carmel had been taken over by the local magistrates to try some of the ringleaders of the 1798 rebellion against the British forces, which had centred on Wicklow and County Wexford to the south. According to local legend, they were hanged in the driveway. Now sixty-two, William intended it for his retirement, but he never made it—he died soon after Jack arrived.

If Jack was impressed by the Clarkes, they do not appear to have taken to him. Bitterness at what subsequently occurred may have influenced their view in hindsight, but in her later life Judith's mother recalled how this 'pushy' young man used to walk up and down past the house hoping to catch the eye of her pretty daughter. Even after he died, no Clarke in Wicklow had a good word for Jack O'Reilly.

Judith was the fourth in a family of six, with an older brother, Michael, who became a priest and a sister who became a nun (three of the six would take up holy orders—not uncommon in Irish families at that time). It was a large, close and extended family which the solitary Jack, who had never found much comfort in his own family, must have envied. A family photograph taken around the time Jack arrived shows William Clarke, square and dignified, soberly clad in his dark suit and waistcoat, with his gold watch-chain—a pillar of local respectability. The most striking person in the photograph, however, is Judith, with her dark red hair falling to her shoulders, and her widely spaced eyes looking levelly at the camera.

How Jack pursued her no one now remembers, or wants to discuss, but pursue her he did, and with considerable success. Some time towards the end of 1927 Judith realized she was pregnant—a huge shock for a twenty-year-old girl from a strict Catholic family where even a passionate kiss outside wedlock was deemed a mortal sin. Quite how and when she told her family is another forgotten secret, but on 2 February 1928 she and Jack were married in the Church of the Assumption in Howth, on the north side of Dublin.

It was not the wedding her mother would have wanted for her, or the wedding she might have expected in other circumstances in her home town, with all her friends and relatives present. Her father was still alive, but ailing, and there is no record of either him or of her mother attending. The couple were married by Judith's uncle, Father Patrick O'Byrne, with her elder brother and sister, Michael and Eveleen, acting as witnesses. Jack's age was entered as 'full' and Judith's as a mere dash. By that stage she was six months pregnant and could scarcely have hidden it from her family, so the atmosphere must have been hostile. Yet the wedding picture shows the couple looking happy enough: Jack, in wing collar and hired morning suit, has a look of slight trepidation, but Judith seems serene and contemplative.

The young marrieds might not have planned it that way, but they were delighted with the way it had worked out. According to what Judith herself later told her children, Jack was deeply in love and desperate to marry her, pregnant or not—and that is certainly supported by the letters he wrote to her, and his attitude to her, at least for the first few years. She certainly remembered it as the happiest of times, and probably it was. The circumstances of their hasty marriage may have been something of a scandal by the narrow standards of Catholic Ireland nearly some seventy years ago, but the young couple themselves did not see it as a disaster. Not only were they in love, but the twenty-two-year-old Jack had a job with prospects: he was now studying hard for promotion, as well as polishing up on his law with a view to taking a degree at Trinity College, Dublin. He had also acquired a home for his new family: a flat in Anglesea Road, on the south side of Dublin.

In later life Judith seldom talked about the marriage, but when she did she described how similar their views were—they had the same ambitions, the same hopes and the same likes and dislikes, she told their children. He had a good voice and often sang to her. For their honeymoon they went to London, where Jack insisted on visiting the Old Bailey to observe the barristers at work. This was where his ambition really lay, and she sympathized and supported him.

Back in Dublin their first child, Judith Mary (later known as Juliette), was born in May, to be followed, just over a year later, by another girl who would be known as Ria. Their third child, Julian Patrick, was born on 15 December 1930. This imposed the first serious strain on the marriage: Jack, according to what his wife told her family, did not like children, and three babies in a small flat got on his nerves.

They moved home several times, presumably in search of better quarters, and two years after they were married they were living in Monkstown, on the southern edge of the city. After working in his customs office all day and going to law lectures in the evening, Jack would arrive home late and tired, but prepared to rise early the next morning to get on with his studies. Judith related how in the summer, as the examinations approached, Jack would get up at 5.30 and go out into the garden where he wrapped a towel around his head. With considerable wonder and admiration for what she described as his 'brainpower', she told of how the perspiration rolled down his brow as he concentrated. No one, she reckoned, had a mind like his.

The children, however, disturbed him, and he frequently sent Judith back to her family in Wicklow, leaving him free to study as hard as he liked. When William Clarke died his widow moved to the big house on the hill where there was plenty of room for her children and grandchildren, and Judith started to spend more and more time there, or with an aunt or a sister. Jack insisted on the arrangement, yet often found it intensely lonely. Late at night on 4 February 1930 he sat down to write her a love letter of extraordinary poignancy and tenderness, a letter in which he laid himself bare before her, unreservedly offering her his love and his soul. Even to an outside observer over sixty years later, it is a letter so intimate as to be almost painful, and one can only imagine the joy it must have given Judith, equally in love, at the time—and the pain it would give her and her children later.

Written on the pages of a lined notebook, it was probably directed more to himself than to his wife, analysing on paper his most secret thoughts and feelings which were almost too private to be read by anyone, including Judith.

> Juie darling, this is the 4th of February I am writing this. We are two years and two days married today, and tonight I am here alone thinking of you.
>
> Darling, you can never know all that you have meant to me since we met. It seems such a short time since I saw you first with your youthful bloom and glorious hair streaming down your back.
>
> There are few women in this world like you dear. People say the love-sick always see their loved ones in a favourable light but God help me I am [indecipherable] to see anyone [indeci-

pherable] this very plainest setting. Taking that for granted, I
still say you are the sweetest most charming and adorable wife
a man could have and t'is only of late I realise the cause of
your great popularity, with young and old, both sexes, alike.

Your purity and charity, and above all your womanly and
sincere affection make me feel ashamed of my own unworthi-
ness, and I often wonder why God has treated me with such
special favour in giving me a life partner of such outstanding
qualities.

Juie love this is not a letter. I am just writing this here alone
at the fire, and in years to come we may read it over and feel
happy to think that I was impelled from within to set down
here in this little book my sentiments towards you this very
night.

I have just now finished my rosary and put up my books. It
is 11.30 and I must go to bed.

Darling wife, you asked me in your letter today to say my
rosary each day for success. That request and the way it was
made touched some hidden chord in my heart on the spot. Yes
love, I'll pray as I never did before. I will not miss my rosary
a single night from now on and I will study with all the power
of my soul to raise you to the heights you deserve. I know God
will hear my prayer. He has refused me nothing so far, and in
that belief I will start from now on to strive for all that means
happiness for you dearest.

Good night dear heart. You are asleep by now, but I feel as
though you were just telling me some little secret of the day's
events. Good night.

The unsigned letter, written on a cold Dublin winter's night, is
written in a neat, fluent and educated hand. It tells us a great deal
about Jack, and about his relationship with Judith, for whom it was
the most important note she ever received in her life. It shows him
capable of deep and tender affection, and unreserved commitment:
'I often wonder why God has treated me with such special favour in
giving me a life partner of such outstanding qualities.' It also reveals
him to be a religious man—probably not profoundly so, but the
recitation of the rosary, compulsory in almost every Irish home at
that time, takes a full ten minutes of kneeling and requires a certain
degree of commitment and discipline to perform alone. Jack's gener-

ation was brought up in the belief that, contrary to their actual experience, almost anything could be achieved, including success in examination, if you prayed hard enough; in his mid-twenties Jack still clung to that belief.

Above all the letter shows, whatever went before and came afterwards, that Jack O'Reilly at this moment could not be more in love with his wife: he admires her appearance, her charm, her popularity, her grace, her 'purity and charity', her womanliness and her goodness. Yet, for all his love and adoration, why does he consider himself unworthy? Despite the impression that at this lonely and depressed moment there is no one in the world—particularly not his children, who are not even mentioned—for him other than his wife, has his eye already strayed? If he misses her so much, how can he bear to be parted from her? Whatever the truth, within two years he had left her, sending her, bewildered and heartbroken and pregnant with their fourth child, back to her mother's large house in Wicklow.

What had happened? Essentially Jack had discovered a new life, delighting in the company he found at Trinity. He spent every spare moment there, arguing and discussing the politics of a Free State which was gradually becoming a nation. The Great Depression had arrived, hitting Ireland even harder than Britain, which had over three million unemployed, and the American slump had dammed up emigration. De Valera, after a year in jail for his role in the civil war, had emerged to become leader of the Fianna Fail party, and, in 1932, of the Free State, ruling in an uneasy coalition with the Labour party. But Jack had a secure and undemanding job in the Customs—a department which, like every other part of the Irish civil service, was generously overmanned, and by student standards he was relatively well off.

But more importantly he had fallen in love. Most people in Dublin who knew something of the story always believed that Jack left his wife for the woman who bore him his second son, Tony O'Reilly, but it is not true. He actually left her for a fellow student, a girl called, according to the Clarke family legend, Petite O'Hagan (presumably because she was small). Trinity in the 1930s was essentially a Protestant university, with a handful of Catholics among its student population which was then less than a thousand (today it is over ten thousand). It was also a university where the richer Anglo-Irish and Northern Irish families sent their children, and it had a strong contingent of English and Scots who preferred its more intimate and scholarly atmosphere to that of Oxford or Cambridge. Jack, however, seems to have fallen for a Catholic girl, devoting to her some of the same passion as he had to Judith. The relationship did not last long, but it was long enough to end the marriage.

It was by no means a clean break. At one stage Judith actually met Petite O'Hagan, whether to confront her or by accident is not known. At any rate, the young student made it clear that her relationship with Jack was over. 'You needn't worry about me,' she said, as related by Judith later. 'I've given him up and am going into a convent.' She did, but within a year she had developed a brain tumour and died.

Jack's daughter Eveleen, his fourth child in five years, was born in Wicklow on 12 May 1932. Too many children in such quick succession had taken their toll on Judith, who remained in hospital, seriously ill, after a perforated appendix. She remained in hospital for almost a year. Even when she emerged, she was in no position to look after the children. Nor was Jack, with his work during the day and his study during the night—not to mention his extra-curricular activities. Judith's aunts and mother rallied round, but four young children were too much for any relative.

Jack's solution was a formal separation which split the family. He took the two older girls, Juliette and Ria, into his custody and sent them off to a French convent, Le Bon Sauveur, at Holyhead in North Wales. Why he chose that particular convent is not clear—he certainly never told the girls and they never dared to ask—but there were other Irish children there, including the daughter of the Lord Mayor of Dublin, Alfie Byrne. Its one advantage was that it was at the end of a direct ferry trip from Dublin, but it does seem as if Jack was trying to hide them away. The O'Reilly children were tiny, aged five and four, and they hated it. Even during the holidays, he either insisted on their staying at the convent or farmed them out to his own relations. Several times they went to Drogheda to stay with their paternal grandmother, which they found worse than the convent. On other occasions they had to wait until he found a boarding house near his own home—they never actually stayed with their father. The two younger children, Julian and Eveleen, remained with Judith, all four children growing up in the belief that the normal practice when a marriage broke down was to divide the children between the parents. It wasn't until the outbreak of war in 1939 that they were united as a family in the big Clarke family house, where Judith now lived with her mother and aunt.

By that stage Jack's life had taken an altogether different direction, permanent and lasting—and probably fulfilling. After the O'Hagan affair he took lodgings with a family called O'Connor, and there he met the daughter of the house, Aileen, whose father was a former Royal Irish Constabulary policeman. They were from Ballyforan in County Roscommon, in the west of Ireland, and her father had probably taken his payment from the British government and used it to buy a house in Dublin where they took in guests. The O'Connors were a large family—there were ten children—who had been much more directly involved in the events that led up to Irish independence than ever the Reillys were. Aileen's brother Tony, after whom she would name her son, joined the Irish Free State (National) army in 1922 at the outbreak of the civil war and reached the rank of sergeant. Bitterly opposed to de Valera, he related, in a novel which he wrote fifty years later, the true story of how he was selected as a member of a firing squad to execute his boyhood best friend, who had joined the IRA. His cousin Rory commanded the firing squad in Portobello Barracks in Dublin which executed Erskine Childers, the English-born, former Clerk of the House of Commons (and author of *The Riddle of the Sands*), who also fought on the republican side.

Like Judith, Aileen was tall, auburn-haired and attractive, but she was warm and vibrant where Judith was gentle and unassuming. 'She was a very beautiful-looking woman,' recalls a family friend. 'Very charming, and witty.' The O'Connors were a closer and rather more bohemian family than Jack O'Reilly had been used to, and he was dazzled by it—and by Aileen.

Did she know he was already married, with no possibility of a divorce in a country where it was illegal? Possibly not until later. Judith stayed in Wicklow, firmly believing—as she would for most of her life—that Jack would return to her. His children were invisible, and to all intents and purposes he was a single man, a rising civil servant who had qualified as a barrister and was now studying to become a chartered secretary and preparing for his surveyor's examinations in the customs.

By 1933 or 1934 Jack and Aileen had moved into a flat at 100 Pembroke Road in Ballsbridge, on the fashionable south side of Dublin. They pretended they were man and wife, although it would be thirty-eight years before that was legally so. For several years they moved from flat to flat, as Jack always had, before buying a house in Griffith Avenue, on the other side of the city. They were living there when Aileen bore the only child of their union: Anthony John Francis O'Reilly was born on 7 May 1936 to a couple who called themselves Mr and Mrs John O'Reilly, with Jack, for some odd reason, putting his profession down as 'traveller'. Jack was thirty, Aileen twenty-two.

2

A Child of Dublin

WHEN HIS SON TONY WAS BORN JACK O'REILLY WAS WELL INTO THE middle grades of the Irish Customs service, with a lifestyle which by the standards of 1930s' Dublin was not at all bad. He and Aileen were proud parents, treating this little red-haired boy as their only child and denying him nothing. Jack still studied, but now it was for the sake of improving his mind rather than for any thought of a different career: any ideas he nurtured about leaving the civil service and taking up the law seem to have been abandoned with the arrival of his son. The legal profession in Dublin was over-educated and under-employed, and such clients as existed were jealously husbanded by a closed establishment. As a single man Jack might have risked it, taking whatever position he could get and hoping that his energy, personality and outgoing nature would make a mark. He lacked neither ambition nor confidence in his own abilities, but he had a safe job, and safe jobs were rare in 1930s' Ireland; they were not to be abandoned lightly, particularly by a man who now had two families. His hankering after a law career would lie dormant for many years, only being realized after he retired from the civil service thirty-two years later. Aileen, given the vulnerability of her unmarried state, must also have appreciated the benefits of his good promotion prospects, guaranteed pay increases every year, and a pension at the end. Outside the professions it was a cold, hungry world, with not much room even for the bold and ambitious.

Jack cut himself off from his old life, seeing his first family only

occasionally and devoting himself to this new woman and the child
in their lives. He had gone prematurely grey, and his bearing was
increasingly that of the respected, distinguished and slightly pomp-
ous senior civil servant in a time and place where civil servants carried
a considerable degree of respect. Presumably because of his manner
and his law degree he became known as 'the judge', a nickname he
would retain all his life. His friends called him Jack or 'Johnno', but
he was never a chummy, friendly man among his peers and always
retained a certain dignified distance.

Aileen, beautiful, lively and naturally hospitable, was the opposite.
She was taller than Jack, and much more sociable, a country girl
attempting to create an Irish village atmosphere in the heart of suburban Dublin. 'If Dublin had a queen, they used to say it would be
Aileen O'Reilly,' says a former neighbour. 'She was that stately—
people used just to stare at her she was so beautiful.' She loved people
dropping in and, proud of her house, her man and her little son,
greatly encouraged it. She persuaded Jack to hold little musical gatherings where they would gather around the piano and sing John
McCormack songs, Irish ballads and the rebel songs that the Irish
had used to keep their spirits up over the centuries. Jack, with his
pleasant, tuneful voice of which he was inordinately proud, probably
needed little encouragement.

Jack travelled by bus every day the two or three miles to his office
on the North Wall, while Aileen, in an age and in a community where
few women worked, stayed at home. Indeed, even if she had wanted
to get a job there were not many to be had. The Depression had
fallen hard on the Irish Free State as it struggled to achieve some
kind of commercial independence from the overpowering might of
its neighbour. Before 1922 Irish business had never had to stand on
its own, and its few factories had access to the markets of the British
Empire in the same way that factories in Scotland, Wales or Cornwall
did. The Troubles and the Civil War had been tough times in which
to build an industrial base, and within five years of the end of the
fighting came the crash of 1929. The Free State's exports, always
vulnerable to the marginal spending power of its fragile markets, fell
by a quarter in 1930 and 1931, and so-called invisible income—
the money sent back by Irish labourers in America and England—
dropped disastrously. On top of everything else, de Valera's new
Fianna Fail government, which came to power with a small majority
in 1932 (and would stay there for sixteen years), insisted on going

to war with Britain. This time it was the 'Economic War', with Ireland erecting tariff barriers and Britain retaliating by imposing special restrictions on Irish agricultural products. The result was to make a poor nation even poorer. In the twelve months before Tony O'Reilly was born, unemployment rose to 20 per cent of the working population; it was to remain there for the rest of the decade. Even that was an understatement of the true position: there was serious under-employment also in rural areas, where young farmers and farm la-bourers hung around the crossroads killing time. In 1936, when Tony came into the world, the agricultural industry was in a state of deep depression despite a mass of state subsidies. That year alone some twenty-two thousand young Irish people emigrated, mostly to America. It was a pattern which would continue right up to the 1960s, by which stage Tony O'Reilly himself would follow them.

It was not all bad news, however, particularly for those, such as Jack, who had steady jobs. Housing and the cost of living were cheap, and even a lowly paid civil servant could afford a house, a small car and a maid. Economic expectations in a nation which had always been poor were low, and in the country, at least, the Irish could feed themselves. In Dublin and the cities, disenchantment caused by unemployment was largely drained off by emigration, which speeded up sharply after 1936 as the American and British economies recov-ered. De Valera had threatened radical, even revolutionary change to Irish society, but apart from modest state welfare (unemployment assistance was first introduced in 1933) and his drive to create indus-trial jobs, little changed. It was also a time of relative peace in a country which had witnessed internal turmoil for centuries. By the mid-1930s the IRA was a spent force, barely active, and in June 1936, a month after O'Reilly was born, de Valera dealt them another blow when he declared them illegal after they had carried out two particu-larly callous murders of a woman and an old man.

There were other events around the time of Tony O'Reilly's birth which would influence his upbringing and his later life. De Valera had been working on a new constitution and in July 1937 put it to the country in a referendum on the same day as he presented himself for re-election. This was the Constitution that would have implica-tions which are still relevant today, and which would help shape the lives of O'Reilly and his generation. The now famous Articles 2 and 3 claimed the constitutional right of the Dublin government to exercise jurisdiction over the whole thirty-two counties of Ireland, though confining the exercise in practice to the twenty-six counties of the South 'pending the reunification of the national territory'. Oddly enough, in the light of later events, the Constitution did not proclaim Ireland a republic (that did not come until 1949), basically because de Valera was nervous of the reaction in the North; but it did recognize the special position of the Catholic Church 'as the guardian of the Faith professed by the great majority of the citizens' (the wording was actually a snub to Rome which had expected more). This would become a major cause of tension between North and South until it was expunged in 1972, although de Valera and his followers always defended it by arguing that the same article in the Constitution also recognized the other Churches then existing in Ireland, including 'the Jewish congregations'—a gesture, they felt, of some courage in the anti-Semitic climate of the late 1930s from which Ireland, with its tiny Jewish population, was far from immune.

O'Reilly's parents, like most of their generation who had been through independence and civil war, would probably have raised no great objection to the changes. They were Irish Catholics in an Irish Catholic country which still resented its colonial past and felt the festering hatred of the Calvinists to the north. They would have supported the Constitution, which was, of course, never submitted to the full 'national territory' to which it claimed rights, but only to that section 'of the Irish people we can consult on the matter'—which meant the twenty-six counties of the South. Few people in Ireland seriously thought about the inevitable consequences, which were to make partition, seen as only a temporary affair by the British in 1922, more deeply entrenched, giving the Protestants of the North all the justification they needed to cling to their status as part of the United Kingdom. De Valera further alienated them by seizing upon the abdication of Edward VIII in December 1936 to eliminate all references to the King and the British Governor-general in his Free State Constitution, and in 1938 went further. In return for assurances that he would not allow Ireland to be used as a landing-ground for hostilities against Britain in the event of war, he secured the return of the three naval bases that Britain had retained after 1922: Berehaven, Cobh (Queenstown) and Lough Swilly. This, sixteen years after the Free State came into existence, was a watershed in the evolution of the modern Irish state, and probably de Valera's greatest political triumph. It was the final recognition that the Irish Free State had moved from humble dominion status to sovereignty. Without it, Ireland would have been forced to enter the looming European war. But with independence at last a reality the country was able, as de Valera intended, to opt for neutrality. It also strengthened de Valera's hand to move finally and decisively against the IRA, who in 1939 started a bombing campaign on mainland Britain and clumsily sought to open up contacts with the German intelligence service. A series of tough measures passed against them in Dublin, including internment without trial and the death penalty for treason, reduced their numbers to a handful by the mid-1940s.

But in many ways it was the social dream of de Valera which coloured the Ireland in which Tony O'Reilly spent his earliest years. De Valera himself was an ascetic, unworldly intellectual, whose concept of the Ireland he wanted was austere and almost socialist in nature, in many ways alien to the culture of most Catholic Irish. He introduced land reform, semi-state companies and other changes, but under his hand Irish life, already deeply conservative, became more so as he tightened the existing censorship laws on books, films and literature which might offend the delicate sensibilities of the Catholic priests. His political party, Fianna Fail (meaning 'Warriors of Fal', an ancient name for Ireland), was also subtitled 'the republican party', and it stood for a self-sufficient nation, (the original meaning of Sinn Fein) which would speak Gaelic as a first language and would look to the ancient Gaelic culture, which he saw uniting in a seamless stream the heroics of the mythical giant Cuchulain with the sacrificial victims of the Easter Rising.

In the late 1930s, de Valera's vision of a Gaelic Eden was hotly debated in the circles that Jack O'Reilly inhabited; many Irish intellectuals were increasingly disenchanted with what they perceived as a narrow, restrictive and oppressive climate. The writer Sean O'Faolain, returning to Ireland after a long period abroad, openly stirred the debate by insisting that Gaelic Ireland had died in the eighteenth century and that there was no point in trying to resurrect it—Ireland was far better off embracing the new rather than the old. There were many, mostly the intellectual, educated Irish, who agreed with him. Another writer, Frank O'Connor, who like O'Faolain and O'Reilly's Uncle Tony had fought in the liberation struggle, acidly described the Ireland of the 1930s: 'After the Revolution . . . Irish society began to revert to type. All the forces that had made for national dignity, that had united Catholic and Protestant, aristocrats . . . Labour revalationists . . . and writers . . . began to disintegrate rapidly, and Ireland became more than ever sectarian, utilitarian . . . vulgar and provincial.' O'Connor bitterly noted that every year that had passed since de Valera took over had 'strengthened the grip of the gombeen man, of the religious secret societies like the Knights of Columbanus, of the illiterate censorships. . . .' Contrast that with de Valera's own vision, spelt out in a St Patrick's Day address in 1943: 'The Ireland we dreamed of would be the home of a people who valued material wealth only as a basis of a right living, of a people who were satisfied with a frugal comfort and devoted their leisure to the things of the spirit.' In the Ireland of the late 1930s, there was all too much frugality but not so much comfort.

Like all children at the time, from his earliest days O'Reilly lived and breathed the living history that his parents and uncles had only recently witnessed, and which was talked about endlessly in a newly independent nation, the first of many to break away from the British Empire. The visible effects of insurrection and civil war were all around him, pointed out to small boys on trams and British-made double-decker buses as they travelled through the main streets of Dublin, past the GPO in O'Connell Street, and the Four Courts where the IRA had held out against Collins, where the marks of bullets and shells were permanently etched in walls and statues.

The house in Griffith Avenue, on the road to Drogheda, not far from the site of Dublin's future airport, was by no means grand, but it was adequate for a young couple who aspired to something better as soon as they could afford it. They were there when war was declared in 1939, ushering in a strange period of neutrality in a country which over the next five years grew even more isolated. Ireland's insistence on staying out of the conflict that now swept across Europe would not easily be forgiven by Britain, or by many of the Anglo-Irish who still lived in the country. In fact it was not only predictable but perfectly consistent with what de Valera publicly stood for. 'Neutrality in a world conflict is the ultimate exercise in national sovereignty,' wrote the Irish historian John A. Murphy. There was nothing particularly anti-British about it—on the contrary, the Irish approach amounted to a form of pro-British neutrality, even if the Irish ports were not officially available to British convoys coming in from the Atlantic. Secret intelligence and strategic liaisons were made with Britain and the USA which were not realized at the time and are still not widely understood today. Churchill never accepted the concept of Irish neutrality, attacking the Irish constitutional position as 'anomalous' and the Irish strategy as 'at war but skulking'. Yet in a number of speeches before the war, de Valera had spelt out his clear intention to keep the country neutral, and when Germany invaded Poland he was supported in the Dáil without even a division. That does not mean that Ireland wanted Britain to lose, although there was satisfaction in some circles at the early reverses, but de Valera probably felt at the early stages that Britain would indeed lose the war, and was positioning himself cautiously. At one stage Hitler entertained an option of an invasion of the North, imaginatively timed for the twenty-fifth anniversary of the 1916 Rising in April 1941; but he abandoned it as impractical.

Although the country was neutral, the Irish authorities felt that rudimentary precautions had to be taken in case they should become embroiled. At the outset of the war, Jack O'Reilly was appointed group leader of the security force for North Dublin—suggesting that, whatever his marital status, no scandal attached to him. It was an undemanding role: he was a sort of firefighter, ready to lead the local effort should bombs fall on Dublin. He actually built a rough-and-ready air-raid shelter in his garden, a ten-foot-deep trench with boards on top and the soil thrown back over it, which he stocked with oil-lamps and iron rations, ready to fend off the blitzkrieg that was never remotely likely. 'Mr O'Reilly used to joke about it,' says John McKone, who lived a few houses away. 'He used to be always moaning, in a good-natured way, about my father who had a big crowd of kids but no air-raid shelter. My father was a total pacifist and Mr O'Reilly was the head man in the local security force.' The neighbours also remember Aileen, in uniform, issuing gas masks on behalf of Jack's auxiliary force.

In Ireland the war years were officially known as 'The Emergency' but in comparison with what the citizens of the North went through— Belfast was bombed heavily, devastating its shipyards and war machine—they were more inconvenient than dangerous. Ireland's only direct damage was when German planes, led astray by jammed radios, bombed Dublin in May 1941, killing thirty-four people. There was a blackout in Dublin, which Jack O'Reilly was supposed to impose on the north side; but he never took this too seriously, and slept through several of the air-raid warnings that came at increasingly irregular intervals. In any case, it must have seemed pointless to him: the great joke, told endlessly by Jack, was that on the one occasion of serious bombing, the occupants of every house in Dublin put their lights on and stood at the windows to see what was happening. One of Tony O'Reilly's earliest recollections is of a picnic with his parents when a Spitfire chased a stray German Messerschmitt in the skies above them, and Aileen worried that a stray bomb would spoil the bacon and eggs she was cooking. Other than that, there were fuel shortages and food rationing, but Ireland was essentially a disinterested observer on the edge of the greatest turmoil in world history.

There was, however, a long tradition of Irishmen fighting in Britain's wars, and this would be no exception, although the basis would be different and the numbers fewer than in World War I. Aileen's brother Tony O'Connor, young Tony's favourite uncle, joined the Royal Air Force in 1939 and became a squadron leader in Fighter Command. After the war he would become secretary to some of the best-known gentlemen's clubs in London, including the Cavalry Club in Piccadilly, the facilities of which would always be available to his favourite nephew.

At home in Griffith Avenue, Jack was, at least in these early years, a slightly distant father, but Aileen made up for it, devoting all her energy and affection to her son. If she felt insecure and vulnerable, she hid it well. She compensated for Tony's lack of brothers and sisters by inviting his young schoolfriends home and keeping virtually open house, a habit she would continue until he left home twenty years later. In her old age she used to relate how her son had attempted to leave home much earlier: at three and a half, after a rare reprimand from her, he announced that he was going and would take the family labrador, Peter, with him. 'There was a big stream in front of the bungalow, and there were two tennis courts which were let grow wild,' she recalled. 'And he walked across the tennis court, holding Peter by the ear. An hour and a half later he was back, with one shoe missing.' It was one of his few acts of rebellion.

Unknown to the young Tony—and probably unknown to Aileen—Jack O'Reilly was keeping in spasmodic touch with his first family. Life for Judith in Wicklow was not easy. At first she stayed with her sister, and later in the big family house with her mother. When she recovered from her year-long illness after the birth of Eveleen she got a job as a social worker in Dublin, renting a house and hiring a maid to look after her two younger children. Her family were against it, insisting that the children would get a poor upbringing. 'Well, at least there's a home for Jack to come back to,' she responded. When the two elder girls were in Holyhead, every holiday Jack would take the ferry from Dun Laoghaire, pick them up and bring them back to Ireland. But he never brought them home to Aileen. None of the children met their young half-brother, and Tony would be in his mid-teens before he had any inkling that he had any brothers or sisters (even then, it was to be many years later still before he met them).

Judith, meanwhile, had given in to family pressure and gone back to Wicklow, where she was short of money. 'She really did have an awful time when we were very little,' says her daughter Eveleen. 'She had very little money because my father gave her very little—he didn't earn that much to keep up two households.' She was very dependent on the goodwill of her relatives, for the small farm which she had inherited made little or no money in the 1930s. 'She had this very submissive position in her family,' says Eveleen. 'It was humiliating for her in many ways, and she didn't have very good health for years.' The children remember family conferences taking place after Sunday lunch. 'Everybody sat around the table and decided who should pay for what, and how much it would cost, and who was going to contribute for uniforms and books and so on,' says Eveleen. 'And they were wonderful to her, but it wasn't easy for my mother, and sometimes her spirits were very low.'

She and Jack stayed in touch, talking on the telephone and occasionally meeting when the children were brought to see their father three or four times a year. Judith had heard about Tony's birth and had followed, through friends and relatives, the progress of the second O'Reilly family, but she had never discussed it with Jack until they met by accident on the boat coming back from Holyhead. Judith had gone to see the children at their convent and so, separately, had Jack. Judith later told her children of a poignant incident which took place on the ferry. She was now fully restored to health, and with her long chestnut hair swept into coils around her ears, in the height of current fashion, she was even more striking than the teenager with whom Jack had first fallen in love. According to Judith they began talking, and well before they reached Ireland were seriously discussing resuming their lives together. Jack told her he had another child. 'I've known about the baby for some time,' she replied. 'But bring him too. Little Tony would fit in naturally after Julian and Eveleen, and we could all be together again.' Judith later told her children that, by the time they reached Dun Laoghaire, Jack had agreed to resurrect their marriage, bringing all five children under the same roof. 'He said he thought it was the right thing to do,' she told them. Jack apparently went off to Griffith Avenue to tell Aileen, while Judith went back to Wicklow to await him. He never came, of course, and probably never intended to. Jack's relationship with Aileen, although stormy at times, was essentially a happy one and there is no evidence, other than Judith's story, that he ever thought of changing it. Judith may have read too much into this meeting, or later built it up into something it never was. At any rate, according to the family story he later contacted her to say he was not coming after all, partly because he was not able to bring his son with him. Aileen was reported to have told him very firmly: 'In no way am I going to lose both my son and my man in one go.'

Jack did agree to some changes in the family, however. When war came, Judith persuaded him that continually sending the two older girls across the Irish Sea to Holyhead was dangerous, and that they should be kept in Ireland. Jack found it hard enough to manage them in the holidays, and had no way of looking after them in term-time as well, so he agreed that she should have all four. To their delight Juliette and Ria, now aged eleven and ten, were brought back to Wicklow. Because they had been educated outside the country they spoke no Irish, and a desperate catching up process was instigated. It would be some time before they could settle down as a family, but for all the children life, although not easy, now began to improve.

From the outset it was Aileen who encouraged her son's sporting activities, making it her job to have a clean kit for him at all times, and cheering him on from the sidelines. Jack had never shown any facility at sport, and not much interest in it either, but Tony always displayed a natural talent. 'When we played tag in the school yard at lunchtime, nobody could ever touch O'Reilly,' says Frank Turvey, one of his earliest school mates. 'He was awfully good at all sports—running, swimming, rugby, cricket.'

There were holidays with his uncles and aunts, mostly on his mother's side. One uncle and aunt kept the post office in Balbriggan, and Tony often spent summers there. As a little joke on her customers, his aunt Judy used to hide him inside the large post-box in the wall, encouraging him to grab the letters from unsuspecting hands as they were pushed through the flap. Balbriggan is on the main railway line to Belfast, and Tony has keen memories of lying on the platform listening with his ear to the ground for the first signs of an approaching train, and then, as it roared through the station, screaming with delight and simulated terror.

During the war years he was also sent by train to Sligo in the west of Ireland to stay with relatives of Aileen's in the summer, but essentially he was a city boy, growing up in the suburban streets of north Dublin. The occupants of Griffith Avenue were by no means limited to middle-ranking civil servants, although a number did live there. John McKone, almost the same age as Tony, lived a few doors away and recalls their upbringing:

> Across the road from us you had a complete block of houses built by a co-op of English civil servants, and they had a number of Irish people who had worked with them in London. And you also had one of the top IRA men, who was the father of one of my pals, who had nearly scuttled the Treaty negotiations—spent all his time growing vegetables, mostly cabbages. And across the road was a very close friend of Tony's, Robbie Hayes, and Robbie and Tony and I were quite close, growing up together. Robbie's father was a person who got telephones to work, and he was a total and utter alcoholic. I never remember seeing him sober—every evening he would arrive home in a taxi and fall out of it, and Robbie's mother would come out and tow him in.
>
> Now on our side of the road, which was Tony's, we had all sorts of people. My father was manager of a shop. Our next door neighbour was a dairy farmer, and he kept twenty cows in a yard and a number of pigs, and he delivered milk from a pony and trap. The pigs were fed from offal from hotels—a fellow with an ass and cart went around the hotels and picked up what we call slop. Then we had another guy who was in the Department of Agriculture. Then next to that was Tony, and next to that a guy who was involved making shoes—that was another English civil servant. It was a great mix, but there was a stability, as people didn't change at that time.
>
> Twelve of us in that very small area, including Tony, had been born in 1936, and then as we got older and a bit more adventurous there were more fellows up the road, so there was a large gang of us and we played soccer—one fellow down the

road played for Ireland eventually. And Tony later played for Home Farm, which was just down the road, and could have played for Ireland too.

Although Griffith Avenue was a main thoroughfare there were few cars: not many could afford them, and there was also rationing of petrol, tyres and spare parts. So the children played uninhibitedly and without danger on the street. No one was rich, and everyone did what they could to earn something extra. Anyone who had a garden, including Jack O'Reilly, dug and planted it. 'It was unthinkable not to grow food,' says McKone. 'In fact it was always a source of envy with us: one of the fellows had grass and laid out a pitch and putt course on his lawn. But that was the exception, and we were all on this tack of growing food.'

McKone remembers O'Reilly's mother starting up her own little private venture immediately after the war, importing boxes of beads from Czechoslovakia. 'And she lined up all the local people to string them together in a certain order—I couldn't do it—and then you put on this special clasp.' After that she helped in a drapery shop in South George's Street, near the city centre. He also remembers Jack being involved with an engineering company, probably as an adviser. 'Everybody was trying to have some sort of sideline, because that's the way it was,' says McKone. 'Lots of people were cutting turf.'

The O'Reillys, like many city-dwellers, had their own little patch in the Wicklow Mountains where they would go each summer and cut turf, leaving it to dry and then taking it back to Dublin for the winter. Ireland had little coal of its own, and supplies from the Welsh mines had dried up with the onset of war—Britain needed all the coal it could produce for the war effort. Oil and gas were almost unavailable, and the only sources of heating were turf and wood. To the young Tony, as to many others, cutting turf from the bog was an adventure, even if it was also hard work.

Whatever the financial stresses Jack was under, Tony remembers these early days as exceptionally happy ones. The O'Reilly home became something of a musical centre. The writer John D. Sheridan lived nearby and would drop in, and the tradition in those pre-television days was to sing the evenings away. Every household and every pub in Ireland sang, and a good voice such as Jack's was highly appreciated. To his eternal regret Jack had never learned to play a musical instrument, but from the moment Tony was big enough to reach the keys he encouraged him to play the piano.

In September 1942, aged six years and four months, O'Reilly was sent to his first—and only—real school, the Jesuit-run Belvedere College on the north side of Dublin. It was by no means the grandest of the Irish Jesuit colleges looked down on by those who went to the more prestigious Clongowes Wood, in the valley of the River Liffey, which had been established by the Jesuits at the end of the Napoleonic wars as a school for the sons of the Catholic gentry. Although the Pope banned the Jesuit order for most of the eighteenth century, Dublin had a very old tradition of Jesuit education. In O'Reilly's day, the priests liked to boast of how, in 1540, their founder, Inigo Lopez de Loyola, gathered together some of the brightest and best-educated brains in the Roman Catholic Church with the object of creating an order which would, among other things, become the 'schoolmasters of Europe'. Among the schools eventually founded— many years later, although the priests in Belvedere glossed over that—was a small establishment in Hardwicke Street, near the centre of Dublin. In 1841 it moved to much larger premises, worthy of the title 'college'. The elegant Dublin townhouse owned by Lord Belvedere in Great Denmark Street, a few blocks from O'Connell Street, Dublin's main thoroughfare, became available and the Jesuits bought it to create, with their typical thoroughness and energy, a school which would produce many of Ireland's doctors, dentists, lawyers, and civil servants—as well as future generations of Jesuit priests—over the next 150 years. Where Clongowes, a boarding school, got the sons of the rich, Belvedere, a day school, got the sons of the middle classes who lived on the poorer side of the city. James Joyce moved from Clongowes to Belvedere in 1893 at the age of eleven, where the Jesuits took him on free of charge on the grounds he was bright enough to win prizes for the school. The school was proud of its former pupil James Joyce, even if Ireland was one of the few countries in the western world where *Ulysses*, his greatest work, could only be bought under the counter. O'Reilly arrived over forty years after Joyce had left, but the school had not changed much, either physically or in its manner of education. The townhouse of Lord Belvedere, with its large, elegant rooms decorated with wonderful plasterwork, faced down North Great George's Street, but the school proper, which was the part that O'Reilly would mostly see, was across the garden and the actual classrooms were small, shabby and functional. The chapel, in which O'Reilly would spend many hours, was in this second building. A door opened off it into a gym which was also a theatre—Belvedere was proud of its theatre and the school play (or musical in O'Reilly's day) was the feature of the summer term.

Because he had a May birthday and was bright for his age, from the start of his school career O'Reilly was the youngest in the class. So when he arrived in Belvedere he was too young even to have made his first holy communion, a solemn ritual which in the Irish Catholic Church takes place at the age of seven (the 'age of reason'). He was the only entrant that year who had not gone through this seminal ceremony, and later the myth would grow, which he himself would foster, that he was the only new communicant in Belvedere's history—a little bit of one-upmanship to illustrate how exceptional he was even then. But the story is not true. 'Most years there were two or three who had not made their first communion,' said Father Michael Reidy, who was to teach O'Reilly mathematics and English and also to coach him in rugby. 'Most of the boys had made it before they came, and he was the only one that year. But there were two or three the year before.' When he turned seven the following summer, his communion was marked with a photograph in the annual magazine, the *Belvederean*, showing O'Reilly wearing an Irish tweed suit, short pants, proud grin and his holy communion medal. 'It was quite an unusual bit of publicity,' says the architect Sam Stephenson, a couple of years ahead of O'Reilly at Belvedere. 'But then he was a very unusual boy to start with.'

The occasion also created one of the lasting legends about O'Reilly which is still related in Belvedere to this day—and a story which he himself has told on many occasions with suitable embellishments, to illustrate his early commercial skills. In honour of the occasion the Rector of Belvedere, Father Gubbins, presented O'Reilly with a much sought after gift in wartime Ireland: an orange, illicitly obtained by the priests from the North, where there was a supply from the convoys coming across the Atlantic. 'That's very valuable,' he told the puzzled seven-year-old. 'The peel is too.' O'Reilly, along with most of his schoolmates, had never seen an orange and had no idea how to eat it. He would later joke that, having eaten the centre, 'I sold the peel for one penny per piece, thereby showing a propensity for commercial deception which has not left me since.' The tale always gets a laugh, particularly in Ireland, but it is not quite how others remember it. 'We hadn't ever seen an orange and we didn't realize you ate the inside,' says Frank Turvey. 'We all gathered around, and we all paid, but we thought you ate the skin—that's a fact. I got a bit of skin, and I paid a fair price for it, and Tony was left with the inside. I don't think Tony copped on for a while—he didn't realize, any more than we did, that he was on to something.' Kevin McGoran, another of O'Reilly's early friends at Belvedere, is convinced that it was only as he examined the inside of the orange that it dawned on O'Reilly what a good deal he had done. In fact the story says little about O'Reilly's latent business skills but quite a lot about his confidence and self-discipline—most seven-year-olds would simply have wolfed the orange, peel and all, whereas O'Reilly calmly worked out how he could get the most out of it.

It is difficult now to establish how much he did stand out in these early days, because his later fame coloured everyone's retrospective impression of him. In those first years, he was noticed as much for his extreme youth as anything else, and for his mop of bright red hair; but he never shone academically at Belvedere, doing just enough work to keep him in the first or second division through his school career—Belvedere had four divisions in each year—and only accelerating his effort as an examination approached. He read from an early age, and did so well and rapidly; he also had a retentive memory, which allowed him to keep up with his class despite the age difference, but it was not regarded as exceptional at this stage. He was effortlessly good at English, and even more effortlessly popular with both masters and fellow pupils. 'He was a boy of great confidence without being bumptious,' recalled Father Reidy. 'There are some boys who can talk to a master without in any way giving offence, and Tony had that gift. Even as a teacher you could relate to him. A number of boys have that, but Tony had it to an extra degree.'

Reidy and other teachers remember him as a calm, self-possessed and humorous boy, seldom in trouble, usually surrounded by a group of friends who were often older than him, taking part in everything that was going on at the school, from chess to dramatics and debating. From an early age he was keenly aware of the currents and eddies in the school, an organized and attentive boy who moved easily with the flow. 'I can't ever remember seeing Tony annoyed or angry,' said Reidy. 'He had a great gift for mixing with people, even as a boy. And he could mix his bricks—play and study.'

Belvedere was not a place for rebels, but O'Reilly never showed any inclination to be one, even if he had been given the opportunity. The Jesuits imposed a tight discipline, which O'Reilly would absorb and learn from, but which he never objected to. Father Reidy recalled the strictness of the regime under Father O'Riordan, headmaster of the junior school: 'He used to line the boys up in the yard at the school break and examine their shoes to see they were properly polished, and examine their nails to see they were properly manicured. He looked rather terrifying—he always reminded me of a Garda [policeman], but the boys took to it at that.'

Apart from the discipline and study, all Belvedereans were expected to learn the rituals of the Catholic Church, which meant starting as an altar boy and serving mass every morning before breakfast. Mass was still said in Latin and O'Reilly, like all boys of his time, learned it by heart. In his first few years at Belvedere he arose early in Griffith Avenue, jumped on his bicycle and rode straight to school, where mass started at 7.30. Then he would ride home again, where Aileen would have a breakfast of bacon and eggs ready for him, grab his schoolbooks and ride back to school by 9.30, when lessons began. The school's playing fields were well away from the city centre, at Jones's Road, and he would ride off there for rugby practice, then back to school, and back home in the evening.

O'Reilly never minded the rigours of being an altar boy, enjoying the 'odours of sanctity'—as he later referred to the incense which he generously distributed—as well as the liturgy. The Jesuits cleverly made membership of the various sodalities in the school a competitive affair, with each new member democratically elected, and O'Reilly, like all the others, was keen to join. There were prayers in the chapel several times a day, but it was a pleasant, undemanding ritual. O'Reilly was happy enough to pray along with everyone else.

There were other rituals, too, which had to be observed—including the learning of the Irish language. Church and State relied wholly on the schools to teach the language, knowing that no one, outside the Gaeltacht (Gaelic-speaking) areas of the west of Ireland, spoke it at home. But the Jesuits, their system modelled much more on the lines of the better English public schools than on those of the modern Irish ones, had a healthily sceptical attitude towards the mission of successive Irish governments to revive Gaelic as the universal tongue of the country, and went along lukewarmly with the compulsory requirement to teach it. They were much more interested in Latin

or even maths, and Belvedere numbered some fine English teachers from whom O'Reilly, with a natural flair for language, benefited. But Jack and Aileen believed their son should at least attempt what all of Ireland was being urged to do—to learn to speak what they told him was his own language. By the late 1940s it was clear that the policy of reviving Irish had failed, but even so examinations in Irish had to be passed at every level of school, at entrance to university, and of course—and this must have influenced Jack—for entry into the civil service, even though only a handful would bother with the language after that. In national schools there had been an attempt to teach in Irish, since abandoned, and most Irish schools taught Irish six days a week, except for the Jesuits, who taught it on only four.

To make up for it, the young Tony was sent by his parents to the Gaeltacht, a primitive but native Irish-speaking area heavily supported by government grants, which was supposed to embody the frugal, clean-living, Irish-speaking, Gaelic culture of de Valera's dream. The western islands and the far west of Ireland were still seen as specially significant in Irish life, as something almost mystical, set apart from the rest of the country as the true heart of its culture and language. All children were supposed to experience it, and learn from it, to think of it as the way of life to be preferred above the more materialistic world of the east coast and the richer parts of the country whose culture was too tainted by the English. The harsh realities of life in these areas was very different: they were already suffering from a new wave of emigration which in the war and immediate post-war years had emptied parts of the countryside, and life there was far from noble. The tradition was that schoolchildren would go to the Gaeltacht, live with a local family and speak nothing but Irish, attending the local schools and learning the old ways. O'Reilly, like many an Irish schoolboy before and since, hated it. Within days of arriving he was writing to his parents pleading to be rescued. 'It was the first time I thought they had failed me. I wrote and begged them to come and take me away, but what I didn't know was that the people whose home I was staying in had confiscated the letters.'

He was in a small village in the mountains, miles from anywhere, and the young boys were at the mercy of a local population which showed neither love nor sympathy for these English-speaking immigrants. 'The focal point of my hatred was the schoolhouse and the teacher who, although he didn't touch me, used to beat the other

children very badly, in a savage way. And he had a set of false teeth that I remember clearly, and he used to almost salivate as he was about to beat these children. He was an extremely cruel man.' O'Reilly felt so strongly about it that, when he returned years later to show his children the now deserted schoolhouse, his sons borrowed the guns from the Special Branch men guarding him and pretended to machine-gun it.

His time in the Gaeltacht was one of the few unhappy memories of his school career. Belvedere would give him a rounded education of a high standard, teaching him the disciplines of languages (English, Latin and Irish—not French or other foreign languages, which were barely taught until Ireland decided to join the European Economic Community in the early 1960s), plus a range of subjects which included chemistry, physics, history, geography and, of course, Christian doctrine. But for O'Reilly all of them were secondary to what had become the principal love of his life: sport in general, and rugby in particular.

3

Learning the Game

TONY O'REILLY WAS SIX WHEN SPORT, IN AN ORGANIZED SENSE ENTERED his life. The first rugby match he has any memory of was played, as were so many of his early matches, on the back pitch of Jones's Road, the playing fields of Belvedere which were over a mile from the school. Aileen had bought him a rugby shirt but had misinterpreted the requirements, much to her small son's frustration and embarrassment. The Belvedere teams played in black and white horizontally striped jerseys and Aileen assumed that anything in black and white would do, with the result that Tony turned out for his first match in a jersey that was all black, with just a white collar. He felt horribly conspicuous, trying to hide himself in the mass of small figures running aimlessly about the pitch. He was small for his age, but his mismatched shirt and bright red hair made him stand out, and he ended the match trodden on and roughed up. A picture taken afterwards shows a tearful, muddy boy, anything but happy with his introduction to the game of rugby.

Only one mother was there to watch the scramble of small boys in total chaos, and that was Aileen, lustily cheering her boy on to greater things. There was a priest in charge and towards the end of the match she went up to him. 'Well, Father, what are they like?' she asked him. He had no idea who she was, as he turned to her after briefly surveying the heaving mass of little bodies. 'The red fellow's the best,' he said. It became one of her favourite stories and, much later in their lives, one of their private jokes. Almost the last thing

O'Reilly said to her, when she was on her deathbed and he tried to make her smile, was, 'The red fellow's the best.'

In Griffith Avenue he still played soccer, a game frowned on by the Irish authorities as British and un-Irish, certainly not part of the Gaelic culture which de Valera (who had played rugby at Blackrock) sought to re-create. Ireland had its own national sports, hurling and Gaelic football, which were officially fostered by the state to the point where the overall sports body, the Gaelic Athletics Association, actually banned its members from playing soccer or rugby. Rugby in Ireland was essentially a middle-class game, mostly played, at junior level, between twenty or so fee-paying schools, by the sons of the professional classes. Few of the national schools, those of the Christian Brothers, or the diocesan colleges financed by the Catholic Church played it—indeed they actively discouraged rugby, even if they did often take a keen interest in the progress of Ireland's international team. Soccer was even more taboo, played usually by youngsters kicking a ball around a street as O'Reilly and his friends did in Griffith Avenue.

Father Reidy, the priest whom Aileen had observed at the match, put him in the under-nines, an unruly and undisciplined gaggle of young boys who barely knew the rudiments of the game. 'At that stage, your job would mostly be to keep them on the pitch and teach them the elements,' he said later.

> And we had to try to get eight forwards, and sometimes we'd have nine or ten. I remember on one occasion we were playing and one of the forwards was late so a substitute came on, and then the boy who was late turned up, didn't see me or the referee and just added himself to the team, so we had nine forwards. And at half-time, one of the boys said to me: 'Father, I think we're playing an extra man!'

In these early days O'Reilly was just one of the mob of young players, but by the time he was eight he was starting to make his mark, although not so dramatically as he would later. He was still not particularly big for his age, but he was fast and strong, with a good pair of hands and a natural flair for the game. Reidy made him captain of the under-nines, and put him in the key position of out-half where he could use his running abilities. At times he over-used them: Reidy recalled one game against another school when Belvedere were leading by 30 points to 6 at half-time, most of the scores coming from O'Reilly.

> So I called him over at half-time, and I said: 'Now look, Tony, we must pass the ball. First of all, that score is far too high, that's not fair. Secondly, this is not an individual game, it's a team game, and we must train the others. I'm going to move you to centre and you must play your winger—you must give them all an opportunity to play.' And then Tony said: 'Ah, Father, you're only wasting your time. If I pass it they'll just knock it on, or drop it.'

The early school reports of his rugby progress give no real hint of the potential he would display by his mid-teens. O'Reilly remembers he was 'a little better, not much, but a little better than the others', despite being a year younger than most. But that was all. There was no feeling that he was exceptional. He moved up from being captain of the under-nines to captain of the under-elevens, and was still aged ten when he played for the under-twelves. The 1947 *Belvederean* records that the team had had a 'very short but successful' season, playing eight matches and winning all but the first of them, the season coming to an early halt at Christmas because of sickness and wet weather. O'Reilly, it says, was 'invaluable in the backline', but it barely singles him out from half a dozen other promising players, including his friend Frank Turvey. O'Reilly was still slight, showing no sign of the bulk or height he would develop as a senior player. Sam Stephenson, several years ahead of him and one of the stars of the senior team, remembers O'Reilly coming down to train with the older players. 'He was quite a slender young man, and he was rather intimidated by playing with the seniors, but he developed very quickly.'

Halfway through the 1947–48 season, he was taken out of the under-twelves, although he was still only eleven, and promoted to the under-thirteens where, the *Belvederean* reported, 'he served as a very reliable centre for the remainder of the season'. That was no more than could be said for half the team, and the priests were still critical of his tendency to hang on to the ball rather than pass it. But he more than compensated for his selfishness with the ball by his ability to break through the opposing lines, and once he was through, there were few in his age group who could catch him. He also discovered in himself a ferocious competitiveness, which made him a poor (although not ungracious) loser, driving him to train as hard as anyone in the school and to soak up all he could from the older players. Above all, from his earliest days at Belvedere, his eye was fixed on winning the Leinster school cups, junior and senior, which would put his picture on the stairs alongside those of past winning teams. 'I was a sort of hero at Belvedere because I'd been on the schools cup-winning team in 1951,' says Stephenson. 'And the most important thing in anybody's life in Belvedere was to win a schools cup medal—the school got the day off, or two days off, and you were feted.'

There was plenty outside the school to inspire them. These were the golden years of Irish rugby, and Belvedere occupied a special place in it. Karl Mullen, a young doctor nine years older than O'Reilly, was now captain of the Old Belvedere Rugby Club, a senior team composed mostly of former Belvedere boys. He led the team to victory in the Leinster Senior Cup which they won seven years in a row, and in 1946 six of the Old Belvedere rugby team, including several of the Quinn brothers, played for Ireland. Mullen, who would later become O'Reilly's mentor and friend—as well as the deliverer of all six of his children—captained his country to a Grand Slam victory (beating the three home countries, England, Wales and Scotland, as well as France), three International Championship wins, and two Triple Crowns—a remarkable feat achieved by no one else in Irish rugby. In 1950 he led the British Lions tour of New Zealand and Australia and, according to John Griffiths in his history of the Lions, 'his side is still regarded by many New Zealanders as their favourite visiting team since the War'. O'Reilly, along with most of the school, was at Lansdowne Road to watch many of his twenty-five appearances for Ireland.

It was some years before the Jesuits allowed themselves to be convinced that O'Reilly was going to make it as one of their star players. He was good, but he had faults. 'Tony O'Reilly, achieving more bruises than glory, spoiled his play at out-half and centre by being too individual,' noted the *Belvederean* acidly at the end of the 1949 season.

Later, when O'Reilly had achieved international status, his former schoolfriends liked to talk about his astonishing rugby skills from the first moment he ever handled a ball. It never was quite like that. In these very early days, there were three or four others as good as him in the same year at Belvedere, and many more in the schools out-side—Niall Brophy of Blackrock, for instance, who would be his great rival throughout their school careers and for much of their time as internationals as well. Even in his mid-teens he was never a sure match winner—Belvedere lost as many as they won, and all through his career O'Reilly was to find that the big prizes of cups, championships and Triple Crowns, which mattered more to him than anything else, eluded him.

But there were plenty of hints that here was an unusual talent. Early in 1950, although still only thirteen, he was again promoted halfway through the season, becoming the youngest player in the Junior Cup Team, under-fifteens who would, in a few years, form the backbone of the senior school team. It was a daunting step for a boy who was still no more than average size for his age, and considerably smaller than most of the teams he was now playing against. One report of a school match records: 'The diminutive O'Reilly, at full-back, kicked short but accurate touches', but behind that single sentence lay a story of a different kind. The boys were now playing on full-sized pitches, and O'Reilly recalls turning out at Donnybrook, not far from Lansdowne Road where the Irish internationals are played, with the Junior Cup Team, and gazing in awe at the width and length of the field. 'I thought, Jesus Christ, look at the size of it, knowing that if I caught the ball in the middle I would not be able to reach the touchline—I would never be able to punt that far. So whenever I caught the ball I hurtled towards the touchline to get within range to punt. So that was the "short and accurate" touch.'

Full-back was not O'Reilly's natural position, but the school liked to experiment and often moved players around. His special gift was his running ability, and ideally he should have played at out-half, his position through the early part of his junior career, or in the centre of the back-line where he could take advantage of any half-break to run through the opposition. In modern rugby the position of full-back has become more of a running position, but in the 1940s it was essentially a defensive role: the full-back was expected to stand well behind the others, fielding high kicks-ahead, covering the back-line and acting as a tackler of last resort. At the end of the 1949–50 season, the *Belvederean* recorded that O'Reilly had been put into the position 'with certain regrets'. He had, it said, 'all the qualities of a good centre and his passing had improved very much indeed'—this latter a reference to the fact that O'Reilly, after invariably trying to run with the ball on his own, had now learned the lesson of team play. 'We needed, we felt, Mullen's powerful tackle in the centre, and O'Reilly had all we needed in sense of position at full-back. Here he did remarkably well.'

The praise here is not unqualified: clearly the priests were worried about O'Reilly getting hurt by the heavier players, and also by his tackling ability and passing skills—which is presumably why they preferred young Mullen. Through most of his international career, doubts about O'Reilly's tackling would remain, although as he grew heavier and stronger he would become immeasurably more effective. Nor was that year's team a notably successful one, being well beaten by Blackrock, Newbridge and Castleknock. When it came to the much-coveted Leinster Cup the junior team played the favourites, Clongowes, three times, all of them hard, defensive, low-scoring games which allowed O'Reilly little chance to show his running skills, and eventually lost. But he was learning the game, keenly absorbing something from every match for use later.

The following season, 1950–51, his third year in the Junior Cup Team, O'Reilly was made captain and moved back to centre. By now he was a much improved, confident and more talked-about player, although again that year Belvedere failed to win the Junior Leinster Cup, which became an increasingly important goal to O'Reilly as he moved up through the school. The senior team did win, proving themselves the best schools team in Ireland and raising the expectations and hopes of the junior team for the following year.

O'Reilly was now beginning to stand out, but was still far from dominant in a team which included some good young players, all of them keen, all of them drilled and trained by the relentless priests. Father Reidy, who had taught O'Reilly in his first few years, had now given way to the much tougher Father Tom O'Callaghan, known as 'the Bull', a firm and uncompromising coach. 'He never spared himself or the boys,' said Father Reidy. 'He was always down at practices, did hard training, very demanding—but the boys appreciated what he did for them, and he played a tremendous part in their rugby formation.'

'The Bull' lived for the game. He bestrode the touchline with spare rugby balls tied around his neck, shouting loudly at the players, highly critical of every mistake and weakness in his young players. He had a temper which all the boys feared, and, like most of the priests, carried a long cane under his cassock which he would produce to administer punishment for the slightest disobedience or misdemeanour (corporal punishment was universal in Irish schools up to the 1960s, and was administered liberally—but on the hand only). O'Reilly was beaten as often as anyone, although not for rugby.

He began the 1950–51 season in lacklustre form, probably because of lack of fitness after a relaxed summer, but before Christmas was finding his confidence and his stride, flashing through for a series of spectacular tries. He was developing into a powerful runner with the ball, and had also worked on his tackling to the point where the *Belvederean,* previously scathing of his defence, relented: 'Defence as well as attack was excellent and his quick start combined with real pace made him a marked man in every sense of the word. He has one admirable virtue: he is quite unselfish and never hesitated to give his man a run in which to make sure of a try which he has made. We are quite sure he is a player of class in the making.' Father O'Callaghan was grudging with his praise, and often acerbic in his assessments: one player, for instance, was 'inclined to lose his head when in possession' while another was 'at once slow to start and wont to take spasmodic breathers'. O'Reilly was not spared, and the Jesuit priest obviously still had some doubts about the weaknesses in the fourteen-year-old's game: '. . . experience will give him the teaching still necessary . . . not to force the openings.' This presumably meant that O'Reilly, despite all the strictures to play a team game, was still hanging on to the ball too long. None the less, the *Belvederean* records O'Reilly making a 'fine opening' in the first round of the cup against St Mary's for his friend Joe McAleese to score, and a 'brilliant cut through' later in the season at Stillorgan.

By now O'Reilly was thinking about other things than rugby. Academically he was first in his class in 1949, but after that never shone again at school, although he did enough in the summer of 1951 to pass his intermediate certificate with honours, much to the relief of Jack and the joy of Aileen. For the most part he was somewhere around the middle of the class, except in English where he was easily the best when he put in any effort. He was, however, almost as good at other sports as he was at rugby. Saturday was rugby day at Belvedere but Sunday was soccer day for Home Farm, the local team. Urged on by Jack O'Reilly's brother Paddy (one of the few members of his own family who stayed in touch with Jack), Tony was developing into a fine soccer player with an exceptionally talented team who would eventually, as with all poor Irish clubs, lose their better players to the rich clubs in Britain—Joe Haverty went to the London club Arsenal, Billy Ryan to Glasgow Celtic, and Ronnie Whelan to Manchester United, then the top club in the English league, where he was killed in the Munich air crash which wiped out half the team. This group was from a different social class from those who played rugby—they were sons of labourers and of Dublin's artisans—but O'Reilly was as much at home with them as he was at Belvedere, and he formed friendships which he kept for years. 'He loved the *craic* up at Home Farm,' says Kevin McGoran. 'And he loved the repartee with the crowd. He was an outstanding soccer player.'

O'Reilly was a natural athlete who could probably have played for his country in several different sports. Through the year he played one sport or another almost seven days a week—rugby and soccer in the winter, cricket and tennis in the summer. Cricket, a game not much played in Ireland after the British left in 1922 (or even before), was an unlikely sport for an Irish schoolboy, but Belvedere took it seriously enough to employ some of the finest coaches in the game. For several years the legendary West Indian batsman Frank Worrall would arrive in Belvedere on his way to a summer season in the Lancashire League. The result was a team which could hold its own with those of most of the English public schools. O'Reilly's friend Joe McAleese was also a much finer batsman, but O'Reilly acquired a reputation as a useful opening bat who could, according to his captain, Michael Mullen, in his end-of-year report, 'wait patiently for runs while at the same time never missing an opportunity'. Belvedere won the schools junior cup in 1950 for the first time in eighteen years, but O'Reilly's contribution, while solid enough, could not compare with the bowling of the school star, Reggie Jackson, or with the batting of McAleese and Lenehan.

It was an unusually good sporting time for Belvedere, which was sweeping all before it, and O'Reilly euphorically rode on the tide of success. In that same year he was also on the junior tennis team which won the Leinster Schools Cup, and so was awarded his second cup medal. That junior team was unbeatable—and unbeaten, winning all its matches in the cup competition 6–0. O'Reilly reached the semi-finals of the Irish under-fifteens in 1950, but was beaten by his friend and team-mate from Belvedere, Tony Lenehan, an infinitely better tennis player. Neither of them, however, was in the same league as Kevin McGoran, the son of a general in the Irish army, who was another member of their team at Belvedere and the best under-fifteen in the country; over the years he would continue to feature in O'Reilly's life. At the end of the year the *Belvederean* featured pictures of both teams: O'Reilly, still small in comparison to the others, in his cricket cap and whites; and in the other photograph a small, freckle-faced boy, nervously clutching his tennis racket as the team lined up for a picture for the *Irish Independent* after winning the cup.

Aileen enjoyed her son's sporting success almost as much as he did. She attended most of his appearances, keeping him continuously supplied with clean white kit. It was she who applied the whiting to his cricket boots and his tennis shoes, and she who washed, ironed and packed his flannels and the rest of his gear. She also continued to make the family home a centre for Tony's friends where they would gather after a match to eat the pile of sandwiches she provided.

By his mid-teens, O'Reilly had acquired a wide and diverse set of friends. By nature he was courteous and inquisitive, keenly interested in everyone he met. Kevin McGoran became a friend for life when he arrived at Belvedere at the age of twelve. On his first day O'Reilly came over to him, introduced himself and made the newcomer tell him all about himself. By the end of that day they were playing tennis at McGoran's home near Collins' Barracks; they still regularly play tennis to this day. O'Reilly's widening social circles took in friends from rugby, an entirely different set from soccer, some from cricket and some from tennis. He made friends not only with the members of his own team but quite often with the opposition as well, offering to show the visiting teams the high points of Dublin—which in the early 1950s essentially meant the cinemas and new ice-cream parlours which had opened in O'Connell Street and Grafton Street. Often he took them home, forming and cementing relationships which would last a lifetime. Frank 'Porky' O'Rourke played rugby for Castleknock, and after one match O'Reilly took him into the city centre; by their late teens they were—and remain—best friends. O'Reilly loved to be the centre of the crowd, his quick wit and his outgoing, attractive personality easily confirming his position as such. He could sing, too, and play the piano, and loved to gather the others together for a post-match sing-song—often the bawdier verses of rugby songs they had learnt from the older players. No one thought much about it then, but what he was doing was almost exactly what he would do in later life, but which would then be called 'networking'. O'Reilly probably did it unconsciously, simply enjoying being liked and the focus of attention. He was the one who knew what was going on, who loved to hear the gossip in other schools as much as he did in his own, who wanted to compare notes on the qualities of the new players in the rival teams, and who simply had an overpowering desire for more information and more knowledge. He also had a remarkable memory, so that he seemed to be able to recall every game he had ever played in, every movement he had been involved in, and the names of the players on both sides. It was not something he had to work on—it came to him without effort, but it made him, as a schoolboy, a compendium of knowledge on the game.

There was another aspect to his teenage years which would also have a profound influence on O'Reilly. The memory of the Gaeltacht had cooled his interest in the Irish language and old Irish culture, but now it was revived again, in a different form, from an unexpected source. From the age of eight he had made friends at Belvedere with a boy called Peadar O'Donnell, a nephew of one of the leading literary, socialist and republican figures in the country, also called Peadar O'Donnell. Each summer, encouraged by his uncle, young Peadar brought a group of his schoolfriends from Belvedere to Donegal for the holidays; from an early age they included Tony O'Reilly.

Peadar O'Donnell was an extraordinary man in a time of extraordinary people. Born in County Donegal in 1893, he was in his early fifties when O'Reilly first met him, a more reflective but still passionate version of the revolutionary republican he had once been. Originally a teacher, in 1916 he became one of the most active organizers in the Irish trade union movement, but two years later resigned for something even more active. In 1918 he became a member of the Irish Republican Army, and commanded the Donegal Brigade in 1921, the last year of British power in Ireland. When the Civil War began, he was one of the defenders in the Four Courts in Dublin when Michael Collins attacked the IRA. O'Donnell was imprisoned for twenty-one months, and in jail began to write. From then on he divided his life—he lived to be ninety-three—between his literature and his socialism. His best works were books of fictional realism, such as his novel *Islanders* (1928) and *Adrigoole* (1929), which Terence Brown in his book *Ireland: A Social and Cultural History 1922–79* describes as 'essays in rural naturalism and social criticism'. In O'Donnell's writing, Gaelic Ireland became not the narrow, mean-minded desolation which O'Reilly saw but, as Brown says, 'the authentic heroic Ireland', the rural scene occupying 'the same primal, essentially mystic territory as it does in the conceptions of purely nationalist ideologues'.

O'Donnell had married a wealthy American and bought a splendid house between Burtonport and Annagry on the west coast of Donegal, looking out to Aran Island and the Atlantic. From his first visit there O'Reilly adored him, listening for hours as O'Donnell, in his clear, measured and timeless way, talked about old Irish myths and legends, of his socialist dreams for reforming the agrarian system and of what modern Ireland could be. O'Donnell had no time for the Catholic Church or the priests, and even less for the modern politicians who, he reckoned, had made a mess of the country since its independence. One reviewer had described O'Donnell's writing as 'pure as well-water', and it made a major impact on the eager young mind of his new disciple. 'He was truly a silver-tongued Irishman,' says O'Reilly, 'and my time with him was truly a formative time in my life.'

'O'Donnell was a revolutionary, but a remarkably sensitive man,' says Sam Stephenson, another member of the party which visited Donegal. 'He certainly had a great influence on us as schoolboys.' They swam in the Atlantic—O'Reilly was never as good a swimmer as Stephenson, who was international-class—and visited the islands off the wild coast, went to the sailing regattas, and generally enjoyed a type of outdoor life denied to them in the city. But they also absorbed O'Donnell's unconventional views on Ireland, past, present and future.

Irish schools usually broke up in the first few days of June and didn't reassemble until early September, so the summers were three glorious months of freedom. In the summer of 1951 O'Reilly was between the two major examinations, the intermediate certificate which he took at fifteen and the leaving certificate which was the final examination at school. Neither of these caused him much obvious worry. McGoran and his friends noticed that O'Reilly had a rather more relaxed attitude to school work than they did. Says McGoran,

> I remember, just before the intercert, the rest of us were all studying—except Tony. He would be at the piano, playing 'Smoke Gets in Your Eyes'—fifteen years of age and strumming away, not a care in the world. He was extraordinarily confident. He got involved in everything in school, and he could get the

exams without any effort at all. He could cram in a few days before the exam, but mostly he would be sitting back not even reading books—just playing the piano.

The following year there was no major examination, so the pressure was even less, and as the summer approached, O'Reilly began to hatch an ambitious plan for how to spend it. Jack, now in the senior ranks of the customs, was better off and had moved the family to a more spacious bungalow in Santry, not far from Griffith Avenue, immediately off the main Belfast road. He had also bought his son a new racing bike with drop handlebars, the latest gears and lightweight wheels with thin tyres—a revelation to his friends, who had never seen anything like it. O'Reilly, whizzing around Dublin and reading about the Tour de France, became determined to try his new machine on something more daring than the Irish roads. One of his uncles in Drogheda told him of a Dutch cattle boat that left the port every week bound for Dieppe in France, and suggested that perhaps he might like to travel on it—he could arrange it with the captain and it would cost him nothing. As spring wore on, O'Reilly became more and more excited—he had never been abroad, and nor had any of his schoolmates. He bought a map of Europe, found where Dieppe was, and began to dream. On his new bike he could travel for miles— practically anywhere was within striking distance. He proposed that Frank Turvey should go with him.

'I hardly knew where the continent was,' says Turvey. 'I didn't really believe it existed, and knew nobody who'd ever been there. Tony suggested this outlandish thing, that we take our bicycles and go to France, Belgium, Germany, up through Denmark, and if we had time, nip over to Sweden and then back again on our bikes to Dieppe.'

They set off, each with £20 in their pockets, Turvey on his father's old-fashioned heavyweight BSA bike with sit-up-and-beg handlebars, and O'Reilly on his racer, and rode to Drogheda where they boarded the tramp ship. It reeked of cattle and diesel, and O'Reilly soon christened it the *Stinkin' and May Sink*, a corruption of its unpronounceable Dutch name (ten years later it did indeed sink off the north coast of Ireland). The journey to Dieppe took three days as the ship slowly chugged down the Irish Channel, around Cornwall and then up the English Channel to the west coast of France. For other boys it might have been a tedious trip, but Turvey remembers

O'Reilly turning it all into a huge joke, hilariously relating how the crew milked the cows every day and strained the milk through their underwear.

Their first stop was to be Rouen, and the first part of the journey was everything they had hoped for. They had an old teapot and packets of dried milk, noodle soup and tea. 'If it was fine, Tony used to make the soup in the teapot and then swill it out and we'd have our tea,' says Turvey. 'But soon the tea tasted of soup and the soup tasted of tea . . . People thought we were very peculiar, the pair of us,' he adds, 'one on a fashionable sort of bicycle and the other on this ancient model, and we attracted quite a bit of attention.'

Neither of them spoke a word of French, which became a problem when they hit the outskirts of Rouen. O'Reilly's delicate racing bike was taking a punishing and he hit something with his front wheel which resulted in what Turvey calls 'an almighty puncture'. They tried repairing it, but only a few miles further on the tyre went down again. O'Reilly had no spare inner tube, and couldn't find one in the bicycle shops they vainly tried to communicate with—the bike was a new British-made machine, with non-standard wheels and tyres.

At first O'Reilly was furious, cursing the French and the bike for ruining his plans. But he would still make the most of things. They pushed the bikes into Rouen, put them on the train and spent fourteen happy days in Paris before their money ran out. 'That was the only time I ever knew Tony think big and fail,' says Turvey. 'He always thought big and here he wanted to go to Belgium and Sweden on £20, all in a few weeks. It didn't work out, but that was the first and only time it didn't work for him.'

It would not be entirely true.

The season of 1951–52 was to be the beginning of the O'Reilly sporting legend. Still only fifteen, he had suddenly grown, gaining several inches in height and several stone in weight, his mop of flaming auburn hair topping a frame which was the athletic ideal: broad shoulders narrowing down to a slender waist, and long, tapering legs. He now stood well over six foot, and was still growing. He was also astonishingly fast, both from a standing start and in full flight, to the point where he could probably have become an international-class sprinter. To cap it all, he was working on a high-speed swerve which made him one of the most elusive players in the schoolboy game.

In September 1951, on his return from another summer of cricket,

tennis, a month in Donegal with Peadar O'Donnell and his trip to
Paris, he was put into the Senior Cup Team for the first time, his
introduction to serious school rugby. The trainer was now Father
Brangan, less tough than O'Callaghan, but that was only relative—
training and coaching were hard work. O'Reilly was also picked for
the Leinster schoolboys' team, another mark of his rising fame. At
Home Farm, O'Reilly's size, weight and speed had suddenly made
him a serious soccer player, and there was talk of him getting on the
Irish schoolboys' team that year. In addition, after his success at both
cricket and tennis over the summer he was down to play in senior
and junior cup teams in both sports for the following season.

But it was rugby that mattered most. Belvedere had won the senior
cup the year before but now had an almost new team, much younger
and lighter than the old one, which started as outsiders. Before
Christmas there were matches against Heriots in Edinburgh and
Rydal College in North Wales—pleasant trips for the young O'Reilly,
who developed a thirst for touring. But the high point of the season
was, as always, the Leinster Cup.

In the first round Belvedere was drawn against the favourites,
Newbridge. The Jesuits decided it was too dangerous to risk O'Reilly,
still only fifteen and a half, in his customary position in the centre,
so played him on the wing where he would be less vulnerable to the
crashing tackles of boys two years his senior. Here, however, he was
to play opposite a Corkman called Harborne, who had somehow
acquired the nickname Hairpin. Tony Twomey, Newbridge's scrum-
half, remembers Hairpin Harborne as a ferocious, hard-tackling wing
whose reputation went before him outside the school. O'Reilly, new
to senior rugby, was solemnly warned by the more seasoned players
of the terrible injuries that Harborne would inflict on him if he caught
him; they graphically described his particularly fiendish method of
tackling.

The match was to turn into one of the most legendary in Belvedere's history, still talked about by the masters and Old Belvedereans
to this day. Newbridge's pack was stronger and much better disciplined than that of Belvedere, which spent the best part of ninety
minutes pinned in their own half. Three times a Newbridge player
was stopped just short of the line. Then, with only half a minute to
go, the ball came out along the line to O'Reilly, who took off to run
the length of the pitch to score between the posts. The official account
says: 'by . . . sheer pace and footwork he beat four Newbridge defend-

ers to score one of the best tries ever seen at Donnybrook'. O'Reilly's own account, while acknowledging the pace and footwork, is slightly different. As he received the ball, he says, all he could see was Hairpin Harborne bearing down on upon him, while his mind flashed up the dreadful consequences if he were caught now. 'Without that, I'd never have made it.'

It was greeted as a heroic score, and from that moment on O'Reilly, with his auburn-red hair and his blistering pace, would be the man that everyone watched. Yet Belvedere did not win the cup that year, and O'Reilly also missed his chance to play soccer for the Ireland under-sixteen team. Selected for a final soccer trial for Ireland under-sixteen schoolboys, he suddenly found he had a problem: the trial was on a Sunday, and on the next day Belvedere were to play Terenure College in the rugby cup semi-final. After the Newbridge win hopes were high, and the team was training intensively. A football match the day before, however fit O'Reilly was, would affect his performance. Reluctantly, therefore, he cried off, hoping they would still pick him. But his main rival for the position of centre-forward, 'Mousie' Monroe, played well in the trial and was chosen instead.

The next day was another low point. Belvedere were now coached by Dr Karl Mullen, who told O'Reilly he expected big things of him. Terenure, he told the team, had never won the schools cup before, and Belvedere should smash them. In the event, however, Terenure won easily, scoring three tries in the last ten minutes. Belvedere were out of the cup.

O'Reilly gave up soccer shortly afterwards, following an incident between Home Farm and Bulfin United when they were playing at Richmond Park. O'Reilly was marking a man called 'Stykie' Connors, so called because of a cast in his eye. During the game he flattened Connors with a rugby tackle, at which stage Connors' mother dashed on to the field to attack O'Reilly with her umbrella. 'This caused a fundamental reappraisal of the game by Tony,' says Joe McAleese, who played soccer, tennis, cricket and rugby with him. After the match O'Reilly turned ruefully to McAleese. 'Rugby,' he said, 'is fair enough—you only have your opponent to deal with. Soccer you can keep, if it involves having to deal with your opponent *and* his mother.'

Rugby, however, was increasingly his compensation. He played in all three schoolboy inter-provincials for Leinster in the 1952–53 season, captaining the team against Connaught, but it was for Belvedere that he really shone. In twenty-five matches he scored twenty-five tries, more than any player before him, and created many others. Two of them were remarkable for more than O'Reilly's speed and footwork. Just before Christmas Belvedere, after beating the English school Stonyhurst (undefeated in English rugby that season) 10–0, set sail for England for their own tour. The big match was to be against another Jesuit college, Beaumont, just along the Thames from Eton, and the boys were put up in the school dormitories the night before. The Irish ambassador was to be introduced to the two teams on the pitch before the match, and a number of Old Belvedereans who lived in London were coming down especially for what promised to be a big occasion in school rugby.

All this did not impress O'Reilly, however, who began a massive pillow fight as soon as the team went to bed and kept it going for most of the night. Kevin McGoran recalls how O'Reilly found a red eiderdown to match his red hair and called himself Big Chief Red, organizing the dorm into two sides. 'We were all absolutely exhausted the next morning,' says McGoran. 'I can remember standing beside Tony and being introduced to the Irish ambassador, and being desperately heavy-eyed. Beaumont went ahead 6–0, and then Tony scored two tries while the rest of us were absolutely comatose and we drew 6-all.'

Again, however, the fateful cup was to elude him. Terenure had unexpectedly beaten them the previous year, and beat them again this year. 'We nearly scored in the first moments when O'Reilly cut through, punted over the full-back's head to field the ball again, only to slip with the line at his mercy,' reported the *Belvederean*. Terenure won 8–0.

There were other consolations. Among the many activities that O'Reilly had embraced at Belvedere was the annual Gilbert and Sullivan operetta. In his first, second and third years he had played a female role, running through *The Pirates of Penzance, Ruddigore* and *Iolanthe*. 'We knew every word of them,' says Turvey, 'particularly Tony, who took more advantage of the great richness of the language than the rest of us did.' O'Reilly's voice broke when he was thirteen and he had a rest for a couple of years, but he was back in his fifth year with *Patience* and now, in 1953, his sixth year, with *The Mikado*. This was O'Reilly's first starring role, and he made the most of it— some said too much. O'Reilly himself thought he was wonderful, but the Jesuits, as ever, were stinting in their praise, perhaps concerned about the effect it would have on a person they must have seen as

delicately balanced on the edge of letting his success go to his head.
'A. O'Reilly was equipped with every natural gift to play the Mikado,
a fine presence, very good voice, natural ease and confidence,' said
the reviewer in the *Belvederean*. The production itself, he reckoned,
was the best the college had done for many years, but he was not
wholly flattering of O'Reilly. 'He did more than justice to the part
but scarcely full justice to himself. We mean that while the thing was
well done and would do credit to any school acting it was less than
his best. There was a somewhat casual air and approach as if he were
doing this sort of thing every day of his life and had become a little
tired of knowing he did it so well.'

That, he added, did not lessen the audience's appreciation of his
fine singing and good acting. 'We have no kind of doubt that he was
a most impressive Mikado and from every kind of man tribute he
may well expect for this performance,' added the reviewer, punctur-
ing with the most delicate of rapiers the O'Reilly balloon.

That year those same Jesuit priests took upon themselves another
duty, for reasons which can only be speculated about, but which
suggested they were thinking deeply about how to help this young
man in their care. O'Reilly, aged fifteen, finally learned that his father
had another family, and that his parents were not actually married
to each other. He was taken into the priests' study to be given the
news in cool, sympathetic yet straightforward language. Strictly
speaking, in the Church's eyes Jack and Aileen were living in a state
of mortal sin and could not even take holy communion. But the Irish
Catholic Church, so apparently unbending, was remarkably flexible
when it wanted to be. Jack and Aileen were both practising Catholics,
went to mass every Sunday, brought their son up to respect the
Church, his religion and God—what was to be served by standing
on narrow principle? Jack and Aileen behaved as if they were married
in the eyes of the Church, and the priests in turn treated them as
such.

Yet it was the priests who decided, without apparently even discussing it with Jack or Aileen, to tell Tony his own history. It is
possible that Jack might have had a word with them, saying something
like: 'Perhaps you could say something to him . . . it's very difficult
for me', but more likely they decided to protect him against the jibes
he might one day encounter if the truth came out in a malicious
manner. That try against Newbridge had stamped O'Reilly as something special, and there was a keen anticipation that something big

was going to happen to him. He was becoming a well-known figure about Dublin, and within a few years, if he kept developing as he showed every sign of doing, he would attract considerable interest and attention.

Curiously, O'Reilly does not remember being shocked or even particularly moved by the news. He rode home on his bike that evening thinking, 'Well, I wonder will I mention it?' How would he begin? What would he say? Jack and Aileen were there, behaving totally as normal, asking about his day and his rugby, and he told them, watching for some tiny sign that anything was different. He decided not to say anything that day, got up to dash off again—and never did bring it up. He and his parents would not speak of it for another twenty-three years.

That summer of 1953 O'Reilly took his leaving certificate. He himself would often boast in later life that he was only sixteen at the time—another of the little legends that still stick to his days at Belvedere. In fact he had just turned seventeen, a young age, but not unprecedentedly so. He had passed his intercert with honours, but only got a pass in his leaving, which is an average mark—well down the order for Belvedere which produced some fine scholars. He had not excelled academically, except in English where he did so without great effort, and in religious knowledge where he got first place. But then he had not worked hard at his studies, spending every free moment either playing sports or having a good time with his increasingly wide circle of friends. 'He could have been unpopular had he been terribly good at school and terribly good at everything else as well,' says his friend and rugby colleague Frank Turvey. 'But because he was good at the sports side and not all that great at the other side, he got on well with everybody, teachers as well as boys. He was not a teacher's pet, however—I never remember any teachers that treated him that way.'

Yet it was clear to the Jesuits, as well as to O'Reilly himself, that, had he put his mind to it, he could have done a great deal better at his academic work. He had the ability, but not the time. There were so many other things to do, so many games of cricket, tennis, rugby and soccer to be played, so many tours, so many dances and parties to go to that there was no time left, even for a boy of exceptional energy and stamina, for study.

The question now arose: what to do next? Despite his prowess on the rugby field he had still not won the coveted rugby cup, although he had won all the cups he could in cricket and tennis. That irritated him considerably. His father argued that he was too young to go to university. The Jesuits, too, wanted him to stay on for another year, probably reckoning he had developed too fast for his age and that without their discipline he might go wild. They were also extremely keen to keep him on the rugby team for another year. His father and mother must have had doubts, too, about a tall, handsome and very personable seventeen-year-old rising star let loose on the streets of Dublin.

But there may have been another factor which he knew nothing about. Jack was increasingly worried that the more Tony became known, the more chance there was of his secret coming out. All his life he was to persuade himself that no one knew, whereas almost everyone who mattered to him did know. According to his daughters, he told Judith that Tony's rugby career was really beginning to take off, and that he really wished fame and fortune had come to her children rather than to Tony for that reason. His youngest daughter Eveleen, four years older than Tony, was a student at University College, Dublin, and if Tony had gone to university that year they would have overlapped. Eveleen was already encountering embarrassment over her half-brother, a situation which she mentioned to her father at one of their regular lunches. People, she said, kept coming up to her and saying: 'Have you got a brother in Belvedere? You look so like him.' Eveleen found the easiest way out was to deny it, and Jack agreed, but he may have felt it was best to try to keep them apart. Tony, he seemed firmly convinced, knew nothing of his family background and he wanted to keep it that way. He would do his best to persuade Tony to stay on at school for another year.

That July Tony went to England with the Belvedere cricket team, keeping wicket on a tour which took in matches against Stonyhurst, Sandhurst, Plymouth and Wellington—all of whom beat them—and ended up at Paignton in Devon for a week of beautiful summer weather. O'Reilly loved every moment, quick to find a piano after a match and astonishing the English schoolboys with his knowledge of Gilbert and Sullivan and his other range of songs. He was also a considerable mimic and could endlessly lampoon both the other teams and his own, to their considerable amusement. But behind all the hilarity and fun through another long summer lay the nagging thought of what to do at the end of it.

In September he arrived back at Belvedere still not really knowing what he wanted to do. Rugby, of course—he wanted to win that cup, and with five of the previous year's team still in the school he reckoned they had every chance. But what to study while he was doing it? Belvedere had an impressive priest called Father Schrenk who taught philosophy, and it was suggested that Tony should study under him. He readily agreed, and with four others in the class spent an undemanding, pleasant and illuminating year. He was a school prefect for the second year running, but there were few other duties to distract him from his rugby. He excelled in the debating society, and performed in *Iolanthe*. There were dances at the tennis, cricket and rugby clubs, and parties to go to at his friends' houses. For his seventeenth birthday his parents gave him a party, lavish by the standards of the day—they hired a local club and actually brought in outside caterers, an extravagance that was much envied by his friends. He also thought once or twice about becoming a priest, a process that every young Catholic was effectively forced to do in a Jesuit school. He rejected it, but not without serious thought and self-study. 'I found the ritual, the whole liturgy of the Catholic Church, appealing. The chapel was a very important focal point for a Belvederean. We went to church maybe once or twice a day—we would say prayers before lunch, for instance. It was a very important element,' he says.

During his twelve years in Belvedere the Catholic religion was ever-present, but the Jesuits were clever enough not to attempt to force it down his throat. He had moved smoothly up the order of sodalities, and was eventually elected a member of the Sodality of Our Lady (in 1896 James Joyce was elected Prefect of the Sodality, equivalent to the British title, shunned by the Jesuits, of head boy; O'Reilly, although a school prefect, never achieved such distinction). He also attended, without protest, the high point of the religious calendar, which was a religious retreat—three or four days just before Christmas in total silence and contemplation. In his novel *Stephen Hero*, Joyce invests the Belvedere retreat with all sorts of searing novelties, to be deeply feared by those in sin. But in reality retreats were a common feature of Ireland, carried out not just at schools but in whole towns where cinemas, dance halls and even pubs were required to close while the priests were in town. In Belvedere's case, the retreat took place in Rathfarnham, on the west side of the city, not far from Griffith Avenue. 'They were pretty spectacular,' says O'Reilly.

There was a lot of fire and brimstone, and I think everyone was pretty touched at that stage, which was their sixteenth and seventeenth year, particularly about whether they had a vocation for the priesthood or not. I'm sure the kids today don't think the way we did. To this day, if I go back to a place like Rathfarnham, a strange sort of peace descends on me. I loved the certitude of those days, even though there was a certain *reductio ad absurdum*: you know, if I behave and do well, you'll ensure we win the cup, won't you, or you'll ensure I get my Leaving [certificate].

O'Reilly remembers going 'shamelessly' to the pilgrimage centre on Lough Derg, in the west of Ireland, where, he says, 'I put up with that appalling place to make sure I got the Leaving on the basis that it was a done deal. There was a quiet calculus in your mind. Yet having said that, it wasn't all about treating God like a bookie's clerk. There was a quality, a spirituality, about the way the Jesuits approached it.'

After the constriction of studying for his leaving certificate, his final year studying philosophy was almost like being at university, and he and the four others in the class, who included his great cricket chum Reggie Jackson, spent much of their time in the Maple Leaf café beside the Savoy Cinema in the middle of Dublin, 'watching the American sailors chat up the hookers'. A recent arrival in Dublin was the juke-box, which the boys regarded as a wonderful technical innovation and played endlessly.

The rest of the time was taken up with the most intensive rugby training O'Reilly had ever put in. Two years before, when he first played in the senior team, the priests had worried about him getting hurt, but now he was six foot two inches, weighed over 14 stone, and regularly broke 10 seconds for the 100 yards even when wearing full rugby kit. For the 1953–54 season Belvedere, largely because of O'Reilly's presence as captain and most dangerous back, were joint favourites with Blackrock, the dominant school in Irish rugby.

O'Reilly started the season as easily the most talked about player in Irish schools rugby, and ended it a legend. In that final year at Belvedere he scored 42 tries in 21 matches, a schools record. He was so big, strong and fast that in full stride he was almost unstoppable. Surely, in this last season, he must win his coveted cup. It was not going to be easy, however, not least because of the conditions in which Irish schools rugby is played. Paul MacWeeney of the *Irish Times*, for instance, was appalled by one Belvedere match that season:

> Following heavy showers of sleet and snow in the morning, the grounds of Donnybrook became a sea of mud with pools of water lying in many places and throughout the afternoon there was bitterly cold driving rain. Senior club players would not have been asked to go out in such conditions so why should boys have been told to submit to such an ordeal?

But they played, and Belvedere won 6–0. In the early rounds O'Reilly's team swept all before them, reckoning all the time they would end up against Blackrock in the final—which is what happened. It was to be O'Reilly versus his old rival Niall Brophy, whom he had played against dozens of times over ten years. They were now the two leading schoolboy stars of the day, contenders for the Irish international team in a few years' time. This was to be more than just a schools rugby final—the rugby aficionados of Dublin would come. The large crowd at Lansdowne Road included Aileen O'Reilly who, if she were the winning captain's mother, would present the prize. She bought a new wide-brimmed hat for the occasion.

Jack O'Reilly, probably fearing that his son's success would go to his head, had given him a copy of Kipling's poem 'If', drawing special attention to one verse which Tony learned by heart:

> *If you can meet with Triumph and Disaster*
> *And treat these two impostors just the same . . .*
> *Yours is the Earth and everything that's in it,*
> *And—which is more—you'll be a Man, my son!*

'My father had always impressed on me that it's easy to win, but it's hard to lose,' says O'Reilly.

> So we play in this game and Phelim O'Leary boots over an enormous penalty for Blackrock—3–0. I'm marking a very nice but light player called Tom Cleary, and the ball comes out to me and I knock him off and go in under the posts. We miss the conversion. Three all. Then they score a try on the blind

side—6–3. Now five minutes to go and it's been a spectacular game up to this. And the ball is being shipped out along our line towards me—Hugh Duffy, to Tony Lenehan, and I can see the ball coming, and when you're about to take a pass you always know where the gap is, because you can see the movement of the other guy's jersey, and suddenly I see him veer out of the way. So I can see the gap—I can see the Havelock Square end of the ground, and I'm just going right in under the posts and we're going to win 8–6. And what Cleary had done, which he had done the previous year against Clongowes, he'd made the cleanest intercept you've ever seen in your goddam life. Like a rocket he went down that field, scored under the posts—a 90-yard run [in fact it was 40]. They convert, so it's not 8–6 but 11–3 the other way. And the sky is a blizzard of blue and white scarves and everyone jumping all over Tom. So I wait until they've disentangled themselves, and remembering that poem and what my father said, I go over and I shake hands with him. Then I go back behind the posts, they take the kick, they win the cup, Mrs Brophy presents the prize and my mother's new hat doesn't get to present the prize.

There would be an odd sequel to this story. Twenty-five years later, when O'Reilly was president of Heinz, the company ran into a serious problem over a US Federal Drugs Administration test of its tomato ketchup. Heinz's bitter rivals Campbell's had secretly tested the ketchup and complained to the FDA that it did not pass a routine 'rot and mould' test. There was no danger to health, and the test was a notoriously imprecise one, but if the FDA sustained the result Heinz would have to recall all its ketchup in the shops, at a cost of $35 million and untold damage to its brand name and reputation. The decision was to be taken by an FDA committee on which representatives from the major food companies sat. Campbell's voted against Heinz, as did another competitor, the Hunt Corporation. Heinz voted in favour, which left the Del Monte food company with the casting vote. O'Reilly flew out to California to make his case to the president of Del Monte, who at the end astonished him. 'Mr O'Reilly, in my parish in San Bernardino is a parish priest called Father McCarthy,' he said. 'And he was a scholastic when you were playing in the super-bowl many years ago in Ireland. He said you lost a game but you

showed considerable style under pressure. He's a good friend of
mine and he says you were a sportsman and a good fellow—I take
his word. The Del Monte Company will vote with Heinz on this.'

O'Reilly left Belvedere without winning a rugby cup, either junior
or senior. But in no other sense did he leave disappointed. Many of
the profiles written about him years later dwell on his beginnings,
marvelling at the distance he must have had to climb from a modest
Irish home to the top of the American corporate tree. To an extent
he cultivated this idea in his early years at Heinz, sensing that it was
the story the Americans liked to hear. But it is a complete misunder-
standing of O'Reilly's childhood and the Irish education system. In
truth, it is difficult to imagine a better grounding for a future industrialist, lawyer, writer or any other successful man. His parents may not
have been wealthy, but they were intelligent, devoted and motivated.
Their son never lacked for anything, and never missed out on whatever he wanted to do. If anything they may have erred on the side
of spoiling him, but fortunately they never had the money for that.
They provided a stable, loving and totally supportive background
which gave him huge self-confidence and gregariousness in later
life—something very much rarer in wealthier households. The Jesuit
education he received in Belvedere was arguably as good as anything
in the world, and O'Reilly, with his interest in debating, light opera,
chess and the English language, had taken what he wanted from it.
The priests took a considerable interest in him, and he responded.
It had taken him some time to learn to play as part of a team; when
he did, he mastered that skill not just in rugby but in soccer and
cricket as well, which would provide him with an invaluable discipline
for the rest of his life. It was the ideal beginning for what was to
follow.

4

Rugby Star

IN THE SUMMER OF 1954, WHEN HE LEFT BELVEDERE COLLEGE SPORT ranked higher than anything else in Tony O'Reilly's life. He was effortlessly good at everything: he had won schools' inter-provincial honours by playing for Leinster in both cricket and rugby; he had played tennis for the senior school team for the last four years; he had turned out for Home Farm on the soccer pitch; and that summer, encouraged by his father, he took up athletics, sprinting for the Civil Services Club in Dublin, of which Jack was a member. Unusually in Catholic Ireland, Tony was an uninhibited left-hander at a time when priests and nuns beat the sinister tendency out of children from the earliest years, and it gave him a particular advantage in tennis, a game he would play all his life with varying degrees of enthusiasm. In cricket, he was a sound if unspectacular opening batsman and a useful wicketkeeper. He now moved up from schools cricket (in his last year at school he had been reserve for the Schools of Ireland team) to the Leinster Senior second eleven—not exactly English county class, but respectable enough for all that. That summer there were enjoyable games to be played against the English sides who regularly toured Ireland, as well as a tour of England. But cricket and every other sport came second to his rugby, one of the few games which Ireland played to full international standards, and where expectations of his career were high, both in the O'Reilly household and around Dublin. The Irish press was now seriously discussing him as a potential international, not perhaps that season but maybe the next—there was much pontificating about the dangers of 'rush-ing' him too fast.

Yet for all the praise that was now being heaped upon him, Belve-dere's valedictory report on O'Reilly as a schoolboy rugby player still contained, as the school's critiques had done all through his career, a qualification. 'He had almost everything a footballer needs—size, weight, pace, mobility,' said the *Belvederean* in 1954 as O'Reilly left. Almost everything? 'Perhaps he needs a little cooler judgement to make for perfection.' Nothing, it seems, could fully satisfy the exact-ing Jesuits.

Despite his extra year at school, O'Reilly, now just turned eighteen, still had no clear idea what he wanted to do with his life—except that rugby would feature strongly in it. For him 1954 meant another busy summer of cricket, tennis club dances and parties—innocent fun, perhaps, compared to the lives of teenagers a generation later, and with the priests and God-fearing parents never too far away, but none the less enjoyable. He went to the Belvedere summer camp on the beach at Termonfeckin, County Louth, where he and his friends played their own version of touch football on the sand, sang around the fire at night and talked endlessly. It was a carefree, happy time—the last such summer O'Reilly would have.

Back home in Dublin, Jack O'Reilly posed the question which hung over him all year. 'What do you think you'd like to do?' he asked Tony on one of the few days that he was in the house. The young man pondered for a moment, but he had been thinking about it a great deal, ruling out the various options until he was left with only one.

'I seem to be pretty good at debate, and I'd like to be a barrister,' he replied.

Jack had been thinking along the same lines, and very much wanted his son to succeed in the profession he would have chosen for himself. But given the demands that Tony's rugby career was going to impose on him, he was against him going to the bar. His advice was to become a solicitor instead.

'I think you'll need a lot of time off in your life. You can build a practice if you're a solicitor rather than a barrister—you can share the load. A barrister's a piece worker—you're on your own and you can't get others to stand in for you. I think you should be a solicitor,' he told him.

O'Reilly agreed. But how to start? Jack had thought of that too. 'We'll ring the Jesuits,' he said.

O'Reilly's time at Belvedere had plugged him into an order which would now look after him for the rest of his life—and expect him to look after others of its kind. The priests at Belvedere had an instant answer. 'The president of the union is James O'Connor—let's go and talk to him.' Within days the two O'Reillys saw O'Connor, who was equally direct.

'Well obviously, since you were at Belvedere, we should use the old Belvedere mafia,' he said. 'We'd like you to be apprenticed to an Old Belvederean. I shall call Gerry Quinn.'

One telephone call later Tony O'Reilly found himself apprenticed to Gerry Quinn, one of the Quinn brothers who had dominated rugby at Old Belvedere for years. Student solicitors in Ireland normally had to serve a four-year apprenticeship, but on Jack's advice he registered as a student at the law faculty of University College, Dublin, where he would take a parallel law degree. O'Reilly really wanted to go to Trinity, as his father had done at night-time, but that year UCD had started a new course leading to the degree of Bachelor of Civil Law, which was specifically designed for those who wanted to become solicitors. Trinity had no similar degree. There was another obstacle which might have deterred him: the Archbishop of Dublin, John Charles McQuaid, forbade Catholics going to Trinity, which he regarded as a Protestant enclave with too many corrupting foreign influences. Trinity was a much more international university, which took half its students from Britain and overseas, whereas UCD was much more national.

To be accepted as an apprentice he had to sit some basic examinations, but they were fairly nominal and, guided by his father, he passed without trouble. With that settled, he tackled the next decision: who to play rugby for? Niall Brophy and some of the other star schoolboys of his year were also now students at UCD—and the obvious thing would have been to join them on the UCD team. But there was also pressure to join Old Belvedere, which his legal mentor, Gerry Quinn, increased. Out of loyalty to the school and Quinn he opted for Belvedere, a decision he never regretted.

O'Reilly's reputation as a schoolboy star was well known to the club committee at Belvedere, most of whom had seen him play, but because of his youth there was considerable anxiety about how he would measure up to the senior game. There was a world of difference between school rugby and the much rougher, more vigorous senior club rugby. Over the years Belvedere had produced many internationals, but all of them were now past their best and the team needed a new infusion. Even so, the club felt it must not rush this young man. Too many schoolboy stars had fizzled out after being pushed too hard.

O'Reilly was put into the third team, where he played three games. He was relaxed after the summer, and played with no great enthusiasm for a team in which he had no interest, but even so his bursts through the centre, brushing aside all but the most determined of tacklers, confirmed that he was an international in the making. For a time he was as interested in enjoying his new life as a student as he was in rugby, although his energy was such that he could do both. His father replaced his bike with a car, a tiny second-hand Fiat 500 which he never locked and which his fellow students soon discovered could be started with a six-inch nail. O'Reilly didn't mind, good-naturedly going in search of the vehicle and lending it freely to students who had no hope of owning their own cars. He was out in it every night, sometimes all night, and learned to cut the engine a hundred yards from home so that Jack and Aileen would not hear as he crept in just before breakfast. He was already renowned among the young generation in Dublin not just for his rugby, but for the ease with which he could pick up girls. A tall, striking young man, he had wide-set, attentive eyes which missed little but focussed directly on the person he was talking to. His infectious smile revealed a full mouth of even teeth, and he had an even more infectious laugh which rang out often. He was not classically handsome: his complexion was pale, even in summer, and freckled; his nose was slightly too broad; and even at the age of eighteen he had a hint of a double chin and jowls. But when he grinned, as he often did, suddenly he was dramatically good-looking. At eighteen he stood six foot two and a half in his stockinged feet and weighed over 14 stone. His shoulders had filled out, and his thighs were so muscular that in his last years at school Aileen had to cut away the legs of his shorts to give him more freedom to run in—to the point where there were jokes about Dublin mothers complaining to the bishop about how he was tempting the young ladies. His body tapered to delicate ankles and feet, giving him the shape of a long, inverted pyramid, a classic build for a running back.

Women of all ages found him more than ordinarily attractive, a feature which would increase as he grew older. It was not one-way—O'Reilly was drawn to the opposite sex as enthusiastically as it was drawn to him, and from his mid-teens there were always pretty girls around him. He also continued to be extraordinarily gregarious—invariably the first to introduce himself to the players on an opposing team. Aileen had now grown used to thirty or so players descending on her house after a rugby match, and she loved it. Above all, both men and women found O'Reilly great fun, the source of endless anecdotes, banter and joshing.

In October, as the rugby season started, Tony Twomey, who had played scrum-half for Newbridge in that fateful schoolboy match won by O'Reilly's famous try, ran into him in St Stephen's Green, near UCD. Twomey had left school a year ahead of O'Reilly and was, like O'Reilly, studying law at UCD. He was also becoming something of a rugby star himself, already on the first team at Lansdowne, from which height he felt he could condescend to the younger man who he knew had not been chosen for the first Belvedere team.

How, he asked O'Reilly, was his rugby going? 'He told me that he was playing at Belvedere for the third fifteen, which I thought was about the measure for a whipper-snapper like that,' says Twomey. O'Reilly then told him that he expected to be on the first team by Christmas. 'I left, thinking what a pretentious young man,' says Twomey.

He would soon change his mind. From his slow start in senior rugby O'Reilly began to pick up speed. After three uneventful games for the thirds, fate took a hand which rocketed him overnight into the sports headlines, and launched him on one of the more spectacular careers in the history of Irish rugby—or indeed, rugby anywhere. The first Old Belvedere team were meant to play Galwegians in November, but, in an incident which became the talking point of Dublin that season, they got stuck in a pub in Athlone and only seven players turned up for the match. Uproar followed and the wayward players were dropped. O'Reilly suddenly found himself picked to play in the first team in a match against Monkstown, one of the weaker teams and therefore, it was reckoned, an easy introduction to senior rugby. On 13 November 1954 he turned out for his first senior game, playing in the centre opposite Captain Billy Ringrose of the Irish Army Equitation team, a wiry man who O'Reilly remembers as being 'as tough as a coiled spring'. In the very first minute,

Ringrose tackled him so hard that he knocked a front tooth out. 'That confirmed my worst suspicions that this was not a game for an eighteen-year-old,' said O'Reilly ruefully afterwards. Holding his tooth in with one hand, he played on to score the only try of the match.

The rugby writers were generous: it was an 'excellent debut', said the *Sunday Despatch,* while the *Sunday Express* reported that he had given a 'sparkling display'. None the less, O'Reilly was sure in his own mind that he had not measured up to the tougher requirements of the senior game. 'I thought, well, maybe I'll play another couple of games later in the season and that'll be that,' he said. That seemed to be what Belvedere had in mind too, but a few days later the Belvedere winger, 'Bucksy' O'Connor, asked him if he would play for the firsts in Tullamore the day after Christmas, when the team would be short of some of its best players. O'Reilly accepted with pleasure. 'Sure, that sounds great to me,' he said, seeing it as a kind of benediction. Well before that, however, he was in the senior team for good. To his surprise, he was picked the next week to play against the main Cork team, Dolphins, and suddenly it all began to happen.

'It was my day. I just literally ran wild on the park and we scored four tries, and I ran from one end of the field to the other and looped the loop, shook hands with the guy and came back and jumped over him.' Dolphin was a serious team with three or four internationals, including the man who would later become O'Reilly's best friend, Jim McCarthy (the Irish captain—not playing that day), and the Irish scrum-half John O'Meara. To have beaten them so comprehensively was no small achievement. O'Reilly's performance, remarked the *Cork Examiner* the next day, was 'devastating'.

Afterwards he was exultant, all his fears about the senior game dropping away. The whole Irish rugby world was talking about the match and his tries, and Belvedere instantly picked him again, this time for an even more serious test: they were to play Queen's University, Belfast, where O'Reilly would be playing opposite one of the best centres in Ireland at the time, Cecil Pedlow, already the possessor of three caps for his country. Queen's in fact had a full Irish back-line, including Jack Kyle (twenty-nine caps for Ireland at the time) at out-half and Robin Gregg at full-back.

On 5 December he turned out against the Queen's side, nervously glancing at Pedlow, against whom he had played tennis at school and knew slightly. This was only O'Reilly's third senior game, but again it was one that would be remembered and talked about. He had the immeasurable advantage of playing alongside the former international Kevin Quinn, an ageing but superb strategic player who had somehow never repeated at international level the skill he produced for his club. He was a master of creating the half-opening, and O'Reilly's pace and strength were ideal for exploiting them. Pedlow proved far too slow for him that day, and time and again O'Reilly raced past him, making opening after opening and scoring two tries. For his first he ran 40 yards, shaking off two Queen's players on the way and dragging another two over the line with him. For the second the wily Quinn made an intercept and slipped the ball to him on the halfway line; stepping inside the Irish full-back Gregg, O'Reilly beat three or four others to the line with yards to spare.

'O'Reilly takes a lot of stopping and has speed in addition,' commented the *Irish Times*. The selectors thought so too, because they immediately picked him to play for Leinster against Ulster at Ravenhill, in Belfast, the following Saturday. Far from being overjoyed, O'Reilly was appalled. The inter-provincial matches were a build-up to the international season which starts in January, and if a player did well, the next stage would be selection for an Irish trial. This, he decided, was a game in which he should not play. Ulster had beaten Leinster four times in a row, and its backs were far more formidable than anything O'Reilly had yet encountered. Noel Henderson, with nineteen caps already for Ireland, was a burly centre of the Royal Ulster Constabulary famed for his resolute tackling, and he terrified the eighteen-year-old. 'I knew a fair bit about Ravenhill, and I knew what a graveyard it was,' says O'Reilly.

> There were Henderson and Dick Chambers, two gorillas, in the centre—Pedlow had been moved to the wing. So I rang a friend of mine in Belfast on the Tuesday and said, 'What's the weather like up there?' and he said, 'It's absolutely pissing down, it's the worst weather we've had in ten years. It'll be like porridge. If I were you, I wouldn't come near those two fucking gorillas.'

While O'Reilly wrestled with the problem of how to get out of the match, his selection was already causing considerable excitement in rugby circles. Writing in the *Dublin Evening Press* that weekend, the columnist Joe Sherwood waxed lyrical on his abilities. 'I certainly consider young O'Reilly, even after only four senior club games, to be a better centre than any that has played for Ireland since international rugby was resumed after the last world war.' He had, he added, a 'grand pair of hands, taking the awkward pass on the run better than any centre I have seen in Irish rugby'. Others, equally keen on his abilities, had some doubts about the wisdom of promoting him too quickly. 'O'Reilly is still in the development stage of his rugby career,' wrote the columnist 'Rugger' in the *Irish Press*, 'and some rough handling and crash tackling could have the effect of knocking the edge off his present keenness and ability. That's the risk the selectors are taking.'

O'Reilly, meanwhile, had decided that the selectors were taking too great a risk, not with his international career—he had now set his sights on playing for Ireland that season—but in playing against this uncompromising Ulster side. Over the weekend he let it be known he was a 'doubtful starter' because of injuries—he had already been hurt twice that season, once when his tooth was knocked out, once with a kick in the back. 'The player told me yesterday that he doesn't think he'll be able to play next Saturday,' wrote 'Rugger' a few days later.

By then O'Reilly had no intention whatever of playing. There was all downside in this match, no upside. He cried off, pleading his back problem, and instead of going to Belfast he and his best friend at the time, Frank 'Porky' O'Rourke, climbed the Sugar Loaf mountain, south of Dublin. On the way home they turned on the radio in O'Reilly's little car to hear the result. It was everything O'Reilly had feared. 'At Ravenhill Park today,' said the commentator, Sammy Walker, an ex-British Lions captain, before the war, 'the paucity of Irish centres with genuine talent was once again underlined as Chambers and Henderson blasted Jim Morris [chosen to replace O'Reilly] and Derry McCarthy into anonymity in a mud-stained game.' There was no doubt, added the commentator, that 'by default, Tony O'Reilly must be the best centre in the country'. As they headed back towards Dublin late on that wintry Saturday afternoon, O'Reilly and his friend could not help but see the irony of it. 'I've got a new formula here,' marvelled O'Reilly. 'It's called "not playing the game". If you don't play, they say you're the best.'

He would have to play several more matches, however, before he would get picked for Ireland. His next was, in effect, an Irish trial: just three days before Christmas 1954 he was selected for the Rest of Ireland to play the Combined Universities, a match which would include thirty of the best players in the country. To his intense relief he was playing alongside the bruiser Henderson, while his opposing centre was Robin Godfrey, who could not hold O'Reilly in the tackle. He had a good game, and now seemed certain to play for Ireland that season. At the final trial a few weeks later he was in even better form, his confidence growing with each game. The press turned up in large numbers—not just the Irish press but the rugby correspondents from London too, who came over to assess the strength of Irish rugby for the coming season. Just a few minutes into the game, Henderson intercepted the ball underneath his own goalposts and passed it to O'Reilly. There was a full 100 yards to run, but O'Reilly was un-catchable, streaking the length of Lansdowne Road in his white shirt for one of the most spectacular tries of the season. 'I said to myself, all you have to do now is make sure Cormac Greally [his opposite centre] doesn't break through your tackle, and tonight you'll be in the Irish team to play France. So I played a tidy game.' In fact he did more.

The headlines the next day ignored the other twenty-nine players to concentrate on the one who had excited them most. 'O'Reilly stars in Irish trial,' said the *Sunday Chronicle*; 'O'Reilly star of Irish Trial' (*Sunday Despatch*), 'O'Reilly smashes way to a cap' (*Sunday Express*), and so on. The match was covered almost as much by the British press as it was by the Irish, and even the more sober London rugby writers joined in the adulation for 'the 18-year-old redhead'—a phrase which appeared in a dozen different reports—who was not only the best centre in Ireland but the best new player they had seen in years. He had, the press universally acclaimed, scored a 'brilliant try', and then had confirmed his claim to the international side by 'smashing through the defence to open the way for two more'. 'O'Re-illy was a menace every time he got the ball . . . there was no centre on the field quite in his class,' wrote the *Sunday Times*. 'A big lad, he repeatedly crashed through the gaps and this, combined with shattering tackling, made him the outstanding centre of the day.'

A few days later an official envelope brought the news to the O'Reilly house, Auburn, in Santry. The Irish Rugby Football Union had pleasure in advising A. O'Reilly Esq. that he had been selected to play for Ireland against France at Lansdowne Road on 22 January 1955, and would be grateful to receive his EARLY (in bold type and underscored) acceptance. His jersey would be supplied but must be returned 'immediately at the conclusion of the game', otherwise a charge of forty shillings (£2) would be made. 'Each travelling player or substitute,' it added severely, 'should provide himself with training togs, clean white knicks, towel and soap and see that his boots are in good playable condition.'

By the standards of the cosseting that international players would later receive, it was an austere introduction to the top of the game. Rugby of course was, and would remain, an amateur game, but a generation after O'Reilly a player picked for an international side would be provided with everything he possibly needed and more in the way of kit, cars to the ground, superb facilities, free tickets and all the rest. Not so in Ireland—or any other country—in the 1950s, when players were expected to supply most of their own kit, cleaned by themselves (or in O'Reilly's case by a proud mother), and find their own way to the ground where the facilities were anything but luxurious.

None of that, however, dampened the excitement and joy in the O'Reilly household that weekend. Tony celebrated with his friends into the early hours, and the next day the *Dublin Evening Press* sent a reporter and photographer up to the house to capture the first impressions of the new cap. They found congratulatory telegrams pouring in, but O'Reilly asleep. According to the reporter, he 'was very tired and slept late'. His mother finally roused him and he tottered down to be photographed in his Belvedere blazer and tie, reading his telegrams. He gave the reporter a suitably modest statement: 'I am delighted, and, of course, very much surprised. It was most unexpected.' In fact, by then there would have been an outcry if the selectors had not chosen him.

The following Saturday O'Reilly turned up, as requested, with his kit and boots in good playable order at the Shelbourne Hotel for his first pre-international lunch. Despite his youth and inexperience, most of the players were familiar to him—they had almost all played in one of the trials—so he was quickly at home. Jim McCarthy, the wiry, veteran captain, did all the talking in the dressing room, with a sympathetic word for the newcomer. After his tough first game, O'Reilly had found senior rugby no harder than school rugby to excel at, and in each of his games he had been one of the best players on the pitch. But everyone warned him that international rugby was of a different order still. Until a decade before, France had been regarded as the weakest team in the five-country championship, a relative newcomer to the game of rugby, easily beaten before World War II. Recently, however, France had developed a new style of open, attacking rugby, with rolling passes and the forwards linking up with the backs in an adventurous and attractive game which would make them dominant in the championship over the next twenty years. In the eight matches played since rugby relations were resumed in 1947, Ireland had won four, France three. But a fortnight before, France had shown their form by trashing Scotland in Paris, and Ireland started this match as the underdogs. The 'golden years', essentially the period 1947 to 1952, when Karl Mullen was captain, had given way to a more mediocre team, and it was now four years since Ireland had won the championship. Some of the older players, including the evergreen Jackie Kyle and Jim McCarthy, were still around when O'Reilly joined the team, but the last two seasons had been indifferent, and in 1954 Ireland won only one match. However, as the season began there were still hopes, some of them resting on the big new centre. For O'Reilly, however, it turned out to be a shock.

'Against France I began to learn that this thing wasn't quite as easy as it appeared to be,' he said. All had gone reasonably well until the French outside half, Martine, picked up the ball on the halfway line. O'Reilly half went for him, taking his attention away from his own opposite number, Maurice Prat, one of the great French post-war players. Seeing the half-gap, Martine passed to Prat who was past O'Reilly in a flash and racing upfield. 'I thought I'd turn and catch him, but God, this was a quicker game. I suddenly found he was clear.' O'Reilly's superior speed began to close the gap, but before he caught him Prat had passed to Domenech who scored under the posts. Ireland fought back and besieged the French line, and the match ended dramatically. 'Only two minutes remained when the red-headed Tony O'Reilly started a thrilling Irish move down the left-hand touchline,' wrote the *Sunday Express* the next day. 'McCarthy came up in support and tore headlong for the corner-flag. A try appeared certain. As he shaped to dive across the line however, scrum-half Dufau, showing super anticipation, flung the Irishman into touch in goal. So France survived . . .'

O'Reilly's lapse, however, had opened up one of the running criticisms of his play: his defence. He had missed the tackle in a move which had led to France's only (but winning) score, and suddenly Dublin was talking, not about his brilliance, but about his weaknesses.

His next international a few weeks later was against England, where he would be marking Jeff Butterfield, one of the best centres in the world at the time. Could he hold him? O'Reilly, bristling with the criticism, was determined, as he remarked, to 'knock Butterfield all over the ground'. It did not work out that way. Early into the game, the ball came out on the England line and O'Reilly carefully lined up Butterfield ready to launch himself at him. 'I must have shut my eyes, because I can still see myself flying through the air and landing on the juicy grass of Lansdowne Road, and doing a slalom right down the pitch as Butterfield was darting in under the posts.' England scored again a few minutes later, and nine minutes into the game Ireland were 6–0 down. O'Reilly did come back to score a try, his first in international rugby, and the match was eventually drawn 6-all. But he was aware that a major question mark now hung over his game.

'In those days, if you let your opposite number through, you were gone from the side no matter how good you were,' says Niall Brophy (who had not yet begun his international career for Ireland) with a touch of acerbity. 'That was a mortal sin. If you played rugby for Ireland and your opposing number scored a try, no matter what the circumstances, you were out—unless you were Tony O'Reilly.'

O'Reilly had now done it twice and, although he had made up for it in other parts of his game, there was some debate about dropping him until he improved his defence. From these two early games O'Reilly acquired a reputation as a poor tackler which he would never fully shake off. The imputation was that he regarded himself as too precious to commit wholeheartedly to the tackle, a charge he was highly sensitive about. In truth, he was a much better attacking player than a defender, but he was also a fine all-rounder, learning to cover back and to shadow his own opposite number pretty effectively. What he had not bargained for was the quality and quickness of players like Prat and Butterfield.

Against Scotland, who beat Ireland 12 points to 3 a few weeks later, he had a dull match; the Irish tactics of kick and rush were unsuited to his running game. There was no question that, by the time O'Reilly togged out for his fourth international, against Wales, some of the glamour which had attached to him earlier in the season had worn off. It had been a dismal season so far for Ireland, who had played three, lost two and drawn one.

The final game, against Wales, would be a critical one because the selectors for the British Lions team which would tour South Africa the coming summer would be there, and many of the thirty players on the pitch were desperately anxious to catch their eye—including the eighteen-year-old O'Reilly, who at that stage had done just enough to hang on to his place in the Irish team but scarcely enough to get himself into a team which would include the best players from the four home countries. O'Reilly was fortunate in this game in that Bleddyn Williams, the Welsh centre who had dominated British mid-field play since 1947, had retired halfway through the season. Williams in his day was in a different league even from players such as Prat and Butterfield. But even without him Wales was a formidable side, featuring one of the best out-halves of post-war times, Cliff Morgan, whom O'Reilly had met when he worked and played in Ireland—and who would later become another close friend.

In the event Ireland were slaughtered 23 points to 3, but O'Reilly played a blinder. 'I decided there was no point in being conservative about this game, so I'd run all afternoon. All my Christmases came true, and although we were well beaten, I was able to show a lot of skill and a lot of pace.' Next day the press, lamenting the rest of Ireland's performance, was full of praise for O'Reilly. 'Hard as they tried, the centres could never work completely clear,' wrote Mac-Weeney in the *Irish Times*. 'O'Reilly, barely stopped early on when taking Kyle's pass on the burst, made his way clear in the second half, but instead of keeping his direction towards the open space on the right wing, he cut inside and ran into eager and relieved tacklers. His own defence was much tighter than in previous games.' It was the most important game of his career so far, not least because he did catch the eyes of the selectors. The next day, when the British Isles squad of thirty to tour South Africa was announced, O'Reilly was on it.

This was the culmination of one of the most astonishing seasons in Irish rugby. O'Reilly had started it in the Old Belvedere thirds and had progressed, almost game by game, through the first team to the Leinster inter-provincial team, to the Irish probables and into the Irish team, all in a matter of two months. Two months after that he was included in the best team that England, Wales, Scotland and Ireland could produce between them to play against a country where rugby, among the white minority, was a religion. It was promotion beyond the dreams of any schoolboy—even those of O'Reilly, who had learned to dream big dreams.

Of course, it was not all joy. He still had his studies to contend with and, in the excitement of the rugby season, his first year of law had been considerably neglected. His appearances at lectures and at UCD were spasmodic, almost events in themselves because of their rarity and because of the hero status that now attached to him. No one could miss him as he strolled into the college, good-looking and smiling, his height and auburn hair making him stand out above everyone else, always the centre of a group upon whom he bestowed his beaming smile and his little stories about the latest rugby match or dinner he had attended. He lived hard, quite often staying out all night at parties or with one of his many girlfriends, but unlike many of his rugby-playing cronies he had one discipline in his favour: he was not a heavy drinker. Whereas the other players would often consume large quantities of beer after a match, O'Reilly drank only wine, and much preferred, as he more and more often did, to invite the team back to his parents' house in Santry than to adjourn to the pub or club bar. He was not being prudish—he simply didn't like beer very much, and was never at home in the pubs where rugby players tended to congregate. 'Even at that time, he was just that little bit different,' says Niall Brophy, who had tried to persuade O'Reilly to join him on the UCD team.

> He was already thinking further down the line than the rest of us students, because after a match we would be in Hartigan's pub having pints and chasing the girls. But Tony wasn't one of the rugby crowd in that sense—he was ahead of us in Dublin, off somewhere in a smart hotel dining with his girlfriend, who-ever she happened to be at the time, or with business connec-tions who he would be learning more from than we would in Hartigan's.

O'Reilly doesn't disagree.

> I'd no interest in going to those places such as Hartigan's. In that sense I was very much a loner. But you must remember I had arrived at Old Belvedere because of the excesses of the team in the first place, and then I had this amazing series of matches which ended up with me playing against France, and by that stage there was no way I could be one of the lads—or that I needed to be one of the lads.

One of the benefits of that lifestyle was that, when he did turn up for lectures, he might have been tired through lack of sleep—though he needed no more more than a few hours to restore him and often caught up with a long lie-in on Sunday mornings—but he didn't have a hangover.

When he wasn't out on the town enjoying himself O'Reilly was training harder than ever. 'At that stage you were wondering what you had, and how far it would take you, and you trained like a maniac.' His hero was the Irish wing-forward Ronnie Kavanagh, later to become one of the most capped players ever for Ireland, who was apprenticed to a firm of chartered accountants. In Kavanagh, O'Reilly glimpsed what he called 'the personification of controlled violence', a fearless tackler and loose mauler who never gave in. Kavanagh, a teetotaller, was a fitness freak in an age when that was unusual, and tried to persuade O'Reilly to work out to the same almost impossible schedule.

'O'Reilly, are you fit?' he would say when they met.

'Yeah, Ron, I'm fit.'

'But are you hard fit?'

O'Reilly never knew what he meant, but he could get some idea from the tasks Kavanagh would set for him.

> It meant, I think, fording rapidly raging torrents and climbing mountains. He did most of his training up in the mountains, and I used to say, 'Kav, it's not guerrilla warfare, it's rugby we're playing. We're not going to be asked to ford a stream at Lansdowne Road.' But he would have none of it, and he'd say, 'We're going to run to the waterfall at Powerscourt,' and of course you'd run to the waterfall, and your legs would be so seized up you'd be in bed for three days afterwards.

A tour of South Africa would make him stand apart even more. Selection for a British Isles tour was the ultimate ambition for anyone who played rugby in the four countries, and O'Reilly desperately wanted to go, seeing it as the ultimate test of his still-increasing abilities. But it would mean missing his first year's examinations at UCD, forcing him to repeat the year. He tried to negotiate a way round it, suggesting to the law faculty that they might let him sit the examination earlier—or preferably later, when he got back. In later years that would have been allowed, but UCD was unprepared to bend even for the man who was now Ireland's star rugby player. If he went on tour, he would lose a year—it was as simple as that. All the other players were older and under less pressure, although even then some of the best players, including the Welsh scrum-half Rex Willis, would refuse to travel. Jack O'Reilly, proud enough of his son's rugby career but much more anxious about what happened afterwards, was against him going. So was Gerry Quinn, the solicitor to whom he was apprenticed. Ireland, although slowly emerging from the poverty of the 1930s and 1940s, was still far from being a land of unlimited opportunity and Jack was adamant that he must put his studies before his rugby. Even in Irish rugby circles, where the question of the tour was also discussed at length, there were some doubts. O'Reilly had been catapulted, with certain reservations, on to the Irish team at a very young age. Now he was being asked to withstand a tour involving twenty-two matches (two of them in Rhodesia) in four months, with continual travel. The last Lions tour of South Africa, in 1938, was still remembered as one of the toughest and most demanding ever, and although travel had improved—for the first time the Lions would travel by air—this one would demand a considerable degree of stamina.

But O'Reilly wanted to go, and in the end Jack relented. The loss of a year at UCD was not the end of the world, because O'Reilly's apprenticeship with Gerry Quinn was, like all solicitor's apprenticeships, for four years, and UCD degrees took three. Provided he didn't drop another year, he could still finish both at the same time.

He wrote to accept the offer to join the tour, then had a final burst of parties, dating and general socializing. At the end of May it was an excited nineteen-year-old who set off for London to join the team, knowing that for the next four months he could devote all his energies to the game he loved—and to the fun that went with it.

5

A Rampant Lion

IT WAS NEARLY MIDNIGHT ON 11 JUNE 1955 WHEN THE PLANE CARRYING the British Lions team finally touched down at Jan Smuts airport outside Johannesburg to begin what is still one of the best-remembered rugby tours of all time. Even at that late hour the visitors were greeted by a crowd of several hundred—rugby worshippers in a country which that summer went rugby-mad. A swarm of photographers turned night into day with popping flashbulbs as the team slowly unwound from what for many of them—including Tony O'Reilly—had been their very first plane trip. There was a new phenomenon too: the arc lights of the movie camera, used for the first time on this tour which would usher in a number of technical innovations. It had been a long but hilarious plane ride: the team started as they would continue, singing all the way. No one had been airsick, although many, including O'Reilly, had been nervous, but that all dropped away as they stepped out on to the tarmac. In London their departure had barely been recorded, witnessed only by a few doting wives, girlfriends and mothers. But here their arrival was a national event, and the rugby fever which had gripped South Africa for weeks, and which would build steadily for the next four months, was infectious. There was no band to greet them, but Cliff Morgan, the diminutive (five foot seven) Welsh out-half, made up for it. From the moment the team had gathered at Eastbourne on the south coast of England for pre-tour training a week before, he had been rehearsing them in the words and cadences of the Welsh rugger song, 'Sospan

Fach', as well as in the more difficult Transvaal anthem, 'Sarie Marais'. O'Reilly, who loved to sing at any time, had been an enthusiastic recruit to the Morgan choir, and now stood with the others for twenty minutes under the blazing arc lights to give the South Africans their prepared rendering. 'There followed several rugby songs, ancient and modern, on not unfamiliar themes which brought the clubhouses of England to the edge of the African veldt,' wrote one rugby commentator wryly.

Such was the arrival of the 1955 Lions team to South Africa, the first to travel by air, the first to receive extensive media coverage, and the first to carry away equal honours on the field since the turn of the century. Also for the first time they had their own press contingent covering every match: the *Sunday Times* sent its rugby correspondent Vivian Jenkins, a former Lion himself, while the Cardiff *Western Mail* sent Bryn Thomas. As the tour wore on, others came out to join them, and their reports began to find their way off the sports pages and on to the front pages. No previous tour had received such coverage or caused such interest in Britain, but that was muted in comparison to the near-hysteria which gripped South Africa all summer. In many white households, there was no other topic of conversation.

O'Reilly had taken the ferry and train to London with several other members of the Irish contingent, and travelled on south to Eastbourne to be kitted out with his Lions blazer, tie, red shirt and a special kind of rugby boot to cope with the hard South African surfaces. The team was to have all hotel and travelling expenses paid, plus £2 10s (£2.50) pocket money a week each—provided they could produce chits detailing how it had been spent. The British Isles team included five Irish players, including the captain, the big Northern Irish second row Robin Thompson, with whom O'Reilly had little in common. The manager, Jack Siggins, was also Irish (from Belfast), taking on an unpaid and thankless task in the days before touring teams brought their own coaches and support staff. But to O'Reilly's intense delight his friend from tennis days, Cecil Pedlow, was also among the thirty players picked for the tour.

Britain and Ireland had been sending combined teams to South Africa since 1888, but the age when the record would be 'Played 19, won 19' as it was in 1891 had long gone. The early tours by British Isles teams were originally exercises to spread the rugby gospel to the British colonies, but by the turn of the century the pupils had become the masters. The last time a British touring team had beaten South Africa was in 1896, and only three years previously the South Africans had swept all before them in a tour of the British Isles, thrashing Scotland by the remarkable score of 44–0. Since 1906, they had won every single international they had played in either the British Isles or France. But the last Lions team to tour, in 1938— half of it consisting of Irishmen—had salvaged its honour by winning the final Test (international). No one gave this team much hope of doing even that.

From the start at Eastbourne, O'Reilly loved it, quickly making friends with the rest of the team. Many of them he knew slightly from having played against them, but he intended to get to know all of them a great deal better. There was an air of enormous anticipation and excitement in the camp, a group of thirty fit, confident, happy men setting out on the adventure of a lifetime. It was only as they finally settled into their seats in the plane that O'Reilly had his first moment of uneasiness: he who would later spend half his life in aircraft discovered that he was a nervous flier.

Within a day of their arrival, the team began to prepare for the rigorous programme which lay ahead. Previous touring teams had been bedevilled by injuries caused by the hard tackling of the South Africans on bone-hard grounds; with twenty-four games ahead of them, the managers reckoned the best way to combat that problem was with superb fitness and training. The first Test match against South Africa was seven weeks away, but most of the players, including O'Reilly, had not played seriously since the end of the season in March. At their training camp at Vereeniging, on the banks of the River Vaal, they now began a systematic programme of non-stop hardening exercises tough enough, as someone remarked, as 'to raise protests from Rocky Marciano himself'. The England centre Jeff Butterfield, a physical education master at Worksop College, took charge and devised twice-daily exercise sessions which, as Vivian Jenkins noted from his comfortable deckchair on the touchlines, were of such a pace 'as to make the ageing watcher wince'. At sea level it would have been hard enough, but at Vereeniging, 5000 feet up— and even that was 1000 feet lower than Johannesburg, where the first Test would be played—it was punishing.

O'Reilly, with some help from Ronnie Kavanagh, had devised his own personal form of training, designed to improve power as well as speed. In Dublin over the past year he had developed the habit of training in the stands at Anglesey Road, doing hours of repetition running, racing up and down the stand as hard as he could, his thigh muscles, already large, popping under the effort. It gave him an immense power surge from a standing start, which was often just when he needed it in rugby. 'I do a series of sprints over 110 yards, not just 25 yards or so,' he explained to Vivian Jenkins. 'The try scorer is the man who can keep going over a long distance and increase in speed as he goes. So many players peter out after 30 yards.' A picture of the team at Vereeniging shows O'Reilly looking leaner than he had ever been before, or ever would be again: his official weight was 13 stone 10 pounds, a full half-stone lighter than when he had played for Ireland the previous season.

Vereeniging gave them their first taste of the style in which they would live for most of the tour. Fleets of cars with drivers were put at their disposal; they were housed in a luxury hotel; a golf course (none of the team played), cinemas and clubs were all available to them free; and a constant stream of former Springboks came to pay their respects to the visitors. To give the team a feel for what they faced, Siggins and Thompson took them to Pretoria to watch some of the Springboks playing in an inter-provincial match. This also gave them the first real welcome of their tour. On the edge of the capital, they were stopped by the police who grouped their cars into a convoy and then, with motorbike outriders, escorted them into the city with all the pomp of a visiting head of state. Wailing sirens announced their arrival to a crowd which, although it was the middle of the week, numbered twenty-five thousand.

Observing the South Africans for the first time on their home ground, O'Reilly was impressed—and exhilarated. Back home a pack of forwards would get bogged down in the mud; here, in the dry, dusty ground, the forward game was much faster. He watched with a degree of apprehension the speed and lightning side-step of the Northern Transvaal wing-threequarter Karel van Vollenhoven, a short-cropped, bullet-headed man who seemed to waltz through the opposition. But the team returned pleased with themselves. The South Africans, as ever, would probably have much the better of the forward play, but their backs, with the possible exception of Vollenhoven, were reckoned not to be in the same league. The Lions backs were outstanding: Morgan, already being described by the South African press as the best fly-half to visit the country, was a rugby genius, capable of creating scoring openings for his three-quarter line out of nothing. In the centre, Butterfield, as O'Reilly knew to his cost, was one of the outstanding players of his day, while Phil Davies, a broad-shouldered Englishman with a superb outside swerve, seemed the natural choice for the other centre. The Lions had brought two players for each of the fifteen places, so it was going to be hard to get on the team for the four Test matches. If O'Reilly did play, it might have to be on the wing rather than his favoured position of centre. That was no sacrifice. O'Reilly could see that this back-line, capable of feeding him the ball with a view of the line, was perfect for him.

Suffering from the effects of a vaccinated arm, O'Reilly was left out of the first few games; but in early July he was selected to play against the Orange Free State, the toughest team in the Union. Butterfield and Davies had by then tied up the two centre positions, but O'Reilly was chosen to play left-wing, the position where he would make his real mark. This game was a turning point, both for O'Reilly's rugby career and for the tour. 'When Thompson and his men left England,' wrote Vivian Jenkins in the *Sunday Times*, 'it was no secret that most people were sceptical in the extreme about their chances of success in the Tests. This performance puts an entirely different complexion on the matter.' Later, in a book on the tour, he would add presciently: 'That day the Lions played such glorious rugby that it will be talked of on the platelands when Tony O'Reilly, the "baby" of the team, is a grandfather.'

Butterfield scored two tries, Davies one, and O'Reilly got his first playing, as Jenkins remarked, 'some of the finest rugby in this writer's experience'. The Lions won by 31 points to 3, a feat which suddenly made the whole of South Africa realize that here was a team out of the ordinary. Moreover, they had won it with try after try, coming from brilliant running and passing play that was delightful to watch. If the tour had already begun to arouse interest, this match ignited it. A week later they were in Cape Town for another superb game. 'This British Isles team in its flaming red jerseys is blazing a new trail across the African continent,' wrote one commentator. Butterfield was injured, so O'Reilly was moved to the centre where, out of all the players on the Lions team, the forty thousand-strong crowd adopted him. 'O'Reilly, 19 years old and the youngest in the party, was the man who took their fancy most of all,' wrote Jenkins that week. 'With his long legs and auburn hair, the 14-stone Irish boy made a thrilling sight as time and again he thrust down the middle with long runs.'

The tour, although exhilarating, was turning out to be every bit as tough as the pessimists had warned. Although the team had arrived by air, they did most of their travelling by coach and train, covering huge distances over dusty plains, then playing twice a week against rock-hard players who put everything into their rugby and who wanted, more than anything in their lives, to beat the Lions. There were some wonderful stops on the way, trips to the Kruger National Park and to the diamond mines at Kimberley, as well as some of the finest beaches in the world. But they were constantly on the move, coming down from the heights of Johannesburg to the coast, and back up again, singing all the time in coach, plane or train, but all the time finding the schedule gruelling. There were receptions, mayoral dinners, conferences, parties, letters from fans to answer— from an early stage O'Reilly began to receive most of them—and training to be fitted in. By the middle of July fourteen of the party were either injured or sick, and in Port Elizabeth O'Reilly changed position again—this time to full-back, where he had not played since he was ten. The match was a disaster: the Lions were trounced 20 points to 0, with O'Reilly performing, according to the reports, 'as well as anybody in a side which from start to finish were harried from pillar to post'.

It was the low point of the tour. Back in Johannesburg the Lions, although they would never quite regain the joyful uninhibitedness of those first few games, were again rampant. By now O'Reilly was the player everyone wanted to see, and when he stepped on to the field the crowd, immediately spotting his tall figure and unmissable hair, burst into cheers. He was clocking up tries at an unprecedented rate, scoring one of his best against Transvaal—'very fast, he varied an outward swing with a lightning sidestep which beat at least four men to bring him his second try—a superb effort,' wrote Jenkins that weekend. By that stage, the writer added, O'Reilly's exploits were 'fast becoming a legend'. His two hat-tricks, one against North-Eastern Districts, the other against Transvaal, had, he said, 'crammed a couple of seasons' thrills into a few short hours'.

By the end of July, as Thompson came to pick his team for the first Test, the Lions, playing a wonderfully attractive form of open, attacking rugby, had scored an astonishing 60 tries in 12 matches.

O'Reilly had scored 11 of them, and was top scorer with 33 points. There was now no question that he would be in the team to play against South Africa, selected in what was increasingly becoming his new favourite position, left-wing, with the formidable duo of Butterfield and Davies in the centre.

That first Test, on 6 August, was played in the vast bowl of Ellis Park in Johannesburg, in front of a crowd of ninety thousand—the biggest ever to see a rugby match anywhere in the world. The roar was almost deafening as Thompson led them out to the usual skirl of their own travelling piper. But within minutes of the start, O'Reilly and the rest of the backs were desperately defending against the fiercest onslaught any of them had yet experienced. No one thought that playing against the full South African side was going to be easy, but this was even more formidable than they had feared. Yet it was the Lions who scored first and it was an Irish wing who scored it—not O'Reilly, but his friend Cecil Pedlow. Then Butterfield scored again, a brilliant solo effort in which he seemed to beat half the South African team. And just after half-time Cliff Morgan, from a scrum 20 yards out, set off on one of his slanting runs to jink and dummy his way through the whole team and score between the posts. O'Reilly's turn came a few minutes later when he made a long run down the left wing, only to be brought down a yard out. A Lions player, following up, kicked the ball on and fell on it for another try. And immediately after that O'Reilly chased a kick-ahead 'like an express train', as one reporter put it, to pick up and score in the corner, thus becoming one of the select band to score in their Lions debut.

By then the Lions were 23 points to 11 up and the match seemed to be over. But the altitude and pace began to get to them, for they had run themselves into exhaustion. The South Africans came back with two tries in injury time to bring them to within a point. All rested on the final conversion kick which the South African full-back, J. van der Schyff, who had not missed all day, lined up. Two points would give the Springboks victory, and the huge crowd, which had almost lifted the roof off the stands a minute before, now went deathly silent as he ran up. 'Only two-thirds of the way out and we shielded our eyes,' wrote Jenkins in his report for the *Sunday Times*. 'Glory of glories he failed, hooking the ball to the far left of the posts, and a memorable match was over.'

It was a euphoric moment, one of the highest points that O'Reilly would ever remember. The news was flashed around the rugby world, making the front pages in all the British and Irish papers the next day. The British Isles had actually beaten the famous Springboks in a full Test match, and were one-up in the series.

Afterwards, back in the Ellis Road tea room when they had showered and changed, Cecil Pedlow recalls an odd incident which showed a different side of the young O'Reilly.

> There was a very old Springbok there who had played forty years previously, and he was sitting in the corner, very down and leaning on a stick. One of the hosts said to Tony: 'I'd love you to meet this man over here, because he was a great player in his day.' And he took Tony over to this dejected old man and introduced him as 'O'Reilly'. And Tony said: 'It's very nice to meet you. I remember reading of the try you scored against the All Blacks at Wellington on such and such a date to win the game.' And this old man's eyes lit up—for this young fellow even to have heard of him! But that was typical Tony. He'd done some homework, and he had a bit of knowledge and he produced it when he needed it, and this old man walked out of the door feet above the ground. Tony was always doing something like that—he had that extraordinary ability.

What Pedlow didn't realize was that O'Reilly had memorized the names of every South African team since the beginning of the century. He could also recite the names of every team he had ever played against, every Irish team and many others as well.

He and Pedlow had become fast friends, each of them with a gift of mimicry and quick wit which soon turned into a double act. They developed a habit of seizing the stage at the post-match celebrations to lampoon their own officials: O'Reilly did a perfect impression of Siggins' heavy Belfast accent, exaggeratedly conveying the most absurd instructions to the team. The others loved it, and Siggins and Thompson took it in good part. Whenever they could, O'Reilly and Cliff Morgan, a better musician even than O'Reilly, found a piano for the others to gather round and sing the songs whose every word the whole team now knew.

In the second Test, in Cape Town a fortnight later, the Springboks had their revenge, crushing the Lions 25 points to 6. O'Reilly, one of the heroes of Johannesburg, had a poor game in defence. Nine minutes into the second half, the Lions were only 6–3 down and were in with a chance when his opposite wing, the tough little van Vollenhoven, took a ball near the halfway line. He cut inside O'Reilly as if he wasn't there, beat the full-back Cameron with another lightning side-step, and was over for a try. It was the signal for the unleashing of the full Springbok potential, and van Vollenhoven scored twice again before the end.

For the third Test O'Reilly was switched from the left to the right wing, but in a dour, low-scoring match none of the Lions' backs got much of a chance. But they won 9–6 to go one up in the series, with one match to play—which meant that when they arrived at Port Elizabeth in the middle of September they faced the dazzling prospect, which had seemed most unlikely when they set out, of beating South Africa in their own arid and forbidding conditions. O'Reilly had now been tried on both wings, but still saw himself as a centre. Before the final Test there was much debate among the selectors about how best to utilize his running skills. In the last two Tests he had barely received the ball on the wing, and the selectors felt he should play at centre where he would get more of it. However, that meant breaking up one of the most formidable centre combinations the Lions had had in years: Butterfield and Davies. In the end, the selectors decided to take a gamble. Phil Davies, one of the players most feared by the South Africans, was dropped after a couple of indifferent games and O'Reilly was picked at centre, which caused some resentment among the Welsh contingent in particular. Davies was not only popular but one of the most devastating tacklers in the game, and had had an excellent tour. He took it gracefully, but most of the rugby critics saw it as the wrong decision—which it probably was.

By this stage of the tour the Lions were tired, and were finding it harder and harder to lift their game to the heights they had achieved earlier. The long coach, train and car journeys, and the interminable receptions, as well as the constant matches and injuries, were taking a serious toll. The South Africans were immensely hospitable, but expected them to socialize, and often to spend several hours simply signing autographs. O'Reilly loved it, moving easily in the company of senior businessmen, politicians, farmers or just rugby fans. When the other players retired to bed, O'Reilly, who never seemed to sleep, would accept an invitation from the local team to join their party. Word went ahead that he was wonderful company, that he played the piano and sang and enjoyed being entertained, and invitations awaited him at every stop. There were plenty of girls at the parties, too, and he took full advantage of that. According to one of the team, O'Reilly 'had a tremendous following from the fairer sex. All the players were content to follow him and catch the cast-offs.' But he never drank, not even wine—on this first tour he was completely abstemious, drinking only vast quanties of lime and lemonade, or grenadilla juice. Not a drop of alcohol passed his lips from the time he left on the tour to his return.

Slightly over-awed at the beginning of the tour, halfway through it his natural ebullience had asserted itself and it was he who was organizing the sing-songs and the practical jokes. 'He stood out wherever he went,' says Pedlow.

> He always drew attention to himself, not because he was trying to but because he had such a winning way and a quick turn of phrase. Others on the team, and people whom we met, found what I always found with him: he makes you feel better for seeing him. He makes you feel as if it's you who's being funny. And he could go up or down at any level, even when he was nineteen.

In the event O'Reilly had his best Test match of the four Tests playing in the centre. Thirteen minutes into the game the ball came out to him along the line and he passed it to the young Welsh sprinter, Gareth Griffiths, on the wing. Although Griffiths was fast, O'Reilly was still able to come round him to take his pass on the inside. A perfectly placed cross-kick was gathered by the Scot Jim Greenwood, who scored. O'Reilly's pace was just as useful in defence when a Springbok broke through and was clean away, five yards ahead of the field, before O'Reilly gave chase and caught him within 15 yards.

But this was a match where South African tactics, previously inferior to those of the Lions, caught up, and the British pack was soon in disorganized retreat. South Africa scored five tries to the Lions' two and won confortably. In the final minutes of this, the very last match in South Africa, O'Reilly again got the ball and, using every bit of his speed, strength and guile, raced for the corner. He made it and grounded the ball with his left hand—only for a covering South African to hit him with a bone-crushing tackle on his right shoulder blade. O'Reilly's shoulder was dislocated, causing him such pain that he actually howled. Jack Siggins came on and his arm was roughly wrenched back into place, but he left the field with it strapped in a sling as South Africa raced downfield again to score yet another try in the final minute.

At the end of September the team departed for home, full of memories of a tour which had left a lasting impression on South Africa. They hadn't won the rubber, but they had come closer than anyone had ever reckoned they would. 'Any side that wins a single Test match against the Springboks on their own soil causes a stir there,' wrote Vivian Jenkins at the end of the tour. 'When it wins two out of the possible four and, at one time, has the temerity to lead two-one in the rubber it becomes a matter of national consternation, even panic.' There was much discussion about how the British Isles' style of open rugby, with the ball handled rather than kicked, had changed the whole South African approach to the game, causing them to adopt it, highly successfully, by the final Test.

On his first real trip abroad, O'Reilly had travelled 25,000 miles, 11,000 of them in South Africa of which only 7000 were by air. The team had been watched by 730,000 spectators; and it had scored 94 tries, a record which still stands. O'Reilly's contribution was 16 tries in 15 matches, which was also a record. He ended the tour as top scorer. The South African press was generous, too. 'Men like Cliff Morgan and Tony O'Reilly will long be remembered here as rugby geniuses of an order seldom seen even in this country of great footballers,' said the *Johannesburg Star*. 'They will be schoolboy heroes and models for years to come.'

It was in such a mood that he returned to Dublin on 1 October to take up his life again. His mother was allowed out on the tarmac at the airport to meet him, and he hugged her warmly. His right arm was still in a sling, and she anxiously enquired about his much publicized shoulder injury. He dismissed it lightly, but in fact it was to affect him all his life. Already in his rugby career, O'Reilly had suffered the usual crop of injuries and scars, and would in time dislocate both shoulders several times, break his leg, injure his back, have several of his teeth knocked out, suffer a broken nose and tear just about every muscle in his body. In South Africa he had been fitter than at any time of his life—as fit as an Olympic athlete—but it had not been enough to counter the 14 stone of his tackler landing on that shoulder on unforgiving ground. But it made him even more of a hero, the man carried off the pitch—in fact he had walked, his face wreathed in pain—in the dying minutes of the final Test against the mighty

Springboks, having scored a valiant try in the corner. He had set off with dreams of just that sort, and now they were reality.

There was, however, another reality, of which Jack reminded him when he arrived back in Santry. His neglect of his studies was now getting beyond a joke and becoming a serious matter. In his first year at UCD O'Reilly had only turned up for lectures when he thought there would be a pretty girl around. Once he had not got beyond the main entrance lobby after spotting a couple of American girls whom he decided to chat up. More often than not he would get side-tracked by one of the many Dublin beauties with whom he could claim some slight acquaintanceship. At Gerry Quinn's practice he explained he had to be at lectures all day, while at UCD he told the lecturers that he had a tyrannical master who insisted he was in the office all the time. In fact he was at neither, but at the Safari coffee shop at the top of Dawson Street where every day he met his friends and chatted up the girls. In the rugby season he went to Anglesea Road twice a day to train, running up and down the stands, but his law studies were getting severely neglected.

That still did not mean an immediate crisis. Solicitors' examinations in Ireland are exacting—much more rigorous than an ordinary law degree—because the Incorporated Law Society of Ireland is a closed shop, only willing to accept a certain number of new entrants from the many who try. It wasn't a question of grades—it was a matter of those at the top getting in, and those lower down being invited to try again next year. The examinations are taken in four parts: intermediate parts one and two, after two years, and finals parts one and two, normally two years later, in June and September. In theory there was nothing to stop an apprentice taking all four examinations in the same year—the only rule, essentially, was that all of them had to be passed. There were many who took five or even six years over it, not because of laziness but because of the toughness of the examinations and the limited time available to study when they were also working in a practice. In addition, O'Reilly had taken on the extra task of a full university degree, which would now have to be achieved over four years rather than three. And so far he had barely opened a law book.

Jack and Aileen were rather more worried about the situation than Tony was, but in the euphoria of his triumphant return they didn't apply immediate pressure. He was the only apprentice at Quinn's highly profitable practice, and was treated, on the few occasions when he came cheerfully bouncing into the office, with a growing degree of affection and even awe. In the small circle of Dublin, Quinn, who had taken him on as a favour, found it did his practice no harm at all to have him working for him. But O'Reilly could see that this type of law practice, financially rewarding though it was, was not for him. Quinn was the official solicitor to the Irish Permanent Building Society, and the office was basically a conveyancing factory, a legal licence to print money. Quinn lived in some style and luxury, and his plan for Tony was to offer him, when he had qualified, a junior partnership and go on from there. His parents, coming from an uncertain past, were keen on that too. But Tony was beginning to form other ideas.

For the moment, he went straight back to enjoying himself with all the energy and enthusiasm he had spent on tour. Jack gave him a certain amount of money, but Tony, even though he drank little and was often entertained by others, had extravagant tastes. A friend from UCD worked in the evenings as a barman in the Gresham Hotel, one of Dublin's biggest, and that became a place for him to take a girl to impress her without having to pay. A restaurant called Alfredo's gave him a spot playing the piano, when the band went off, in return for dinner—and that was another spot to take his girlfriends without charge. Cliff Morgan told him of the welcome he would get if he played rugby in Wales as a special guest, and each September he went to Wales for a month, charging each club for his travel expenses to and from Ireland (usually from Galway, the furthest point from Wales, even though he had only travelled a few miles), which earned enough to see him through most of the year back home.

After the Lions tour and the brilliance of Butterfield, Morgan and the rest of the back-line, rugby in Ireland was an anti-climax. O'Reilly still had to turn out for Old Belvedere, but again avoided the inter-provincials, and even the internationals that year did not have the same flavour to them. 'I think Tony felt lost after that on the Irish team,' says Karl Mullen, who later became one of the Irish selectors. 'He wasn't your usual carthorse, and if he was playing with a poor side, he just felt lost.' The Lions backs in South Africa were probably among the greatest ever, giving him all the scoring opportunities he could ask for. The Irish backs, by comparison, seldom let the ball out, but kicked for touch and hoisted the ball for the forwards.

But there were bright patches too. On the last day of 1955, O'Reilly

was picked to play for a combined Ireland and Scotland side against
England and Wales, when the four countries played a friendly at
Lansdowne Road to celebrate the opening of a new stand. It was a
day of splendid rugby, with the two great out-halves of the day, Jackie
Kyle and Cliff Morgan, both on top form. O'Reilly too was at his
best, scoring, as Vivian Jenkins wrote the next day, 'two glorious tries
for the losers, rounding Owen on each occasion at such a pace that
one shuddered for any full-back faced with two such "impossible"
tackles'. No one could guess it at the time, but these two tries were
to represent half of all the tries O'Reilly would ever score in international rugby in front of his home crowd at Lansdowne Road.

The Irish team over the next few years was one of the poorest
sides for a generation, and O'Reilly's running talents were starved
as he waited vainly for clean possession and a little space. The crowds
at Lansdowne Road, buoyed up to expect great things after the South
African tour and the four nations match, trailed away disappointed
at the lack of fireworks. O'Reilly still favoured his shoulder through
the season, and was heavier and slower than he had been a year
before following his study period. Ireland were humiliatingly beaten
by England at Twickenham by 20 points to 0, their biggest defeat
ever, giving rise to another favourite O'Reilly story. As they walked
away from the ground he remarked in disgust to the Limerickman
Tom Reid, who had been with him on the South African tour,
'Twenty—nil! That was dreadful!'

'Well,' replied Reid, 'sure weren't we lucky to get the nil!'

This was the time of another O'Reilly story, too—half legend, half
truth. Many of the profiles which have appeared in every type of
publication from women's magazines to the *Wall Street Journal* mention how he was almost picked for the part of Ben-Hur in the movie
of that name, and that the famous chariot race in the Colosseum
might have been won by him rather than Charlton Heston. What
actually happened was this. The previous year the ubiquitous Irish
character actor Noel Purcell, whose huge figure and flowing white
beard seemed to appear in every film made in the 1950s, was in
Hollywood making *Lust for Life*. He became friendly with the casting
director of MGM, Al Corfino, who asked if he had spotted any fine-
looking, unknown young male actors in Dublin. He was, Corfino
explained, beginning to cast for a new film—the story of a galley
slave who rose up against the Romans. 'We don't want any star,' he
said, 'because Ben-Hur will automatically sell the picture.' But what

he did need was someone muscular, preferably an athlete, because of the scenes in the galleys.

It may just have been a casual remark but Purcell took it seriously: back in Dublin he went to see Father Gerry Nolan, the Jesuit priest who ran the Catholic Stage Guild. While waiting in the visitors' room, he picked up a copy of the *Belvederean* annual from the table. It contained a picture of the cast of *Iolanthe*, and O'Reilly, dressed as one of the lords, caught his eye. As he read on he noticed that O'Reilly seemed to feature quite a lot—head of the debating society, rugby captain and so on. 'I just thought, this is the man who could play Ben-Hur,' said Purcell in an interview later. The Jesuit agreed, saying that O'Reilly was intelligent, had a great personality and a good, resonant voice, could act and sing a bit, and 'moved well'. Purcell went up to Santry the next day to explain to a slightly mystified O'Reilly that he had an audition for him. 'He didn't break into a lather,' said Purcell, who clearly expected more excitement. Aileen was rather more interested than her son, and Purcell took away some pictures to send to Corfino in Hollywood.

The MGM director replied a few weeks later to say that he was coming to Europe and would like to see the prospective star. Purcell took him to Twickenham to see O'Reilly in action against England, but Corfino saw little to impress him that day. At the end of the game, O'Reilly had a black eye and hurried back to Dublin with his parents and new friend Andy Mulligan, skipping the party at which Purcell had arranged to introduce him to the American. To add insult to injury, the *Observer* had interviewed O'Reilly for their Man of the Week feature the next day, but after the match they swopped him for Yehudi Menuhin, prompting Mulligan to jeer that his team-mate had been dropped 'for a bloody fiddler'. Corfino never got to meet O'Reilly, but it is doubtful if the American was ever very interested anyway—he probably only agreed to see him to please the persistent Purcell. There were thousands of others competing for the role.

Later, Purcell asked O'Reilly why he didn't follow through on the offer. 'Mr Purcell,' he replied, 'I have two ambitions. One is to qualify as a solicitor, and the other is to play rugby football.'

To his dying day, Purcell regretted O'Reilly's refusal to audition. 'There was every chance he would have got it, and in my book he would have been great for it,' he said. 'He was perfect for the part with his build—he was such a fine-looking young man.' But, he added philosophically, maybe it was better that he hadn't gone into show business: 'It might have taken his mind off what he achieved in other fields.'

The story of how O'Reilly was in the running for the role was picked up by the papers, even in places as far away as Cape Town. Over the years the tale would be changed and exaggerated, to relate how he was actually offered the role but turned it down. O'Reilly rather encouraged this distortion of the truth, basking in the even greater glory it gave him among his friends (and the girls) in Dublin.

The England match was the low point of the season. Playing again at centre, he scored a try against France at Colombes and another against Scotland, while Ireland restored some sense of honour by beating Wales to spoil their bid for the Triple Crown.

That season had introduced him to Andy Mulligan. Born in February 1936, Mulligan was three months older than O'Reilly, a slim, willowy scrum-half and one of the few people in international rugby who was probably faster than O'Reilly on the burst. He was also an elegant man, both on the rugby field and off it, slightly affecting the air of a toff among the less cultured Irish team. He wore a cravat, with a hat or cap worn at a rakish angle—on tour it sometimes became a beret—and behaved like a dandy too. Brought up in England, he was a Cambridge student when he was first picked for Ireland, the eighth man to partner the perennial Jackie Kyle in the half-backs. He was almost as funny as O'Reilly, an equally good raconteur and mimic, and from the beginning the two formed a friendship which was to endure a lifetime.

If anything, Mulligan was wilder than O'Reilly, encouraging him to even longer hours out on the town at night. The two often double-dated girls, vying with each other to see who could be more successful. O'Reilly's foreign travels were opening up new markets for his talents, and at the France–Ireland match in Paris he found a very pretty *contessa* whom he invited to visit him in Ireland. A few months later she did. At the time O'Reilly was penniless, but he was still determined to put on an impressive show. He arranged to meet her in the bar in the Gresham where he grandly ordered drinks, knowing that, as usual, he would not have to pay. His battered little Fiat 500 he carried off with considerable élan—he had outside, he told her, 'an Italian two-seater' in which he was going to convey her to a grand dinner. Unfortunately he forgot to tell her that her particular seat was not actually anchored to the floor, and as he accelerated down O'Connell

Street it tipped up, throwing two elegant legs complete with sexy French suspenders high in the air. He took her to Alfredo's where he was received with his usual pomp, and ushered to a table. He had also neglected to tell her that the cost of the meal was paid for by his piano spot between the bands, but Alfredo, in O'Reilly's confidence, carried it all off. 'We have a very great rugby player here tonight,' he announced to the restaurant, 'Mr Tony O'Reilly, who's just here as a guest tonight, but has agreed to give us a few melodies.'

With the French girl now firmly won over, O'Reilly found he had another problem—he had nowhere to take her afterwards. All he could think of was the UCD building at Earlsfort Terrace, which was closed when they reached it. But they couldn't stop now. A few minutes later the UCD porter, hearing a noise from the shadows on the top of the steps, walked by. 'Goodnight then, Tony,' he called out. 'Good luck to ye!'

There were other girlfriends of longer standing but he kept coming back to one girl in particular, Dorothy Connolly. 'It was quite a vivid time in my life,' he says now with a careful understatement.

The South African tour had brought him fame well outside Ireland. The London *Daily Express*, one of the major British papers of the day, sent over its columnist Carole Findlater to see him play against Wales. O'Reilly, she wrote, was 'the new pin-up of sport', a title she reckoned he had taken over from the English cricketer, Denis Compton who had held it for the past nineteen years. She had, she said, spent the match 'in a nerve-racking frenzy of suspense' watching him on the field, 'praying he would not be kicked, clawed or socked before we had a chance to photograph him the following day'. When they did meet, she confessed herself to be bowled over. 'This tall, good-looking young man with the startling mop of vivid auburn curls, large hazel eyes, and the most perfect teeth I have ever seen, is by no means a brawn, muscle, and no brains boy.' O'Reilly had made another conquest.

All this added to the rapidly growing legend that increasingly surrounded him, later causing the Dublin cynics to remark that he was achieving more off the field than he was on it. However, behind all his fun-seeking and socializing he had retained his ability to calculate and assess his own life, and his own strengths and weaknesses. Twenty years later, in the age of television, O'Reilly would have been accorded such star status that he would not have had to worry too seriously about working for a living afterwards. But in the amateur game of rugby in the 1950s star status lasted for ten minutes after retirement, and O'Reilly had seen too many former great players down on their luck to have any illusions. Jack was absolutely insistent that he must devote himself to law, even if his rugby career had to suffer. His son agreed.

He was now approaching his twentieth birthday. He had proved, to himself as much as to anyone else, that in physical prowess he measured up to the best in the world. But he had not stretched himself mentally yet, and that spring he took the cold, hard decision to put himself through the most punishing study schedule he could devise, partly to make up for his missed two years, but also as a test for himself. His examinations were in September, so he had four full months in which to get ready—not just to pass, but to beat everyone else. The contrast with the same four months the previous year when he had been in South Africa could not have been greater. He said goodbye to his girlfriend, went back to Santry, took the phone off the hook, and for the whole summer refused to speak to anyone other than his mother (and occasionally his father). He never read a newspaper and allowed nothing to impinge upon his schedule; his sole relaxation was a record player and the occasional bit of snowy television picked up with a large aerial from Ulster. During those months he even gave up training—'I looked like Colonel Blimp'— while he kept himself chained to the desk. He developed a daily work plan consisting of three four-hour study periods with short breaks in between; during those work periods he did not allow himself to move from his desk even for a cup of coffee or a visit to the lavatory. 'I reasoned that the person I had to break in this was myself—I was the enemy. There were days when I sat in front of the books and didn't absorb a thing. But gradually the flywheel got going.'

He discovered, half to his surprise, that he was interested in law, easily able to absorb the principles of tort and contract and property and so on. Most of the papers he would take for his solicitor's examinations were similar to those he would have to take at university, but there were extra ones too and the papers were only days apart. In September 1956, a pale and bloated O'Reilly turned up to sit both sets of examinations—and sailed through. The Incorporated Law Society records him as getting fifth place in the country in the intermediate examination.

That was the schedule to which he kept for the next two years. Every September he was in Wales, playing rugby and clocking up his precious financial reserves which would feed him for the next year. By November he was back in Dublin for the opening of the rugby season, for a period of high jollity, and at peak fitness by January when the international season began. From April onwards he was a recluse. Neither Gerry Quinn nor the lecturers in UCD saw any more of him than they had in the first year, but in the autumn of 1958, after another reclusive summer, he took his finals. He was first in Ireland in Part I and third in Part II. 'Having regard to your feats in the rugby field at this time these were no mean academic achievements,' the secretary of the Law Society wrote to him later. In November that year O'Reilly was enrolled as a solicitor. He would never practise.

6

Susan Cameron

WHILE O'REILLY WAS STUDYING AND PLAYING RUGBY AROUND HIM social and economic change, which had come slowly to Ireland in the 1940s and early 1950s, was beginning to accelerate. During his years at school and university, a predominantly rural society was perceptibly becoming an urban one. The Dublin into which he had been born twenty-two years before had a population of 472,000, but by 1958 it had grown to nearly 600,000; and a decade later, including the population of its environs into account too, that figure would top 750,000. And that was only part of the story. The west and south-west of Ireland, the country areas that Valera had seen as the backbone of his idealistic, self-sufficient, self-reliant, Gaelic-speaking nation, were emptying at bewildering speed; young women in particular were leaving the land for the big city and beyond. 'The trains and buses at weekends were packed throughout the 1950s with new urban dwellers returning to maintain contacts with their roots in the countryside,' wrote Terence Brown. Even that small contact would not last, as whole families moved and entire areas emptied.

Dublin was often just a staging post for the migration. Thousands stayed only long enough to become disillusioned with an over-populated and still relatively poor city, before passing on, like the characters in Edna O'Brien's *The Country Girls*, published in 1960, to the brighter prospects of London and the rest of England. In the 1950s, the net emigration from Ireland was a staggering 400,000, reaching its highest point since the days of the Great Famine over a hundred years before just as O'Reilly graduated with his law degrees.

Much else had changed too. The Dublin of Jack O'Reilly's youth had been an elegant, colourful, cultured but down-at-heel colonial centre. Now it had become a duller, albeit more modern, administrative and commercial capital. Many of the fine Georgian terraces for which Dublin was renowned were being knocked down to be replaced with graceless concrete and glass structures, a trend which would become worse in the 1960s, the low point for architecture in Europe generally but Ireland in particular. Dublin was developing a large middle class: its thousands of general labourers were seeking jobs on building sites in England, to be replaced in the population by office workers, many of them in jobs created by the ever-growing civil service. Dublin seemed to have become a city of young secretaries, thousands of young women who took on low-paid clerical work with the government or state-sponsored bodies until in some areas there were three girls for every young man. Whole new estates of semi-detached and terraced houses sprang up on the outskirts of the city, and the streets, almost traffic-free when Tony O'Reilly rode to school on his bicycle, were now clogged with cars.

O'Reilly was not to know it at the time, but 1958, the year of his graduation, was to prove a turning point in the history of his native land, marking the end of the old Ireland, whose traditions and folk-lore he had absorbed from his parents and uncles as well as Peadar O'Donnell, and the beginning of a new Ireland for which he was to become one of the flag-bearers. Across the Irish Sea the British economy was in a post-war boom, offering Ireland's young doctors, dentists and engineers as well as labourers opportunities which seemed limitless. For several decades Ireland simply exported its unemployment: its farm workers and skilled artisans alike moved for the higher wages available in Britain, and the earnings they sent home kept the country's balance of payments above water. This was the period building up to Harold Macmillan's 'You've never had it so good' speech, which had as profound an impact on Irish consciousness as on British, highlighting as it did the British consumer boom and the gap in the standard of living between the two countries. Britain also offered welfare benefits and a free National Health Service many times superior to those in its much poorer neighbour—yet another attraction to large Irish families. 'In the bright dawn of 1934 de

Valera had envisaged a day when the nation's children would no longer be reared for export,' wrote the historian J. J. Lee, 'but that was what more and more of them would be brought up for as his regime tottered to its close . . . His monument was now to be found not in the cosy homesteads, but in the deserted homesteads of the Irish countryside.'

By 1958 even de Valera, now seventy-four and almost blind, his unshakable grip on his party beginning to slacken, was forced to accept that the country had descended into a slough. In May, a devastating report by the Irish Department of Finance starkly spelt out the true position of the nation: an independent Ireland had not delivered what had been promised or hoped for, economically, socially or educationally. Indeed, rural Ireland, it said, had sunk into 'a psychological and economic malaise' where there was growing despair and depression. 'After 35 years of native government people are asking whether we can achieve an acceptable degree of economic progress. The common talk among parents in the towns, as well as in rural Ireland, is of their children having to emigrate as soon as their education is completed in order to secure a reasonable standard of living,' it concluded.

The author of that report was an impressive and deeply thoughtful young civil servant called T. K. (Ken) Whitaker, and he would later play an important role in the life of Tony O'Reilly. Whitaker found a deeply gloomy country encapsulated for him, he later said, in a cartoon on the cover of *Dublin Opinion*, a humorous magazine of the day. This showed a downhearted Kathleen ni Houlihan (the traditional personification of Ireland) asking a fortune-teller, 'Have I a future?' Whitaker would later talk of a community experiencing a dark night of the soul 'in which doubts were prevalent as to whether the achievement of political independence had not been a failure'. The lesson had finally been learnt, but for those who might still doubt, Whitaker bluntly spelt it out: the pursuit of self-sufficiency, he said, 'through policies which fostered inefficiency', offered no prospect of employment in Ireland at an acceptable income for those who sought it.

De Valera had twice been out of power to coalition governments, and a year later would formally pass over the leadership to Sean Lemass, the strongest man in the government. For years, both as finance minister and as the minister in charge of industry and commerce, Lemass had been changing the way the Irish economy was run. He could see what de Valera did not want to admit: that in a Europe increasingly coalescing into large free trade units—the European Economic Community, which Britain was talking about joining, and the European Free Trade Association (EFTA)—Ireland would inevitably be forced to abandon its protective walls and let in the outside world to compete with its over-manned, under-capitalized and feather-bedded industries.

In the circumstances, it was wholly in tune with the times that O'Reilly should choose to take the well-worn path of so many of his generation. That autumn, his law degrees tucked under his arm never to be used, he left for England. He could have had many jobs in Ireland, including a position in Gerry Quinn's legal practice. His contacts by that stage were widespread and powerful, as his rugby colleagues enviously knew. With a certain amount of premeditated hard work, he had used his prominence on the field—and, it must be said, his personality—to effect an introduction to many of the circles of influence around him. In Dublin, rugby opened every door, and there were many who would have been flattered to have had the young British Lions' star work for them.

He left behind an economy still recovering from the crisis in 1955, with rising unemployment and a serious balance of payments deficit. His father was by now nearly at the top of the Irish Customs service, yet his salary, and his standard of living, were less than those of a middle manager in Britain. There were no businesses of any consequence in Ireland, and the biggest were usually subsidiaries of British or American companies. In a country whose entire population was less than a third that of London or New York, the domestic market could sustain few thriving businesses. The few entrepreneurs and businessmen were generally regarded with suspicion and distrust. Whitaker's vision of the new Ireland, in which the state would take a much more active part in productive investment and foreign investment would be encouraged to flow in (in much the way that so many Third World countries, notably China, would do several decades later), did not promise immediate salvation either. There was also another problem for O'Reilly: although his enthusiasm for rugby was beginning to wane, he was still being picked for tours overseas, including one to Canada (where he had spent his twenty-first birthday), which required lengthy periods away from the job. Not every employer would accept that.

So he accepted an offer in the East Midlands of England, some way from the bright lights of London, but close enough for him to get there at weekends when he could get together with a number of his old friends and team-mates. He was not turning his back completely on Ireland—this would be a temporary move, which he would use to gain experience, training and status (training in England still meant something special in Ireland, which was in awe of its big industrial neighbour and disrespectful of its own home-grown product). In Leicester he became a management consultant at Weston-Evans, receiving a salary of £2000 a year, well in excess of anything he could have earned in Ireland. O'Reilly had been recruited by a Scottish rugby international friend, R. G. K. McEwen, and in return he recruited another rugby player, Phil Horrocks-Taylor, who had first played for England earlier that year (although not against Ireland), and had partnered Andy Mulligan at Cambridge where the two formed a formidable pair of half-backs. Although he only ever received nine caps, Horrocks-Taylor was to become something of a legend among the Irish team, mainly because of the story the Limerick man Mick English used to relate, of how he was faced with Horrocks-Taylor bearing down upon him with the ball. 'I tried to tackle him, but Horrocks went one way and Taylor went the other—and I was left holding the hyphen!'

O'Reilly played rugby for Leicester, considerably boosting the prospects for that team in English club football.

He approached the new job with considerable excitement, but for the most part, although he would never admit it, it was dull, repetitive work, standing for hours with a stopwatch at factories making glazed piping. But for a man who would rise to one of the top executive posts in the world, it was to prove an excellent grounding. Over the next two years he learned about standard unit costing, basic accounting at production level and other techniques. He spent much of the time on the factory floor, watching how things were done and devising methods of making them better. Leicester was still the centre of a once great British shoe industry, and was also on the edge of the Potteries, based around Stoke-on-Trent. O'Reilly would learn about both industries: one day he would be advising a factory on how to speed up a production line making ceramic pipes and bathroom fittings, and the next he would be in a building materials plant. It was a steep learning curve, but O'Reilly, despite his youth, was ideal management consultant material. In the small pool that was Ireland he would have been a large frog, but in the English Midlands, where rugby is a minority sport, he was almost unknown. Yet he had immense self-confidence, an extraordinary memory for faces, names and detail, and an inquisitive mind which sought to find out how everything worked. He discovered that he liked and could absorb large quantities of figures and statistics. And despite the distractions of his rugby he had a huge appetite for work, needing little sleep and quite prepared to work through the night. He also made sure he got on well with the people he worked with, using his charm and his quickness of wit to make friends quickly.

During this time he lived in the quaintly named town of Ashby-de-la-Zouch, very different from Dublin, but enjoyable for all that. Again, rugby opened the doors and he was soon leading as busy a social life as he ever had. As soon as the money began coming in he bought himself a white TR3 sports car and roared around the English countryside, often driving to London where Andy Mulligan had a job with the De La Rue company and played rugby for London-Irish, or going to Wales to catch the same ferry from Holyhead that his half-sisters had used all those years ago.

He still played rugby, of course, although Leicester could never be as important for him as Old Belvedere. In the 1957–58 season, his last before moving to England, he had been the top scorer in Irish rugby with a total of 52 tries and two dropped goals—162 points in all, a remarkable total for a non-place kicker. Yet even so, just as the school-boy cups had eluded him, so did the senior cups, and all the time he played rugby—at school, at club level or at international level—O'Reilly never played in a team which actually won a cup or a championship. During all the years he played for Ireland, it never won either the Triple Crown or the International Championship. Was it just bad luck, bad teams—or something more? It would be a subject debated keenly in Irish rugby for as long as O'Reilly played the game.

For the moment, however, he could shrug all that aside in the excitement of his new life. That year he became engaged to marry a girl who had been one of his more serious girlfriends—in between quite a few dozen others—since he was a teenager. O'Reilly first met Dorothy Connolly on the night of the Belvedere—Blackrock schools' cup final in 1954, and had instantly set out to pinch her off her escort, a boy from another school whom he disliked. O'Reilly had a large black eye developing from a rough tackle, and was also feeling desperately deflated after the defeat, but still managed to persuade her to swop partners. Dorothy, he discovered, worked at the Royal Bank in Talbot Street in the centre of Dublin, and soon it was a serious teenage romance—more serious, it must be said, for Dorothy than it was for O'Reilly.

Now, five years after their first meeting, he proposed to her—and she accepted. They agreed to be married the following year when he was established in his new profession; in the meantime O'Reilly would get back to Dublin as often as he could—or she would go to Leicester or London to meet him. In retrospect it was an odd engagement, out of character with O'Reilly's life up to that point, and even more out of character with what came later. If he had found women attracted to him—and vice versa—in his late teens, that was multiplied many times over by his early twenties when he was hailed everywhere as the great star. Dorothy was a pretty girl, outgoing and athletic (she played hockey for Leinster). O'Reilly's friends at the time remember her as 'an explosive personality', well able to cope with her famous boyfriend, but there were very few women who could live alongside him for long. He was not, by nature, monogamous, and he must have known that Leicester and his tours would throw up as many temptations as ever. The relationship was turbulent, with many highs but some lows too. 'I would have been surprised if it had worked out,' says one old friend who saw them often. 'Dorothy was a strong character, but volatile, and so was he.' Ronnie Dawson, later to captain both Ireland and the Lions, also remembers the relationship as sometimes difficult. 'Tony liked her a lot but there were clashes of personality.'

In mid-February 1959 he was back in Dublin for his seventeenth international, another low point in his rugby career. Ireland were playing at home to England, and had failed even to score against them for the past three years. That season they fared no better, losing a dour match to a single penalty goal, despite the fact that their forwards, led by Ronnie Dawson, played brilliantly and destroyed the English pack. It was the backs, who included not only O'Reilly but Niall Brophy, Cecil Pedlow, Noel Henderson and Andy Mulligan, who wasted the ball. The Irish papers the next day were venomous, wondering why O'Reilly could be such a match-winner on tour and so ordinary at home. There were some good reasons, of course: the out-half, Mick English, kicked all day rather than passing the ball along the line; O'Reilly was also a heavily marked man and the opposite centres, Butterfield and Phillips, hardly missed a tackle. But even so it was disappointing and frustrating stuff, for O'Reilly even more than for the spectators. At Cardiff Arms Park a month later he moved to wing three-quarter against Wales, and scored a good try, but Ireland, 6–0 up at half-time, lost 8–6 in the final moments.

Then things began to look up. Early in April, the British Lions selectors chose their team for what promised to be the tour of the decade, an even more prestigious event than the tour of South Africa five years earlier which had made O'Reilly a star. 'A tour of New Zealand is probably the greatest experience that can come a British rugby man's way,' wrote Vivian Jenkins, including in his hyperbole the Irish too. New Zealand had acquired a daunting reputation ever since their first All Blacks team had arrived in the British Isles in 1905 and in 33 matches piled up 868 points with only 47 scored against them—a record that will probably stand forever. They had remained unbeaten since. In a country with a population at the time of only 2.5 million, rugby ruled unchallenged as the national game—a religion for tough, uncompromising players who were even feared by the Springboks. Yet the adventurous, exciting rugby played by the Lions in South Africa four years before had lifted everyone's spirits and hopes, and there was keen anticipation in the British rugby world to see if the same attacking rugby might not also disrupt the traditional All Black style of grim attrition.

O'Reilly's selection came at a good time for him. That season, his first in a real job, had been hard work for him. He weighed 14 stone 7lb—11lb more than he had been on the South African tour four years before—and his career was increasingly getting in the way of his training. He had scaled the heights of the rugby world before he was twenty, and there were not many goals left to achieve, other than cups and the Triple Crown—and these were team efforts rather than individual achievements. A tour against Australia and New Zealand was something very special, however. It would sharpen him up, both mentally and physically, and would also be great fun—three months on the other side of the world, away from the factories of the British Midlands, would be delightful. There would be many old friends on the team, both from the last tour and from the Irish team. His great friend Ronnie Dawson, the Irish hooker, was picked as captain, the fourth successive Irishman to captain a Lions tour; while his old schoolboy opponent, Niall Brophy, was also in the team, as were five other Irish players. O'Reilly was one of only six (out of thirty) players to survive from the tour of 1955.

The tourists were ordered not to play any rugby after 5 April, to avoid staleness and injury before the tour. The Irish team, however, was excluded from this restriction: they still had to play France in Dublin on 18 April for the last of the season's internationals. O'Reilly arrived back in Dublin in time to see Dorothy before the game, and the next day she was at Lansdowne Road to watch him play in a match which turned out to be the best of the season. France was unbeaten that year, and was already assured of the championship, while Ireland was regarded as the worst team among the five. Yet it was the type of situation which brought out the best in the Irish, and that day the team excelled itself, winning 9–5. It was the last international for some of the great players on both sides, including Noel Henderson, who had first been capped in 1949 when O'Reilly was still playing junior schools rugby. Vivian Jenkins, who covered the match for the *Sunday Times*, recorded it as a 'magnificent performance' which 'gave the tour itself a big fillip in advance'.

They took off a few weeks later, to begin the tour in Australia before getting on to the really serious stuff in New Zealand. Four years earlier, in 1955, O'Reilly had been the baby of the tour, an unknown quantity even to his team-mates. Now, in 1959, he was one of the veterans, with twenty caps for Ireland, one Lions tour and several Barbarian tours behind him. 'For a man of 23, he was astonishingly mature of mind,' wrote Terry Maclean in his history of the tour, echoing the views of Brophy, Dawson and so many others. Maclean was greatly impressed with O'Reilly's reading habits ('mostly Irish literature and about Irish revolutionary heroes', although in fact O'Reilly's reading was far more catholic). His personality and wit in any case made him one of the natural leaders of the party, but so did his passion for analysing every aspect of the game of rugby. He could—and did—make life miserable for the managers of the tour, but Dawson found him supportive, a useful man to have on his side. Before the tour even set out, O'Reilly was also the player most talked about in New Zealand. 'After his record-breaking success of the 1955 tour,' said the rugby journalist J. B. G. Thomas, who accompanied both tours, 'there was an air of expectancy in the Antipodes for the arrival of the Golden Boy. For them he was the wing *extraordinaire*—big, strong, fast and handsome.' It would make him a marked man on the field in New Zealand, but also a celebrity—and O'Reilly decided to take full advantage of that.

He had learnt from his previous tours, and came well organized. In London he had met several of the England cricket team which had toured Australia a few years before, who passed on the phone numbers of some of the pretty girls they had met. The trick, he had discovered, was to ring up and say you were a friend of the guy from the previous tour, and ask for a date. In this case, O'Reilly had decided to say he was a friend of the English opening batsman, John Edrich, whose success with women was known well beyond cricketing circles. Armed with Edrich's address book, he arrived in Melbourne and rang a former beauty queen, June Finlayson. He needed the introduction: for all the enthusiasm they were to find in New Zealand, rugby, he found, was no big deal in Melbourne, and no one had ever heard of the Lions, let alone O'Reilly. But the Edrich introduction worked well, and soon he was enjoying himself at parties, dinners and receptions. He had injured his leg against France, and would not therefore be playing in the opening games. So he was on the sidelines to see the Lions play their first match of the tour on 23 May, beating Victoria by a landslide in front of a tiny crowd of seven thousand. Then they were due to move on to Sydney, where they would play two Tests against the full Australian team.

Before leaving Melbourne, O'Reilly asked June Finlayson for the addresses of a few friends in Sydney. 'There's this stunning girl called Susan Cameron,' she said. 'You should meet her.' O'Reilly readily agreed that he would, but then June had second thoughts. 'I don't think she'll meet you because she's got a boyfriend—and I think they're going to get engaged.'

O'Reilly, however, decided he would still try. The team checked in to the Coogee Bay Hotel, five miles from the city, on the edge of one of Sydney's finest beaches, and within a couple of minutes' walk of the Coogee Bay Oval where they trained. Because of his injured leg he would also miss the second match, so he had time to spare. A party was being given for the team at the house of a girl called Di Rose Orr, and Susan Cameron was expected to attend. So he went there eagerly—but she never showed. Instead, O'Reilly met a girl who knew her, Helen Hayes. He wanted to make a date with Susan, he said. Could Helen help? She couldn't, she said, even if she tried. Susan was much sought after. 'You'd be the luckiest man in the world to get a date with her,' she told him.

At the time, Susan Cameron, a beautiful blonde with hazel eyes, was working as a receptionist for a doctor in Sydney. The next day O'Reilly rang her number, and began with the technique which had worked well for him in South Africa, and which he would later perfect in New Zealand where it had the desired effect.

'The top of the morning to you, Susan,' he boomed in his broadest Irish brogue. 'You don't know me, but I'm a friend of June Finlayson, and I'm one of the British Lions touring team . . .'

There was a blank silence at the other end. Susan had not only never heard of him, but to her 'lions' simply meant the large wild animals which lived in Africa—or in Sydney Zoo. She had just broken off an engagement to a polo player, so she knew something about the world of sport, but rugby was a blank. No, she could not meet him, she said. Thinking hastily of an excuse, she said she was going to be bridesmaid to a friend that week and was involved in the preparations—which was true. Then she put the phone down.

That merely acted as an incentive to O'Reilly, who tried again, this time with a different tactic. In a much more refined voice, he told her he was a teacher as well as a rugby player, and invited her to a rugby reception. Again she refused, pleading the friend's wedding preparations. By his fourth phone call he had elevated himself to a professor from Cork University (he had given some lectures there), and finally, half intrigued by the sound of his voice, she gave in and agreed to meet him at Usher's Hotel, in the heart of Sydney, at five that afternoon to go on to yet another reception for the team. O'Reilly donned his smartest Lions blue blazer, and trousers tight enough to show off his finely muscled legs.

As first dates go, it was a disaster, with Susan underwhelmed by her admirer.

> I had never had a blind date in my life, and I had to meet him
> in this hotel where I was likely to see some of my friends, and
> here came this creature towards me in the tightest trousers you
> have ever seen—Australians wore sort of flappy trousers—and
> a blazer with a great big emblem on it, and this red, red hair.
> I thought he looked a bit of a teddy boy, and I was just hoping,
> all the time we were having a drink, that I wouldn't see anyone
> I knew.

O'Reilly, however, was an accomplished conversationalist, interweaving the talk with little jokes and anecdotes, quotations and references to people he had met. On discovering her interest in music he expressed his own passion for it, considerably exaggerating it. Maybe they could go to a concert? She was lukewarm about the idea, but she had given him an opening. He rang her again the next day.

'Ever been to the Sydney Concert Hall?' he said grandly, having just scrounged two tickets for that evening's performance of Tchaikovsky's *Romeo and Juliet*.

'Yes,' Susan replied sweetly. 'I played there last week.' She was, he soon discovered, a fine pianist. Her monumental put-down was an added incentive to Tony's siege.

She finally agreed to go with him and enjoyed it; afterwards they went on the Kings Cross for a coffee. Susan's father was very protective of her and insisted that, if she were out at night, she must take a hire car home. When the car turned up at the appointed spot she said goodbye to Tony and sailed off, leaving him stranded on the pavement.

The next day he tried again. Would she like to go to her first rugby match? The Lions were playing New South Wales and, although he would not be playing because of his injury, his old friend Niall Brophy would be substituting for him. Susan had never been to a rugby match before, and, beginning to warm to him, she went along. Within three minutes of the game starting, they witnessed one of the more bizarre accidents of the tour. Brophy, now an articled clerk, had only been allowed on the tour by his Dublin accountancy institute on condition that he took his intermediate examination immediately he arrived in Melbourne. The plane had taken three days to get to Australia, arrived twelve hours late, and he had to go straight into the examination hall. He missed the first match but now, with O'Reilly still out, he was chosen for the second. Three minutes into the game, he turned to chase a rolling ball and then, with no opponent within yards, collapsed on the ground. He was carried off the field with a broken bone in his instep, and took no further part in the tour. He had travelled 24,000 miles for less than three minutes' play. 'I only turned,' he kept protesting. 'All I did was turn.'

The team moved on again that weekend to Brisbane where O'Reilly scored two tries—and nearly several more—in a runaway victory over Queensland, and then it was on to the first Test against the full Australian international team. Six minutes into the game O'Reilly scored a textbook try, and came close to scoring another two. But it was a rough game on a pitch as hard as iron. Twice he was caught in tackles so hard that the game had to be held up while he received treatment, and he ended up with two grazed knees and bruises all over. It was warm-up stuff for the rigours of New Zealand, though pretty tough for all that. But at least they had won, 17–6. In the next game they ended up with only twelve men, and by the time they arrived back at Sydney for the second Test O'Reilly was limping badly, with blistered feet (he had very soft feet all his life, and on the field wore light, almost slipper-like, boots) and four stitches in his upper lip.

He rang Susan and they went out again one evening, but she was still not interested enough to see him play in the second Test on 13 June when the Lions ran riot in the second half, winning by 24 points to 3. O'Reilly scored one of his best tries when he got the ball 30 yards out. 'How the man ran!' wrote Terry Maclean in his book *Kings of Rugby*. 'Lenehan [the Australian full-back] and two corner-flaggers formed a reception committee a yard or two short of the corner flag. Their greeting was en masse, too. But O'Reilly still hurtled forward and, after impact, sustained his onward drive until he was over the goal-line for a try which could be described as perfect in every particular.' It was to be one of the most memorable of the tour, and one of the best in O'Reilly's career. 'The O'Reilly, in top company, is *très formidable*,' wrote Vivian Jenkins in the next day's *Sunday Times*.

A few days later the team departed for New Zealand and, as far as both O'Reilly and Susan were concerned, that seemed to be that. They had seen each other on and off for a couple of weeks, he had fancied her rather more than she him, but now he had gone on to another country, with lots of matches to be played, lots of cities to be visited and lots of other girls to meet. 'He left swearing undying love, and after that I got two letters and then there was dead silence, and I just got on with my life again,' says Susan. 'But I must say he had disturbed me quite considerably.' What she didn't know was that he was still engaged to Dorothy, and seemed to have no thought of breaking that off, even for someone as pretty and clever as Susan. Nor did she know about the many other women, young and old, he would meet in New Zealand.

Sir Edmund Hillary, the conqueror of Mount Everest and a keen New Zealand rugby fan, saw them off at Sydney airport. He solemnly warned Ronnie Dawson that the opposition he was about to encounter would be a lot tougher than anything he had found in Australia.

After the unenthusiastic reception given to their rugby in Australia, New Zealand was a revelation. They were escorted through the streets in a procession of cars led by a band, with thousands cheering them on. Again, as in South Africa on his first tour, O'Reilly loved it. There were receptions, dinners, speeches and visits to local beauty spots on the way, with time to enjoy them. The Lions team had become as popular off the field in South Africa as it was on it, and Dawson was determined to make sure this team would do as well.

O'Reilly missed the first match but worked himself up to full fitness for the second, scoring two tries. He and Peter Jackson, the English winger, had begun a private but intense needle match for the position of leading try scorer, a battle which came to matter to both of them as much as the result of the overall tour. O'Reilly had got four tries in Australia against Jackson's three. Jackson had gone ahead in the first match in New Zealand with two tries and now O'Reilly, with two in the second, had regained his lead—and so it would go back and forth throughout the tour until the final moments of the very last match.

Both players were hugely competitive, and completely different in their style. O'Reilly was a relatively straight runner, relying on his speed, weight and a ferocious hand-off either to out-run the opposition or to crash his way through. Dawson characterized him as a 'great finisher-offer', his speed and size often enabling him to take two or three men across the line with him, sometimes with tries which changed the whole course of the game. By contrast, Jackson was nearly four inches shorter and 27 lb lighter, a willowy, pale, frail-looking player, with probably the best jink-cum-swerve in the game and a swift, effective inside cut which brought him some of the most spectacular tries of the tour. His running, finely balanced but slow by the standards of some of the other backs, was so elusive that, as Jenkins wrote, he 'brings the crowd to its feet with anticipation every time he gets the ball'. If the nineteen-year-old O'Reilly had been the player the crowds took to in South Africa, in New Zealand he was being outshone by Jackson—and he didn't like it.

The team managers now decided that three of the players, Niall Brophy, Mick English and the scrum-half Stanley Coughtrie, were so badly injured that they should be sent home. Excitedly, Brophy told O'Reilly that he and English would go by sea. They had discovered a cruise-ship on a round-the-world tour which would soon be calling at Auckland, before going on to Europe via Sydney. O'Reilly was all in favour of Brophy taking the slow boat home—he didn't want any rumours of his off-the-pitch activities getting back to Dorothy. None the less he was envious as Brophy enthusiastically outlined his itinerary to him. 'Sydney?' exclaimed O'Reilly. 'I know a smashing girl in Sydney. You must look her up.' He wrote the name 'Susan Cameron' and her phone number and address in Brophy's diary, suggesting, as Brophy later remarked, that 'there could not have been anything between them then'. Brophy never did see Susan, although he rang her; but years later, when he read of O'Reilly's engagement to her, he tore the page out of his diary and sent it with the words: 'Congratulations—I guess I won't be needing this any more!'

If O'Reilly had lost his old mate Brophy, this was more than compensated for by the arrival of his best friend, Andy Mulligan, who flew in to replace Coughtrie. He arrived after a hectic three-day plane journey, complaining that he had only been given twenty-four hours to pack. 'Mother was almost sewing on name-tabs at the airport,' he quipped. Mulligan would also prove a valuable ally in O'Reilly's increasingly competitive battle against Jackson.

Against Auckland he and Jackson got one try apiece, but by 1 July O'Reilly had opened up a gap of three and was impatient for more— too much so, sometimes. 'O'Reilly was apt to go up too early for diagonal kicks-ahead and be given offside,' said one commentator. Both wings were now becoming targets for the hard-tackling New Zealanders, and although O'Reilly, rapidly gaining a reputation as the peer of obstructionists in defence, gave as good as he got, the more delicate Jackson was soon injured. The tackling of the New Zealanders, many of whom wore highly controversial and much disputed leather shoulder-pads, was taking a savage toll on players, and against Otago on 4 July it was a depleted Lions team which turned out. The Lions went down 26 points to 0, and O'Reilly had his worst match of the tour, giving away a vital try when, trying to clear from behind his own line, he miskicked and three Otago forwards pounced on the ball.

While Jackson was still hurt O'Reilly scored twice again in Timaru. But his rival pulled one back three days later, darting and weaving his way past three opponents before touching down under the posts.

By the middle of July they were in Dunedin for the First Test against New Zealand, a match which soured the whole tour. New Zealand won by a single point, all of their 18 points coming from the boot of probably the most lethal place-kicker in the history of world rugby, Don Clarke, the 16 stone bull-like full-back, who landed goals from all over the ground. In those days, before the rules changed, a try and a penalty both counted as 3 points (a try is now 5 points and a conversion makes it 7), and although the Lions scored four tries—one each to O'Reilly and Jackson—they were still beaten. There was fury in the Lions camp at the referee, who gave 21 penalty kicks to New Zealand against 14 to the Lions, and also over-ruled one of the touch judges, Mick English, who decided that one of Clarke's kicks had gone wide of the posts. O'Reilly had opened the scoring with a fine try, and ended the match by starting a movement which nearly pulled the Lions back from Clarke's last devastating hammer-blow. In the dying minutes of the game, he got the ball and kicked determinedly for the corner. The Lions' forwards were on to it, and the Welsh second-row, Roddy Evans, picked up and was almost over the line when the referee awarded yet another penalty to New Zealand. 'That last tremendous rush was one of the great events of the tour,' wrote Maclean. The crowd, he said, 'in its shame', was chanting for the Lions to win.

The penalty was perhaps the most controversial decision (out of many—the standard of New Zealand refereeing was very poor) of the tour, and the film of this particular incident was later analysed and reanalysed, with many independent observers siding with the Lions. 'Evans in his own recollection was quite certain that, having grasped the ball, he would have scored and given the Lions victory—a victory which, had it occurred in that dramatic manner, would have been ranked among the greatest in New Zealand test history,' wrote Maclean. Vivian Jenkins, too, reflected some of the anger in his match report that weekend. "We wuz robbed", I say, and I don't care who knows it,' he said, sparking off yet another controversy as he in turn was accused by the New Zealand press of being a poor loser.

That evening, at the formal post-Test dinner, New Zealand officials talked about winning 'within the framework of the rules' for which, said Gordon Brown, the president of the Rugby Union, in his after-dinner speech, 'no apologies need be offered'. O'Reilly and Mulligan were to seize upon this phrase and, to the huge hilarity of the rest of the team, wove it into the cabaret act they now put on for the others on every occasion. They had developed their own private radio show which they called *Two-Y-Front*, broadcast over the inter-com system of whatever vehicle they were travelling on. The format was a radio interview, derived from the *Goon Show* humour of the time, in which one or other of them would play the part of a well-known rugby character. O'Reilly, in an upper-class English accent, would pretend to be a visiting official, announcing he was 'very glad to be in . . . where are we, my man? New Zealand? Doesn't seem to be many white people down here.' Someone had recorded one of their sessions and, much to their horror, it went out on New Zealand radio—to an enormous reaction. After that they were besieged at airports to provide more—which they were more than willing to do. Some of the coach journeys were seven or eight hours long, and over the intercom the two, sometimes abetted by Mick English before he went home, conducted mock radio interviews with prominent people whom they had met on the trip—or with their own managers. O'Reilly had perfected a South African accent, and often played the role of 'Dr Danie Craven', the South African who was president of the Rugby Federation worldwide, and who had now arrived in New Zealand for the tour. In the evenings, they developed a cabaret act which they called 'Hi-Diddle-Riddle', with Mulligan, who had a good tenor voice, on guitar and O'Reilly on the piano; they were much in demand among the other players. At Whenuapai airport, when the official goodbye speeches had finished, they grabbed the microphone and broadcast to an appreciative crowd, and that too became a set pattern. Mulligan was every bit as good a mimic as O'Reilly, and both had an instant ear for the phrase or mannerism of any potential victim whom they would then ruthlessly lampoon. According to Maclean, 'the stunning success' of the pair as public entertainers had persuaded Mulligan, by the end of the tour, to try his hand in radio or television.

On 22 July, Jackson scored four tries in a runaway victory over a combined West Coast–Buller match, and a further four a week later against another weak team. O'Reilly was not playing in either match, but against the much tougher Canterbury, who beat the Lions 20–14, he failed to score. Jackson was now ahead, and O'Reilly was going through a fallow period. He clawed one back a few weeks later in the final match before the second Test, but then Jackson went down with flu, and it was a desperately under-strength team which finally turned out at Wellington. The Lions were so short of fly-halves that at one stage it was suggested that Mulligan play in that position—but he too was injured, and the Lions took the field without many of their star players. They more than held their own in the first half and then shortly into the second came one of the uglier incidents of the tour.

O'Reilly, following up a deep kick-ahead, gathered the ball and at full speed bore down on the only man between him and the line, the lumbering full-back Don Clarke, over 16 stone of solid muscle and bone. He swerved infield, drawing Clarke with him, chipped the ball over the full-back's head and went to run around him for a certain try. Clarke, however, instead of taking up a chase he would certainly have lost, dropped his shoulder and ran straight for O'Reilly, flattening him in what even the New Zealand supporters saw as a brutal act of obstruction. O'Reilly, at the very least, should have had a penalty try for it, but the referee awarded a penalty which the Lions converted, leaving O'Reilly hurting both physically and spiritually. New Zealand won again, coming from 8–6 behind four minutes from the end to win 11–8 when Clarke partly redeemed himself by crashing over the line for a try.

O'Reilly was now increasingly becoming the target for rough tackling and obstruction. Although he was still smarting over the loss of his try he didn't blame Clarke, and indeed the story told by other Lions was that, even as O'Reilly was crashing to earth, he was heard to mutter: 'Sure I'd have done the same thing myself.' But life on the field for him was getting nasty and dangerous, and it came to a head four days later at Taumarunui against a combined King Country–The Counties side. A few minutes into the game, he tried to dodge his way through but ran into the grasp of the opposing forwards. One of them grabbed his hair and yanked a chunk of it out, while another hit him in the ribs with a right uppercut, just above the heart. As the ruck broke up, O'Reilly was left clutching the bleeding gap in his scalp before toppling backwards like a statue, out cold. The *Taranaki Daily News* accused him of a 'theatrical fainting fit', but in fact he was unable to breathe—and, when he came to, angry. The Lions scored three tries that day, all of them by O'Reilly, one of them the strangest try of the tour. He chased everything and everybody, rattling any opponent who came near him with bone-shaking tackles. But at one stage, running full pelt after a kick-ahead towards the line, he found himself forcibly restrained by a hand holding him back. He was given a penalty try, the first ever awarded to a touring team visiting New Zealand, and another blot on what was developing into an ill-tempered tour—at least on the field.

In Masterton at the end of August he and Jackson got two tries apiece, and then it was the third Test—and New Zealand's third victory, this one a comprehensive 22–8 defeat. Vivian Jenkins in the *Sunday Times* had caused national outrage in New Zealand by labelling the All Blacks a team of 'softies' for wearing their leather shoulder-pads, and the All Blacks now stepped on to the field determined to redeem the national honour. 'The first exchanges were like the cuffs that professional boxers give each other after preliminary pawing,' wrote Maclean. O'Reilly could have had a try in the early stages when David Hewitt, the brilliant young Irish centre, broke clear with only Clarke to beat and O'Reilly outside him. Some of the commentators—

Jenkins for instance—blamed Hewitt for trying to beat Clarke on his own, only to be hauled to the ground by a long and ferocious arm. Others claim the fault was really O'Reilly's who, not for the first time, had got ahead of his centre. 'It was a tragic moment for the Lions and a tragic moment, too, in the career of O'Reilly,' wrote Maclean.

The series was now lost beyond recall, the Lions 3–0 down with only one to play. But various players remember well the next morning as the tired, battered and dispirited team boarded the plane at Christchurch to fly to Wellington. The instant they were airborne, Andy Mulligan and O'Reilly grabbed the microphone off the steward-ess to announce the next instalment of the *Two-Y-Front* show. 'Never had they been in better form,' said Jenkins, 'with their mock radio interviews of personalities high and low.' Many of their targets were on the plane, including the president of the New Zealand Union, Gordon Brown, plus a number of All Blacks flying home. The pair kept it up for nearly an hour and the flight, recalls one player, 'was a long gale of laughter'. The All Blacks, he says, could scarcely believe their eyes. 'I can't get over it,' said Brown on the plane. 'Here's a team that has lost three Test matches in a row, and you'd think they'd be in the depths of despair. Yet they're behaving like this. I think it's marvellous.' The team landed in Wellington in much higher spirits than they had left Christchurch.

They were now in the final stages of the tour, with just four matches to be played before the final Test, which they were determined to win to regain their honour. O'Reilly scored two splendid long-distance tries in the first of them, causing Jenkins to comment: 'Though he had done very well on this tour and scored his full quota of tries, the flying Irishman had never quite produced the kind of runs that had brought him such fame in South Africa in 1955. Now at last he showed he could still do it.' Yet he entered the final Test—and the last match of the tour—just one try ahead of his arch-opponent, Peter Jackson. He had scored 16 tries in New Zealand (on top of four in Australia) to Jackson's 15 (plus three in Australia). All depended on this final match.

Half an hour into the game Jackson drew level with a classic try in which, ironically, O'Reilly had a major hand, coming in from the blind side to make the crucial overlap. Jackson, in his swallow-like, unpredictable run, beat his own winger with a perfectly timed instep and then seemed to float around Don Clarke, to score in the corner before being buried under a crowd of beaten defenders. Now it was 16 tries each.

It was at this moment that Andy Mulligan, who had had a superb tour, took a hand. From a scrum five yards from the All Blacks' line, Mulligan looked first to the right, then noticed a yawning gap on the blind side with O'Reilly perfectly positioned. 'So I took out the New Zealand back row, and there he was, right where he always was, and I put it down his throat,' says Mulligan. There is an excellent film sequence of this try, showing Mulligan breaking on the blind side, drawing O'Reilly's opposite winger, MacPhail, and then timing his pass perfectly with O'Reilly only half a dozen long strides from the line. It was a move they had practised for hours the previous week, and at that distance O'Reilly was unstoppable. He was ahead of Jackson again.

In the next passing movement, he decided, he would again come in from his wing to the centre, but instead of passing it on in the way which had led to Jackson's try, he warned David Hewitt he would have a go himself. 'Don't expect a pass,' he told Hewitt. 'You never give me one anyway,' retorted Hewitt. A few minutes later, the perfect chance seemed to have come. Mulligan again made a break, running right to the open side of the field, with O'Reilly running flat out to get into the line, ready for the pass which would see him, he hoped, scorch through a defence which would be shifting over to cover Jackson. The whole New Zealand line moved to that side, but, as he had done many times at Cambridge, Mulligan slipped a reverse pass behind his back to the fly-half Risman who was 15 yards clear before the All Blacks (or O'Reilly) realized what was happening. Chased by half the All Blacks team Risman made it to the line for one of the best tries of the tour, leaving O'Reilly and Hewitt in the middle of the field sharing their private joke.

The Risman try won the match 9–6, and the Lions had finished the tour on a high note. It was one of O'Reilly's best games, and his try put him in the record books. His fellow Lions carried him shoulder high from the field. He had scored 17 tries in New Zealand, a record that still stands, and was one of only five players who had played in all six Test matches in Australia and New Zealand. The team went home via Canada where O'Reilly picked up another try, taking his tally to 21 for the tour in 23 matches—more matches and more tries than anyone else in the entire team. He had written a few times to Susan Cameron, but she was pushed to the back of his mind as he arrived home at the end of September, to be greeted by his fiancée Dorothy Connolly on the tarmac. Susan seemed to be forgotten.

———————7
A New Life

'IT IS THE CLOSEST YOU CAN GET TO GOING TO WAR,' SAYS WILL Carling, probably England's most successful post-war rugby captain. 'You are playing a very physical game and you look after each other— if someone is on the floor being kicked, you go in there, you get down to basics, you get close to each other, you have respect for someone who is taking it alongside you.'

Carling played a generation after O'Reilly, but the principles of the game had not altered. Since he was seven, O'Reilly had played or practised most days of the week for at least six months of the year, and even more on the four-month tours of South Africa and New Zealand. It had shaped him mentally and emotionally as well as physically, causing him to take for granted the warm camaraderie of team play, but also to accept for granted the hard knocks and bruises of the game. O'Reilly was born competitive, but years of playing rugby at high levels had honed and sharpened the urge to win to the point where it infected most areas of his life. At the same time he had been forced to learn how to lose, another invaluable preparation for a life which, however gilded, was going to include its shares of disappointments and setbacks.

Rugby had given him a degree of fame and adulation (at one stage in New Zealand he had received fifty-seven fan letters in a single day, another record for the tour), which he was aware would be transitory and confined to a comparatively minor element of the world's population. But besides those elements which Carling talks

Born in Drogheda on March 14, 1906, John Patrick Reilly changed his name and his age to join the Irish civil service in 1925.

Marriage in February 1928 to Judith Clarke by whom he would have four children before he left her.

Reunion with his still legal wife for the marriage of their eldest daughter Juliette.

Jack O'Reilly in retirement.

Young Tony with his mother Aileen at Griffith Avenue and (below) Aileen aged about 30 wearing the "Mario wave" hairstyle fashionable in 1940s Dublin.

First rugby match, and a tearful O'Reilly kitted out in the wrong shirt. Aidan Doyle (centre) and Michael Mullen are still friends. Below, with the Belvedere Newsboys Club, designed to provide recreation and amusement for some of the poorer boys of Dublin, at summer camp in Termonfeckin, Co Louth.

In the office of the solicitor Gerry Quinn on the day he was first picked to play rugby for Ireland.

Below, Christmas party at Leicester in 1958.

Action man: the hand-off was an essential part of O'Reilly's game (top left) as was his punting. Below, O'Reilly, weighing more than 14 stone, could break 10 seconds for the 100 yards in full rugby kit. Here he races outside Clem Thomas of Wales.

O'Reilly touches down over the Springbok line in the last minutes of the final Test in 1955 for his sixteenth try in fifteen matches. A second later he was hit on the right shoulder, dislocating his shoulder, one of many injuries he would suffer in his rugby career. The Lions manager Jack Siggins (bottom) helps him off the field.

Close to the line, O'Reilly's speed and weight made him almost
unstoppable. Top, the field littered with South African players as he scores
in the corner and bottom, crashing in for his final try for the Lions in 1959 in
the Fourth Test against New Zealand. It established a new record of
seventeen tries for a tour.

Dunedin, 1959, and O'Reilly has to beat the New Zealand full-back Don Clarke to the line in the First Test. Below, he makes it.

O'Reilly's weight fluctuated when he wasn't in strict training. In 1957, top left, 1959 (top right) and right, in training for his twenty-ninth and last international for Ireland in 1970, fifteen years after his first.

On the 1959 tour of New Zealand Andy Mulligan and O'Reilly created their own entertainment duo for the amusement of their team-mates – and discomfort of the officials. Here they seize the public address system to amuse the crowd at Whenuapai. Below, engagement to Susan Cameron, outside her Chelsea flat, on August 31, 1961.

Marriage in April 1962.

Below, Jim McCarthy, left, was the best man, and the bridesmaids were Susan's friends (from left) June Finlayson, Helen Hayes and Sonia Walsh. Ronnie Dawson and Andy Mulligan were never far away.

Left, Jack and Aileen at the wedding.

The O'Reillys produced six children in four years – including triplets, born in December 1966. The proud father sports a black eye from a tough rugby match.

Executive meeting at Bord Bainne to plan the launch of Kerrygold. Joe McGough is on O'Reilly's right and Jim Kenny on his left.

O'Reilly the food
marketer: in 1967
as head of the Irish
Sugar Company
and its disastrous
affiliate, Erin
Foods.

Pittsburgh, the city of the Mellons, the Fricks, the Carnegies – and of John Henry Heinz, founder of one of the great food companies of the world. After over 100 years of existence, it was worth less than $1 billion in 1979 when O'Reilly became chief executive. A decade later it was worth ten times that.

The young Heinz executive in England, where he was picked out by Burt Gookin to be his successor. Below, chief executive and the 37-year-old president changed the shape and direction of the 'Ol' Pickle Company'.

about, it had given him immense self-confidence, which some of the contemporaneous assessments of his character identify. 'At a long-range guess,' wrote Terry Maclean at the end of the New Zealand tour, 'one felt reasonably sure that he would in time become president or premier of the republic,' which, although not correct, was not a bad guess. In his summing up of each of the characters of the tour, Maclean described O'Reilly as 'astonishingly mature of mind', adding, less generously,

> one can only hope that the remarkable possibilities of this young man as student and thinker would not be harmed by too great an affection for witty display and by a strange regard, almost amounting to envy, for those fortunate folk [and there were many in the team] who move through the world with a lordly calm based upon a secure place in the scheme of things.

By that, Maclean presumably meant the lackadaisical upper-class English on the team, typified by the winger John Young, who cultivated a laid-back attitude to life. It is an interesting observation of O'Reilly, reflecting the mild sense of inferiority that his Irish upbringing had given him towards the aristocratic English.

It was one of the few chinks in his otherwise fairly complete armour. To his fellow players, O'Reilly was full of good spirits, energy, wit and bonhomie, the instigator of so much of the teasing and name-calling of other players, so often the leader in setting the level of team morale, by far the best public speaker of any of the players. And he had every reason to feel well about himself. Up to this point in his life, he had never failed at anything to which he had set his mind. After the New Zealand tour, no selector would deny him an automatic place in a World XV rugby team. Team success might have eluded him—even he could not expect to lift the whole Irish team out of the doldrums and lead it to victory in the Triple Crown that year—but even when playing for losing teams he had excelled individually. At school he had been a boy wonder, the first to be picked in any team, always promoted to the next team up, always reaching for a new challenge, and always discovering he could respond to it. Adored by his parents and liked by many others, O'Reilly carried with him all the physical and moral wellbeing of a supremely fit and fulfilled young man, brimming with his own masculinity and simple good health. It would have been astonishing if that self-confidence had not spilled over into arrogance and hubris at times, and it did, but part of O'Reilly's charm was to disarm the impact of that too. His need to be liked was more powerful than any desire to crow.

By the time he returned from New Zealand, O'Reilly had probably learnt as much as he ever would from the game of rugby—which was just as well, because although he had not yet fully understood it, his career was now effectively over. The tour had given him a second wind in a career which was flagging, but once he was home it began to run down again. He would play another nine times for his country, but six seasons at the top of the game and two major tours, each lasting four months, had been enough. Despite the effort demanded, rugby was an amateur sport, and the players were required to get on with their lives and careers outside it. Unless he trained hard every day O'Reilly's weight went up rapidly, and lack of fitness in turn made him more prone to injury. His shoulder, so painfully put out by that tackle in the dying moments of the last Test in South Africa, plagued him more and more, as did other old injuries, as well as some new ones. The matches now seemed longer and harder to him, his interest really only kindling when the internationals came around, and sometimes not even then. The truth is that he was no longer enjoying the game very much. He had had his blaze of glory, and it had been enormous fun, but after the New Zealand tour there was nowhere to go except down, a fact he would come to accept only reluctantly.

Back home in the autumn of 1959, he broke off his engagement to Dorothy. He would later tell Susan it was because of her, and certainly he hoped he would see her again, but he made no attempt to contact her in Australia. But meeting her had helped persuade him that Dorothy was not the girl with whom he now wanted to spend the rest of his life. It was a blow to her, but she must have been half-braced for it, since rumours of O'Reilly's activities had permeated back from Australia even before the tour returned. They remain firm friends to this day, but life together was not for them.

In September the now twenty-three-year-old O'Reilly returned to his life in England and his job as a management consultant, getting down to London when he could to team up with Andy Mulligan and other friends who had congregated there. He also zipped to and from Dublin to see his parents whenever possible, but these were the days when air travel was still rare, and the road or rail journey took the best part of a day.

The best of his rugby career might now be behind him, but he still played, turning out for Leicester as the new season got under way. He avoided the Irish inter-provincials and trials, and in February was at Twickenham for the first international of the season. Against an England side which went on to win the Triple Crown that year Ireland had their best match of the season, scoring their first try at Twickenham in six visits. But they still lost 8–5, and in the second half O'Reilly, hurled to the ground under a mass of players, hurt his troublesome shoulder and had to be carried off. He did not play again that season for Ireland, who lost every match.

However there were other things to occupy him. He had been working in England for two years when he returned one evening to the house in which he boarded to find a letter sitting on the mantelpiece. It was from a London businessman, Sir William Ramsay, president of the Rugby Football Union, who had taken a proprietorial interest in O'Reilly's career. Ramsay's letter announced that at his London club he had met a man who needed a bright young executive to take on the running of a subsidiary in Ireland. Ramsay had obviously sung O'Reilly's praises because, he said, 'he wants you to become managing director of an engineering business called Stephenson Clark in Belfast'. The man was, he added, contactable through Powell Duffryn, a large engineering and fuel distribution company, at its London headquarters. When O'Reilly made contact he found the position was very different from that described. The job was not with Powell Duffryn but with a rival, William Cory; it was not in Belfast but in Cork; and the job was not managing director but assistant to the chairman. Furthermore the company, John M. Sutton & Son, had nothing to do with engineering but was a general builder's merchant—and one of the biggest fertilizer, seed and coal merchants in Munster. None the less, O'Reilly was ready to come home, and the job fitted very well with what he wanted to do. The salary offered was an impressive £2000 a year, which would mean that, at the age of twenty-four, he would be earning more than his father after a lifetime in the civil service. Jack O'Reilly urged him to take the job, persuading him that it was a good time to come back to Ireland where the economy, under Lemass, was beginning to move forward and all the talk was of joining the European Economic Community. He accepted.

O'Reilly knew Cork moderately well, mostly from playing rugby there, and liked it. It was very different from Dublin—only a third of the size, even though it was Ireland's second city. It was also a much more closed society than Dublin, with little of the literary and artistic tradition associated with the capital; it was provincial but self-confident, with its own very definite social strata and pecking order. O'Reilly's particular friend there was Jim McCarthy, holder of twenty-five caps for Ireland which he had led to victory in the Triple Crown. Their rugby careers had barely overlapped, but McCarthy had captained Ireland in O'Reilly's first game, and he had never forgotten the enthusiasm and aphorisms of the man, with his team-rousing talk which never stopped all the time they were changing—or through the game. McCarthy ran a family paint business and lived, to O'Reilly's eye, in the height of opulence. When the newcomer arrived in Cork he called on him and, as McCarthy would remark wryly afterwards, refused to leave. 'He dropped in for a cup of tea one afternoon, and two years later I called up his mother and told her to get him out of the place because everyone in the house had fallen in love with him.' McCarthy hospitably offered him a room, shared with his young son James, and although O'Reilly soon acquired his own flat, he preferred staying at the McCarthys'. 'When Tony first came, he would always refer to "*your* house, Jim, and *your* children and *your* wife", but he soon switched from "yours" to "ours". I didn't mind him saying "our" house, and "our" kids and "our" dog, but when he started saying "our" wife I was glad Susan turned up.'

O'Reilly's impact on the Cork social scene was immediate and considerable. He appeared in his white Triumph sports car, roaring into town as if he were arriving on an official visit to a rugby-mad city in New Zealand. If his personality seemed large in Dublin, in Cork it was considerably larger. Within days he had more invitations than he could handle as Cork's hostesses vied with each other to entertain this new arrival in their homes.

The job itself was nothing special to begin with, but O'Reilly set to with enthusiasm to make it so. Sutton's had been an old family seed business which had gradually spread to sell coal and building materials; most of its customers were farmers, who came in from miles around to discuss their needs—and expected the head of the firm to visit them. It was a prosperous, unspectacular business, still run by Jack Sutton although he had sold the family shares to the British-based company, Cory. Sutton had little interest in expansion and listened with mild-mannered amazement to the plans produced by this young man who, on the basis of two years as a trainee management consultant and work study observer in England, was trying to tell him how to run his business within a week of arriving. But the two of them got on well—Sutton was happy enough to let O'Reilly channel his energy into new methods of increasing coal sales—he did so by putting them into smaller sacks which could be sold at shops and petrol stations, a forerunner of a system that later became widespread—and of seeds and feedstuffs to the local farmers. He travelled all over Cork and into Waterford, Tipperary and Kerry, talking to farmers and potential customers for Sutton products, and the legend of his name opened all doors. It was his first real contact with the Irish farmer, and later he would refer to this period as 'the beginning of the beginning'. Coming on top of his experience in England, it was the perfect training for what was to happen next.

On his first day at Sutton's, O'Reilly encountered one of the women with whom he was to form a relationship as lasting as anything in his life. Olive Deasy was a small, neat, taciturn woman who oversaw the Sutton office with such efficiency and control that nothing happened without her approval. Officially she was Jack Sutton's secretary, but in fact she 'did' for everyone, as she primly told the newcomer on his first day. From the beginning she treated O'Reilly with a mixture of faint disapproval and affection. If this man expected adulation—and on the whole he did—he would never get it from Olive. Over the next two years he would come to depend on her to the point where he could not conceive of running his life without her, and she in turn built her life around him, devoting herself to his interests. She fielded the dozens of telephone calls which came into the office for him, ran his busy engagement diary and talked to the farmers who were demanding to talk to the famous rugby player about their seeds or the delivery of corrugated iron for their new barn roof.

Work as a consultant in England had whetted O'Reilly's interest in management techniques, a subject which everyone in Ireland was talking about as the country struggled to bring its industry into the modern world. If British management was reckoned to be behind the best practise of the 1960s, Ireland was positively Stone Age, and in the land of the blind a young man with even two years' training was a king. O'Reilly was determined to learn more—and to teach what he knew. As part of his original deal, he had arranged to become a part-time lecturer in industrial management at the Department of Applied Psychology at Cork University, an interesting precedent for his dual life in later years. His lectures were soon among the most popular in the university, not necessarily for their content but because of O'Reilly's reputation. He enjoyed the task, putting considerable effort into it and working up his own knowledge of management theory as much as he did that of his students.

He had been in Cork a matter of months when, in August 1962, Andy Mulligan rang him from London with some momentous news. 'Hey, Rooikop,' he began in the South African accent they often used between them. 'Do you remember that bird you fancied in Sydney? Well, I hope it's a blow to your not insubstantial ego to know that she's been in London for three weeks—and she hasn't called you yet!'

It was now more than a year since O'Reilly had met Susan Cameron, and after a few letters he had not been in touch. They had talked vaguely about her plans for doing what so many Australian girls of her age did, which was to go to London for a period, and they had talked about seeing each other then. But given his silence, Susan had no intention of making contact—although she still hoped he might find her. O'Reilly had not been lonely during that time, finding Cork full of attractive and compliant women, but Susan Cameron had been something special.

O'Reilly enquired how Mulligan knew about her arrival. 'I met Sandy Hone who said he'd seen her at the Oversexed Visitors' Club the other night,' replied his friend, using the term which he and O'Reilly used to describe the Overseas Visitors' Club in London's Earl's Court area, a favoured hunting-place for both of them. This was bad news. Not only was the club a danger spot for the girl of his dreams, but Sandy Hone, an Australian rugby player, enjoyed a reputation as something of a sexual athlete.

O'Reilly had to get to London quickly. Fortunately it was the start of the rugby season and there was an imminent tour of Britain by the Irish Wolfhounds, an international side which he had helped put together several years ago. Its first match was in Cornwall, and they were to catch the overnight train from Paddington. Mulligan was given strict instructions to find out where Susan was, and O'Reilly rang her from Dublin to say he was on his way. 'There's a rugby tour going to Cornwall—why don't you come along for the weekend?' he suggested. Susan coldly responded that she would do nothing of the kind, but O'Reilly said he would drop by to see her in any case.

He took a taxi from the airport straight to her small mews flat in

Bywater Street, off the King's Road, which she shared with two of her friends, Helen Hayes and Sonia Walsh. It was not a dramatic new start to their relationship, for as O'Reilly went to pay the taxi, he discovered he had no money on him. He rang the doorbell and Helen appeared, with Susan standing in the door behind her.

'Fantastic to see you again,' he boomed enthusiastically. 'Have you got three pounds for the taxi?'

Susan, still annoyed with his calm assumption that after all this time she would simply go to Cornwall with him, refused to help him out. It was left to Helen to pay off the taxi.

Inside, he heard all their news. Helen had fallen for Ronnie Dawson, the Lions captain, and she and Susan had decided to travel to Europe together to catch up with him—and, possibly, with Tony. But they had been in no hurry. For £100 each they bought themselves 'boomerang' tickets, which allowed them to go to London and back to Sydney nine months later; towards the end of 1959 they set off on an Orient Line passenger ship, enjoying their first real taste of freedom away from home. In Singapore they teamed up with Sonia, who persuaded them to stay for a time. In the event the ship sailed without them and they spent three months there before all three of them continued to London, where initially they stayed in the Overseas Visitors' Club. They had moved to the mews when Susan got herself a job at the *Daily Telegraph* in Fleet Street, as secretary to Maurice Green, later the editor. Helen became a waitress at what she referred to as a very 'in' spot in Notting Hill Gate.

O'Reilly, however, did not have much time. Unwisely, he pressed his invitation to go to Cornwall with the rest of the team, but Susan very firmly told him she would not. Contact had been re-established and he was determined to pursue it. A week later he was back, and this time she agreed to go with him to one of his rugby matches and have dinner in the evening. He told her enthusiastically about Cork, the friendliness of everyone, the job he was doing with the farmers, about the McCarthys, and of the many friends he had made in his new life. Why didn't she come and visit him there?

Her first visit to Ireland was to watch him play for Ireland at Lansdowne Road. She stayed with his parents for the weekend. A few weeks later she went on a longer visit, this time to Cork, and fell under its spell, as he knew she would. If the sun is shining, West Cork is among the most beautiful coastlines in the world, and by now O'Reilly knew every bay and inlet. He took her in his sports car along the coast to Kinsale, Glandore and Castletownshend, and on around the Ring of Kerry to Sneem and Waterville—beautiful, unspoilt small towns with lush semi-tropical gardens growing in the unexpected warmth of the Gulf Stream which runs along the coast. On the way he told her some of the history of Ireland. He stopped at Derrynane House, home of Daniel O'Connell, leader of the Catholic emancipation movement, who created the first political mass movement of the Irish people, admitting members for a fee of a penny a month. O'Connell, a lawyer with an extraordinary command over great crowds, was one of O'Reilly's particular Irish heroes. Susan knew nothing at all of Ireland or its history, but if she was to marry Tony—which she was now seriously considering—she thought she might convert to Catholicism. The seaside home of the man who finally won Irish Catholics their right to practise their religion was an important landmark for her.

Susan was now a long way from Bendigo, the town 70 miles from Melbourne in the Eastern Highlands where she had been born in the same year as O'Reilly. Her father, Keith Cameron, was a mining engineer and celebrated oarsman who had moved with his family, first to Kalgoorlie, a mining town stuck in the middle of the desert, then to Broken Hill, where some of Australia's biggest mining houses were based, and later still to New South Wales, where he was sent to resolve a long-running dispute with the coal miners. Susan and her sister went to school at Fensham in Mittagong, 100 miles south of Sydney, and on graduation she did what many girls of her generation did: she took a secretarial course. In Sydney she got a job in an advertising agency, and was soon enjoying one of the busiest social lives in the city. Then O'Reilly had appeared on the scene—and here she was walking on the big wild beaches of the west of Ireland with the man she had fallen deeply in love with.

At that Lansdowne Road match she had watched a few weeks earlier O'Reilly had got his twenty-second cap for his country. The next day the rugby writers talked of him being 'now completely fit' after his injuries, and of playing with 'refreshing determination' and interest in the game, which Ireland won. But he missed the next two games because of yet another injury to his shoulder, and the season which had started with such hope for Ireland soon deteriorated, that victory against England being their only one of the season.

But in the summer there was another tour, this one by the Irish team only, to South Africa. It was a much less elaborate and lengthy affair than a Lions tour, but O'Reilly had decided it was time to do something other than play rugby on these tours. After the trip to New Zealand two years before, it had struck him that the interest and goodwill shown to the players could be turned to a profit. He roped Mulligan into his little scheme.

'Ireland should be doing a lot more in the way of promoting and selling its manufactured goods abroad,' he told him one day. 'Very few of our manufacturers seem to be awake and alive to the interest overseas, and I think you and I should form a company, which we would call, say, Ireland International, marketing Irish goods on the tour.'

It was a radical thought which probably no other Irish player, before or since, could have got away with, but O'Reilly's standing was such that Mulligan knew no one would try to stop them. The firms, when contacted by them, were enthusiastic enough, and they set off on the tour with order forms for everything from Irish whiskey cake to tweeds and hand-knitted woollen sweaters made in Donegal. They even had specially tailored business suits made up. In each city they took a suite of rooms, laid out their samples and displays and invited the locals to a reception.

It worked, after a fashion, although the other players on the team became more resentful as the tour wore on. 'I have a vivid memory of Tony, when he was supposed to be training, standing with his foot on a case of whiskey trying to arrange an Irish coffee cocktail party for the night after the match,' says Ronnie Dawson, who captained the short tour. Yet the resentment never lasted long and O'Reilly joked and charmed his way out of any gathering problems. His reputation in South Africa was considerable from the 1955 tour, and the cocktail parties proved popular. They even received some orders, which they passed back to the manufacturers in Ireland. 'We ended up with a cash balance of £1000 in our favour,' says Mulligan.

They blew it all on a dinner they gave for the bank manager who had backed the operation, Tom Casey of the Munster and Leinster Bank in Cork. The Caseys were O'Reilly's second favourite family after the McCarthys and he spent much of his time in one or other of the two households, hardly ever using the flat he had rented except when he had female company. Casey was more than an ordinary bank manager; he was one of the characters of Cork, a big man who had quickly taken O'Reilly under his wing, advising him on how to deal with the farmers, how to expand Sutton's and how to keep

control of the financial position. At the expense of the fledgling
Ireland International he and his wife were brought to London, put
up in a first-class hotel, given a magnificent dinner and taken to a
rugby match. As a result the pair of would-be entrepreneurs had a
thoroughly loyal and happy bank manager—but no money.

O'Reilly didn't mind. That summer his relationship with Susan
strengthened and deepened, and they were now talking seriously
about marriage. O'Reilly still held back from the final commitment,
but Susan was clear about what she wanted: either he married her
or she returned to Australia. She had, she pointed out, been in England for a year and, despite his protestations of undying love, she
was not prepared to hang around as just another girlfriend. They
became engaged on 31 August 1961, a year to the day since his
arrival outside her door with the taxi-meter running. They would
get married in Dublin the following spring, they agreed. Tony had
never met her parents, and her father flew to Dublin to check on
this young man. He stayed with Jack and Aileen, immediately hitting
it off with Jack who took him on inspections of the border with
Northern Ireland (then remarkably peaceful). Aileen joked to Susan
that the so-called border expeditions were really Guinness inspections. For Susan it was a delightful time. She had now quit her job
in London and moved permanently into the O'Reilly home, which
was the centre for dozens of family and rugby friends to drop in.
She loved the Mullens, Karl and Doreen; the McAleeses; and Ronnie
Dawson (with his wife Wendy—he never did get together with Helen
Hayes) and many others.

Jack, whom she called 'Papa', was initially suspicious of her and
remained aloof, but Aileen enveloped her. 'She was a very strong
person, very much an earth-mother, and I felt as though she was
protecting me in some way,' Susan would recall later. 'She just embraced me, which was amazing, because this golden light was her
son, and here was this girl from overseas come to marry him.' At the
beginning Susan was a little in awe of her.

> She was so capable. She didn't have much money for
> housekeeping, but she would produce these gargantuan feasts.
> She grew everything herself—she had amazing green fingers—
> and anybody could turn up at the front door for a meal. She
> was the pivotal person in the house, the force you felt, but she
> was doing it all for other people, never for herself.

At times she noticed considerable tensions in the house, with Jack and Aileen not speaking to each other. She had no idea of the cause, and put it down to the normal rows of any married couple. In his eternal search for self-improvement Jack was learning Italian, and there was a very pretty Italian teacher around the house whom Aileen clearly hated—possibly with good reason. But she never spoke to Jack out of turn, and never talked to Susan about anything other than domestic details. In front of their son, the O'Reilly couple tried to be as united and loving as possible, and nobody except the two of them would ever know what torment Aileen in particular went through. She must always have wondered if their neighbours and friends knew of their marital status, or worse still, if Tony knew. What if this beautiful, innocent young Australian girl found out? What would she—and her father—think? It was not until old age that she knew the security of marriage, and all these years she must have wondered whether Jack would leave her, as he had done Judith, for one of the other women she heard rumours about.

While Tony simply adored his mother, he had a more complex, intellectual relationshp with his father. He liked to go off for long walks with Jack when they would discuss his career, or the state of the country and Irish politics, and Tony listened respectfully enough. Jack was a shrewd, learned man, narrow in some ways, a product of his time rather than of the new Ireland, who found it hard to bend, but as father and son they were—and would remain—close.

Tony's relationship with Aileen was very different. 'He would almost flirt with his mother,' says Susan. 'He'd play the piano and she would adore him so much, and he'd become a little boy with her and it was very sweet. Nothing was too much trouble for her. Their relationship was touching and warm, and he really admired her.'

Tony was still working in Cork, driving up every weekend, and Susan often went down to stay with the McCarthys. But there would be bumps in this engagement just as there were in Tony's first. Several times Susan threatened to break it off when he didn't turn up, or left her in Dublin while he was playing rugby in England. Finally they set a date for 5 May 1962 at the University Church on St Stephen's Green.

Then his life changed in a way he could not have expected. On a wet, windy night near the end of 1961 Jack Sutton, mistaking an articulated truck for a single one, went under it and was killed. Suddenly life at Sutton's altered. O'Reilly was considered too young for promotion to his job, although he wanted it and reckoned he could do it. Sutton's brother took over, but O'Reilly didn't have the same enthusiasm for him. He was also still suffering from the after-effects of a back injury which lingered on and on. At Jim McCarthy's insistence he had joined the local team, Dolphins, and had trained there as usual at the start of the new season. But playing against Blackrock in November he was regarded as barely a passenger, and a week later he cried off at the last moment. His shoulder was bad again, too, and the medical advice was gloomy: it would never get better, he was told, unless he gave it complete rest—not for a matter of weeks, but months. Picked to play in an Irish final trial in December, he cried off, telling the secretary of the Irish Rugby Football Union that there was some doubt if he would be match-fit that season. For the first time since he was eighteen he did not play at all for Ireland that year, and newspaper comments began referring to him as the 'former' Irish international rugby player. That by itself was a cruel blow—he prided himself on never missing a game, and he and the iron-hard Welsh forward Rhys Williams had been the only two men to play in all ten Tests on the Lions tours of 1955 and 1959. He now had twenty-five caps for Ireland, but had missed half a dozen because of injuries. O'Reilly was moving towards the end of his career as an international rugby player—although he still had some surprises left in him.

Still wondering about his future at Sutton's, early in the New Year of 1962 he was approached for a job he thought he would like more than anything he had ever done. In the newly emerging industrial Ireland, it was clear to the planners that one of the first targets must be the modernization of the country's backward agriculture, the mainstay of the economy and responsible for more than 50 per cent of all exports. Ireland produced large quantities of milk, but little of it was exported, and most of that only when a butter surplus arose. Under de Valera the drive had been to keep imports down rather than increase export markets. That was no longer good enough: now every resource had to be properly harnessed. But the Irish dairy industry was hopelessly fragmented and divided, and Britain, the most obvious export market, still imposed tough quotas on Irish butter, a hangover from the economic wars with de Valera. Over the years farmers had formed themselves into co-operatives, but they were isolated, uncoordinated and inefficient. O'Reilly had seen for himself the waste in the rich farmlands of Munster, some of the finest grazing land in the whole of Europe, where surplus milk was fed to calves if the local creamery had more than it could use. In 1936 the Irish government had created the Butter Marketing Committee basically to sell surplus butter abroad, and that was about all it did—dump it on the market without much thought for quality, consistency or value-added.

Irish dairy exports in 1961 brought in a mere £7 million, a tiny contribution to the balance of payments, and it was clear to Sean Lemass and his government that there was far more potential in the area if only they could bring it out. Two years earlier a key report, arguably the most important ever produced on Irish agriculture, had been prepared by the Advisory Committee on the Marketing of Agricultural Produce; it paved the way for the change which was now taking place. One passage, which O'Reilly would later learn by heart, set out the questions to be addressed:

> The fundamental point to be decided is whether this country should be an exporter of whatever temporary surplus of dairy produce may arise from time to time or whether the country should be a long-term and regular exporter of dairy produce. If it is the intention that the country's export trade in dairy produce should continue to be merely the export of whatever fluctuating surplus may arise from year to year there would be little point in altering radically the present marketing arrangements.

At the time there were surpluses of dairy products in many European countries, but the committee was adamant that Ireland must export more of its butter or else the economy would go backwards again. 'Dairying is an essential feature of the small farm framework of Irish agriculture and, in our opinion, increased milk production and an expanding dairy industry are vital to the development of a growing national economy.'

In 1961 the old Butter Marketing Committee was dissolved and a new organization was formed 'to improve and develop the marketing of milk products outside the State'—in other words, it had no function on the home markets, its sole object being to sell as much Irish milk and milk products as possible on the world markets. It was called

An Bord Bainne—the Milk Board. Its first objective was to find itself a smart general manager who knew something about marketing, particularly marketing to the British housewife who was, despite the quota problems, to be the main market for Irish butter. O'Reilly's name was on the list, although he was still only twenty-five and would be by far and away the youngest head of any state-sponsored body in Ireland.

With the death of Jack Sutton, O'Reilly was in the process of looking for a new job in any case. His father suggested one: there was a vacancy for deputy director-general of the Irish Tourist Board, Bord Failte, and he suggested that Tony should apply for it. Tim O'Driscoll, the current head, was a friend of his. He was thinking about that when he received a telephone call from one of his new friends, Jim Foley of the Dungarvon Co-Op, a man who had actively encouraged his staff to attend O'Reilly's lectures at Cork University. 'Paddy Power is the chairman of a new body called An Bord Bainne,' he told O'Reilly. 'He's the most powerful man in the Irish dairy industry, and he'd like to see you.' O'Reilly knew about Power, who ran the Ballyclough Co-Op in Mallow, County Cork. Sutton's sold him their products, but O'Reilly had never met him. Foley arranged for the two men to meet in Mallow that Friday night.

O'Reilly climbed into his little white sports car and drove up from Cork on a road which even in Ireland was notorious for its bends and camber (the local joke was it was half a mile longer one way than the other). He arrived at the appointed bar, sat down and was joined by a giant of a man with a great wave of grey hair, huge bushy eyebrows and a face which seemed to be carved out of Connemara granite. In his measured Cork accent, Power told him he had heard great things about him from Jim Foley, a man he respected greatly, and would like to put him forward as the man to run Bord Bainne. Taking a stubby pencil out of his pocket, he began to draw out on a napkin his plans for the new board. 'The whole thing is to get milk out of butter and get it into other things— chocolate crumb and cheese, and powder where the support levels are less, and therefore the cost to the country is less,' he explained to an incredulous O'Reilly.

Finally, at the end of their dinner, Power turned to the young O'Reilly. 'It could be arranged,' he said, 'that I get you an interview in Dublin. But on no account are you to indicate that you have ever spoken to me.' O'Reilly didn't understand the thrust of this remark, but didn't query it. Power obviously had his own way of doing things, and the important fact was that O'Reilly would go forward as his choice, however secretly.

A few days later he was called for an interview at the Dublin District Milk Board in Leeson Street, a frugal little place, where four men, all of them twice his age, sat around a board room table shooting questions at him. They were all powerful men in the agricultural community: Dick Godsil, the managing director of Cadbury Fry and one of the biggest users of milk products in the country; Martin J. Mullally; Tony Hennerty of the Department of Agriculture; and Captain David John Barry, who liked to boast that he was a veteran of the Easter Rising.

At the end of the interview O'Reilly was asked to appear for a final interview the following Thursday. This was chaired by Power, who gave not the slightest indication that he had ever met O'Reilly before or that he was his personal choice for the job. Towards the end of the meeting he stirred his giant frame and suddenly asked O'Reilly: 'You know a bit about the import and export business—you're an importer of Polish coal, aren't you?' O'Reilly agreed that Sutton's of Cork was. 'Well, would you mind telling me what would be the price at which you import the coal?'

It might have been a trick question, and O'Reilly treated it as such, even though this man regarded himself as his mentor. 'Mr Power,' he said, 'if this interview turns out to be unsuccessful from either of our points of view, next Monday I'll be trying to sell you Polish coal. I'm not going to tell you what the margins are on Polish coal to get this job or any other.' He laughed as he said it, taking the sting out of it, and the rest of the nine-man board chuckled with him, enjoying this unexpected put-down of the normally dominant Power. Power too allowed himself a chuckle, and let it pass, as one of the board later put it, as 'a fine demonstration of independence on the part of this young man'. Power, O'Reilly could sense, was used to getting his own way on this board and some of the others resented it. This little incident, although it puzzled him, appealed to them.

That evening, O'Reilly flew to London to watch Ireland play England. He was only a spectator, still nursing his shoulder, but he went to give Mulligan and his old friends support. When he walked into the Irish Club in Belgravia he ran straight into Dave O'Laughlin, a former Irish rugby international, who was then the manager of one of the bigger co-ops in Ireland, Goldenvale.

'Well, you're the unanimous choice for the job,' he greeted him. O'Reilly was to be the first general manager of Bord Bainne.

He arrived in Dublin to take up the job on 1 April, insisting on one condition: Olive must accompany him from Cork. He didn't know how to run his life without her, and for her part, with Jack Sutton dead, she would have felt lost without O'Reilly. His salary was £3200 a year, an enormous sum in those days for Ireland, where a large country house with 20 acres could have been bought for less. He also got his first company car, a big black Mercedes to replace the increasingly battered TR3 sports car which he had driven to death.

Five weeks later he and Susan were married in the wedding of the year. The crowds were so dense outside the church in St Stephen's Green that they stopped the traffic. There was a bus strike in Dublin, and that morning a march of students protesting at the busmen ran into the crowds outside the church. When the marchers heard who was getting married, they stopped to add their good wishes in an atmosphere of good cheer on all fronts.

In addition to Jim McCarthy, his best man, Ronnie Dawson and Andy Mulligan, his groomsmen, Tony had invited more rugby friends to act as ushers. They were Cecil Pedlow, Joe McAleese, Ronnie Kavanagh, Syd Millar, Gordon Wood, Niall Brophy and Frank O'Rourke. The line-up on Susan's side was of a more attractive nature. All former Australian schoolfriends and flatmates—June Finlayson, 'Miss Australia' of 1956, and O'Reilly's first date in Australia thanks to John Edrich, Sonia Walsh, and Helen Hayes who had returned from Paris where she now worked as a model. Following up this bevy of beauties was Jim McCarthy's young son acting as pageboy and carrying the ring on a satin cushion. The Irish *Evening Mail* described the event as being 'like something from a film production.'

The happy couple departed for three weeks in Portugal, and nine months and five days later their first child, Susan, was born. Within three years there would be five more.

8

Kerrygold

'THE BIGGEST SUCCESS OF MY LIFE WAS INDISPUTABLY KERRYGOLD,' Tony O'Reilly would say many years later. 'There were few jobs I've had before or since that remotely excited me so much.'

General manager of the Irish Dairy Board does not, on the face of it, sound like the obvious route to the top for one of the world's corporate high fliers of the late twentieth century. Yet O'Reilly's four years there were to transform him from sports star to serious business success, invite offers from some of the world's major corporations, and point him like an arrow towards the top of the corporate tree. From unpromising raw material he created one of the most successful food brands in the world today, changing along the way the perception of the Irish agriculture sector and preparing it for the 'agribusiness' mentality needed for the modern world. The launch of the Kerrygold brand was the subject of his PhD thesis submitted to the University of Bradford in 1980—in which he gloomily concluded that the Irish farmers did better out of state subsidies than ever they would out of marketing butter, however successfully—and the kernel of a number of lectures and talks he has given on marketing over the years. BBC Television later turned it into a case study for a programme in its *Powers of Persuasion* series.

For O'Reilly, it was an exhilarating moment in his life when he discovered that the same energy and commitment which he had channelled into rugby could be used in his professional career. Over these four years he would measure himself against the competition as he had done so often on the rugby field, and realize that he could stand alongside the best. He would learn many lessons, notably that enthusiasm and single-mindedness could carry him only so far, and that meticulous planning and attention to detail were just as vital. But he would learn them well—and enjoy almost every second of it.

The job turned out to be perfect for him—and he for the job. Because he was the first general manager in an ill-thought out new state organization, he was effectively given a blank slate on which to write his own agenda. He was presented with a huge problem too, of course, but it was a problem with a solution; once he had found the key to it, it simply became an exciting challenge. This period was one of the few in his life when he would start with modest targets and no great hopes, and end up achieving a great deal more than he could ever have imagined.

He was not quite twenty-six when, with only very hazy ideas of how this half-baked organization would work out, he began work. His initial impressions were not auspicious. He had realized that he would have to become involved in the dark and tortuous politics of Ireland's farming community, but he had not bargained for the difficulties of dealing with the harsh, mean-minded men who would fight their local corners out of pig-ignorance and self-interest. Many of them were from Gaelic backgrounds, preferring de Valera's policies of state subsidy and self-sufficiency to market economics, and others simply resented change. Although there were also some enlightened people in the industry, he found it a hotbed of intrigue, prejudice and an exaggerated sense of its own local importance. If the new Ireland of Sean Lemass and Ken Whitaker was dependent to an unhealthy extent on their contribution to export-led growth, Irish farmers and the co-operatives neither knew nor cared about it. Their attention was bent only on the guaranteed price which An Bord Bainne would pay the creameries for their butter, and the floor which that in turn placed under the basic price passed on by the creameries to Ireland's hundred thousand dairy farmers. Paddy Power, himself one of what O'Reilly soon learned to recognize as the 'agricultural barons', took him aside after O'Reilly complained he could not persuade the co-ops to support him. Putting one of his huge arms around O'Reilly's shoulders he leaned towards him conspiratorially. 'Tony,' he said in his slow, deliberate voice, 'let me tell you one thing about the Irish co-operative movement—you'll get fuck-all co-operation from it.'

A person less optimistic or with less going for him than O'Reilly might have been discouraged, but he was, at least at this stage in his life, immune to depression or failure. He also had an overpowering confidence in his own persuasive charm, believing that, if he worked on the farmers long and hard enough, he would eventually talk them round (and to an extent he was right). But even on his own board he had men, in the shape of Hennerty and Barry (Mullally became a great friend) who would continue to treat this young upstart, and his English-inspired ideas of efficiency and marketing, with suspicion and distrust.

These were niggles in what was otherwise a near-perfect existence. At this time of his life O'Reilly seemed to be blessed by the gods. 'I remember meeting him then and thinking this man had everything,' says one Irishman.

> He was incredibly good-looking, with a wonderful self-assurance and an amazing personality. He seemed to stand head and shoulders over everyone in the room, with people crowding to get closer, almost touching the hem of his jacket. He was this great rugby star, who was also incredibly bright, who had come first in his solicitor's exams, had a beautiful wife and one of the best jobs in Ireland. He was also amazingly funny, so that he drew you towards him rather than make you resent him. He was the nearest thing to a living god I've ever seen.

The weekly farmers' magazine carried a cartoon which epitomized what the Irish farmers must have thought of O'Reilly at the time: it showed a rugby scrum made up of New Zealanders, Australians and Danes, with O'Reilly emerging from it looking like Superman, but with a baby's dummy in his mouth.

Yet what even close friends never glimpsed was something which O'Reilly did not talk about—not to his parents, not to his closest friends, and not to Susan. Since the Jesuits had first told him about his father's marriage and first family, O'Reilly had never spoken of it to anyone. He was haunted by the knowledge that out there, somewhere in Dublin, probably watching him play rugby for Ireland (which occasionally they did), were three half-sisters and a half-brother whom he had never laid eyes on. Jack's façade was so forbidding, even to Tony, that he dared not even raise the subject, suspecting—and he would have been right—that Jack would have exploded in anger and indignation. In any case, if the subject were ever to be raised it was for Jack to raise it with his son; if he had, Tony, worshipping his father as he did, would have tried his best to understand. But Jack never said a word, and he so dominated Aileen that she, an innocent party in the situation, never said anything either. The subject festered among the three of them, a big black cloud that hung perpetually over Aileen, which must have haunted Jack and from time to time thrust its way into the forefront of Tony's mind.

Jack O'Reilly was now a big figure in Dublin, not just because he was the great Tony O'Reilly's father, but because of his own senior position in the civil service. He knew everybody, and there were many who knew about his past. There was no way it could lie hidden. Judith was still alive, still his legal wife, and they still talked often on the telephone. She had made no demands on him, even when she couldn't afford the school bills, and again and again had turned to her own family rather than to Jack. When her mother died she lived on in the big house in Wicklow. All her four children were now married, and she was a grandparent, but Jack seldom saw his grand-children. Their son Julian had moved to Canada where he was a well-to-do businessman with his own construction business; Ria, the second eldest (she had been paralyzed with polio), had moved to New Zealand; and Eveleen had gone to London where she later married a Pole, Eric Gorniok. When Juliette married a farmer from Kilkenny in 1953 Jack had carried out his formal duties as father of the bride, making a long speech in front of hundreds of guests and posing for pictures afterwards with Judith on either side of the bride and bridegroom. It must have been highly uncomfortable for him, but he did it, and Judith tried not to embarrass him. His wife and children treated the situation with an extraordinary degree of discre-tion and delicacy, but over the years the circle who knew about it had steadily widened. Tony's fame, and the constant references in the papers to him being the 'only child of Mr and Mrs John O'Reilly', had heightened interest, yet somehow it never surfaced publicly; and even more surprisingly, somehow it remained a 'secret', known to many but, largely out of respect to Judith and her four children, still treated with a remarkable degree of consideration.

Tony himself never acknowledged the situation. If the matter ever surfaced in his presence, which it did from time to time, he either denied it or treated it as a gross impertinence. Shortly before they were married he took Susan to Wexford where, at a dinner dance, someone said to her, 'I'm a friend of Tony's brother.' Susan, confused, replied that Tony didn't have a brother. The man, embarrassed, retreated, muttering that he must have been mistaken, but she was puzzled enough to raise it with Tony afterwards.

'You'll hear a lot of stories about me,' he said tensely. 'Don't believe them.'

She never mentioned it again, and for the next fifteen years of their married lives, she knew nothing about her husband's half-sisters and -brothers, several of whom lived only a few miles from them.

What effect did it have on Tony? Quite probably a major one. Susan, trying to account for the forces which drove him almost demonically at times, later attributed much of it to the fact that he secretly knew he had been born illegitimate, and had to prove to the world he was better than anybody else. His conscious reaction was to try not to think about it, but it must always have been there, never too far from the surface, coming to the fore when he saw his father make his mother unhappy and continually nagging at him. If the gods had blessed him in many other ways, they had also given him this burden to carry.

As he drove around the muddy lanes of Ireland in that wet spring of 1962, O'Reilly did not feel at all god-like or superhuman. Pulling into the yard of yet another co-operative creamery, he half regretted not taking the offer from Bord Failte, the Irish Tourist Board, with its promise of foreign travel and sunshine. But as he settled in, he was soon wholly absorbed in a challenge which would stretch him to the limit. He turned up for every creamery dinner dance he could manage, made countless speeches, looked at endless piles of churns and spoke to thousands of farmers in their own cowsheds. O'Reilly was a quick learner, but at no time in his life, before or since, would he ever have to absorb so much so fast. He read up on the history and structure of dairy farming in Ireland, Britain and continental Europe—Denmark was of particular interest; studied what sketchy details he could find of the butter market; and began to rough in the parameters of a plan of campaign.

From the time of the industrial revolution Britain had been the main export market for Irish butter, with Cork as the centre of what at one stage had been a thriving international trade (indeed, the price of graded butter on the Cork butter market was recognized as the world price). In the early years of the twentieth century Irish butter exports were around 40,000 tonnes, mostly to Britain where Irish butter competed head-on with Danish and New Zealand butters. Then the economic war with Britain and the depression of the 1930s hit the industry hard. In 1951 the industry was so reduced that the Irish Dáil debated whether to reimpose rationing on butter or bring it in from abroad (Danish butter was allowed in for a fortnight, leading to a huge public furore and a political crisis). In 1956 only a miserable 100 tonnes of butter was exported, and even as the industry recovered, the Irish policy was to be in and out of the market as and when it had more than enough butter for its own consumption. There was no such thing as continuity of supply. Chocolate crumb, the basic ingredient for milk chocolate, had become the big growth area of the 1950s, but the dairy industry was steadily becoming more efficient, the surplus was getting larger and the big potential for exports was still butter.

The outline of the task that faced him was straightforward enough. An Bord Bainne was a semi-state organization (the other half represented the dairy industry) whose allotted role was essentially that of an intervention agency: it would subsidize the farmers and guarantee them both a price and a market for their product, and then it would export the surplus. The farmer wanted the highest possible price for his milk, and the manufacturer wanted to buy it as cheaply as he could. The Irish government, through An Bord Bainne, would have to pay for two-thirds of the difference between the two. The Irish Second Programme for Economic Expansion, which had followed Ken Whitaker's highly successful first one and was to prove vastly over-optimistic, demanded a dramatic increase in the number of cattle intended for export, which also meant an increase in the dairy herd needed to produce them. A concomitant of that was a dramatic increase in the supply of milk—O'Reilly worked that figure out in the first few days—which it was his job to sell, maximizing the revenue for the taxpayer. Butter could never be sold at a profit, but it could command a higher price than it currently fetched and the extra revenue would have the effect of reducing the burden on the government's strained purse. He also realized, a little awe-struck, that, including their dependants, the lives of some 500–600,000 people would be directly affected by his decisions.

In the game that would follow, O'Reilly held some powerful advantages which he would exploit to the full. He came to the job with no vested interest, representing no one other than himself, and if he could avoid being drawn into one of the camps on the Bord Bainne board he could in effect divide and rule. His reputation gained him a serious hearing everywhere, and if that failed, the fact that he signed the cheques for the milk subsidy—it came to £1 million that year—gave him a huge power in this community. Yet it was not always an easy ride. At the end of one meeting, a farmer stood up angrily to argue with the basis of O'Reilly's lecture on the inefficiencies inherent in having too many small farmers, and too many small creameries, and on the need for centralized marketing—for which the farmers would have to pay. 'We've been listening to you now for an hour and you've got figures for this and you've got figures for that and an answer to everything—all of them wrong. Sure, I've seen figures which show that 80 per cent of Irish farmers are above the average.'

A puzzled O'Reilly queried the mathematics of this. 'The average of what?' he eventually asked.

'The average of the other 20 per cent,' replied the farmer.

O'Reilly spent the first few weeks getting together his organization. He had inherited a tiny staff—'a man, a dog and a bicycle', he would later say, but in fact it was twenty-two people—and urgently needed a deputy, an experienced administrator with a knowledge of the civil service departments, but outside the existing bureaucracy. In this, as in so many other areas of his life at this time, he was fortunate. Born in 1919, Joe McGough was seventeen years O'Reilly's senior. A qualified lawyer—he had been called to both the Irish Bar and to Lincoln's Inn in London—in 1940 he had joined the Irish army, in which he served for nearly twenty years. Still in his early forties, he had retired from the army as a judge advocate and was set to join the British colonial service, but changed his mind when he found his first posting was to be to Nyasaland.

When O'Reilly advertised the job of secretary to the board, McGough happened to be in bed with a cold. Browsing through the appointments sections of the weekend papers, he came across three jobs on offer which interested him. When his wife came up with a cup of coffee, he handed her three letters. 'Would you ask the kids to post those as they're going out,' he said. They were, he explained, job applications.

'But you've only just retired,' she complained.

When he told her about the jobs, she said: 'With your sort of luck, you'll probably get the three of them. Why don't you just apply for one?'

She was right—he did get the three. At Bord Bainne he was inter-viewed by the full board; the huge bushy-white head of Paddy Power led the questioning, while O'Reilly sat attentively at the bottom of the table. Despite the formality, McGough, his big moustache twitching comically, was relaxed and funny, displaying a sharp wit and confi-dence which appealed to O'Reilly in particular. When the tea-lady wheeled in her trolley, Power courteously proffered McGough a cup, saying, 'Do you take sugar?' No, he did not, said the candidate. Power picked up the milk jug and pointed it at him threateningly. 'Well, you'd better take milk!' O'Reilly joined in the laughter.

At the end of the meeting, Power asked if there was anything he wanted to ask them. Yes, said McGough, he was telling them the truth when he said he had already been offered two other jobs, and he would like to know soon whether or not he had been successful, because time was not on his side. They agreed to give him a quick answer.

That evening the telephone rang and the unmistakable voice of Tony O'Reilly came down the line. 'Is that the secretary of Bord Bainne?' he asked.

'Speaking,' replied McGough instantly. It was the beginning of an excellent working relationship.

McGough arrived on 11 May to find O'Reilly on honeymoon and a full board meeting scheduled for that afternoon. Worse still, the main subject to be debated that day was the size of the milk levy to be paid by the farmers for handling their marketing. It had been a subject of considerable controversy in the farming community for the past year, and had caused half the board to storm out of previous meetings. This was McGough's rough introduction to the divided world of Irish agriculture. He watched in some bemusement as four of the nine board members present walked out before the levy order was eventually signed.

O'Reilly returned two weeks later tanned and bubbling with plans and ideas. That summer he set a cracking pace, adding new staff to his rapidly growing team, touring the creameries, spending endless hours with government officials and trying all the time to make enough sense of it all to formulate a strategy for the way ahead. He discovered a kindred spirit in McGough, a sharp observer of the social scene who would return from his army club meetings and regale him with hilarious stories. Years later, O'Reilly remembered the two of them as 'the happiest comedy team since Abbott and Costello'.

In his first few weeks he had realized that what he needed more than anything else was a full assessment of the British butter market, the only market that would seriously matter to him, at least in the early years. A month into the job he had drawn some tentative conclusions, different from those of Power, which would dictate his future actions. Butter, not chocolate crumb or cheese or dried milk, was the answer. In the post-war years Britain followed a policy of 'cheap food' which allowed world surpluses into its market on a controlled basis; this meant, in effect, that the New Zealand, Danish and Irish taxpayers were subsidizing the British consumer. Britain was a huge butter importer, the biggest in the world, absorbing virtually all the world's butter exports: some 410,000 tonnes that year, of which only 12,000 tonnes was Irish. Furthermore, butter consumption was a growth market, rising from 14 lb a head in 1954 to 20 lb a head by 1962 as Britain's prosperity grew. Because of its large population and small dairy industry, there was little prospect that Britain was ever going to supply itself.

There was another obvious point: if the aim was to absorb and export as much milk as possible, butter had other advantages, at least in the short term. It was not only the most widely consumed milk product, but it was also the biggest user of milk—it required 5100 gallons of milk to produce a tonne of butter as opposed to 2000 gallons for a tonne of cheese. So here was the opportunity: butter, sold to Britain.

But how to capitalize on it? In 1962 Ireland ranked among the minor suppliers of butter to Britain, way behind New Zealand, which sold 158,000 tonnes a year, Denmark (93,000 tonnes) and Australia (63,000). New Zealand and Denmark sold branded butter, which commanded a premium price. Ireland's supply simply went to agents who used it to blend with other butter (to bolster the quality), before selling it on as a branded product.

He commissioned the Economist Intelligence Unit, a research group run by the *Economist* magazine group based in London, to prepare an initial assessment of the British butter market, with particular reference to selling a branded Irish butter into it. The unit was intrigued with the problem, and within days was working on a profile of the demand and consumption characteristics. O'Reilly had not yet worked out a way of tackling the market, but at least he would know what he had to tackle. A visit to any British food shop—supermarkets were just beginning to come on the scene—showed him the widespread success of New Zealand branded butter and the Danish Lurpak brand. He spent hours with the various agents and distributors in Britain who handled butter, instantly liking a man called Fred Adams, who ran a respected and long-established public company in the British Midlands and sold butter under the slogan 'Adams Butter—spreading everywhere'. Adams was full of useful advice.

'All you have to do is get a pack for the butter, Tony,' he said. 'You are being exploited, because your butter is simply coming into England and being used as a blending butter for everybody's else brand—for Unigate's brand, for Express Dairies, and all the others.'

O'Reilly was rapidly reaching the same conclusion, but was still nervous about taking the leap into branding. And yet he could see that simply selling more Irish butter in 56 lb unbranded packs would be pointless—it would simply push the price down and make more quality butter available for the blenders in Britain. There was another problem he would have to confront: image. 'While we may have been seen as having many charming characteristics, Ireland's rating as a possible food supplier was not high,' said a Bord Bainne executive later. Irish products did not enjoy much of a reputation in Britain, and the task of changing British consumer perceptions seemed the most daunting task of all. He would be starting from scratch against the established power of the New Zealand and Danish brands, not to mention the big British food companies, and even if he could reach the British housewife direct, how would he persuade her to buy Irish?

In June he was in London again, this time in search of an advertising agency. He settled on Benton & Bowles, part of a large American-controlled agency, which had a reputation for solid but unimaginative creative work (O'Reilly did not know enough about advertising to assess it—he was recommended to the firm and they accepted him, and that was enough). His account executive was Ivor Samuels, who, like McGough, was to prove one of the successes of the operation.

The EIU's report was to prove pivotal, clearly highlighting the potential for Irish butter in Britain. By 7 July, less than four months since he had arrived (and he had taken three weeks of that for his honeymoon), he had committed himself. He would launch an Irish branded butter in a carefully selected region of England. If it worked there, he would eventually sell it nationwide. Apart from the expense, there was a good reason for this. Of the UK quota of butter imports available to Ireland, 6000 tonnes went to the Six Counties in the North, the other half to mainland Britain. That was not enough for a national launch, and in a detailed report in August, Samuels recommended they concentrate on a single area to begin with— north-west England, around Liverpool and Manchester, the Winterhill Television franchise area. Here 7 million people lived, transportation costs from Dublin would be low, and there was a large Irish population. If Bord Bainne got a 10 per cent share of the region, that would absorb the entire annual quota, although they were not too concerned about that—the quota was adjusted every year and they had every reason to believe they could get a solid increase the next year.

O'Reilly now prepared to face his board with the proposition of launching an Irish branded butter in England. First of all, however, he had to take some hard, lonely decisions, with nobody in a position to advise him. If he was going to build up a brand product in the British market, the first essential was to ensure a guaranteed supply of butter. The history of Irish butter-making was so erratic that he could suddenly find himself going from surplus to short supply, in which case everything he had achieved would be thrown away. He went directly to the dour Minister of Agriculture, Paddy Smith. Would he agree to allow the import of foreign butter into the Irish market if Bord Bainne ran short of butter for export? O'Reilly was keenly aware of the political delicacy of the request, but he persuaded Smith it was unlikely ever to happen—it was just a safeguard, and a demonstration to both the customers in Britain and the farmers in Ireland that he was serious. Smith, although he knew that Irish governments had fallen for less, reluctantly agreed.

O'Reilly's next decision was a harder one, which he would have to do battle over with his own board. The only way O'Reilly could get the distributors in Britain to handle his new brand was to let them pack it in their own blending plants. He was proposing to take away their blending butter, but as compensation he would be offering them the margins on the contract packing of what should be a growing brand. Fred Adams had agreed to make his sales force available on this basis, and also to handle the physical distribution.

Early in July he made his presentation to the board. He had rehearsed his arguments and his case, and showed them graphs and tables, quoting the Economist Intelligence Unit findings, using every bit of his guile and persuasive powers in a way he had rarely done up to that moment but which he would do again and again in his later career. It was no easy ride. Many of these men represented the co-ops, each of which had their own tiny packing operation, and there was considerable resentment and anger at O'Reilly's proposals to let the British distributors have the job. 'A hundred and fifty seven co-ops packing half a ton here, a quarter of a ton there is a logistical nightmare,' he argued. 'How would we pull it all together? How would we guarantee the evenness of quality? And even if we did, how would we sell it in Britain? We can't afford a sales force, and we can't do our own distribution.' Packing in England, he insisted, was the price the British distributors had demanded as a minimum for handling an Irish brand. Without them, there would be no market.

Power, impressed by the logic of O'Reilly's arguments, was prepared to go along with it, but not everyone was. Tony Hennerty of the Department of Agriculture opposed it, and would continue to object to almost everything O'Reilly did for the next four years. Hennerty had been chairman of the disbanded Butter Marketing Committee and O'Reilly felt resentment oozing from him. At one stage Hennerty leaned across the table to hiss at him: 'Young man, you are proposing to bring the Irish farmer face-to-face with the British housewife—and they are patently unsuited to one another.' But Power and the board backed him, agreeing to his plan for an advertising budget of £75,000 for the new brand—less than a third of what New Zealand spent annually promoting its butter in Britain. He was ready to go.

And then they had to decide on a name. There had been much debate about this, with everyone producing his own list and everyone else rubbishing it. In London, Benton & Bowles wrote down its preferred candidates for the brand name, and O'Reilly, McGough and everybody else chucked in others until there were sixty possibilities. Many of them were stage Irish names such as Blarney, Colleen, Leprechaun and Shillelagh which O'Reilly rejected out of hand (Blarney is now used by Bord Bainne on a cheese). And yet the name had to suggest lush green pastures, the beauty of the Irish countryside—and quality. 'We have looked for a name which has a definite Irish sound with overtones of richness and purity,' said Benton in its report. Three names survived on to the shortlist: Dairy Churn, Shannon Gold and Kerrygold. The first, although it wasn't a bad name for a butter, was rejected as 'not Irish enough'. The second suffered from the fact that most British housewives thought about Shannon as an airport rather than a river, and was therefore ruled to be 'too modern and too mechanical in tone'.

That left Kerrygold which, with some misgivings, O'Reilly settled for. The full name would be Kerrygold Irish Creamery Butter, sold in half pound packets with a green and yellow wrapping. It was not greeted with universal enthusiasm, particularly among the old Gaelic-speaking community. Everyone in Ireland knew that of all the twenty-six counties in the Republic, Kerry, with its wild mountains, lakes and moorland, had very few milking cows. 'Sure, there's no butter in Kerry,' said someone. 'The British housewife doesn't know that,' O'Reilly snapped back. The writer Myles nag Copaleen (whose real name was Brian O'Nolan and who was the author of *At Swim-Two-Birds*, one of the classics of twentieth-century Irish literature, under a third name, Flann O'Brien) thought it was the most hilarious thing he had heard in years. He wrote a beautifully crafted satirical column in the *Irish Times* every week which sent up life in Ireland, and now his eye alighted on Kerrygold. This, he said, was a venture doomed from the start. Everyone knew, he went on, that a brand name had to be short and brisk—like Omo or Daz or Tide. Yet the idiots at Bord Bainne had come up with this absurd name.

'I can see the board of An Bord Bainne,' he wrote, 'fifteen black-faced, bandy-legged Kerrymen with ten rejected three-act plays stuffed in a trunk under their beds, and their revenge on the Irish taxpayer is to launch the unpronounceable "Kerrygold".'

There was opposition from another quarter, too. Major-General Michael Joseph Costello was one of the most influential men in Ireland in the 1950s and early 1960s and would become one of O'Reilly's most outspoken enemies over the next decade. At this stage he was the general manager of both Erin Foods and of its parent, the Irish Sugar Board, another semi-state organization which had subsidized Irish farmers to grow sugar beet in de Valera's rush for self-sufficiency in the 1930s. He was a formidable, brooding presence over the whole of the state sector, and soon made it clear that he too was suspicious of what O'Reilly was planning. The two men ran into each other at a reception where the general fixed O'Reilly with his steady, unwavering gaze. Trying to sell Kerrygold branded butter in Britain was a big mistake, he told him bluntly. It was a highly competitive market in which the big operators were all large, sophisticated companies who were never going to let him get a foothold. Erin Foods had achieved good sales in the Irish market for its innovative accelerated freeze-dried foods, but Costello had not dared tackle Britain. An Irish company, from its little base, could not compete with Heinz, Unilever and Knorr, he said. 'You'll surely fail,' he said. 'The English will teach you a lesson.' O'Reilly replied that he thought otherwise and politely disengaged himself. But Costello's remarks rankled and, although he was not a vengeful man, O'Reilly from that moment was no fan of the general.

If the pace had been fast before, now it became hairy. O'Reilly and McGough barely slept, shuttling between London and Liverpool as they worked on the details of what had to be a superbly well-run launch. O'Reilly knew all too well that he would not easily get a second chance, and there were plenty of people even in his own organization waiting for him to trip up. They toured the agents who handled Irish butter to explain to them what they wanted to do. Some of them were not keen, because they were making the margin they wanted by using the butter as a blend, but Fred Adams offered ten full-time merchandisers to help with the distribution in the crucial first four weeks of the campaign. O'Reilly's relationship with him had become vital, as indeed had his working relationship with the Benton team and with the EIU. He tried to re-create the same kind of rugby team spirit he had experienced on tour in his launch team, and to a degree it worked. A new launch was something that neither O'Reilly nor McGough had ever done before, so they were dependent on Samuels and his team at Benton, who as the summer wore on came into their own. 'They were captivated by it,' says McGough. 'But then Tony was an amazing person to work with. You cannot but fall immediately under his spell. He carries you with his enthusiasm and his tremendous ability, and his remarkable recall for items, events and so on. That launch was really a most exciting time for us all.'

O'Reilly wanted to get the new brand launched by Christmas, and with a six-week campaign that meant Kerrygold had to be in the shops ready for 1 October 1962. The television campaign (which was budgeted to cost £4871 for air time and newspaper space plus £500 for making three commercials—a figure which seems absurdly low by contemporary standards, but which reached 72 per cent of all households in the area—would begin two weeks before that. O'Reilly was determined to make it a memorable event—something more than just another new product launch. 'Normally when you think of things done quickly, you think they're done carelessly,' says McGough. 'But this wasn't. It was done with great attention to detail all along the line. Tony was a tough taskmaster, and really stayed on top of it.' They would make some mistakes, notably a lack of liaison between the advertising agency and market researchers, but as a campaign it was a textbook exercise with some interesting novelties thrown in. O'Reilly was keen to bring as Irish a flavour to it as possible, reckoning that that would mark it out from other brands, and Samuels agreed. They held long sessions, sparking off each other, outdoing one another with outrageous proposals and ideas. They decided to use dairymaids to promote the product, but they would be special dairymaids: five of the prettiest models in Ireland, including the then Miss Ireland, Olive White, and Helen Joyce (later Mrs Terry Wogan). The girls toured the retailing outlets on a schedule worked out by the advertising agents, acting not just as promoters but also as market researchers and sales agents. Their feedback was an unexpected bonus as they were bright enough to evaluate the different outlets, recording this one as a 'dud' and others as worth extra effort. As a result, an embarrassed Benton & Bowles was forced to extend the campaign for a week longer, until finally they had the outlets right.

They spent days working out clever incentive devices to cover everyone from agents and merchandisers to store managers and consumers. In the case of the store managers, the Irish dairymaids called in their green cars and, dressed in Irish folk costume, went into the shop to judge the display of Kerrygold butter. If the display merited it, they presented the store manager with a gold pen; then they told him, if they came back some days later and found the display still there, he would get double points—and a gift twice as good.

There were other incentives, too. The Bord Bainne people had brought over some Irish linen as prizes for consumers, who were asked to send in the corner of a Kerrygold wrapper and complete the slogan: 'I have just tried Kerrygold Irish Creamery Butter and I think it is excellent because . . .' The Irish linen factory in the North of Ireland had also produced little leprechaun dolls, and these too had been brought over to Liverpool. The Irishmen were embarrassed by them, basically because the Taoiseach (Prime Minister), Sean Lemass, had that very week made a speech to the Irish Institute

of Management in Killarney saying that Ireland had to get away
from symbols such as the harp, the wolfhound, round towers—and
leprechauns. They needn't have worried. The various sample prizes
were lying scattered on a table at a meeting in the Adelphi Hotel in
Liverpool when the tea-ladies came in. 'They all went "oooh" at the
sight of the leprechauns,' says McGough, 'and we then forgot all
about the embroidered Irish linen. And it became a tremendous
thing, with people writing in to say their luck had changed from the
moment they got their Larry the Lucky Leprechaun.'

There were only a thousand of them, and to win one consumers
not only had to send in a wrapper but also to find as many words as
they could from the word 'Kerrygold'—and then make a slogan of
it. There were too many entries for the staff of Benton & Bowles to
handle. Eventually McGough brought the job back to Dublin, where
the girls who handled the *Irish Press* crossword puzzle moved into
the Bord Bainne offices and worked through the entries in a single
night.

The supply of butter was soon gone. In the first four weeks Kerrygold achieved a market share of 18.5 per cent, well above its target.
Follow-up research showed not only that its brand had registered,
but it had already built up a brand loyalty, even though it was selling
at a premium on New Zealand butter (their great day came when
they were able to sell Kerrygold for more than the high-priced Danish
butter). They had to slow the campaign down and eke out supplies
for the rest of the year, but the following year, 1963, they got an
increased quota of another 600 tonnes and O'Reilly opened Bord
Bainne's first overseas office, in Manchester.

The shades of Ireland's past occasionally intruded into the otherwise smooth upward march of Kerrygold. O'Reilly had to tread warily
in the board room, staying in the no-man's land between the various
factions. The disgruntled Hennerty remained a dedicated enemy on
the board, and Captain David John Barry, a stout, coarse man, tried
to enlist O'Reilly's support against the chairman, Paddy Power. When
O'Reilly refused, he turned on him. Barry's oft-repeated boast of his
involvement in the 1916 rising, where he claimed to have been in
the Post Office, was treated with scorn by some of the board—several
of whom had been active IRA men at the time. 'If he was there at
all,' said Martin Mullally one day, 'all he did was wave his rattle from
an armour-plated car.'

Barry turned up for the opening of the Manchester office prominently wearing a medal awarded to him for fighting the Black and Tans in 1921. There was to be a large lunch, with toasts to the Queen as well as to the President of Ireland. Hearing this, one of the Bord Bainne people almost fainted. 'Holy Jesus!' he said. 'Barry'll never stand for it.' For a moment there was consternation, but O'Reilly thought quickly. He got hold of McGough who, just before the toasts were to be made, appeared on the balcony and shouted down: 'Captain Barry, there's an urgent call from America for you.' In fact it was one of the secretaries ringing from Dublin, but she held him long enough for the toasts to be made. When Barry returned he was actually wearing not one but two medals—the second had been awarded to the Irish emergency forces in the 1939–45 war.

'What are the two medals you're wearing?' asked a *Sunday Times* reporter.

'One is for fightin',' replied Barry. 'The other is for not fightin'.'

Later that year, 1963, General De Gaulle gave his famous '*non*' to Britain and Ireland joining the Common Market, and the impetus to find new markets for Irish butter became even more intense. Kerrygold was right up against its quota ceiling in Britain, so they started marketing it in Gibraltar, Malta, Cyprus, the Middle East and America. By 1964 they were selling it in twenty-five countries. O'Reilly went to the International Food Fair in Leipzig, East Germany, and came back with a contract for 500 tonnes of Kerrygold butter. He waved off a ship with the first ever consignment of Irish butter for the Italian market. He launched the brand in Trinidad and the Lebanon, all the time reducing the dependence on Britain even as the quotas were going up. O'Reilly was expanding the company into other areas than butter, too. That year he asked for and got the export rights for cheese, cream, condensed milk, milk powder, chocolate crumb and butteroil, giving Bord Bainne a monopoly of all Irish dairy products. He could boast, as he did, that there were now no surpluses of dairy products in Ireland, since all of them went for export. In three years Bord Bainne's sales trebled to £20 million— nearly 10 per cent of Ireland's total exports. By 1965 Kerrygold had spread to London and he gave a party for five hundred at the Hilton Hotel to mark the occasion. Its quality had now been accepted beyond question. By 1966, when O'Reilly moved on, it was sold nationwide in Britain, which now consumed 22,400 tonnes (a figure which would go on rising until well into the 1970s). Today, Bord Bainne has the largest turnover of any Irish enterprise, with exports of over £1.2

billion a year sold to more than eighty countries; less than a quarter goes to the UK. Ireland now exports almost as much milk in the form of cheese as in the form of butter (both are being challenged by a new business, begun as a sideline in O'Reilly's day—cream liqueurs, notably Bailey's Irish Cream). In Germany, Kerrygold is now the number one brand. That country alone takes 16,000 tonnes of Irish butter, nearly three times the quota for mainland Britain in 1962. By 1973, seven years after O'Reilly had left, the export of Irish dairy foods was so large that the subsidy given to the Irish farmer to produce it was almost 5 per cent of the Irish budget—and would have bankrupted the country had it not been passed on to the EEC in 1973.

The impact of Kerrygold's success was far wider than a marketing one. O'Reilly had forced considerable change on the Irish dairy industry, dragging it from its fragmented and backward state into a position where it could play a full part in the new Ireland towards which Sean Lemass was struggling. He did not do it alone, of course, and nor would he claim to have done. These were the years when, as Terence Brown wrote, Lemass was 'arousing his people to a new mission which he believed could do more to achieve the country's most profound aspirations—genuine political independence and unity between north and south—than the previous decades of economic isolation and cultural self-regard'. Ireland in the early 1960s was finally infected with what Professor David C. McClelland called a 'mental virus', which was necessary in order for a society to modernize itself. O'Reilly was one of the major carriers of that virus, spreading it liberally into the most backward corners of what was, in the 1950s, probably Europe's most backward society. It was a time when Ireland was at last allowed what Brown calls 'free, almost explosive, expression' as traditional Ireland and its constraining ideologies faded, and although O'Reilly was never one of the ideological leaders of that change, he was certainly a symbol of it.

The Kerrygold period represented O'Reilly at his best, his enthusiasm limitless and his imagination unblunted by the daily grind of running a large corporation. Never in his career would he find the same set of uniquely satisfying conditions which only come once in a lifetime—if you're lucky.

Yet what precisely had he achieved? Fifteen years later he would mull over that as he wrote his PhD with the same concentration which he had devoted to those months of study for the examinations of his youth. It is a thoroughly researched, well thought-out document whose conclusion is actually deeply depressing. True, he had created a premium for Irish butter, which had until then been sold as a commodity. He had also created new markets outside the traditional ones. And, he hoped, he had helped make the whole industry more efficient and outward-looking. But at the end of the day, the premium was only a modest part of the large increases which had taken place in farmers' incomes over that period. By far the most important element was the subsidy, first from the Irish government, later from the EEC. 'An Bord Bainne was set up primarily to increase the returns available to the primary producer from milk production,' he concluded. 'The leading edge of the strategy . . . was the creation of a brand in Ireland's main market, the UK.' The strategy had been highly successful in conventional marketing terms, he said. Yet the £10 million net premium created by Kerrygold between 1962 and 1972 amounted to only £100 per dairy farmer, or £10 for each year. 'The net premium as a proportion of the farmer's average milk price was typically less than 1 per cent.' On the other hand—and this was his final sentence—the success of Kerrygold had, in twenty years, put the Irish dairy farmer 'within reach of being one of the most efficient producers and marketers of milk products in the world'.

Years later, when he was fifty and looking back on his life, O'Reilly analyzed his own PhD thesis, of which he is intensely proud. He had wanted to see, he said, if the whole Kerrygold story was merely the creation of a market image, or whether it actually helped the farming community financially. 'The answer I found, to my dismay, was— not as much as I thought. In the short term, plundering the public purse, either domestic or EEC, was a much more effective way of increasing the net worth of the farmer than consumer marketing.' On the other hand, with the imposition of basic milk production quotas in Europe 'it now appears . . . that added value and consumer marketing are the only road to increase prosperity for the Irish dairy farmer'.

9

Erin Foods

IN MAY 1966 O'REILLY CELEBRATED HIS THIRTIETH BIRTHDAY WITH
a large party for friends and business acquaintances at his house in
Mount Merrion, on the south side of Dublin. His life since he joined
Bord Bainne had changed considerably. He was now the father of
three children, and Susan was in the early stages of pregnancy with
what would prove to be triplets. He was not yet rich, but by the
standards in which he had grown up he was prosperous enough,
with his handsome house, his expense account and his big black car.
He was not as fit as he used to be, but he kept in reasonable shape
with tennis and running. Life was good, even if there were certain
elements he missed. A fair impression of how he struck people and
how he lived is given by one interviewer, Michael O'Reilly, who first
met him at his Bord Bainne office at this time.

> There is no mistaking the tall, burly, red-haired figure, dressed
> in an Irish tweed suit, white shirt, dark blue tie, that sits behind
> a vast expanse of desk in Merrion Square. The lush green
> carpet; the light-green walls and white ornamental Georgian
> ceilings; the big coal fire in the ornate grate; the Paul Henry
> over the carved mantelpiece; these are the trappings of a suc-
> cessful man.

The interviewer went on to note: 'The round face in the huge
body is still very boyish; the voice cultured but determined; long

technical words shoot into the telephone with amazing speed; the manner commands respect—and obedience.' At the house in Stillorgan, he went on, 'paintings by Jack Yeats and the French impressionists decorate the lounge and books are very much in evidence'. Even by that stage, still living on the pay of a salaried employee of a semi-state body, O'Reilly had come a long way from the boy from Santry— although that was where his roots still were.

His rugby career had stuttered to a disappointing close, or so he thought, and all cups and prizes had evaded him. He had returned to it in the month before he joined Bord Bainne, his shoulder strong enough for him to turn out for Dolphins against Shannon in Limerick in March 1962. The following season started promisingly enough— playing for the Rest of Ireland against the Combined Universities, he scored one of his typical tries with a burst of speed which left the defence stranded. Then in January he played in his twenty-sixth international, against France, and scored only his second try for Ireland at Lansdowne Road with a run from 30 yards. It was classic stuff: the little French winger, Jean Dupuy, was knocked on to his back by a fierce O'Reilly hand-off, and he hit the line with three French players hanging off him. But Ireland went down 24 points to 5, and for the next match the selectors decided it was time for changes. For the first and only time in his life, O'Reilly was dropped.

'Seldom can the slings and arrows of outrageous fortune have afflicted anyone in rugby as severely as O'Reilly,' wrote Paul McWeeney in the *Irish Times*. 'In the 21st minute of Saturday's match, he was the hero of his native land and received a tremendous ovation as he ran back after scoring his try—less than 24 hours later, he is cast into outer darkness.'

For O'Reilly it came as a jolt to a self-confidence which had received remarkably few. Between 1955 and 1960 he had played twenty-two consecutive games for Ireland—more than any other player. Injury had then forced him to cry off, but now he was fully fit and, he believed, back at his best. It seemed all the more ironical that he should be dropped after scoring this special home try. 'Even if his work in the centre was hardly distinguished,' wrote McWeeney, 'it comes as a shock to find his name omitted from one of the wing positions, for he proved on Saturday that, given an opening, his speed is unimpaired and greater than that of any of the Irish three-quarters.'

There were many who thought he had been treated disgracefully, while others reluctantly agreed with the selectors. But on one point even O'Reilly himself had to agree: he had never shown the same form for Ireland as he had for the Lions, or even for the clubs he played for. There were all sorts of views and analyses of why this was so, most of them focusing on the quality of the Irish back-line and its inability to give him the ball in positions from which he could score. What is probably one of the best analyses comes from the Welsh rugby historian John Griffiths who, writing on an England–Ireland match, said: 'The Irish were unlucky to lose to England. Their forwards earned plenty of good possession, but the tactical approach of the backs was ineffective. The extent of their enterprise was tossing the ball to O'Reilly and expecting the big man to burst through the massed opposition. Effective tackling prevented Ireland's plan working.'

It wasn't true just of O'Reilly—it was true of other great Irish wingers as well. Niall Brophy, in many ways as good a wing as O'Reilly, scored seven tries in twelve appearances for the Lions in South Africa; but in twenty appearances for Ireland he scored only four tries. In twenty-six internationals so far, O'Reilly had scored five tries for Ireland, one of them on the tour of South Africa in 1961. Yet in only ten Test matches against South Africa, Australia and New Zealand he had scored six times. There were some good reasons for this: as he once remarked to Brophy, 'Niall, the only time we touch the ball for Ireland is afterwards when we autograph it.' The rules allowed direct kicking to touch is those days, and Ireland in O'Reilly's time never played a running game. The modern game, with its abundance of broken field possession, would have suited him much better.

His dismissal from the Irish team was the only talking point in the rugby clubs and pubs that weekend. But he got another chance in February when Brophy cried off and he was picked to play against Scotland. In a lacklustre game, Scotland won 3–0. He stayed in the team for the last match of the season, against Wales, and this time he was back at his best, continually charging at the Welsh defence in his most aggressive fashion. It was his twenty-eighth cap for Ireland— and his last for seven years.

He was now playing for Old Belvedere again and the club asked him to captain the senior side for the 1963–64 season. He accepted willingly, seeing this as his last serious chance to win one of those medals which had eluded him in every Belvedere side for nearly twenty years. Three months before the season began he sent every player in the club a personal note, setting out a rigid training programme which he expected them to adhere to. Practice would begin in July, and there would be trial matches at the end of August. The players reacted enthusiastically enough, but rugby for O'Reilly was not what it used to be. Although still younger than many of the senior side, he had a very different lifestyle, hosting large lunch and dinner parties, attending constant meetings, flying to and from all the countries where he was opening up export markets. At club level in particular, lesser players were dazzled simply by being in his presence, and stories began to spread of his grandness and aloofness. He had a tendency to roll up in his Mercedes minutes before the game was due to start, or travel in a separate carriage in the train, dictating to his secretary, Olive, all the way. There were stories of referees being asked to hold up the game until O'Reilly, dashing from a meeting (and always a poor timekeeper in any case) finally arrived. He could be vengeful, too, particularly if he were hand-tripped, an illegal tackle which involved catching the boot of the opposing winger and could be devastating to a player of O'Reilly's weight and speed (and vulnerability to injury). His favourite tactic if this happened was to chip the ball ahead for the offender to field it, whereupon O'Reilly, following up at full speed, hit him with the full force of his 14 stone. He was accused of getting in front of his own out-half too often, of looking for the ball too selfishly with the cry 'thank you, thank you' echoing across the field when he wanted it, and total silence when he didn't.

There were niggles and carping, but there was another side too. O'Reilly still loved the game of rugby, and as club captain certainly put more back into it than he took out. He thought continually about the game, and at Belvedere introduced a system which he had been considering since the Lions tours: the variation in the length of a line-out throw-in, from long to short, which is a regular part of the modern game. He coached the youngsters and drilled the senior players, passing on many of the lessons he had picked up on tour.

Then as the 1964 season began he was injured again and had to cry off for the rest of the season. In 1965 he was just getting into his stride when he tore his Achilles tendon, and to all intents and purposes that was the end of his career. He barely touched a rugby ball for the next three years.

In these years there had been crises and moments of self-revelation, too. A week after baby Susan was born, in February 1963, O'Reilly went to Limerick to play for Old Belvedere against Old Crescent (they beat them 30–8 with O'Reilly scoring a rare drop goal). He excused himself from the big dinner afterwards, and drove on to Cork to stay overnight with the McCarthys. He set out for Dublin after lunch on Sunday, intending to visit Susan and the baby in hospital that evening. His Mercedes 220SE was doing over 80 miles an hour between Urlingford and Johnstown when O'Reilly was half-dazzled by the lights of an oncoming car. Suddenly there was a noise like a bomb going off, a strangled scream and a blast of cold air blowing on his face. He braked to a stop 100 yards down the road to discover he was at the wheel of what had been transformed into an open tourer—the whole cab of the car had come off.

He looked back down the road, slowly taking in the scene. He had, he realized, hit a cyclist (the scream had come from his uninjured pal) whose body was now lying in the middle of the road. 'That was the moment when I realized the cowardice in all of us, because my first instinct was to drive off—to hit and run,' he said later. He found himself holding on to the rocks on the side of the road, saying, 'You've got to go back, you've got to go back', but unable to move or even to think clearly. Slowly, reluctantly, he dragged himself back towards the scene of what he felt had to be a dead body, with people and lights already gathering around it.

'I remember seeing this bloke lying there in the road, blood pumping out of him and my whole life passing in front of me. I was twenty-six years of age, running Bord Bainne, we had just had the launch of Kerrygold, I had become a father—and now this.'

A few minutes earlier the road had seemed deserted. Now women, all dressed in Irish country black, materialized out of the hedgerows to gather round the stricken body. 'He's going fast,' they were muttering as O'Reilly limped up. 'He's going fast, we'll have to get a priest.'

That snapped O'Reilly out of his trauma. 'Jesus Christ, don't get a priest!' he shouted. 'Get a doctor. Get an ambulance.'

The priest still arrived first and started anointing the unconscious figure, who O'Reilly could see was still faintly breathing. Someone stopped in a car and, recognizing O'Reilly, invited him to sit inside while they waited for the police to arrive. A *garda* sergeant appeared a few minutes later and came over to him. 'Are you the footballer?' he asked sympathetically. O'Reilly said he was. 'Well, that fellow's got eight brothers down the road and we'll have to be a bit careful.' He gave O'Reilly the clear impression that it wasn't him they might attack, but the stricken brother for daring to get in the way. When the ambulance finally appeared over an hour later it was driven by another great Irish sports star, Ollie Walsh, the Kilkenny goalkeeper-hurler. By that stage O'Reilly was surrounded by half the local community, all of them telling him how the young lad, James Neary, was always being hit by cars, riding in the middle of the road at night on his way to the pictures.

O'Reilly finally arrived back in Dublin at midnight and went to his parents' house, where he was staying while Susan was in hospital. He needed them badly that night. Jack could often be tiresome and trivial, but on this occasion he was magnificent. Had Tony been drinking? he asked immediately. No, he'd taken nothing. Jack went into action. They rang the Kilkenny general hospital to discover that the county surgeon, Dick Power, was another old O'Reilly acquaintance from university days. Jack summoned him to the phone for Tony to talk to. 'Jesus, Dick, the chap who's just been brought in by ambulance—is he dead?' asked O'Reilly.

No, said Power, he was alive. 'But he's got a four-inch hole in the back of his head which is so big we can see him thinking.'

It was Jack who organized for a local solicitor to call on the boy's family the next morning, and he who arranged to keep the event as quiet as possible. No newspapers reported the incident, which was astonishing given the level of O'Reilly's fame. A week later the local paper, the *Kilkenny Journal*, carried a single paragraph stating that James Neary had been involved in a 'collision with a motorcar', his second in a year. He had no lights or reflector, and was on the wrong side of the road.

Even in Ireland, there had to be some repercussions. O'Reilly was formally charged with driving with undue care and attention and a few months later appeared in court, when he was fined £4. His insurance company met the damages of £2841. Even that judgement never made the papers, which by an astonishing coincidence started a national strike that day.

O'Reilly, although he was unhurt he was deeply shaken, as much at that self-revelatory moment of fright and cowardice as at the event itself. From that time on, his pleasure in driving disappeared and for the rest of his life he would employ someone to drive him, particularly at night.

By 1965 the success of Kerrygold was conspicuous enough for O'Reilly to have become a figure on the international business stage. That year he was approached by Lord Netherthorpe, a large British farm owner who was chairman of Fisons, then a large British fertilizer and chemical company, to take charge of its African interests. Once again it was rugby which opened the door, this time through the Fison's chairman Lord Netherthorpe who had seen O'Reilly play in South Africa. At the time Fisons had become deeply involved in a large phosphate development at Palabora in partnership with Shell and a local company; they needed someone to run it, as well as their other African businesses. The salary offered was £25,000 a year, a fortune in 1965, and O'Reilly was tempted, both by the money and by the prospect of living in South Africa.

He decided to seek advice, not just from his father (as he invariably did on these occasions) but from someone else too. There were two major Irish political figures in his life, both of whom had become friends, and both of whom were very influential in government and in the smooth running of Bord Bainne. Jack Lynch, the Minister of Finance, was a mild-mannered, pragmatic, shrewd politician who had been a boyhood hero of O'Reilly's for his sporting prowess (he had won six All-Ireland medals in Gaelic games—five for hurling, one for football—and had captained County Cork). Born in 1917 in a working-class family in the Cork suburb of Shandon, he would take over from Lemass the following year to become, as one commentator remarked, 'the first Irish leader who did not have to explain to the Irish electorate where he was at Easter 1916.'

O'Reilly's other political friend was Charles Haughey, who in 1964 had become Minister for Agriculture and O'Reilly's immediate boss. Haughey, probably the most charismatic and astute politician of Ireland's post-war years, was a clever, self-serving, tenacious man seldom far from a scandal involving either his womanizing or his financial affairs—or both. He had married Lemass's daughter, giving him a powerful position within the Fianna Fail party, which he had consolidated. In 1965 he was seen as the favourite to succeed his ageing father-in-law (de Valera, now blind and doddery but still serving as Ireland's President, remarked that he was also a man who would destroy Fianna Fail).

When the Fison's approach came, O'Reilly went to Lynch rather than Haughey to tell him about it. Lynch saw himself as something of an O'Reilly sponsor, keenly interested in his career and ambitions, and they had often discussed a potential career in politics, which seriously tempted O'Reilly. Lynch was wholly opposed to the Fisons job, advising O'Reilly not to take it and arguing that he had an almost limitless future in Ireland. He was not yet thirty, he told him, and if he waited another year he could join the Fianna Fail government in almost any position he wanted. As an inducement to stay, he offered to raise O'Reilly's pay—he would put him on the board of the Irish Agricultural Finance Corporation and of Nitrigen Eireann, two state-sponsored organizations, at £500 a year each. That would take O'Reilly's annual earnings above £4000 a year, plus his car and various other perks—he could live well on that.

O'Reilly was still thinking about it as he drove up to Santry that evening for one of his regular visits to his parents. He turned on the car radio to hear the white Rhodesian leader Ian Smith declare his country unilaterally independent from Britain. Rhodesia was to be an important part of his territory at Fisons, and now Britain was going to impose sanctions and a blockade. He decided to stay at Bord Bainne.

A year later, in September 1966, Lynch rang O'Reilly in London, finding him at a moment when he was deep in battle with several of the big British food companies. One of Kerrygold's friends in the business had tipped him off about a secret request from Unigate to the distributors asking them not to handle Kerrygold any more, but to replace it with their own brands. A furious O'Reilly faced them directly with this information, and they agreed to meet at the Institute of Directors in Belgrave Square to discuss it. They were at the height of the row when O'Reilly was summoned to the telephone. It was Lynch. 'I need to see you straightaway,' he said. 'Can you come home?'

As it happened, Susan, heavily pregnant with triplets, was on her way to join O'Reilly in London the next day *en route* to the Costa del Sol for a holiday, and the last thing in the world he wanted at that moment was to return to Dublin.

'Come home to what?' he asked.

'We have a major problem with the Erin Food company,' said Lynch. 'We have just had these reports done which are quite shocking. It needs a new man to go in there as soon as possible—a heavy-hitter. We'd like you to do it.'

O'Reilly knew a little about the problems of Erin Foods and its parent, the Irish Sugar Board, which for over twenty years had been run by the man he detested, General Costello. The news that Costello was to resign had broken a few days before, but no one had taken it too seriously—Costello was in the habit of threatening even Irish prime ministers with his resignation threats, knowing they could not afford to lose him. This time, however, it was for real—Lynch wanted him out. The position at Erin had become so bad that Lynch had indicated he would bring in legislation to split it off from the Sugar Company and put someone else in charge.

'Jack, I've no interest in Erin Foods,' said O'Reilly. 'If you asked me to take over the Sugar Company, I might, because the Sugar Company controls Erin. But look—my wife is wildly pregnant, we're on our way to Spain, and I really don't see why I should do it.'

Lynch however was persuasive. 'Tony, please, for me, come home.' Reluctantly he agreed to fly home the next day, and went back into his fractious meeting. The following evening Charles Murray, assistant secretary at the Department of Finance, arrived at the O'Reilly house in Mount Merrion clutching a large mass of papers from a firm of management consultants. 'I have here six reports from Arthur D. Little,' he began.

> And I want you to read them and then consider seriously taking control of something which is very clearly completely out of control and which if we don't downsize in Britain will bankrupt the company. Last year we lost £3 million on sales of £2 million, which must be a world record, a Harvard Business School case study, *Guinness Book of Records*, achievement by Costello.

Murray was highly uncomplimentary about the general. 'You're the only person who is credible enough in the agricultural community, thanks to Kerrygold, to challenge him and take this on. We want you to run the Sugar Company,' he said.

O'Reilly was flattered. Clearly things had shifted overnight. Now, instead of Erin Foods, he was being offered one of the biggest jobs in all of Ireland, much bigger than Bord Bainne, with direct control of its own manufacturing process, a large prestige office on St Stephen's Green and a high profile to go with it. There was also an attraction in stepping into the shoes of this strange, powerful and slightly sinister man. Ever since O'Reilly could remember, Costello had been a part of Irish history, a man involved with almost every stage of the country's development since independence—and before. There were more stories about him, many of them mythical, than almost any man in Ireland.

Born in 1904, two years before Jack O'Reilly, in Cloughjordan,

County Tipperary, Costello had become a full-time member of the IRA in 1920 when his father was arrested by the Black and Tans. In 1922 he joined the national army as a private, and in the Irish Civil War, fighting on the opposite side to de Valera, he was promoted with a speed which even he later admitted had been 'misguided'. Shortly before he was killed Michael Collins made him colonel-commandant—he was still only eighteen—a rank equivalent to general, basically because, he said later, 'I was one of only two survivors of an ambush party whose twenty-three members surrendered to us.' In the 1920s he became the head of Irish army intelligence, then chief staff officer and, after an Irish military mission to the USA, he set up Ireland's Military College in 1930. There was a legend that, while at West Point, Costello had scored a decisive victory over Erwin Rommel (later Field Marshal) in the academy stakes, a myth which Costello did not try to deny but which was wholly untrue (in fact he never even met Rommel). In the war years de Valera, trying to keep him out of harm's way, gave him the task of defending the Irish ports from German attack. There were persistent rumours during the war, with which Jack O'Reilly was certainly familiar, that Costello was plotting a military coup to instal himself as dictator. He refuted them vigorously—'I fought a civil war to assert that the will of the people would prevail'—but they stuck.

In 1945, when he was still only forty-one, Costello was put in charge of the Irish Sugar Company (Comhlucht Suicre Eireann), largely to deal with its appalling industrial relations record. Since its formation in 1933 the Sugar Company had averaged two strikes a year, but in his first year Costello put down the biggest strike yet—largely by threatening to open the Irish ports to foreign sugar. Industrial peace reigned for the next thirty years.

Erin Foods, launched in 1959 as a partnership between the Sugar Company and the local co-operatives, was to some extent a blueprint for An Bord Bainne two years later. It was under-funded from the start—the £25 million promised by Lemass turning into only £5 million—yet for a time it seemed to offer a bright future. Several able young scientists at the Sugar Company's research facilities in Carlow had fastened on to a new system of freeze-drying food, vegetables in particular, so they could be reconstituted simply by pouring boiling water on them, and they had taken this innovative idea several stages further than any other food company. Until that point Ireland had never been a big vegetable-growing country, but, as it had originally done for beet sugar, the company now set out to create an entire new Irish industry. There were joint ventures with co-ops in Middleton, Skibbereen, North Kerry and Glencolumbkille in Donegal which began growing fresh vegetables, putting them through the accelerated freeze-dried (AFD) process, packaging them and marketing them as a substitute for imports. Costello poured large quantities of Sugar Company money into the project, building a series of large plants around the country and advertising his new soups and vegetables heavily. In the age before domestic freezers, Erin Foods were a hit— or they seemed to be. What no one, particularly not the general, had considered was the costs, which were buried deep in the arcane accounts of the Sugar Company.

Costello was evangelical, almost fanatical, about the new process and his new foods, seeing in this the chance to regenerate large parts of rural Ireland which had been devastated by emigration and poverty. When he had conquered the Irish market—which took only a few years—he began to look abroad. He had once mocked O'Reilly's marketing efforts in Britain, but in 1964 even he had to admit that Kerrygold had proved him wrong. He set out to emulate this success, but chose a different route. He would not give his packaging or his distribution to a 'foreign' company, but would hire his own sales force. Erin Foods would do it itself. That was when his whole edifice began to unwind in a dramatic and embarrassing way.

'He fell in love with the AFD process,' says O'Reilly now, analyzing it from his position as head of a world food company—and as the person who inherited the mess. 'From a marketing point of view you must never fall in love with the process—there's always another way to do it. What matters is the presentation, the recipe, the taste, the capacity to engage the customer's excitement and imagination, and to deliver consistent high-quality good taste. His products didn't deliver.'

Until 1966 that hadn't mattered—Costello covered the losses of Erin Foods from his cushion of profits from sugar, which seemed to be guaranteed because the Sugar Company was a monopoly business, the only supplier of sugar in Ireland. However, over the years even sugar profits had been abused, with sugar beet contracts becoming a powerful political weapon, given almost exclusively to farmers who supported the Fianna Fail party. Sugar made from beet grown in the inefficient farming community of Ireland was an expensive commodity compared to cheap cane grown in the Caribbean, so Costello kept the acreage of Irish beet down and imported large quantities of cheap cane sugar which he then blended, getting the guaranteed sugar beet price for the mixture. In the early 1950s, Cadburys, Rowntrees and the other chocolate companies went into the manufacture of chocolate crumb in Ireland, setting up their own plants which Costello supplied with sugar (it is a little-known fact that 50 per cent of all the chocolate bars eaten in Britain are based on an Irish-produced ingredient) from two huge plants at Mallow in Cork and Rathmore in Kerry.

Costello was gambling that the price of world sugar would stay low, and for years he got away with it. But his cover was blown in 1963–64 when their was one of the periodic "spikes" in world cane prices, which left him with pre-priced obligations to the chocolate crumb manufacturers which he had to fulfill from world priced cane sources. It was to prove his downfall. Suddenly, the profitable Sugar Company was plunged into massive losses. An internal report projected a severe cash crisis ahead for Erin, and Costello reluctantly went back to the Department of Finance to demand more money. Charles Haughey, however, refused to give it to him, and sent in Arthur D. Little to examine the situation. The consultants' report was damning: accumulated losses had already reached £4 million, and a further investment of £15 million would be needed to sustain Erin Foods. Even then, there was no guarantee that it would do much more than break even at best. The accelerated food-drying process was already being overtaken by frozen foods, competition was getting rougher, and there was no way that vegetables could be grown in large parts of Ireland competitively, it added. The scandal rebounded on Lynch as well as Costello, and O'Reilly found his political mentor in a hole. He was wary about getting involved, but Jack Lynch was insistent, the job was an obvious promotion—and it was an even bigger challenge than the Dairy Board. He agreed to think seriously about it.

He called a friend of his, Tom Gallagher, who was the advertising agent for Erin Foods, and invited him down to Glandore, the beautiful little fishing village in West Cork where he and Susan now went every summer. For three days he and Gallagher walked for miles along the unspoilt beaches at Roscarbery, examining the situation from every angle. He showed Gallagher the Arthur D. Little reports and reanalysed them himself. At the end of the period Gallagher said: 'Tony, it's a tough one to call, but I think you should take it.' He took it.

On 6 December 1966 O'Reilly left the Dairy Board with considerable regrets and took over the Sugar Company, in an instant going from the best job he ever had to the worst. By then Lynch had succeeded Lemass as Taoiseach, the compromise candidate against the much more thrusting Haughey and Colley. 'He came quietly through on the rails, giving the impression that he was merely out for a canter, while his frothing rivals churned up the ground in the centre,' wrote J. J. Lee, who also added that with the departure of Lemass the pace of change in Ireland began to wind down. Lynch was a temporizer, a man who, says Lee, 'having no strong views himself . . . preferred to lead from behind'. But whatever his failings—and Lynch was to lead the Fianna Fail party, in and out of power, for the next ten years before Haughey finally succeeded him—O'Reilly now had a friend and supporter in very high places.

He exacted very tough conditions for taking on the new job. He wanted to be managing director of the Sugar Company at a salary of £12,500 a year, more than three times what he had been earning before. In the twenty-one years he had run the organisation Costello had only ever held the title of general manager, but O'Reilly insisted on being managing director. He had also heard rumours of Costello's highly generous contract, so when the Department of Finance asked him what sort of contract he wanted he said: 'Exactly the same as what Costello had. Whatever he had, I want.' It turned out to be an astonishingly generous one: Costello had a contract for life, which meant that if O'Reilly had left the job after six weeks he would still have been entitled to two-thirds pension until he died. He also got a chauffeured Mercedes, driven by Arthur Whelan (or 'Wheels' as he became known to the O'Reilly children), who joined him in October 1967 and still drives him today. The indispensable Olive would also, of course, accompany him.

Even before he made the move, he had discovered that the situation at Erin Foods was even worse than anyone outside had imagined. There was at the time considerable controversy in the public press about his taking on the job, and one day Olive put through a telephone call from a man who said he had something special to tell him about Erin. He introduced himself as Vincent Ferguson, finance director of the Sugar Company. Although O'Reilly did not know it at the time, Ferguson was the man who had projected the huge cash shortfall at Erin Foods and the Sugar Company, and whose report had resulted in the appointment of Arthur D. Little. 'I'd like to come and see you,' he said.

'Sure,' said O'Reilly, 'come down.'

So Ferguson walked from his offices in St Stephen's Green to the Bord Bainne office at 13 Merrion Square, a few hundred yards away, and appeared before O'Reilly. He was older than his new boss, with heavy glasses and the careful, deliberate manner of a born accountant. 'Before you arrive, I'd like to talk to you,' he began. 'The first thing you have to know is that this company is a nightmare—I really can't believe how bad things are.'

As O'Reilly arched his eyebrows in astonishment Ferguson began to take him through the financial structures, the systems, costs, difficulties and possibilities of achieving the company's goals. O'Reilly was spellbound. Here was a man who clearly understood the accounts of the company in a way that was well beyond even O'Reilly's grasp. 'I formed the opinion that this guy was one of the most financially literate guys I had ever met,' says O'Reilly. 'He wasn't just an accountant, he was a fellow who had the architecture of finance in his head, who understood a lot of moving parts, and really understood about money. I formed an extremely high opinion of him then, which I maintain to this day.'

The picture painted was pretty dismal, persuading O'Reilly that, even if he could get it, there was no point in pumping more money into Erin Foods. He had to find a different solution. A few days later he went to London where he met Bob Norman, a former purchasing officer for H.J. Heinz who was now the UK manager of Erin Foods, to receive even worse news. Norman was close to despair.

'Tony, my boy, you have no chance at all,' he told him on the first day. 'You've got to close this thing down. It's a disaster. Do you know last week's sales were exceeded by last week's returns? We've actually got negative sales!'

'I've never heard of negative sales,' said a puzzled O'Reilly.

'I'm telling you,' said Norman vehemently. 'The tomato soup is coming back by the bucketful—it looks like blood plasma. There's more coming back than is going out.' The only choice, he went on, was to sign up with a major corporation, as O'Reilly had done on the Dairy Board. 'Sales administration and distribution are costing us about 120 per cent of the product price—and that's just for the sales, never mind the product and the packaging. We've got a hundred people, a hundred expense accounts, a hundred goddam motor cars, and we've got all sorts of concealed costs that we don't even know about.'

O'Reilly heard him through and finally said. 'OK, so what do we do?'

Norman suggested what Arthur D. Little had also recommended: a merger with another food company.

> You have this enormous overhead here, and you can transfer that on to them—they've got fixed costs for their sales force, they've got their distribution structures, they've got their sales assistants and their administration. Let's get a list out, we'll talk to everybody. Let's talk to Brooke Bond, Oxo, Unilever, Knorr, Heinz ... we have to find a credible way to get rid of this overhead in Britain.

In the end they talked to eighteen companies, but the only one which expressed serious interest was Heinz.

It was Bob Norman, with his Heinz background, who arranged for O'Reilly to travel out to Hayes in Middlesex to see Tony Beresford, managing director of Heinz in Britain. Beresford was a veteran of the food industry, who had started at the age of sixteen at Heinz in 1932 and sold cans of beans, tomato soup and baby food across half of England. After a colourful war record he had returned to work his way to the top. He had seen O'Reilly on the rugby field, but knew nothing else about him.

'My first thought was: how am I going to get rid of this man politely,' says Beresford. 'But as he went on talking, I suddenly thought: you know, this man is a bit different, and I ought to sit up and pay attention to what he's saying.' By the end of the conversation Beresford was hooked, not so much by the prospect of selling Erin foods through his sales network, but of using Erin as a source of raw vegetables and meat for his factories in Britain. There were intriguing possibilities here. They agreed to talk further in the new year.

O'Reilly had other things on his mind that month. On 17 December Susan gave birth to triplets—delivered, as were all his children, by his old mentor at Belvedere, Karl Mullen. They called them Caroline, Gavin and St John Anthony (who would be Tony Junior). As soon as Susan was up to it, on 12 January 1967, O'Reilly took her off on holiday to the Canaries. Charles Haughey, now Minister of Finance, joined them there, and he was in continual touch with Vincent Ferguson, who was working on the deal with Heinz. O'Reilly was nervous because he had never dealt with a big multi-national before, and he and Ferguson were both concerned that Heinz would run financial rings around him. Over the holiday they worked out between them what they wanted in the way of a partnership, trying to think through every angle of it. What they came up with was a joint company, Heinz-Erin, to which Erin Foods, as the manufacturer, would sell its products at a gross margin of 35 per cent over cost. The product would then be sold by Heinz, which would charge Heinz-Erin a 9.5 per cent fee on everything, leaving a net margin of 25.5 per cent. Heinz had its own sales force in Ireland but that would be disbanded, and Erin's existing sales force would sell all Heinz products for a fee of 16.5 per cent. That in the event was the basis of the deal and Haughey, involved in much of the detail, wholly approved what both men knew would be a controversial announcement.

In Ireland, largely because of his Kerrygold reputation, the general belief was that O'Reilly would build and strengthen Erin, rather than cut it back. Costello had created the impression that Erin was a big success, and if it had now run into problems, then O'Reilly seemed the ideal person to take it to the next stage. The magazine *Business and Finance* noted in November 1966 that O'Reilly 'should provide the necessary marketing expertise to help Erin Foods achieve the ambitious targets' set in the A. D. Little reports. This, it went on, involved investing another £15 million in Erin before it showed a return. A week later the magazine, normally informed, added: 'Mr O'Reilly's appointment is being hailed in trade circles in Britain and Ireland as the start of a determined bid by the government to expand the entire marketing range of Irish processed food products in export markets.' A note of caution crept in to later issues, but the seed was sown: O'Reilly was expected to expand rather than contract. Few knew he was negotiating what would be regarded by many, notably Costello, as a sell-out of a fine Irish concern which with the right money behind it might still succeed.

The O'Reillys were back in Ireland on 1 February ready for a state visit from the Heinz team to the Erin factories. As he waited for them at Cork airport, O'Reilly suddenly realized he was going to be showing them around plants that he himself had been too busy to go and see.

Three of them arrived including Tony Beresford, the managing director of the British company. O'Reilly was to be their official escort at factories in Mallow, Thurles and Carlow, and all day long he tried to stay two yards ahead of them, rushing forward to grab the managers, trying to drown out their greetings by taking them rapidly aside. 'If you don't mind, just pretend I've been here for most of the past month,' he kept saying. Mallow and Thurles were modern production plants, and at Carlow the Heinz people found impressive laboratories and the bright research and development team which had refined the AFD system.

The Heinz team liked what they saw, reckoning that, whatever their shortcomings, Erin Foods would be a useful extra arm to their product portfolio. But suddenly they hit an unexpected snag. Beresford and his team in London wanted to do the deal, but Heinz's head office in Pittsburgh did not. 'By this time I was very impressed with his personality, and I suddenly realized here was a person full of ideas and imagination who had a personality and an attitude I could very happily work with,' says Beresford. But Beresford's ultimate boss, Burt Gookin, was not so happy with it; nor was his own UK board. Beresford was told he could not go ahead; but he refused to give in easily, arguing that he had gone around the factories in Ireland, seen the raw materials available, and believed there was every chance that Heinz could make a success of it. He was in a strong position because at that stage the British end of Heinz was making around half the group's total world profits, while its major US operations made nothing. 'They didn't really want to upset me by saying no, you can't do it,' he says. Finally, Gookin agreed on condition that two senior Heinz men went on the Heinz-Erin board to watch over this young Irishman on whom Beresford reported so favourably but who was regarded with some suspicion in Pittsburgh.

Charles Haughey then announced the deal to the Dáil, insisting that it was 'clearly in the national interest', countering the expected outcries from the opposition by pointing out that there was no other course, and the Heinz link guaranteed a future for Erin. But in the farming community the announcement was received with mixed feelings. 'I thought I'd done a damned good job,' says O'Reilly now.

> I was able to dismiss the sales force in Britain, close down the
> entire operation, get rid of an expensive, prestige office at
> Slough, and within a year we had the company back in profit

again. What we'd done was downsize the whole operation, and we had basically recognized that climatically Ireland is not the ideal country to be able to grow vegetables at anything like the comparable cost structure of say, southern France, or parts of Holland or California—and then dehydrate them and expect to be competitive internationally. They just weren't. Costello also had an enormous social experiment that he was conducting covertly under his great cover profit gleaned through the cheap sugar cane prices, and he had put plants into improbable places which were hostile to growing vegetables. You just can't grow vegetables competitively on the hillsides of Donegal.

O'Reilly and Haughey had been concerned about how the statement might be received and had put a lot of work into preparing the ground. On the day O'Reilly did a great deal of briefing, and to an extent it worked. The agreement, wrote Hugh O'Neill in the *Irish Times*, was 'a better solution for the farmers' predicament than anyone could have foreseen' and had got the government 'off an unpleasant hook'. He concluded that 'many parties could take pleasure out of the deal' adding that O'Reilly had proved himself a 'formidable negotiator in bringing such a complicated arrangement to a successful conclusion within three months of the first round of talks'.

Costello, watching his dream of a highly profitable vegetable-growing industry die before his eyes, saw it in a different light. He savagely condemned the deal as a betrayal and a sell-out, a cave-in to the 'foreigners' and the British in particular—a theme he would go on expounding for years.

It was not a comfortable few weeks for the new managing director. Expectations had been so high that the result seemed something of a let-down. O'Reilly worked hard to alter the climate, talking about the huge overheads in Britain and the advantages of being linked to a major company such as Heinz. But his reputation as a superman had been dented, and would never quite recover to the impossible levels it had reached at Bord Bainne.

A few weeks later he was to run into another thorny problem, this one bringing him into direct conflict with Charles Haughey. As Minister of Agriculture Haughey had had a rough time with the farmers, particularly when a seamen's strike cut off exports to Britain, and the EEC, with Ireland still outside, decided not to take any more beef from beyond the Community. The beef industry, which had been through two boom years, collapsed, and the leaders of the National Farmers' Association (NFA) marched on Haughey's office to demand help. He refused to meet them, and nine of them camped on the pavement outside for the next three weeks. It was not his fault, but in the charged atmosphere, and because he had handled it so badly, he got the blame, and it probably cost him the premiership. Lynch then moved him to the Department of Finance, but he was still boiling with rage at the farmers when O'Reilly's problem broke.

He had been at the Sugar Company less than two months when two of his advisers, Matt Rowlette and Maurice Sheehy, came to see him. The Beet Growers' Association (BGA), they explained, was under enormous pressure from the twenty-six thousand Irish farmers who grew beet to change its rules of election. At present, because of the arcane rules which no one fully understood, only six thousand voted, and the NFA was insisting it be changed. They were threatening, they told him, to stop all supplies of beet to the Sugar Company, and close him down. Only in Ireland could this have significant political implications, which the two Sugar Company advisers explained to O'Reilly. The BGA was a Fianna Fail–dominated body, with beet contracts awarded as political patronage. Democratic elections would change that—and the government would never stand for it. Yet the NFA was prepared to march on Haughey's office again and picket the place, and the Sugar Company as well. 'I wasn't concerned about protecting Fianna Fail's control of the beet growers,' says O'Reilly. 'But I was concerned that the Sugar Company should not be politicized, and that we got our beet in and our vegetables grown.'

O'Reilly left Ireland a few weeks later for his first-ever visit to Pittsburgh, travelling on the last voyage of the *Queen Mary*. With him he took a biography of Harold Macmillan—and the rules of the Beet Growers' Association, which he discovered were even more complex than he had suspected. By the time he got to New York he was an expert on both subjects. In Pittsburgh he met Burt Gookin, the chief executive officer of Heinz, for the first time and liked him instantly. He spent a week in meetings, playing tennis and seeing some of the local sights, pleasantly surprised by the friendliness and professionalism of the company. But the problems back home were never far from his mind. The Sugar Company, he decided, had really no choice but to allow a free election—which, even if the Fianna Fail candidates lost, wouldn't matter too much. The Sugar Company would still control the contracts.

Back in Dublin he indicated that this was what he wanted to do, and then sat back to await the storm. It came within hours. Haughey came through on the telephone first. 'I suggest, Tony, you drop these elections,' he said. O'Reilly explained that he could not do that, that he really had no choice, and he would like to bring along his two advisers to explain why. 'Have you got any time today?'

'I'm seeing an old bollocks at seven at Iveagh House,' replied Haughey. 'Meet me there at 6.30.'

Before he got there O'Reilly received another message, this time passed on by an acolyte of another politician. 'He says to tell you that, if you allow these elections, he'll coffin ye,' said the man.

O'Reilly tried to laugh it off. 'That's a verb I've never heard of before. Is that spelled with one or two Fs—as in cacophony?' he asked. But he didn't regard it as funny.

When he saw Haughey that evening he brought along Sheehy and Rowlette, the two civil servants who knew the politics of the beef industry better than anyone. They could scarcely believe their ears. The Finance Minister was almost leaping off the ground in his rage. 'These fuckin' farmers have been hounding me, and doing terrible things to my family, and they're not fuckin' going to get away with it,' he shouted. 'There will be no election. No election!'

O'Reilly decided there would, and the next day began to outflank Haughey. He first went to see the Minister of Land, Sean Flanagan, and persuaded him that a BGA election was the best route to go. Then he went to Lynch, whose immediate reaction was the same as Haughey's—why wreck this bastion of Fianna Fail support? 'Jack, this is an issue you just can't win,' said O'Reilly. He took Lynch through the argument at length and in great detail, insisting that, unless they took the democratic route, Lynch would be faced with a crisis he couldn't handle. In the end, the Taoiseach reluctantly agreed.

By the time the issue came up in the Irish Cabinet, O'Reilly and the farmers between them had done some impressive lobbying. The vote was eight to seven in favour of allowing a BGA election, without Lynch himself having to vote. Haughey took it philosophically, sourly remarking to O'Reilly a few days later: 'I thought the Taoiseach was unconscionably well informed on the issue.'

When the elections were held, Fianna Fail lost 58 of the 60 seats on the BGA, an indication of the pent-up anger among the beet growers. O'Reilly had just heard the news when he bumped into

Haughey in the Russell Hotel. 'Have you heard what's happened in
the election?' he asked him. Haughey hadn't, and when O'Reilly told
him he threw his head back and roared with laughter. 'This'll break
Blaney's fuckin' heart,' he said.

His relationship with Haughey, who O'Reilly liked very much,
endured an amusing episode a few months later. One day, for some
reason, O'Reilly was driving Susan's family car, still full of toys, sticky
sweets and the rest of the paraphernalia associated with six small
children. He bumped into Haughey after a lunch and offered to
drop him back at his office so that they could have a quick chat in
the car. Haughey duly stepped out of the car and walked with dignity
up the steps of the ministry, acknowledging the salute of the *garda*
officer. Watching him go, O'Reilly was horrified to observe a series
of little round coloured objects stuck to the back of his jacket and
trousers: the remains of a packet of Smarties that one of the children
had left on the seat. Hastily, he put the car in gear and drove off.

In the spring O'Reilly went to Donegal to see the Errigal Co-op
Society which had been formed by an energetic priest, Father James
McDyer, in an effort to keep what remained of the farming community from emigrating. Bravely, in the hostile climate of north-west
Ireland, they had tried to grow vegetables on some of Ireland's poorest land. McDyer had been encouraged and subsidized by Costello,
and had become almost a saint to the locals who depended on him
for employment. Now there was only trepidation in the community.

McDyer greeted him courteously enough, but when O'Reilly started
to explain why he'd come the priest cut him short. 'I know why you've
come,' he said. 'You've come here to close us down. I've heard all about
you—you're the hatchet man from Dublin, a faceless man from the
Department of Finance. We know who you are all right.'

O'Reilly was stunned for a moment, but he had come prepared.
'Listen to me for a moment, Father,' he said.

> Let me tell you something. We've got fifty people working in
> this plant, we've got seventy farmers growing for you—it's a
> small enterprise. I'll guarantee you that you'll be able to keep
> those fifty people working in this plant if you let the Protestants
> grow your crops, because the Protestants have all the good
> land. It's over in the Lagan Valley, it's 90 miles away, but if
> you get a couple of good farmers growing for you you'll have

all the raw materials you need at competitive prices, with suede
turnips as big as basketballs. And you'll be, possibly, the lowest-
cost operator in the entire system. We'll keep the plant open.

'Do you tell me that?' said the priest. 'Do you tell me that? Aye, the
Protestants have the good land all right. You may be right, we may
do that.'

O'Reilly went on to argue, from his Bord Bainne experience, that
the hillsides were fine for cattle and sheep, but there was no way
they could grow carrots or cabbages competitively. He made a speech
to the workers and farmers stressing the same points, although more
delicately than he had with McDyer. 'It is essential that all Irish
producers, including Errigal, appreciate that the international marketplace is the supreme discipline in their activities. Heinz-Erin provides such a challenge. It could provide one of the most powerful
market forces in the UK, provided cost and quality are right.'

In some ways he came to have a reluctant respect for Costello, who
might have had no time for the 'supreme discipline of the foreign
market,' but was, according to his own lights, an Irish patriot who
had done what he could to keep the farmers on the land and improve
their prosperity. But the cost was enormous. O'Reilly discovered another Sugar Company venture in the west of Ireland where Costello
had attempted to grow high-quality grass for seed on the peat bogs.
The technical people reckoned it was possible, and on a pilot plot
they raised some very high-quality seed. But a larger operation, abandoned long before O'Reilly came on the scene, failed dismally, and
the legend was that £2 million worth of equipment had disappeared
into the bog. There had been a big opening by the minister, and
gigantic American-made harvesters, better suited to the prairies of
Kansas, had set off blessed by the Bishop of Tuam. One of the
agricultural officers explained to O'Reilly that, when the bishop and
dignitaries went off to the bar, one of the machines had sunk without
trace. 'John-Joe Moriarty set off on his quivering Lilliput for his last
journey,' he told him graphically. 'His last journey—all they ever
found of him was his hat!' It was apocryphal, of course, but the bog
had indeed swallowed up large quantities of valuable resources.

In that first year O'Reilly removed costs of £850,000 from the Erin
Foods operation, and by the following year had stemmed the outflow.
In the December 1968 issue of *Business and Finance* magazine, which
named O'Reilly 'Man of the Week', it was reported that Erin, which

had been trading at an annual loss of £2 million two years before, was now about to break even on cashflow for the first time in its eight-year history. 'The link with Heinz is beginning to show its paces, with sales soaring from £3.2 million to £5.5 million and acreage of vegetables up by 50%.' The tide of opinion was turning.

O'Reilly's lifestyle over these years had become steadily more prosperous. The house in Merrion Road, Stillorgan, proved too small once the triplets arrived, and they had moved again, this time to a house of O'Reilly's dreams. Columbia, in Delgany, County Wicklow, was described by the estate agents as 'one of the most interesting residential properties in Ireland', which was only a modest exaggeration. With acres of grounds and woods on the edge of the sea, plus views down over the village of Greystones and the Wicklow coast, its own gate lodge and a long, tree-lined driveway, the handsome Georgian house was less than an hour from the centre of Dublin. As he grew more prosperous he added a tennis court and a swimming pool, and covered two acres with glasshouses in which he grew tomatoes commercially, bringing into his life another of his indispensable staff, his farm manager, Jim Kelly, who like Olive and Arthur, the chauffeur, would stay with him wherever he went.

Susan loved the new house, but it meant she was less often able to join O'Reilly at the dinners he attended in Dublin most evenings. In any case she was continually tired, since the task of looking after six children under the age of four occupied all her time. Jack and Aileen came down most weekends to see their grandchildren, attending the large lunch and dinner parties which O'Reilly insisted on holding at these times. Jack must have made these journeys with mixed emotions: Wicklow did not have happy memories for him, and at Delgany he was only a matter of miles from the territory of his in-laws.

But O'Reilly was working hard for his success. The Heinz deal continued to fester, with Costello talking bitterly about the 'servile role' played by the Erin Food sales force he had built up in Ireland, now used to promote 'the sales of products made in foreign factories . . . produced in foreign countries . . . at prices higher than those paid to Irish farmers. The widespread goodwill for Erin Foods is being used to promote a foreign-owned brand name.'

Costello blamed more than just O'Reilly—he blamed the government for short-changing him and his concept of Ireland as an intensive vegetable grower along Dutch lines, which he reckoned he was on the verge of achieving when the rug was pulled from under him.

O'Reilly, knowing the figures and the projections, could only wince. 'I've never commented publicly about Costello, but I will comment now,' he says. 'Costello was a patriot, but he was also a bully. His patriotism blinded him to the commercial realities of the marketplace. He knew how to look after himself by way of the most remarkable contract I have ever seen. There were elements of his character you could admire, but he was not a good general manager of the Sugar Company.'

O'Reilly stayed for nearly three years, a time for him of consolidation and learning, laying, without knowing it, part of the foundations for his later career. These were probably among the least spectacular years of his career, yet they were far from fallow. He could later boast that the price paid to Irish farmers rose every year under his management, and profits too rose each year.

In the early days he could talk about a 'bright future' for Erin Foods, but in reality there was little future for such an enterprise in the international food business, even with Heinz as a partner. He did get the joint company Heinz-Erin into modest profit, and after five years there was a shareholders' distribution of a couple of million pounds. But Erin Foods continued deep in the red, and Costello's over-bold experiment would eventually die in the ferocious new world of open borders and competition. Its poor performance would leave a blot on the O'Reilly reputation. In November 1971 two years after he left, the company announced losses of £777,000, double the previous year's figures, provoking an acid comment in *Business and Finance*.

> What Tony did was to cut Erin Foods' losses by scrapping the field force in Britain and handing the direct retailing of convenience foods over to Heinz-Erin. Now we find that the Heinz-Erin sales targets haven't been met. While Heinz-Erin broke even, the Sugar Company is left carrying the can, i.e., Erin Foods' production losses and greater increased stocks. Heads, Heinz-Erin wins, tails, Erin Foods loses.

O'Reilly vehemently rejected such criticisms, presenting another side of the picture. The Joint company, he argued, all this time distributed all Heinz's foods in Ireland for a charge of 16.5 per cent, contributing £1m to the Sugar Company's overheads. It also continued to trade for fifteen years after he left. When it was eventually dismantled and closed, he angrily condemned it as a 'singularly stupid act'.

But by that stage O'Reilly had moved on.

10

Entrepreneur

AFTER TWO YEARS AS MANAGING DIRECTOR OF BOTH THE SUGAR COMPANY and Erin Foods, O'Reilly was getting restless. The Sugar Company was back on an even keel (it would be privatized, twenty-four years later, as Greencore—a profitable and successful company), and he had done what he reckoned in the circumstances was a good job for Erin. His salary for doing both jobs was £12,500 and materially he was doing well, but it was clear to him that neither company was ever going to provide anything like the same type of explosive excitement as the launch of Kerrygold. His role at the two semi-state bodies had drawn him more and more into the political network of Ireland and he liked this arrangement, moving easily in the circles of ministers, senior civil servants and the dozens of apparatchiks that surrounded them. He was naturally good at this kind of thing, and he got considerable satisfaction from it. But he was no longer stretching himself, as he had done all his life so far. Ireland's semi-state organizations were essentially extensions of the government, which already played a larger part in the 1960s' Irish economy than in that of any other country in Europe. Decision-making was painfully slow. In retrospect, O'Reilly realized he had been exceptionally fortunate at Bord Bainne. Because he had been the first general manager there were no rules and no guidelines, and before the organization could impose them he wrote his own.

But that was not possible at the Sugar Company, which was tightly restrained by civil servants and ministers. O'Reilly's capacity to work up to eighteen hours a day—and more—and getting by on four or five hours' sleep left time and energy to spare for something else. What interested him more and more was the concept of risk-taking, something almost unknown in the Ireland in which he had grown up. Despite his basic middle-class aspirations for security and certainty, O'Reilly wanted to become an entrepreneur.

The excitement of the Lemass surge which had begun in 1958 had subsided by the mid-1960s, as the second programme for economic expansion proved much less successful than the first. Ireland now entered a period of economic drift which would last through most of the 1970s. There was still an explicit policy of going for economic growth and the creation of an industrial sector in Ireland which could withstand the winds of European competition when—and it was only a question of time—the country joined the EEC, and there were innovative attempts to create jobs by attracting foreign firms to invest in the country. But some of the hope which had blossomed with Lemass had given way to the realities of taking into a new age a country still unhealthily obsessed with questions of religion and politics rather than those of economics.

O'Reilly led or participated in many of the endless discussions and debates about Ireland's economic future in the universities, in government departments, around dinner tables or simply on the top of a Dublin bus. Everyone had a view, but O'Reilly, examining his own motives and background, was slowly concluding that what held Ireland back more than anything else was the antipathy at every level towards risk-taking. Even the education system, with its emphasis on standardization and the disciplines of scholarship, discouraged flexibility and the use of imagination and individual talents. The journalist Tim Pat Coogan, in a phrase which seemed to catch perfectly the mood of the time, talked resentfully about 'the brash young men in their mohair suits' taking over the country in 1958, but a decade later it was clear that tradition and prejudice were beating them. Far from embracing the free market, Ireland was becoming an increasingly state-controlled economy with total government spending rising from 29 per cent of gross national product in 1958 to 40 per cent in 1972 (and an astonishing 67 per cent in 1982). In Britain, where government expenditure was out of control in the 1970s, the highest it ever reached was 48 per cent. In the twenty years from 1958 the number of Irish civil servants rose from 110,000 to 230,000. 'The tendency for . . . government to bulk ever larger in

national activity has been common to many western countries,' wrote
T. K. Whitaker, the civil servant who was one of the principal architects of contemporary Ireland, 'but nowhere, I believe, to a more
marked degree than in Ireland.'

O'Reilly's frequent visits to Britain brought him into contact with
a very different kind of ethos, one which may have proved in the
longer term to have been more froth than substance, but which was
very attractive for all that. The City of London, the financial centre
around which Dublin's minuscule banking and stockbroking frater-
nity revolved, and which many like him in Ireland followed closely
in the British financial press, had entered what became known as the
'Slater era'. It was a time when bright young men, instead of seeking
their fortunes in manufacturing industry, traded stocks and companies instead. The age of the conglomerate and the hostile takeover
had arrived in Britain, to become the single most fashionable economic force until the oil crisis and the stock market crash of 1974
brought it all tumbling down again.

The conglomerate had its roots in America where its arch-priest
was a Dallas-based entrepreneur called Jimmy Ling, who combined
the aeroplane-maker Chance-Vought with Temco, a ball-bearing
maker, to make LTV, whose stock soared through the mid-1960s.
Ling's philosophy was a simple one: spot a company with under-
valued assets, move in on it, cash some of the assets and use the profit
to bankroll the next deal. Properly done, conglomeration could be
a beneficial force for industrial rationalization and efficiency. Taken
to extremes, as it all too soon was, it became little more than asset-
stripping. In Britain the man who epitomized it in 1968 embraced
both its good and bad aspects. Jim Slater was the uncrowned king
of the financial world in the late 1960s, a financier with hair-trigger
market reactions and an almost uncanny feel for market trends. He
began using his high stock market rating to issue shares for under-
priced assets. Slater depended for his success, as one observer remarked, on 'a certain claret-grouse-and-port-induced somnolence in
British boardrooms—failure to earn a reasonable return on capital
employed, and indifference to the fact that many corporate assets,
notably real estate, had a current value much higher than the figure
in the balance sheet'.

Slater, an engaging man with one of the best (if flawed) financial
brains that the City of London had seen for decades, took over a
little company, H. Lotery, for £1.5 million and seven years later

expanded it to a market capitalization of over £200 million. Only after he had done the deed did he set about justifying it with a rather bogus philosophy which argued that 'fear of the predator was an essential discipline for many boards, as without it they would have tended to rest upon the laurels of their predecessors'. For a time it was persuasive. Writing in the *Sunday Telegraph*, the columnist Peregrine Worsthorne welcomed Slater and others of his generation as the Mr Efficiencies, the meritocrats who would change the face of British industry, hacking away the dead wood, revolutionizing the ingrained and old-fashioned habits of management, and producing from the industrial mess a new and invigorating Britain.

O'Reilly didn't know Slater, but he read about his activities almost every day of the week. There was hardly a deal he was not involved in, taking share stakes, spinning off satellite companies which he financed, putting companies together, taking them apart again, and all the time building a bigger and bigger empire. The fact that the empire would be exposed by the mid-1970s as having nothing at the centre didn't matter—this was high fashion, which caught the imagination of the best and the brightest as well as the spivs and opportunists. Three young entrepreneurs in particular learned the art of the hostile takeover from Slater: Jimmy Goldsmith, James Hanson and Gordon White all at one stage or another revolved in his orbit. It was scarcely surprising if there were not some 'mohair suits' in Ireland who were tempted to emulate them.

The concept of creating his own Irish conglomerate was not an original O'Reilly idea. Michael Smurfit, another bright young Irish businessman, was already beginning a series of takeovers which were to take his family company, Jefferson Smurfit, to a size where it became the biggest maker of cardboard boxes in the world. Others, too, were starting to stir, and the Irish banks began to create their own merchant banking offshoots to participate in the new boom.

The man who first put the idea to O'Reilly was Vincent Ferguson, his right-hand man at the Sugar Company and Bord Bainne. Ferguson took as his role model not Slater Walker, but a more staid industrial holding company called Thomas Tilling, which had made a series of acquisitions and had grown its earnings impressively. When he suggested to O'Reilly that the two of them should create their own mini-Tilling, O'Reilly jumped at the concept. 'That sounds fantastic!' he enthused. Over the next few weeks they developed a plan. They would find the right type of asset-rich public company, preferably with some cash in it, get a bank to agree to back them, and then persuade the management to let them use it as a vehicle for even bigger deals—very much the Slater, rather than the Tilling, formula. Ferguson drew up a short list of candidates, the most attractive of which was McGuire & Patterson, which made most of Ireland's safety matches—the Friendly Match. Its chairman was Professor James Meenan, professor of economics at University College Dublin, who for three years in a row had stood up at his annual meetings to tell his shareholders that he was looking for projects for diversification, and was saving up the company's cash for that purpose. 'But we should not diversify for diversification's sake,' he said, and the cash continued to grow.

O'Reilly rang him up and invited him to lunch. He expounded his concept to the economics professor, explaining that he and Ferguson had a bank (they didn't, although they hoped to get one) which would back them with cash which they would like to inject into McGuire. Then, using the new cash along with McGuire's cash, they would propose to take advantage of their own high share price to take over other companies. The match company would in effect be the 'shell' into which they would inject a whole series of other companies, creating Ireland's first serious industrial holding company.

Meenan listened in stunned silence as he realized that the deal being put to him would mean this young duo getting a majority stake in his company. 'I'm not quite sure where to place this,' he said finally, 'but it's somewhere in between improper and impertinence. I do have to tell you that my initial reaction is to say no.' He then left. A few days later Meenan publicly announced that he was giving the company's cash back to its shareholders through a special dividend. He had obviously been planning that long before the lunch, but had given no hint of it. The chagrined pair of would-be conglomerators went back to the drawing board.

Before they could get their company off the ground, however, O'Reilly received an offer he found hard to refuse. Heinz-Erin was a tiny company to Heinz, its importance—which was minor at that—being its role as a source of raw material for its UK factories. It was O'Reilly's presence which had sold it first to Tony Beresford in London and then to Burt Gookin in Pittsburgh, but as a company inside the world empire Heinz-Erin never did rate better than an 'all right'. What no one had quite foreseen was the prominence that O'Reilly himself would assume in the Heinz joint venture. Later, when he became chairman of Heinz, O'Reilly was able to see his own personnel file which showed that as early as October 1968 Gookin had targeted him, not just for the UK job—which was senior enough—but for an even more major role in Pittsburgh. Gookin had been won over when O'Reilly went to see Heinz in Pittsburgh—according to one senior Heinz man: 'He charmed us all off the trees. We all thought he was a terrific fellow and Gookin, who had been against the deal, now believed Heinz Erin was going to be a big success.' Heinz in the UK, for so long the engine-room of the group's profits, was running out of steam and in 1969 Gookin decided it was time to make some radical changes.

Gookin first broached the subject with Beresford in London. 'How would you feel about young O'Reilly taking over from you?' he asked. Beresford, although he was a fan of the Irishman, was startled, expecting Gookin to have chosen a more traditional product of the Heinz system. But he was supportive. 'It's fine by me,' he replied. 'I think he would be extremely suitable. But he'd need to have quite a bit of exposure to the British company before he actually took over.' Gookin suggested that Beresford stay on after his sixtieth birthday as vice-chairman to keep an eye on the newcomer, and Beresford, accepting the need for a new generation, willingly agreed.

On one of his regular visits to London Gookin decided to go on to Ireland to talk O'Reilly into the job. It was his second visit and so O'Reilly rolled out the red carpet, organizing a schedule of visits to the factories. Gookin, however, had another interest. He was a fanatical golfer, with a scratch handicap, and liked to play some of the courses in Ireland. When the US boss had arrived several years earlier on his first visit O'Reilly, who has never played golf in his life, watched in amazement as his huge golf bag, wrapped in a shroud, came out on to the luggage turntable. It was handled so reverently that some of the Irish onlookers, believing it was a body, blessed themselves.

The Heinz president and chief executive officer—Jack Heinz still retained the key position of chairman—was a tough, no-nonsense manager with a Harvard MBA who had joined Heinz in 1945 and had run its finances tightly ever since. Steely-eyed and tough, he was known in the company as 'the shiny-arsed accountant'. At this time he was three years into the job of pulling Heinz back from the brink of collapse, and badly needed some help back in Pittsburgh. His plan, although he did not divulge it until years later, was to phase O'Reilly in through the UK operation, important though that was, and then

take him back to Pittsburgh where within a few years he could be
one of the runners for his own job—if he performed.

In between his rounds of golf, Gookin told O'Reilly about wanting
him to take over in London. The salary would be $75,000 plus a
large slug of share options, the whole package worth a minimum of
$100,000 a year—three times O'Reilly's already generous salary.
Heinz employed twelve thousand people in Britain, twice the workforce of the Sugar Company, and of course it was an immensely
more profitable concern. Gookin also hinted strongly at the further
prospects.

O'Reilly was ambiguous. There were so many things in Ireland
that he wanted to do. He was just on the verge of getting his company
with Ferguson off the ground, and that could make him seriously
rich if it went according to their embryo plans. There were still things
to be done with the Sugar Company and Erin Foods. And there was
the political career which Jack Lynch still kept talking about to him.

He rang the Taoiseach's office and asked for a meeting with Lynch,
in much the way he had four years before when he had had the
Fisons offer. Lynch could fit him in on his way to a dinner, and they
met in his official car in the car park of the Sugar Company. O'Reilly
told him about the Heinz offer, and, as he had done before, Lynch
tried to persuade him to refuse. 'Don't take it, don't take it,' he kept
on saying. 'You have a big career in politics here.' He explained his
plans for O'Reilly: Desmond O'Malley, the young star of the Fianna
Fail party, he said, was 'a great bit of stuff'—Lynch's highest acco-
lade—but he was too young, even younger than O'Reilly, although
he was already in the government. 'I think a lot of O'Malley, but I've
got problems, and I'm going to need help.' He didn't explain what
the problems were, and it was only later that O'Reilly realized he
must have been referring to his early intelligence of accusations,
which were never proved in court, that two senior members of his
party, Charles Haughey and Neil Blaney, had been involved in gun-
running to Northern Ireland, a scandal which, when it broke, would
seriously embarrass the government.

'If you stay, I'll make you Minister of Agriculture,' said Lynch.
'You could come into the Cabinet on the Taoiseach's Senate Panel,
where there will soon be a vacancy.' That meant he would not have
to stand for election in a local constituency.

O'Reilly was torn. This, he understood very well, was a turning
point in his life. If he stayed in Ireland, which he wanted to do, there

was no reason why his career should not continue to progress, and he might be able to make the type of money he wanted—and play a role in government, as he did now. He had a good life already, and it could become even better as Ireland's economy expanded. On the other hand, if he was to prove himself in the world of business, in the way he had proved himself in rugby, he would have to leave Ireland eventually. Until that moment he had not thought of going beyond Britain, which seemed big enough, but the Heinz job opened up the prospect of America as well. If he could make it there, he would be an enormous figure in his native Ireland.

That evening he talked it over with Susan, the person who, along with the children, would be most affected by his decision. Although normally the most placid of people, she recoiled fiercely at the Lynch proposal—she could stand for most things, she told him, but not a career in politics, which secretly she felt was what he wanted to do. She was quite taken with the job at Heinz in London, although she was more than happy to stay where they were. Susan had her hands full with six young children, the house in Delgany, Tony's parents and the continual dinner parties which she either had to attend or organize. She was tired, but she was loyal. She would leave it to him, she told him.

They talked until late into the night. 'We have to think about it,' he kept saying. Long after she had fallen asleep, O'Reilly lay awake pondering. Jack Lynch's offer had its attractions, despite Susan's opposition. Many of the aspects of politics appealed to him. He enjoyed the intrigue and the gossip and the tensions, and understood very well how the civil service and the bureaucratic system could be made to work in his favour. He also loved making speeches, basically because he had discovered in his schooldays that he was good at it, and had worked hard on it ever since. He had averaged several speeches a week since going to Bord Bainne, and was already one of the most popular after-dinner speakers in Ireland, and in rugby circles in England and Wales too. He was almost a professional entertainer, hoarding and secretly practising his jokes and his timing, using little props and apt quotations which his astonishing memory could produce when he wanted them. He had an instant rapport with an audience, which thrilled him, and he devised little tricks to get them on his side before he even began.

Finally, in the very late hours, he made up his mind. He would go to London and take the Heinz job on a five-year contract, but he would also create his own business in Ireland with Ferguson, who he proposed should succeed him at Erin Foods, just as McGough had done at Bord Bainne. That would give him an anchor in Ireland. He would leave Susan and the children in Delgany, and return every weekend, until he sorted something out in England. He would work for Heinz for five years, learn all he could about a big international corporation, make some money—and then come home. He would still be only thirty-seven, he would be independently wealthy if his options paid off, and it would not be too late to enter politics.

In the first week of November 1968 he told Gookin and Beresford that he would join them, but on certain conditions. His letter of acceptance was to have considerable importance in later years, as O'Reilly made clear he intended to maintain his outside interests. He fully accepted his responsibilities in Britain, he said, but he also wanted to retain close contact with Ireland where his 'emotional and intellectual involvement' lay. He wanted the right to have separate commercial interests there—which, he promised, would in no way conflict with the interests of Heinz. Instead of playing golf at the weekends, he added, in an aside which Gookin would understand, he would be playing 'Celtic monopoly' in Dublin. He also wanted to bring both Olive and Arthur. And he could not join until he had fulfilled certain commitments—which meant 1 May 1969.

The terms were agreed without argument, and just five days short of his thirty-third birthday, he arrived in Hayes in Middlesex, not far from Heathrow airport, to begin his new job. Heinz in Pittsburgh treated his arrival as significant enough to devote a section on him in its third quarter report. 'The appointment marks another step in Heinz management's long-range program of developing and as-signing executives with broad international experience to leadership in the company's multinational operations,' it said. O'Reilly's experi-ence at that stage had scarcely been 'broad', although he had travelled extensively in promoting Kerrygold. Soon afterwards, Heinz was re-porting that O'Reilly had instituted some 'fundamental changes', in-cluding 'a methodology for close inspection of all costs, the elimination of all activities judged insufficiently productive, a thor-ough re-examination of the company's functions and organisation' and much else. 'There was a real buzz coming out of London,' says a former Heinz director. 'It was our most important business, and Tony revved it up.' He inherited a strong but declining position: none of Heinz's seven main product lines had less than a 55 per cent market share, and some had more than 90 per cent. It was the dominant baby food producer, but also brand leader in salad cream, baked beans, ketchup, pickles, spreads and canned soups. In his first year all the brands improved their market shares, partly as a result of some heavy television promotion. He also inherited a $30 million investment programme in new plant and equipment, designed by Beresford—and approved by Gookin—to increase efficiency across the group, but he himself added to it and improved on it.

Yet he never found the job of running the Heinz operation in Britain challenging, despite its newness and its size. It was a well-ordered company, running on lines set in Pittsburgh, and it was no great task to whip some new life back into its flagging sales force. It was stimulating enough, but for other reasons than the job itself. 'He was very excited by the challenge of England,' says Susan.

> You could see it pleased him very much to be asked up to the City for a lunch, and he always felt they were just slightly condescending because he was Irish, and he would come back feeling wonderful because he had run rings around them all intellectually. So it was a very challenging time for him personally there, but it was a personal challenge of proving that he was superior to most of the people he was mixing with.

Although he kept the house at Delgany he brought Susan and the children over, moving them into a large, very English house in Farnham Common, a half-hour from the office by chauffeur-driven car. Susan didn't mind. 'Moves did not worry me at all. Having made my first big move for him from Australia, it didn't matter where we went after that.' She was very happy in England, although she adds, 'I can't tell you how much my life was internalized by this enormous family I had. I had no life outside it.' O'Reilly moved his driver Arthur into the house, where he became a useful baby-sitter for her. Later Olive moved in too, never to move out again of the O'Reilly household. 'I thought, that's another baby-sitter,' says Susan, 'so that's quite good. And at that stage I realized, very early in our marriage, that we were not going to have too many intimate dinners alone together. There were always hundreds of people around'.

Tony's life, she adds, had became 'much more sophisticated' with the move to England. He was continually at dinners in London, travelling around Britain or flying to Pittsburgh or New York, in between frequent short hops to Dublin. The Heinz management met in different—and usually exotic—parts of the world for intensive budget sessions, and O'Reilly always went carefully prepared, making sure that his presentation would be remembered. 'We had a management meeting down in Sea Island, in Georgia, at a resort called the Cloisters,' recalls Don Wiley, then the company's general counsel—not actually on the board (he was later) but in a pole position to observe what was going on.

> That was the first time Tony came, and he was delightful. Everyone took to him immediately. But I don't recall any of us thinking he was designated in any formal way as Gookin's successor. He was obviously headed for higher things, sure, but Gookin didn't tell any of us what he had in mind. When Burt appointed him, I had thought—as most others I talked to did—that it was a gutsy move on his part, hiring a young Irish Catholic out of Dublin to go and run that bastion of British industry, the Heinz UK company. But they really needed someone like Tony over there.

At that first conference meeting O'Reilly played tennis with Wiley, ran and swam with the others, and also showed off his skills on the piano and as an entertainer, giving them Gilbert and Sullivan as well as some Irish songs. As he had done all his life, he very deliberately found a point of contact with each person there, including the wives. Susan joined in his new life as a corporate man without complaint, actively enjoying some of it, putting up with the rest, and concentrating her efforts on her demanding children.

O'Reilly, by contrast, seemed to be supercharged. His energy levels, far from diminishing as he grew older, seemed to increase. When he joined Heinz he also decided he would take up serious rugby again. In the middle of October, fifteen years since he had first played for Ireland, he turned out for London Irish against Bath for his first game in first-class rugby in five years. He was thirty-three, weighed 15 stone and should long since have hung up his boots—but none the less there he was panting up and down the wing. He had an undistinguished game, but in front of a large crowd who had come to see this legend of the game he didn't disgrace himself. He did have one good run when he dashed up the right flank, handed off an opponent and crossed the line, only for the try to be disallowed.

'I really enjoyed that moment,' he told a reporter afterwards. 'It made me feel that I must get back into top-class rugby. I think I'm going to have great fun playing for the Irish.' By that he meant the London Irish—not the full Irish team.

Yet five months later, in the middle of February 1970, that is what happened. He was in Annabel's nightclub in Berkeley Square late on a Thursday evening when Ronnie Dawson, now coaching the Irish team, called him on the phone. 'We've been trying to find you everywhere, Tony,' he said. 'You're to be at the grounds of the Honourable Artillery Company in the City tomorrow morning for training. Billy Brown's hurt his ankle, and we want you as a reserve.'

Only slowly did the implications of this dawn on O'Reilly and his group of happy revellers. It meant that after seven years he could be back in the full Irish team. Ireland's match against England at Twickenham was only thirty-six hours away, and he had invited a party of friends and colleagues (he never missed an international if he could possibly avoid it). Now, instead of watching, he might be on the pitch. He had played only eight matches that season, averaging less than one game a fortnight, and in none of them had he shown outstanding qualities. Yet the selectors, short of available wingers and knowing he was in London and playing again, had turned to him, and while he had been drinking champagne the news was already rocketing through an astonished rugby world.

He slipped out of a board meeting the following day, and Arthur, at the wheel of the Heinz Mercedes, drove him to the City to the HAC grounds where the Irish team was practising. The press had already gathered to see this momentous event, and the sight of the uniformed driver opening the car door for O'Reilly to step out was irresistible. Arthur played up to the occasion with a salute, which made most of the newspapers the next day.

O'Reilly changed and joined the others, self-conscious about his weight and shape and hoping that no one would notice. Most of the team was new to him. Tom Kiernan, the full-back, had been a youngster when he last played with him, but was now the veteran. Ken Kennedy the hooker and Sid Millar the prop were also old hands, but he had never played with Mike Gibson, the best centre that Ireland had had for years. The huge Willie-John McBride, the Irish captain, looked him up and down, a sardonic smile on his face.

'Well, Tony,' he said in his thick Ulster accent, 'in my view your best attacking move tomorrow might be to shake your jowls at them.'

Billy Brown, the winger from the Malone club, was already running up and down the snow-covered turf, moving with apparent ease, but at the end of half an hour decided he dared not risk his injured ankle in a match. He cried off, and Dawson came over to O'Reilly. 'You're in the team, Tony,' he said. Few commentators could credit it. 'To say this is the most bizarre situation in international rugby for many years is to make an understatement,' wrote Paul McWeeney in the *Irish Times* the next day. 'This is a gambler's throw and there must be many who are apprehensive as to its value.'

The match itself was every bit as disappointing for Ireland as might have been expected. For O'Reilly the tension was lightened briefly by a remark made by one of his friends on the England team as they ran out: 'Tony, we'll never be able to get past you—there just isn't room on the field.' Fortunately for O'Reilly, both fly-halves chose to kick for most of what was a scrappy, untidy game, and the ball seldom came near his wing. 'O'Reilly never came under the spotlight at any stage of the proceedings,' reported McWeeney. 'No pass was thrown to him; his duties were reduced to covering defensively and delivering the ball to his forwards at the line-out, and it must be said he did not carry out that task with distinction, the referee adjudging the throw to be crooked on numerous occasions.' England won 9–3.

It was his twenty-ninth and last cap for Ireland, and did at least give him the consolation of providing one of his funnier—and only semi-apocryphal—stories in his repertoire of rugby stories. He tells it like this:

> At the very last minute I was suddenly reduced to bravery. A long English rush was terminated when—completely out of character—I dived at the feet of the England pack. As I emerged from momentary unconsciousness, I heard a loud and, I must confess, Irish voice, shouting from the crowded terrace: 'And while you're at it, why don't ya kick his fuckin' chauffeur too!'

His energies were channelled in other directions besides rugby. A few days after that match he received a letter from a former financial journalist called Nicholas Leonard, who had learnt his trade on the City pages of the British press before going back to Dublin to become the first new-style financial editor of the *Irish Times*. Leonard brought a different type of financial journalism to Dublin which gained him many enemies but also considerable respect. He had left the *Irish Times* to start up his own magazine, *Business and Finance*, and O'Reilly had first met him when he came to interview him for a cover story in September 1965 in the middle of a newspaper strike. 'He came to attack and remained to become a good friend,' said O'Reilly later, although in fact the meeting had been set up by the advertising people as a publicity puff for Bord Bainne. For his part, Leonard says his first impressions of O'Reilly were 'those which I still have today—a person of enormous energy and an ability to direct the charm and energy in equal proportions, to achieve goals which most people would regard as impossible'. Leonard was invited to the celebration after the christening of the triplets, where he sat on the same table as Jack Lynch, and over the years they became good friends. Leonard, like Vincent Ferguson and O'Reilly himself, was a keen observer of the business world, and had followed, just as closely as either of them, the takeover waves in both the American and British markets. Independently, he had decided it was time for putting together something similar. Nowhere, he believed, was business more ripe for a conglomerator than Ireland, with its sleepy old family-run companies, under-valued and under-utilized assets and good growth prospects. An enterprising company could access the sophisticated capital markets of Britain to raid the Irish corporate sector to its own considerable advantage.

By that stage Leonard was working at a new investment bank, Allied Irish Investment Bank, set up by the large AIB group. By coincidence, O'Reilly was a non-executive director of it and, taking advantage of that and of their old friendship, Leonard suggested they might create a venture capital company in Ireland. 'I knew that, with his involvement in it, my chances of getting the thing off the ground were a great deal better than going on my own.'

O'Reilly wrote back a few days later to say he had been having similar discussions with the person in the next room to Leonard: why didn't he talk to him? He meant Vincent Ferguson, who after a short spell as general manager of Erin Foods had resigned and also joined this new investment bank. Both Ferguson and Leonard were part of a team recruited by Martin Rafferty, a smart young man who had left the Irish Management Institute to start up the merchant bank. Leonard went next door for a chat and discovered that Ferguson was much further down the road, and was already increasing the pressure on O'Reilly to revive their venture, fearing that he would soon go to the USA and it would be too late. 'Remember that idea we had back in '68?' he asked O'Reilly. 'We should be looking at this again. If we're going to do anything at all, now is the time.'

O'Reilly was enthusiastic and suggested that Leonard and Ferguson begin work straightaway. In June 1970 the three of them got together around the swimming pool at O'Reilly's house in Delgany for what was to be the crucial meeting. All three of them committed themselves to working together as partners. Ferguson and Leonard would continue to work at the bank, where they would secretly work out the structure and business plans to show the banks, and feel out the right deals—the first one would be vital. Meanwhile, O'Reilly in London would make contact with one of the big British banks and line up the cash they needed.

The three of them continued their secret meetings, mostly in a downstairs room in the Russell Hotel. It was there that they decided on their target: the list was in alphabetical order, with Crowe Wilson, a wholesale drapery company headed by one of Ireland's leading eye surgeons, Dr Alan Mooney, at the top. Crowe Wilson, they agreed, was as good a starting point as any. Before they even had the money in place, or had formed a company, they approached Crowe Wilson with a proposition: they would inject £500,000 into it, take management control and use it as their vehicle to go on to greater things. 'We had no money to throw away on forming companies,' says Ferguson. 'Nick and I needed to work in the bank, and we told them Ulster Bank were here with all this pile of money, and we told the Ulster Bank we had this public company which would welcome us with open arms—all of which was not strictly true. It was finely balanced for quite a while, and there were lots of surreptitious meetings that took place.'

On the other hand, it was almost the truth. In London O'Reilly had persuaded National Westminster Bank, which owned Ulster Bank, to agree in principle to support his new venture, and Crowe Wilson, for its part, was not against the idea of being taken over by this dynamic trio. Over one of their regular dinners they chose a name for their new company, almost at random: Fitzwilliam Securities, named after the elegant Dublin Square which housed the city's equivalent of the All-England Tennis Club at Wimbledon. 'It seemed a slightly Anglo name that would gain approval,' says O'Reilly. It would have a capital of £100,000, and he would own 32.5 per cent of it; Leonard and Ferguson were to get 22.5 per cent each; and the Ulster

Bank, which eventually agreed to invest £25,000 and lend another £400,000, would get the rest.

Before they could get Crowe Wilson fully aboard, however, both Ferguson and Leonard had lost their jobs. They held one of their private sessions with the Crowe Wilson directors at the Gresham Hotel in O'Connell Street on a Sunday evening, thinking no one would be around at that time. Unfortunately, the Gresham put up a sign in the lobby indicating that there was a meeting of the Allied Irish Investment Bank in the Sheraton suite. Martin Rafferty, the bank's chief executive, chose that evening to pop in for a drink after a football match at Croke Park, saw the sign and caught them red-handed. 'We had to accelerate our plans,' says Ferguson. For two weeks he and Leonard were unemployed. Jack O'Reilly, now retired from the civil service and working as a solicitor at long last, gave them office space, and on 1 April 1971 Fitzwilliam was born. A couple of weeks later the shareholders of Crowe Wilson approved the deal which would give Fitzwilliam a 54 per cent stake.

The deal created considerable excitement in the Irish financial community, and unleashed a whole stream of similar operations. Fitzwilliam paid 42p a share for its stake, which within two months had risen to 72p. O'Reilly already had a capital profit, if he wanted to take it, of £100,000—a bigger gain in eight weeks than his total earnings to date, and more than his father had earned in a lifetime. Everyone wanted to join in this new game of conglomeration, and within a year ten would-be industrial holding companies were spawned, including one by Rafferty who took over Brooks-Watson, the old Brooks Thomas store (about three have survived). For months there seemed to be a deal a day, with the revitalized Crowe Wilson leading the charge. By September the shares topped 100p as the acquisition spree accelerated. They bought the Coca-Cola franchise for Ireland, a guaranteed cashflow business, Chemist Holdings in Britain and a couple of other textile companies. They now owned the White House department store in Portrush, a symbol of Ulster Unionism, and added another Ulster stores group to it. Then they made their first mistake, taking over the long-established Thomas Dockrell, a group of builder's merchants. O'Reilly immediately added the Cork-based J. S. McCarthy to it, bringing in his best friend, Jim McCarthy, as managing director of the whole Dockrell business. Profitable at the beginning, Dockrell was to prove an albatross which would bring them close to disaster.

All this time, however, they were stalking something bigger. O'Reilly had long been eyeing the large fertilizer company W. and H. M. Goulding, one of Ireland's largest and most prestigious businesses. It was run by a wonderful Anglo-Irish eccentric, Sir Basil Goulding, whom he had met many times at functions and dinners, and who lived in a large house not far from his own in Delgany. As the shares of Crowe Wilson continued to zoom skyward—fifteen months after it was launched O'Reilly's stake was worth almost £2 million—Goulding began to come within his range.

Long before he could do anything about it, however, his life had changed again. In the summer of 1971, two years into his five-year contract, Burt Gookin told O'Reilly he wanted to move him to Pittsburgh. It was a signal to everyone, including O'Reilly, that he intended bringing him right into the centre of the group where he would be groomed to succeed Gookin. It was also an indication that O'Reilly had made his numbers in Britain—as indeed he had. In his second year, despite a recession, Heinz had moved ahead in almost all product areas, with twelve of its products now market leaders. Heinz soups commanded 64 per cent of the market, a new record, while ketchup's share reached the highest point in its history. There were new products, new factories and new advertising campaigns. He had passed the first test.

The man who strongly recommended him for the Pittsburgh job was not so much Gookin as Junius F. Allen, who, although based in Pittsburgh, had been his immediate boss through his London years. In these two years Allen had become both a fan and a powerful champion on the Heinz board, independently reinforcing Gookin's own, still private, view of the young Irishman. O'Reilly's only serious rival in the race to succeed Gookin would be a man called John Connell, and he was relieved when Gookin told him they would switch jobs, with Connell taking over in London and O'Reilly joining the main board of Heinz with the title of 'senior vice president—North America and Pacific'. O'Reilly would be by far the youngest on the board and, equally important, was one of the select ten people at World Headquarters who controlled the business. After only two years O'Reilly would now be in the inner sanctum of Heinz, and already on the fast track to the top.

The O'Reilly family moved to the United States *en masse* and in high spirits. He wanted to make it an occasion for them to remember, but also to send a signal of a different kind. Too many Irish had travelled this same sea route in tired old freighters, leaving behind famine and poverty for the New World. He would travel in the grandest style possible, in a manner whose significance would not be lost on his father in particular. In August 1971 he, Susan, six children, a nanny and his parents set out from Southampton aboard the *QE2* for the voyage to New York and on to Pittsburgh. Little Susan was now seven, and the youngest—the triplets—were four, and every evening Susan led this long crocodile of people into the dining room. 'You could see the couples seated at tables for two gaping at this, thinking: Jesus, they must have another potato famine in Ireland, they're coming at us in waves,' says O'Reilly. It was an important moment for an Irish family.

Before he left, he had insisted to Gookin, as he had done before, that he retain his business interests in Ireland which, he said, he could run from anywhere in the world. He also brought Olive, who would continue to live with the family in Pittsburgh. Only Arthur, unable to drive in America, stayed behind, but he would drive for Fitzwilliam and be available for O'Reilly on his frequent trips to Ireland or the UK.

A new chapter in his life was now beginning, unravelling in a way, in both Ireland and America, that he could not foresee. Success and disaster equally would soon be staring him in the face.

11

57 Varieties

'Here was the very heart of industrial America, the centre of
its most lucrative and characteristic activity, the boast and pride
of the richest and grandest nation on earth.'

Henry L. Mencken on the city of Pittsburgh

THE PITTSBURGH WHICH MENCKEN WITNESSED IN THE 1920s HAD
changed by the time the O'Reilly family arrived in the summer of
1971, but his impression of 'wealth beyond computation, almost beyond imagination', coupled with 'human habitations so abominable
that they would have disgraced a race of alley cats', was one which
would take generations to dispel. It was still the residual image in
the minds of Jack and Aileen O'Reilly as they stepped off the private
Heinz jet which had flown the whole family from New York.

Their daughter-in-law Susan had been to Pittsburgh before, but
for her, too, this was a new experience. She had made a fleeting visit
when they had stayed with the Gookins, and she had gone house-
hunting in the lush hills of Fox Chapel. That visit had been a succession of dinner parties and visits to magnificent country clubs and
some of the even more magnificent homes of the Heinz directors.
William P. Snyder III had held a dinner for them at his elegant
house, where Snyders had lived since it was built a century before
from a fortune made in steel, and Jack Heinz, the sixty-four-year-
old chairman and grandson of the founder, had received them with
exquisite courtesy, prompting O'Reilly to remark that the well-educated, rich American was far more of an archetypal old-style gentle-
man than anything that either of them had ever seen in England or
Ireland.

But there had been little time then to absorb anything more than
an impression of this city which was now to be their home. Pittsburgh,

they found, was very different from the pre-war town in which a thousand steel mills and factory chimneys belched so much smoke into the air that the sun was blotted out at noon. Even people in their twenties remembered the smog and the all-pervading fumes that made them choke. 'The skies were dark. Traffic was in a snarl. The days seemed like nights. White shirts turned into black within minutes. There was smoke and smog and grime,' wrote the historian Stefan Lorant in his widely acclaimed *Pittsburgh: The Story of an American City*.

Now the smoke and smog were gone, exposing a city whose godfathers had put up fine monuments and stone buildings in a setting which, once they could be seen, were of some distinction. Pittsburgh was built on a series of hills steeper than anything in Rome, falling away down to the two great rivers, the Allegheny and the Monongahela, which joined here to make an even greater third, the Ohio. Driving in from the airport on the way to Fox Chapel that first day, the O'Reillys suddenly found themselves in a town which seemed a maze of rivers and steel bridges, a visible demonstration of prodigious and profligate use of locally produced steel used to cross the rivers every few hundred yards. A fountain played at the point where the Ohio began, just below the site of a fort built by the British, named after the statesman William Pitt, and an older French version, Fort Duquesne. Everywhere there was visible evidence of the work of the town's two post-war heroes, the banker Richard King Mellon, and a visionary mayor, David L. Lawrence, who used their different powers and influences to push through tough smoke control laws and begin the city's renaissance. The black grime of generations had been scoured from the buildings, the rivers which had regularly flooded the town were harnessed, tenement shacks had been removed to build the new Gateway Center, and dramatic new office towers had sprung up. 'Point Park emerged as dramatically as spring after a hard winter,' wrote Lorant. 'Mellon Square Park was chiselled into the heart of downtown Pittsburgh, skyscrapers shot up like pole vaulters at the Olympics. There was a will, there was excitement to build a new city—a city their grandfathers never dreamed possible . . . The grimy milltown was transformed into a sparkling metropolis.'

In the early 1970s Pittsburgh was, as it had always been, a working place, 'a town of business, a town where money was made'. Some of the biggest fortunes in America—and the world—had been made here and were still based in the city. The Mellons, descendants of another family of Irish immigrants, owned half of Pittsburgh's big business: they controlled Gulf Oil, Koppers and Alcoa as well as the Mellon Bank, all with their headquarters in Pittsburgh. But there were other international companies too: Pittsburgh Plate Glass (or PPG), Westinghouse Air Brake, US Steel—and of course Heinz.

To the O'Reilly family Pittsburgh was a revelation. Tony had been there often in the past two years, and had tried to tell them it was something more than a large steel town, but even so nothing had prepared them for the Pennsylvania countryside, with its rolling, wooded hills and deep, verdant valleys. In the centre of the city, the Golden Triangle between the rivers was a mass of tall buildings, competing with each other in both design and structural ingenuity. Alcoa had built its headquarters out of aluminium, US Steel used steel for the tallest building between New York and Chicago (which O'Reilly would eventually move into), while Pittsburgh Plate Glass was planning a glass palace in the air. Jack Heinz and the Heinz family had rebuilt the old Penn Theatre movie house at a cost of $10 million and donated it, as a centre for the performing arts, to the city. There were also Carnegie museums, universities, new hospitals, galleries and libraries. It was the home of two of the best sports teams in America, the Steelers football team and the Pirates baseball, each forming a central part of the city's architecture and culture. On through the town towards their destination, the Fox Chapel area, the river was still lined on both sides with giant steel mills. In 1971 Pittsburgh was on the cusp of losing its position as the steel capital of the world, the 'forge of the universe', but it was still a mighty steel town, with 120,000 steelworkers. Within a decade there would be a mere 10 per cent of that number, bringing profound economic, social and physical change.

Yet the biggest surprise was the fact that the O'Reillys were here at all. At the last moment, O'Reilly had almost changed his mind about going. In the summer he had taken a house on the sea at Bettystown, near Drogheda, largely to please his father who remembered the beaches there as a child. In July, Tony, who flew back from London every Friday night, was just about to leave his office when he got a call from Pittsburgh. There had been a startling event at the company: Burt Gookin had appointed a new chief financial officer, and had even put him on the board. Franklin E. Agnew was a graduate of Princeton and Harvard, son and scion of the chief executive officer of Pittsburgh National Bank, a golf-playing friend of

Gookin—and young to boot. Suddenly O'Reilly seemed to have a rival, only a year older than him, with what sounded like a better inside track than he had for the top job in Heinz.

His father, as always, picked him up at the airport and on the drive north tried to calm him down. 'I was absolutely fit to be tied,' O'Reilly recalled later. 'He had brought me in as the new guy, I was coming to America with my whole bloody family, and I was going there to make the top spot at the company within three to five years, and bang, he brings in someone who on paper was a real rival and is now a little ahead of me.' That evening an angry and disturbed O'Reilly arrived in the house at Bettystown and went for a walk on the beach with his father. 'I'm not sure I want to go now,' he told him. 'This is a highly competitive situation they're putting me into. I'm cutting my links with the UK and Ireland, and I'm going into an unknown country, and maybe I shouldn't go.'

He had, he said, committed to go to America—'and that's a big decision on my part'—because he wanted to head Heinz. 'Everyone else is over fifty years of age and I am thirty-five. And now Franklin E. Agnew III of Princeton and Harvard has been appointed, out of the blue, never having been in the company before. And he's been put on the board—and I'm not on the board yet. That's a whole new set-up.'

This was the type of decision which his father could help him with more than anyone else—more even than Susan. Jack intuitively understood his ambitions and his need to be stretched more than the women in his life did. To an extent, Jack increasingly lived his life by proxy through Tony, his own ambitions for himself finally realized—and more—through this extraordinary son of his. They talked it over all weekend, and O'Reilly finally decided he would go for it. It would be too ignominious to back out now with all the announcements made, the farewells already being said, and the arrangements made on the other side. He would take his chances with Mr Agnew. What neither of the O'Reillys knew at this moment was that Gookin had appointed Agnew for entirely different reasons from the ones they suspected. Agnew had resigned from his job at North American Rockwell after a board room row; Gookin subsequently offered him the Heinz job, not with the immediate prospect of promoting him, but as a means of replacing his existing financial officer, Bill Mewhort.

On the journey the family's natural good spirits reasserted themselves, and it had been a happy group which had disembarked from the *QE2* in New York. It was the first time the family had been to America, and O'Reilly wanted to show them New York before moving on. For a week the entire party stayed in the Berkeley Hotel—a party of twelve plus the two family dogs—before the Heinz plane took them on to their final destination. O'Reilly was again expounding the merits of Pittsburgh which, he told Susan, she would discover 'the most international village in America'. They would all find it warm and friendly. 'It is the modern equivalent of Rousseau's Greek City State—a very civilised place to live.' There was a large Irish community—the mayor was called Peter Flaherty—and many Catholics from other nationalities in a city that had its separate Greek, Russian, German and Italian communities.

For their few days in Pittsburgh they would stay in the O'Hara Holiday Inn in Blawnox, with its impressive views out over the rivers and the Pennsylvanian hills, but within a week they had moved into their own comfortable house in Fox Chapel which someone at Heinz had found for them. Jack and Aileen returned to Dublin, the children went to their new schools and Susan found that affluent American suburban life suited her. She played tennis every day, made a lot of friends and, with the children now slightly older, life became easier for her.

O'Reilly took to his new career in Pittsburgh as if he had been born to it. Compared with the complexities and sensitivities of dealing with the Irish civil service, the politics of Heinz were child's play. It took him no time at all to work out where the power lay, where the levers were and who pulled them. He made his own assessment of the strengths and weaknesses of the various players. Agnew, he decided after the first meeting, was a perfectly pleasant man, a fine financial technician, but had no great desire to be chief executive— so his mind totally relaxed on that score. Don McVay, a slight man with short-cropped hair and deep wrinkles around his eyes, was his biggest supporter, the man who, after his first meeting with O'Reilly in 1967, had sent a memo to Gookin to say they must keep an eye on him. McVay, he decided, was the *éminence grise* of the company, on whom Gookin relied heavily, and would now help him. Don Wiley, the general counsel, also quickly became a supporter. There were a few rivals, too: John Crossen, in charge of Europe and South America, was his most obvious competition. But he was fifteen years older and never a serious challenge. The only other potential rival had been John Connell, but Gookin had already moved him to London where he was out of the race. There seemed to be a clear field.

As for Gookin, the more O'Reilly got to know the dry accountant, the more he liked and admired him. Gookin was the man who had transformed Heinz from a deeply troubled and almost bankrupt family business in the mid-1960s into a meritocratic, marketing-oriented and profitable concern, laying the groundwork for O'Reilly to take it on to greater things. From the start O'Reilly worked very closely with him, in and out of his office all day when he was in Pittsburgh, and in continual contact by telephone when he was not. His own office was at the other end of the building, next to Jack Heinz's chairman's suite, while the office next to Gookin was occupied by Agnew. But that didn't matter. Gookin was an early starter, getting to the office around 7.30; O'Reilly would arrive at around the same time or even earlier, read his post and wander down to talk with him for about an hour over a cup of coffee. O'Reilly would tell him which parts of the business he was concentrating on, they would discuss personnel, O'Reilly would show him the letters he was writing and the assessment reports and budgets he was preparing. Don McVay often joined them at these sessions, which set the agenda for the rest of the day.

If O'Reilly's personality had been a bonus to him in Ireland and England, it was doubly so in Pittsburgh. 'We were all a bit awe-struck by this guy who had been a great sportsman, had arrived at the top of Pittsburgh so young, and whose range of abilities seemed endless,' says Dick Beattie, one of the senior Heinz executives. 'He had this huge personality, and quick wit, and was the best speech-maker I ever heard in my life. He could sing and play the piano, tell jokes, quote Oscar Wilde or Churchill—and he knew more about your business than you did.' O'Reilly made the most of it, using his ability to charm and entertain people outside business hours as well as in the office. Finding the first house too small, he moved the family to a bigger and grander one in Fox Chapel which would allow him to entertain on a much more generous scale, and he soon developed the habit of holding weekend dinners for his senior executives which often turned into late-night strategy sessions. If he wasn't in Ireland over the weekend, the house was filled with Heinz executives and their wives, the men at some point getting down to a serious discussion of the latest knotty problem that O'Reilly wanted to tackle.

The house was not special by Heinz director standards, but it suited

Susan and the family perfectly. It had been owned by Mrs Mary Louise Maytag McCahill, a devout Catholic who had even built a private chapel downstairs, and on whom the bishop had called most weeks. On either side lived Irish-American Catholic families almost as large as the O'Reillys, prompting Tony to christen the area 'No Pill Hill'. It had a formal Japanese garden, but, most important of all in hilly Pittsburgh, it had a flat expanse of garden at the back that was big enough for a rugby pitch.

Soon after he bought the place for $250,000, O'Reilly began a tradition which was to last for years—a game of touch American football to be played between teams from the management of World Headquarters and Heinz USA. It was an idea copied from the Kennedys, but it soon took on a flavour of its own. In the first year it was more of an impromptu effort, but after that it was taken so seriously that both teams—particularly O'Reilly, who liked to show off his running and tactical skills—trained seriously for it. There were allegations that some managers were recruiting people solely on their footballing merits, and resentment at the fact that Mike Manganaro, O'Reilly's burly chauffeur and a former professional football player, was allowed to play (on O'Reilly's team, of course). Even at this level, O'Reilly hated to lose. Wives and families were invited to the O'Reilly house, a buffet, bar and entertainment for the children was laid on all day—and then came the big match, soon known in Heinz as the 'Souperbowl'. Gookin or Don Wiley were brought in as referee or linesmen, but the whole event revolved around O'Reilly, whose day this was. 'It was great for bonding,' says David Scully who joined Heinz in 1974 in time to play in the second game. 'Everybody talked about it and everybody looked forward to it, and it was just a great day, when you mixed a certain amount of business—there were always meetings which coincided with it—and pleasure.'

The company had some big problem areas, but none more so than its USA operations, some of which were actually losing money in that year. The whole of Heinz US, which today makes $375 million on the same case volume, made nothing in 1972, and Ore-Ida, which represented its frozen food business and which has since made over $170 million in a single year, lost money. O'Reilly decided he would concentrate his early efforts there. On one of his first self-appointed missions, he flew up to the Ore-Ida plant where he sat in the offices of Paul Corddry, the vice-president of sales and marketing. Corddry offered him the usual tour of the plant which all new executives got, but O'Reilly was curt. 'I don't want to hear all about that,' he said abruptly. 'I want to know why your cashflow has been so poor.' For the next few weeks he sat with the management of Ore-Ida, building up the budget line by line, making sure he understood and agreed every item on it. None of them had ever seen anything like this before.

'Tony could just sort of take a look at our reviews and zero in on the one or two things that really mattered,' said Corddry. 'And he remembered everything you said.'

'My recollection is that within two or three hours, maybe it was longer but not much, he seemed to have focused on every problem that we had—problems that we had probably been struggling for three years to identify, he ferreted out in three hours,' says J. Wray Collings, Corddry's number two at Ore-Ida at the time.

> It was the start of a unique relationship between Tony and that company, because we were all somewhat contemporary. He could see that the company was turning around, and the poor performance we'd had there—a poor performance which, by the way, was what we'd been sent there to correct—was now nearly behind us, and this was an opportunity for him to associate himself with a pending success. And out of all that came a bond between Tony and Paul and me and some others, and we went through a lot of good times, and some bad times, but we all had that special relationship which went back to Ore-Ida.

The team that Gookin had put in under Corddry had already begun to effect serious change at Ore-Ida, but O'Reilly accelerated it and was not above claiming the credit—which Gookin, good manager that he was, never really denied him. In his first year both major US companies, which were to be the engine of the company's growth through the 1970s and 1980s, broke into profit.

From these early visits came another O'Reilly innovation which was to evolve, like the game of touch football, into a tradition. Gookin had already instituted a system under which the senior vice-presidents produced an annual business plan which they had to present, but O'Reilly developed the habit of taking them away, studying them carefully, and then sending back a detailed critique which often ran to twenty-five pages—sometimes longer than the original business plan. He got Olive to block out a full week in his diary to do it, locked himself away and wrote letters which still read remarkably well today. Ned Churchill, who was head of corporate planning, witnessed the process and was so awe-struck that he spread the story of O'Reilly as corporate superman.

> Tony would get these huge presentations, which were like books, with charts and graphs and appendices and inserts and whatnot, and I remember watching him write one of these long letters, and he would just kind of leaf through the report and he would dictate, and Olive would be sitting there just taking down this stream of consciousness that would come out the other end of the typewriter almost like poetry, with Churchillian phrases and quotes that he seemed to pull out of his amazing memory at will. And I used to apply that test: Could I do that? Later, as I grew professionally, I could respond in that context, but at that time, although I had been to the Harvard Business School and I was only a year younger than O'Reilly, I could not.

The reports fall some way short of Shakespeare, however, and anyone who knew O'Reilly well—which the Americans didn't at that point—would have recognized a number of the phrases and jokes as vintage O'Reilly. His art was to exploit his *bons mots* to considerable effect, both in his speeches—which were actually far better than his written words—and in his letters, as in this example from one written to Dick Grieb: 'Don't take my leg-pull on pollution too seriously. A rural newspaper in Ireland once achieved the unique double positive by commenting on the opening remarks I delivered in a speech as follows: "The speaker's jocose remarks were entirely jocose." ' Or, in a letter to Grieb's successor, Dick Patton:

> My general views on the American plan this year reflect the self-satisfaction of Sir Winston Churchill when the Viceroy of India urged him to bring his views on India up to date by talking to some Indians. He remained immovable. 'I am quite satisfied with my views on India,' he said, 'and I don't want them disturbed by any bloody Indians.'

O'Reilly went on to urge him to stick to his first simple plan and not get blown off course by the complex series of suggestions being made to him.

The annual assessments of the presidents of Heinz USA (Dick Grieb in 1972, followed by Ray Good a year later, and Dick Patton in 1977) tell the story of the revival of a company emerging from its problems but continually, and in great detail, being exhorted to do more. After getting one of these letters, no manager could ever complain that he was not given clear instructions on every aspect of his business, from new investment to marketing, financial objectives, product mix and everything else. Nor could they be in any doubt where they stood in O'Reilly's personal assessment of their management abilities. Less than two weeks after his first session, he wrote to Grieb with astonishing self-assurance for a young man who had just arrived in America in his first senior job, commenting, sometimes critically, on every single point that the Heinz USA president had raised in his business plan. Even on such a serious subject as the criteria to be applied for new investment O'Reilly leavened the tough, uncompromising analysis with the odd little joke. Grieb, he said, should only invest in new product development if he could get his money back in two years, and on existing products he should look for a return of 35 per cent. It was a style of management new to Heinz, and one which O'Reilly would make his own over the years he was to run the group.

There was a third US arm in which O'Reilly didn't need to get very involved at this early stage, basically because it was the one operation in the USA which kept the whole operation together: Star-Kist was one of Gookin's first acquisitions (in fact, one of the first acquisitions ever made by Heinz in the USA) and one of its best ever. In 1963, Star-Kist brought into the company not only $70 million of sales at a time when Heinz's US sales and earnings were at an all-time low, but also Joe Bogdanovitch. Always known as Joe B, Bogdanovitch was a tough-talking, irreverent, free-wheeling entrepreneur, who had taken over his father's California cannery and turned it into an international tuna canning operation, in the process making tuna America's most popular fish product. O'Reilly soon learned that Joe B was the character on the board, a man who reckoned all his men at Star-Kist were infinitely superior to their counterparts at Heinz. He was as colourful as his history: his father, a fisherman from the

Dalmatian coast, had arrived in California in 1908, and by 1914 had a fleet of boats operating out of Terminal Island. Joe B learned the business the hard way, working in the cannery in the winter and on the boats in the summer, and had been running the business since 1937. When he sold his company to Heinz, Joe B became the biggest shareholder after the Heinz family, and while he made his numbers, Gookin left his business pretty much alone. O'Reilly developed an immediate rapport with him, and it was mutual; Joe B was to prove an important ally in the years ahead.

But he found the man in the next office to him, Jack Heinz, harder to fathom. Henry John Heinz II, named after the firm's founder, was always elaborately civil yet distant, very much the patrician figure in a town he almost regarded as his own. He was suave, handsome, trim, athletic, beautifully groomed and with exquisite manners. He looked every inch what he was: a product of the best education— Shadyside, Choate in Connecticut, then Yale and finally economics at Cambridge—who had been reared in a hugely wealthy family which prided itself on its taste and dignity. He was also adventurous: in his lifetime he had swum the Bosporus, toured the Soviet Union twenty-two times, been married three times and owned twelves homes. In London he dined with the royals (he was knighted in 1979 for his contribution to Anglo-American relations); he was a friend of the Aga Khan and the Onassises, and moved in French, Italian, Greek and international jet-set society just as easily as he did among his peer group in Pennsylvania. He was genuinely interested—and knowledgeable—in the arts, a major collector of paintings (on his office wall, among others, were three Gauguins) and a promoter of music. He was also a skier, a gourmet and a wine expert. One of Heinz's little boasts was his story of how, as a young man, he visited Winston Churchill who advised him to start at the top of Heinz 'and work your way down'.

Jack started at the bottom, but when his father died suddenly in 1941, he stepped directly into his shoes, talking full control of the company which he then ran energetically and autocratically. 'He was more than president and CEO,' says a former director. 'He was the lord and master.' Another director, now retired who joined the board in 1958 remembers how, at his first board meeting, Jack sat at a desk on a little platform, while the others sat in a semi-circle around him. In an office where first names were universal, everyone called Jack Heinz 'Mister'. Until Gookin replaced him, bells still rang at the corner of Heinz and Progress Streets four times a day to mark the beginning and end of work—and the lunch hour. Smoking in the office was strictly forbidden. O'Reilly, slightly over-awed at the beginning, found him a man of 'stratospheric elegance'. He was interested in advertising and public relations, in quality, in nutrition—and in the taste of the food he sold—but had little feel for figures.

Unfortunately his taste was not necessarily that of the great American public. When the small family grocers were overtaken by the self-service stores and supermarkets in the late 1950s, Heinz was slow in adjusting. 'In the early Fifties, the sweet smell of success turned somewhat sour,' wrote *Forbes* magazine in a 1964 profile of Heinz, entitled '57 Varieties of Trouble'. 'Heinz is not doing nearly as well as most of its competitors in the US and, without the European market, it would barely be getting along.' The company began to lose market share in all its key products: soup, baby food, ketchup and pickles.

Heinz finally hit its crisis in 1963, as profits in the US operations disappeared. Other than tomato ketchup and vinegar, it had no brand leaders, and was being killed by its rivals in almost all its product areas—Gerber, for instance, was smashing it in baby foods, and Campbell's in soups. That year, although Star-Kist had just been taken over, Heinz UK supplied 85 per cent of group profits. It was time for change. 'Jack was a remarkable man in that the people in the company loved him,' says Bill Snyder, who was brought in as one of a new crop of non-executive directors in order to force change on the company.

> He'd walk into a plant and he was Mr H. J. Heinz of the H.J. Heinz Company, and everyone would want to say hello and shake his hand. And there is a lot of difference between your name being on the door—and it was on the smoke stacks and above half the factories in Pittsburgh—and being a hired hand. I had occasion to walk around the factory with Henry Ford II, and that was the nearest thing to walking round with Jack. But he was not a professional manager, and the company needed professional managers.

Gookin, who handled the purchase of Star-Kist, was put in charge of US operations in 1964, but it was another two problem-filled years before Jack was finally persuaded, after considerable pressure, to move aside and to become non-executive chairman.

Although his power was broken, he still continued to regard the group as something of a private fiefdom. He resented Gookin, who he felt excluded him more and more. His son, H. John Heinz III fell out with the Heinz management and left the company to go into politics. He became a member of the US House of Representatives and later a Republican senator in November 1976; he was killed in a plane crash in 1991, the last Heinz to be involved in the business. O'Reilly, reckoning he would have to work with Jack long after Gookin was gone, made sure he got on with him.

Gookin had done his job well, cleaning up the mess he inherited from Jack, closing down old and inefficient factories, building new ones, beginning a series of strategic acquisitions overseas, and creating a much more international management structure—the prime example of which was O'Reilly himself. Heinz now operated forty factories in seventeen countries and territories, marketing its products in more than 150 countries. Sales doubled between 1964 and 1971 and were now just short of the $1 billion mark, while profits after tax, although they had trebled, were still a modest $42 million. O'Reilly, watching the group's sales go past the $1 billion mark for the first time in its 102-year history, calculated that that was 75 per cent of the entire Irish budget. But despite Gookin's efforts, and his detailed expositions to the Wall Street analysts, the company was rated as a dull, conservative and unexciting investment, its shares commanding a rating half that of the food sector, and the whole operation capitalized at only $500 million.

O'Reilly found that the Heinz tradition went deep in Pittsburgh, where there were many memorials and markers to the man who had founded the firm. Someone gave him a book on the company and he avidly devoured it, fascinated by the history of the place and the company in the same way that he was fascinated by the history of Ireland (and Britain when he lived there). H. J. Heinz was one of the original 'Lords of Pittsburgh', the five hugely powerful figures who ruled the city in their time and still remained legends in the modern day. Four of them, Carnegie, Frick, Westinghouse and Mellon, all made their fortunes in industries traditional to the area: coal and coke, iron and steel, aluminium and oil, railroads and heavy engineering. Heinz, a small man of prodigious energy and large mutton chop whiskers, was the only one to make his by feeding people.

A Methodist, he had begun business at the age of seventeen bottling horseradish, then fashionable as an appetite sharpener and for its supposed medicinal qualities. 'Freshly grated horseradish made dull food palatable and good food—such as beef and raw oysters—better,' wrote his biographer Robert C. Albertus in *The Good Provider*. 'Multitudes swore by it as sure remedy for grippe, catarrh, and dyspepsia.' There was quite a trade in horseradish, which was sold in coloured bottles, usually brown or green (the natural colours of glass). The legend, which O'Reilly heard a dozen times in his first week, was that Harry Heinz sold his horseradish in clear glass bottles, thus proving that it contained no leaves or turnip filler, and that this was of the highest-quality root. This little parable, which was at least partly based on fact, was meant to symbolize the principles for which the modern-day Heinz still stood. 'The youthful Heinz believed in the purity of his product and the right of the customer to see what she was buying,' said Gookin in a major speech to America's big glass container manufacturers a few weeks after O'Reilly arrived. 'Horseradish sales grew rapidly in the clear glass bottles. The enterprise prospered—and eventually became the company as we know it today.'

In fact the original enterprise, after a rapid period of expansion, ran into the recession of the 1870s. Seven years after he started Harry Heinz was bankrupt, arrested and charged with removing his goods to defraud creditors. The schedule of bankruptcy filed against him was two inches thick, showing assets of $110,000 and liabilities of $160,000. But he cleared his name and started again, recording in his diary the fearful slog of the next two years. 'Very close run for money. Can't see how to get along and not a man or friend will give us a cent, even a chattel mortgage or any other way . . . Money hard to get. Am very much worried to keep our heads above water.'

But he won through, and for nearly half a century he was one of the great food pioneers, revolutionizing American agriculture with new methods of processing which changed the kitchen habits of a nation. 'He carried his company's products and his own industrial philosophy to four continents with a promotional flair and showmanship that probably have never been surpassed,' says Albertus, with only mild hyperbole. Pittsburgh during these years was the scene of some of the worst industrial strife in America's history, but Heinz braved the wrath of his fellow employers to build a large factory complex on such paternalistic principles that it became a case study for sociologists, who flocked to Pittsburgh to see it, prompting debate on whether Heinz had found the solution to the conflict between capital and labour.

In 1971, even the hard-headed Gookin paid more than lip service to the traditions of old Harry Heinz. He had every reason to. 'Quality has first priority at Heinz,' he said, and if in truth quality took second place to profit, the two were closely intertwined. An image for quality helped sell food products, and that meant increased profits. Over the years, the Heinz company had discarded those bits of the tradition that were no longer convenient, but kept the bits it wanted and marketed them hard—including Harry Heinz's famous '57 varieties', which still appeared on many of its brands. By the time O'Reilly arrived, acquisitions had brought in some other major brand names: Ore-Ida, America's biggest producer of frozen potato products, was aboard, as was Star-Kist, the most profitable subsidiary after Heinz UK. But the biggest-selling product, if not the most profitable, was still tomato ketchup.

By the middle of 1972, some nine months after he got there, O'Reilly had made it clear he wanted to run the operating side of the whole group, and Gookin, uneasy in the world of marketing, was happy to let him do it. 'He had a lot of confidence Tony was going to change things,' says one former director. In October 1972, just over a year after he arrived, he was formally promoted to the position of executive vice-president and chief operating officer. That raised him above all the other vice-presidents, and clearly indicated to all concerned that Gookin was grooming him for his own job. At the age of thirty-six O'Reilly was now the number two executive in the whole of Heinz worldwide. His salary was raised to $250,000 a year.

The move was not received with unanimous delight among all his colleagues. Crossen, for instance, resented it, putting it down more to O'Reilly's excellence at self-promotion than to his ability at the job. 'His ambition was so patently obvious,' said Crossen later. 'But you had to admire his skill. He was a very charming guy—in the Irish way.'

O'Reilly's responsibilities now covered the world, and he started another tradition at Heinz: a week-long management session at which each executive had to present a paper on the past year, the immediate plans and budget for the next year, and a 'wish list' for the future.

These were intense, gruelling sessions, lightened only by O'Reilly's jokes and humour, but tough on those who had to present to him. Dick Beattie remembers the tension before those meetings.

> Tony was really challenging and penetrating, and we weren't used to that, and you really had to be on your toes, because he knew your business better than you did, and he had this amazing memory which could produce things you had said months ago, and take up on conversations where you had left off last year as if it were just a few minutes. And he would sit there speed reading your report, and he would get well ahead of everybody else, and I'm there looking at Tony, and the rest of the room is following the presentation but he is ahead of it, and I thought to hell with the rest of the room, I'm staying with Tony, so he's speed reading and I'm speed talking, and it's kind of uncomfortable.'

It was after one of these sessions that O'Reilly decided that action was needed to tackle the most urgent problem in the group: the Mexican operations were losing the group $4 million a year, 10 per cent of total profits. He went into Gookin's office to show him these figures.

'Burt, this is totally unacceptable,' he said. 'I just cannot believe that the marketplace will accept this type of money being lost in Mexico each year. I'd like to go down there, and I'm going to tell you at the end of the trip whether we should or should not pull out of Mexico.'

Gookin looked embarrassed. 'This is kind of an emotional decision for me. You see, I made the investment in Mexico, and it's hard for me to close it down.' O'Reilly argued that if they had made a mistake, they must face up to it.

'Well,' said Gookin finally, 'off you go. You go do it.'

O'Reilly arrived in Mexico City on 10 December 1972 and met the new Heinz chief executive, Manuel Alberon, who had just been employed from Coca-Cola for the incredible salary of $250,000 a year. They were later to become good friends, but on this first occasion O'Reilly got straight to the point:

> I'm here more or less to close you down, although you've just been appointed, because I have a feeling when we look at the

books here we're going to head for home. You've four factories, in Los Robles, at Guadalajara, at Salamanca and one here in Mexico City. And the stories I hear about them are fantastic, unbelievable. The balance sheet says we've got fixed assets but I gather when we started the season here for pineapples, the factory's gone, the entire goddam factory has been taken away for the winter—the roof, the walls, everything, taken away by the peons. Inventories are disappearing, everything is disappearing. You know, Manny, you may just be leading the retreat from Moscow.

The Mexican was undisturbed. 'Well, whatever it takes,' he said philosophically. 'So long as I'm well enough paid, I don't mind.'

John Crossen, the Heinz director with direct responsibility for Mexico, joined them as they worked their way through the reports and figures. O'Reilly proposed closing Mexico immediately and taking the write-off on the balance sheet, but he and Crossen disagreed on how it should be done. It was one of their periodic battles which would continue until Crossen finally left the company. That evening O'Reilly insisted on ringing Frank Bretholle, the group's financial expert who knew every number in the whole group. 'Frank, we're getting out of this country, and we're going to have to take a $25 million write-off. Now what we have to do is work out the best way of doing it.' Once he had got over his shock, Bretholle could only agree. There were a few other write-offs he had been wanting to take, including a factory in Britain, and this could be the time to lump them all together and get them out of the way. The markets, he reckoned, would probably welcome the move, seeing it as a sign that Heinz really was cleaning itself up.

Back in Pittsburgh, O'Reilly insisted to a reluctant Gookin that they must go ahead, take their hit and withdraw completely from Mexico. 'Burt, we're going to have to do it. We have to take it up to the January board meeting.'

Gookin gave in, knowing the case was unarguable. 'If you don't mind, Tony, I think I'll play golf that day,' he said.

It was the only board meeting that Gookin missed while he was running Heinz, and was to mark the beginning of a shift in power towards O'Reilly. The retreat from Mexico was by far the biggest commercial decision that O'Reilly had yet taken, and he prepared the ground carefully, outlining the position to the board in persuasive detail. At the end of it, no one, not even Crossen, objected. When the announcement was made, the market was equally approving and the shares rose.

The move, clearly mostly O'Reilly's doing, brought him fully into the board's focus. Jack Heinz, now sixty-four, Bill Snyder, from one of the old Pittsburgh steel families, and the others all looked on approvingly. Mexico was Gookin's mess, and O'Reilly got the credit for sorting it out. There was also now enormous excitement inside the company that a formula had at last been found to make Heinz USA profitable; much of the credit went to Gookin, but O'Reilly was seen as taking up his efforts and carrying them on.

By this stage O'Reilly was in a commanding position, almost able to dictate his own terms. In Ireland Fitzwilton had taken off like a rocket, and O'Reilly's personal stake in it was worth £3 million. He was under some pressure from Leonard and Ferguson to devote his entire efforts to the venture, on the basis that they could turn it into a large, multi-national industrial holding company, taking over companies in the UK and possibly even the USA. In March 1973 he had also become a newspaper proprietor, having bought the Irish Independent group, and there was much work to be done there. His capital assets were becoming substantial, but so was his borrowing, and all of them were in Ireland. There was, he decided, no point in flogging away at Heinz unless his position became very clear.

He went to see Gookin to explain where he stood. 'I've increasingly been making a critical constitution here,' he told him. 'But I've got these two very exciting vehicles in Ireland, and there's a strong temptation to go and look after them. There's not a lot of point in me staying, unless you make me president. But it's entirely up to you, and I'll fully understand if you don't want me to make it. I'm happy to go home.'

Gookin didn't argue. His calculation was that he had now put a considerable effort into recruiting and promoting O'Reilly, who was proving his worth. If his protégé left, he would have to start again, find someone else, train him, and then perhaps be faced with the same problem. In the meantime, he himself would have to work much harder, taking back the tasks he had surrendered to O'Reilly. 'Burt thought, "What the hell, I'm still CEO and I'm going to be CEO until I'm sixty-five in six years' time," ' says a former director, 'and what he really wanted was to remove Jack Heinz from the position of chairman.'

In July 1973 Heinz announced that O'Reilly was to be president and chief operating officer, a move that was well received both inside and outside the company. The *Wall Street Journal* noted that he would bring 'marketing drive' to the company. He was now becoming a figure on the American national stage, singled out as one of the brightest of the emerging young executives in the country. He had been with the company four years, and of that only two years had been spent in America. He was thirty-seven years old, the youngest president of any major corporation in America, a millionaire (at least on paper), with a handsome salary and heir apparent to one of the top jobs in America by his early forties. Life was good. No one could have forecast the problems he was to hit over the next few years.

12

'There Are Two Me's'

IF BURT GOOKIN HAD NOT BECOME AN ACCOUNTANT, HE WOULD HAVE been a professional golfer. Every Friday at four he left the Heinz office for the golf course where he spent most of the weekend, practising a game which had been a passion for him since he was a small boy. Tony O'Reilly left the office shortly afterwards, but with a different kind of weekend in view. Once a fortnight, by six o'clock he was at Pittsburgh airport boarding a commercial flight for New York, and at eight he was aboard Aer Lingus flight EI104 headed out across the Atlantic. Early on Saturday morning he was in Dublin, starting his meetings the moment he was off the plane, and working right through the weekend, sometimes without sleep. At six o'clock on Sunday night he was in the air again, and by 7.30 on Monday morning he was in Gookin's office in Pittsburgh, alert and cheerful, ready to begin another busy week. 'How was the golf?' he would ask innocently, as if he too had been at the club all weekend, and Gookin would tell him of the putts he had sunk and the matches he had won. He never asked O'Reilly what he had been doing.

O'Reilly kept it up for five years, creating an incredibly punishing schedule which took its toll even on his iron constitution. He learned to grab a few hours' sleep in the air, but a voluminous pile of papers and reports continually demanded his attention. These were busy days at Heinz, and, hard as he worked during the week, there was always more to be done at the weekend. In Dublin there were speeches to give, formal dinners to attend, meetings to chair and ageing parents to visit. Even so, O'Reilly's love of fun was such that, with Susan back in Pittsburgh, he often partied through the night. In Pittsburgh, when he wasn't working on Heinz business he was seldom off the telephone, even when he was at home, developing his use of the instrument into a fine art. Some days he talked to Ferguson and Leonard, took part in conference calls to Dublin, talked to the bankers, the Irish brokers, the newspaper journalists who covered his financial affairs in Ireland and Britain, to politicians and many others. Before the days of the portable telephone, O'Reilly perfected a system which allowed Olive to get hold of him wherever he was. If he was travelling or in meetings, he could learn about crises either in Heinz or Ireland very quickly. He also developed the habit of travelling with different briefcases, one with Heinz papers, one for Fitzwilton, perhaps another one for general reading, all stuffed with papers carefully arranged by Olive (when he travelled in the Heinz plane he would have up to eight separate briefcases, each containing all the papers and library material he could possibly need on each subject). Press clippings, relating not just to his own businesses but to anything else which was of interest, were carefully cut and sent to him. He meticulously worked his way through them, making notes here, and putting others away for filing in a system which only Olive understood but which allowed him to retrieve anything he wanted almost immediately.

An interview in the *Irish Times* in early 1973 gives an idea of the effect of his lifestyle:

> A snarl-up in London traffic had delayed his flight a few hours. He was tired, but still ready for work. The strain of his lifestyle is beginning to show, but only a little. He keeps fit playing tennis twice a week and jogging in Pittsburgh. The pace is getting a little hectic though, even for him. In 1972, he travelled around the world four times and made 20 trips to Ireland.

In this interview O'Reilly repeated something that cropped up a lot at this stage, but would never be mentioned in later years: his dislike of flying. 'I'm a devout coward in that respect. It does compound the strain.'

Was he happy with the way he was living? 'The thing I resent most is that I've got myself into a lifestyle that is really grinding. While there may be an aura of romance, success, all that nonsense, the realities of it are grinding hours, lack of sleep, detailed analysis of financial reports, business planning cycles, absence from home . . .'

He was seeing less and less of his young children, something about which Susan was increasingly complaining. 'My children are almost a memory at this stage,' he said. 'That to me is a minor tragedy that could escalate into a major tragedy. I don't believe I can keep up the pace I am working at the moment for the rest of my life.'

He also went to some trouble to keep up with his old contacts. He tried to time his visits to Ireland to take in the international rugby matches when his old friends would be there, and talked most days to Jim McCarthy, now running Dockrell's for him, who was his eyes and ears on the Dublin scene and passed on all the gossip within hours. He saw a lot of Andy Mulligan, Lockie Butler and other old friends too. He had also invited his old boyhood friend from Griffith Avenue, Sean McKone, now a successful builder, to sell part of his company to Fitzwilton, and the kernel of the large group which would attend him on his Irish visits in later years was coming together by this time.

It was not just a busy life, it was almost schizophrenic. 'You could almost say there are two me's,' he told an interviewer, and in effect there were. In many ways, he found the Pittsburgh executive the less difficult half. 'It's easier to manage a business like Heinz with the enormous momentum it has, brand names which have been established over 70 years, substantial cashflow, confident managers and highly predictable growth patterns,' he told *Irish Business* magazine. O'Reilly the Irish entrepreneur was a more demanding role, which he had not yet fully got to grips with. Here, life was wholly unpredictable, there were fewer back-up systems and staff, and everything he had, including his reputation, was at risk. He had different objectives, too: at Heinz he wanted to leave, as he put it, 'a benchmark of my professional competence', which mattered a great deal to him. In Ireland he was trying to build a corporation which would survive him, to establish a reputation in business as large as he had had in rugby—and make himself some money at the same time.

By the end of 1972 he was already one of Ireland's biggest—and certainly most active—businessmen. Fitzwilliam Securities had grown and changed in a more dramatic fashion than even its three progenitors could have imagined. The string of acquisitions, which had included a chemist's chain in the North of England, had culminated in the summer of 1972 with the big one. For years, ever since he had run Bord Bainne, O'Reilly had been watching the huge fertilizer firm of W. & H. M. Goulding. O'Reilly had come across the company again and again, selling Goulding's fertilizers to Irish farmers when he was in Cork, and encouraging the co-ops to use more of the company's products when he was at Bord Bainne and the Irish Sugar Company. It was an old, family-run, profitable concern, and in comparison to his own companies, Fitzwilliam and Crowe Wilson, a giant in terms of both balance sheet and prestige. It was part of the Irish Protestant establishment, a company too large and too grand to get on Ferguson's early target list. Over the years it had diversified, mostly into the Dublin market, building a large new office block, Fitzwilton House, on the canal, and a shopping centre in Dun Laoghaire, south of Dublin, but fertilizers remained its base. Even with the growth of the O'Reilly business in Ireland Goulding was still many times bigger, but its eccentric head Sir Basil Goulding was getting old and O'Reilly wondered if he might not pinch another idea from the British experience: the reverse takeover bid, whereby Goulding, as the bigger company, would bid for Fitzwilliam, but the Fitzwilliam management would take charge. It seemed worth a try.

They were still thinking about it in June 1972 when someone else struck first. O'Reilly was at a convention in the Greenbriar Hotel in White Sulphur Springs, West Virginia, when his father rang on a Saturday morning. It was his busiest period at Heinz, and he was deeply involved in meetings, but he took the call. 'I'm sorry to tell you this,' said Jack O'Reilly, 'but last night Basil Goulding and Con Smith signed an agreement to form a new company. They're merging.'

O'Reilly, although disappointed, mentally shrugged. He was frantically busy, life at Heinz was going well, and there would, he reckoned, be plenty of other opportunities. His father, on the other end of the line, echoed his thoughts. 'I wouldn't worry about it,' he said. 'One door closes, another opens.'

But O'Reilly was still irritated. He would dearly have loved Goulding's, which would have taken him, the lad from the modest house in Griffith Avenue, right into the heart of the Irish Protestant-dominated establishment. It would also have given him the size and balance sheet support he had only dreamed of. He found it particularly galling to be pipped by Con Smith, who had been a rival of his all the way through university and had been setting an even hotter pace in the Irish business world. A brilliant salesman, Smith had created a group based around motor distribution, acquiring the valuable Renault franchise, and his star had soared even faster than Crowe Wilson's. Sir Basil, needing a fresh injection of both capital and management, had chosen him rather than O'Reilly, and that irked him.

At six the following morning his father rang again with an even more dramatic development. A British European Airways Trident airliner, with a party of twelve senior Irish businessmen aboard bound for Brussels, had crashed at Staines shortly after take off. Everyone had been killed. O'Reilly knew many of them—including Con Smith.

Two days later, Sir Basil Goulding rang. Would O'Reilly be interested in a similar arrangement to the one he had agreed with Con Smith? The following Saturday he was in Sir Basil's large, elegant house at Delgany. Goulding had some of his senior directors with him: Jack Good and Robert Mollard, people whom O'Reilly regarded as 'the old sort of very good chaps', Dublin Protestants to a man. He was instantly captivated by Goulding. 'Old Basil had a wonderfully engaging manner, and he was tremendously witty, a true, gentle, Irish eccentric. He and I fell madly in love with each other.'

Goulding outlined the proposal, which over the next few weeks Leonard and Ferguson converted into a workable formula. They would set up a new joint holding company into which they would both inject their interests. Goulding's would end up with 70 per cent of it, Fitzwilliam with 30 per cent and an option to increase it. O'Reilly's team would take over the management. They would also change the name. The proposed company with Smith would have been called Ardagh Holdings. Goulding suggested they called this one Fitzwilton, after his prestige office block—a name close enough to that chosen by O'Reilly for his own company. O'Reilly, who would become deputy chairman, would personally own 1.3 million shares, three times the holding of Goulding, who would stay on as chairman; Leonard and Ferguson would also be major shareholders. The joint company would have sales of over £50 million and profits of over £2.5 million. It would be one of the biggest deals ever done in Ireland, creating a large new company with the asset base of Goulding and the excitement and management of Fitzwilliam. How could it miss?

When the news was announced, most commentators read one particular message into it: O'Reilly was on the way home. And that was how it looked to many inside the company. In his chairman's statement that autumn, Goulding, noting that O'Reilly was executive vice-president of Heinz, commented: 'Until he shall vacate the latter office I have been asked to remain as chairman.'

But O'Reilly, as we have already seen, was now doing so well at Heinz that he had no intention of returning. Yet in Fitzwilton he had one of the largest companies in Ireland, employing 4400 people, created from nothing in two years. He seemed well on the way to becoming Ireland's biggest industrialist, as well as chief executive of one of America's major corporations—and he was not yet forty.

A few weeks later he gave a major interview to the *Sunday Press* in Dublin, which provides a useful snapshot of him and his focus at the time. Flanked by Leonard and Ferguson in their favourite Russell Hotel, he looked 'extremely fit' after stripping off several pounds through constant training in Pittsburgh. The interviewer, John Kelly, asked what made him tick. Was it power, glory, money, ego, a new sort of patriotism? It was a question which many were asking at the time, and would go on asking for years to come, however many times O'Reilly tried to answer it. 'It's a cocktail,' he replied on this occasion. 'It's a combination of commitment, family, people, ego, institutions, country and to some degree money—though I don't think that is the primary catalyst.' It was an honest enough answer, as far as it went. In truth, O'Reilly himself has probably never fully understood what drove him into a work schedule which would have killed most people. In Pittsburgh he was not only staying the pace with some of the best-paid and most high-powered executives in the country, he was actually outpacing them. In Ireland, he ran a rapidly growing industrial empire which again would have been enough in its own right for most people. The fact that they were 3000 miles apart was just an extra obstacle to be surmounted. Nothing seemed to faze him, or disturb his high good humour and equilibrium. However long the plane trip—and often he was delayed by fog or traffic or breakdowns—no one at either end recalls him being ragged.

When he was disturbed, his outward reaction was to become icily calm. In this interview, Kelly put to him some of the criticisms that Irish people were making at the time—and to which he seemed highly sensitive. For instance, he stood accused of abandoning the Irish Sugar Company to go abroad rather than stick with the task—in effect, of deserting Ireland for riches overseas. How did he react to that? 'I would hope that the criticism is sincere,' he answered in the low, even tone that those who knew him well were familiar with when he was angry. 'And I would hope it is researched. People can translate one's motives in a very tortuous way to suit their own ends.'

Far from cutting back on his involvement in Ireland, he said, he had actually increased it. 'The entire thrust of my personal investments have been in Ireland. This, I think, betokens some measure of confidence in the future of Ireland.'

A few weeks before, Kelly had interviewed General Costello and tempted him into an attack on O'Reilly, and now he raised some of the points, already more than familiar, made then. O'Reilly, back on safe ground, grinned: 'If you've ever played football for Ireland, you will quickly learn, one to accept the criticism, and secondly that your best match is the next match.' But he was not going to be drawn, even by a clever interviewer, into a slanging match with his old enemy. 'I have a very considerable admiration for General Costello . . . the fact that his views and mine don't always coincide is a matter of his judgement and mine as to how economics operate.'

But he went to some pains to try to defuse the issues of Erin Foods and his link-up with Heinz. 'I estimate that Heinz will do $20m of business here—and that's a hell of a lot of business.' It had grown from almost nothing and would go on growing, he insisted. In terms of his own long-term plans, he felt Ireland was 'the best country in the world to settle in', but he was making no commitment about coming back soon. Ireland, he reckoned, had a great future inside the Common Market 'if it could manage its assets and reap the benefits to the greatest extent'.

Leonard and Ferguson enthused about the opportunities of managing those assets. But all three of them were keen to dispel some of the flak they were now attracting, prompted by the change of fashion in Britain where conglomerators were increasingly being depicted as 'asset-strippers', with Slater, now at the height of his financial power, turning from City hero to public villain. 'There have been a number of uninformed political comments about companies of this nature,' said O'Reilly, 'and we don't accept this phrase about a "shell company" which has been bandied about.'

In fact, Crowe Wilson had been nothing more than a 'shell' when the trio had bought into it, so to an extent they were trying to rewrite history. But in the sensitive atmosphere of the time they felt the need to defend it, although years later a more confident O'Reilly would have argued that there was nothing at all wrong with what he was trying to achieve. In Britain groups such as Hanson and BTR, now world-class companies, had started in the same way and were only a few years ahead of him. In America, many of the new generation of companies which grew up in the 1970s and 1980s also started from similar beginnings. But 'shell' was increasingly being equated with 'asset-stripping', and in the narrow world of Irish business that was a nasty insult. Fitzwilton, Leonard was fond of saying, was modelled on the British conglomerate Thomas Tilling, a company of impeccable repute, and not on Slater Walker.

'We are the third largest industrial company here and as such a barometer within the economy,' O'Reilly told Kelly. 'If we don't do well, then a lot of other companies will be in difficulty too.' Aggregation of financial power, he went on, did not necessarily have to result in asset stripping 'but should be used as a catalyst for expansion and production both at home and abroad'.

Early in 1973 he was planning an even more ambitious move, this one outside Fitzwilton, adding a third arm to his already over-extended personal interests. O'Reilly had always been an avid reader, absorbing books (mostly history or biographies, but also novels), magazines and newspapers even while keeping up his busy schedule. He had learnt to read rapidly, and could get through mountains of material every day. Newspapers were of particular interest to him, and wherever he was in the world he bought and read everything that was available. Increasingly he had been looking at newspapers with a different eye, that of the businessman. In 1972 he had been much impressed by an article written in the *Irish Times* by Garret FitzGerald, then the leader of the Fine Gael main opposition party and later the Irish Taoiseach, which forecast the end for many of the industries that de Valera and Lemass had tried to foster behind tariff walls. Car assembly, textiles and shoe manufacturing, he forecast, would die in Ireland. Among the only industries that would prosper inside the Common Market were those which were indigenous, or had a local franchise of a unique nature: grassland management, for example. He didn't mention newspapers, but to O'Reilly the point was obvious. There was no more unique local franchise than a newspaper—the Japanese or the French were never going to compete in the Irish market (although the British could—and did).

The company he had in mind was the Irish Independent group of newspapers. It would be an opportunist, once-in-a-lifetime bid, because newspapers such as the *Independent* didn't often come up for sale. Ostensibly, the *Independent* wasn't even on the market, but O'Reilly, knowing Ireland as he did, believed it could be bought by the right person at the right price. But he felt that person should be him, on his own, without his partners in Fitzwilton. He talked it over with Ferguson and with Leonard, who knew a lot of about newspapers, setting out his strategy and plans. Fitzwilton was at full stretch after the Goulding's takeover, he emphasized. 'I would like to run this myself,' he said. 'You guys have Fitzwilton. I'll do this on my own.' He had other reasons for going in that direction. He was now earning $300,000 a year at Heinz, and reckoned his reputation would allow him to raise the money he needed without help. If he could do it personally he could keep control, whereas by doing it through Fitzwilton he would be heavily diluted. He wanted to be an absolute monarch in this role, seeing it as his power base if ever he left Heinz to take up a career in politics.

The *Independent*—or the 'Indo' as it was always referred to in Ireland—was more than just a newspaper. O'Reilly, like most middle-class Irish, had been brought up to regard it with a mixture of tolerance and respect. Jack O'Reilly read the *Irish Times*, which was a more highbrow paper, but in the country regions the *Independent* was the universal paper. Ireland had three national newspapers, all with their different constituencies: the *Irish Times* was the most serious, in 1973 still the preserve of the Protestant population, the civil servants, the business community and academia; the *Irish Press*, much less serious, was owned by the de Valera family, and uncritically supported the government and the Catholic Church; and the *Independent*, which had a readership of a million (a third of the population), traditionally supported Fine Gael, and presented itself as Ireland's family newspaper. It outsold the *Irish Times* three to one, covering local as well as national issues, but with a much more sober tone than the tabloids, which had not yet arrived in Ireland.

Like all educated Irishmen of his generation, O'Reilly was also keenly aware of the prominent role that the *Independent* had played in Irish history. It had been founded by William Martin Murphy, who in some ways was the Tony O'Reilly of his day and, by coincidence, had also attended Belvedere. Murphy was born in Bantry, County Kerry, in 1844, and took over the family building firm at nineteen when his father died. Like William Clarke in Wicklow, he benefited from the great Catholic building boom which came along twenty years after emancipation, and constructed churches, schools and bridges all over the country. But he expanded beyond Ireland's shores, winning contracts all over the world: railways on the West Coast of Africa, tramways in England and Scotland, and even the first tram-tracks in Buenos Aires. A brilliant financier, he acquired the Imperial in O'Connell Street, one of Dublin's leading hotels, and also owned the country's biggest department store, Clery's. He was on the board of every single tramway and railway company in the country, and, even though he was a Catholic, was elected president of the Dublin Chamber of Commerce, which consisted almost exclusively of Protestant businessmen. W. B. Yeats despised him, scornfully dismissing his preoccupation with making money as 'fumbling in a greasy till' and adding 'the halfpence to the pence'. But Murphy seemed not to mind, insisting that making money was as respectable an occupation as writing poetry.

Inevitably Murphy was drawn into Irish politics, and in 1885 was elected to the Westminster Parliament as a Nationalist. He sided against the great political figure, Charles Stewart Parnell when the party split over the Kitty O'Shea divorce case, and helped finance a new newspaper, the *National Press*, in opposition to the pro-Parnell *Freeman's Journal*. After he was thrown off the board in one of the many bitter personality squabbles which pervaded Irish politics, in 1896, he founded his own paper, which he called the *Daily Nation*. For a time there were three Nationalist dailies, all of them at each other's throats, all of them losing money. When the *Irish Daily Independent* went bankrupt, he bought it and merged it with his own, running it at a great loss—more than £100,000 on one account. He didn't seem to mind that either. When asked why he did it, he replied that 'some men have as their pastimes hunting, gambling or some other frivolity, but the *Independent* gives me the necessary relief from the hard and prosaic world I have to face as a man of business'. Three-quarters of a century later, Tony O'Reilly could understand that.

Impressed by the success of Lord Northcliffe's newspaper empire in London, in 1904 he changed the character of the paper, replacing the dull, worthy format with less type, more pictures and more digestible stories and columns. Taking another leaf from Northcliffe's book, he cut the price to a halfpenny, and as sales increased he began charging for advertisements, soon turning it into the best-selling and most profitable paper in the land. He added an evening paper, the *Evening Herald*, and a Sunday edition. He also continued to wage war on his former colleagues in the Irish parliamentary party, causing one observer to note: 'Of all the many agencies which finally broke down the Irish Party and led to the regime of Sinn Fein, the *Independent* and Murphy behind it must be regarded as perhaps the most potent.'

In Dublin, however, his memory would forever be coloured by his leading role in the great lock-out of 1913 by employers who were opposed to recognition of the trade union movement led by the socialists Jim Larkin and James Connolly. Twenty thousand men were thrown on to the streets of Dublin in some of the most depressed times that the city had ever seen. 'It brought even deeper misery into the hideous Dublin slums, and provoked the creation of the Irish Citizen Army that November to raise the morale of the unemployed,' wrote the historian J. J. Lee. Three years later Murphy denounced the Easter Rising, calling for the execution of Connolly. Only when Connolly was safely dead did he demand the end of the executions. By that stage the *Independent* buildings in Middle Abbey Street, opposite the Post Office, were in ruins. Murphy became so influential that Lloyd George asked for a meeting with him, but he remained a ferocious opponent of home rule, arguing that Ireland had to have its own identity and nationality. He died, still fighting the cause of nationalism, while Britain still ruled in Ireland.

The paper atrophied after his death. It remained in the hands of the Murphy family, developing into a conservative, staid but still profitable organization. His son, William Lombard, took over and then in 1943 T. V. Murphy, simply known as Tommy, became the third generation to run it. It was the classic story of clogs to clogs in three generations, except that Tommy, even though his fortunes had declined drastically, wasn't quite reduced to clogs. He had been clever enough to appoint two good managers, Bartle Pitcher as managing director and Liam Healy as finance director. They had expanded the group, adding the *Drogheda Independent*, the local paper in Jack O'Reilly's old town, the *Wexford People* and the *Kerryman*, each a power in their own communities. Between them, the papers comprised by far the most powerful press influence in the Republic. The paper had not paid its owners a dividend for years, but in Tommy's case that barely mattered: he ran his Rolls-Royce on the company and lived in some style in Carrickmines outside Dublin. In 1973 he was seventy-one, and his sole management object was to get his thirty-five-year-old son Rodney to succeed him.

In this he was being thwarted, not just by the management but by his own family—which was where O'Reilly came in. O'Reilly had discovered through his own private contacts that the family was split. As well as a son, Tommy Murphy had two daughters, one of whom had married Peter Young, a huge second row rugby player who had captained England. Young had moved to Dublin and worked for a firm which had recently run into financial trouble, and word reached O'Reilly that they wanted cash. The other daughter was married to a friend of his, Jim Buckley, with whom he had played tennis, and they too wanted some of their capital out of the paper.

Independent Newspapers was a public company, with a quotation on the Dublin stock market, but like most things connected to the third generation Murphys it had an archaic and undemocratic voting structure. The Murphys, and another family, the Chances, held control through the A shares which, although they made up only 4 per cent of the equity, had 100 per cent of the votes. The B shares, which were the ones traded, consisted of the other 96 per cent of the equity and had no votes. O'Reilly's plan was to prize loose the voters.

Privately he made his approaches through Tommy Murphy's closest financial adviser, Russell Murphy, offering £10.95 a share for the 100,000 shares. There was no resistance: both the Murphys and the Chances agreed to accept. He set about borrowing the £1.1 million, and organizing the necessary legal documents and other paperwork. The news that there was a bidder in the offing leaked in February 1972, catching him with his arrangements still incomplete. The company put out a statement formally saying it had received an approach, and the non-voting shares zipped up 55p to 200p, capitalizing the whole group at £4.8 million. The rumours whirled in the hothouse of Dublin: Rupert Murdoch was coming in, Michael Smurfit was bidding and Fitzwilton was going to have a go (Fitzwilton formally denied it, truthfully, although it would later agree to take a stake). In Ireland nothing could remain secret for long, and soon the market had identified the buyer as O'Reilly, who was known to have been in Dublin over the weekend and to have seen Tommy Murphy.

Even as O'Reilly was flying back to Pittsburgh there was a taste of what he would have to tackle in Ireland, where industrial relations in the 1970s were among the worst in the world. The *Independent* journalists demanded details of the reported takeover, and when they were not forthcoming, staged a sit-in. The paper didn't appear and all 180 journalists were sacked. The other Irish papers all struck in sympathy.

O'Reilly, meanwhile, had hit a snag which was threatening to derail his entire carefully constructed deal. He believed he could get away without bidding for the B non-voting shares, which he couldn't afford, but the takeover rules had recently changed in Ireland, and the Stock Exchange interpreted them much more strictly than his advisers expected. By buying the A shares, he was told, he had gained control of the company and would therefore have to extend his bid to all shareholders, voting and non-voting. For ten days he and the bankers argued furiously with the takeover authorities, who refused to yield. O'Reilly's normal calm deserted him during this period, and he became angry and resentful. The shares he had agreed to buy sold at a huge premium on their actual value solely because of their voting power. In terms of dividends, they ranked alongside the ordinary shares. So in effect he had paid £1.1 million for 4 per cent of a company which was worth less than £5 million in total. The authorities were now insisting he put up another £4 million for the other 96 per cent.

But there was a way round it. The man from Allied Irish Investment Bank came up with a clever scheme whereby O'Reilly would make a straight offer for the B shares which he hoped not everyone would accept. In the event, 47% did, and the other 53% stayed in (and were greatly enriched in the process). The 47% was then purchased or placed with institutions including Fitzwilton. The overall effect, at the end of the day, was that O'Reilly personally ended up with 30% of the company—enough to give him effective control.

On 16 March 1973 the bid was finally announced, and O'Reilly went to Abbey Street for the first time in his new role as press baron. The journalists were still on strike but that didn't seem to bother anyone—someone was always on strike in that plant. As he stepped out of his car, the evening's television news was already leading on his latest purchase, the first shake-up in the Irish newspaper world for generations. Bartle Pitcher, the chief executive and Liam Healy, were waiting for him downstairs and took him up in the lift to the board room, where he was introduced to the senior managers. It was the first time most of them had ever seen the legendary Tony O'Reilly at close quarters, and he appeared every bit the superstar they expected. He put them instantly at ease with a few of his little jokes, warm handshakes and reassurances that he was not going to change the editorial line of the papers but would carry on the policy of editorial independence. Nor did he envisage any redundancies. He had plans, he said, for building an international communications company with the *Independent* as its kernel. He moved on into the news room where he made similar reassuring noises, and on through the print works. It was a heady moment for him, which he savoured.

Once again, as with the Goulding's bid, the takeover was widely interpreted as a signal that O'Reilly was leaving Heinz and coming home. The *Financial Times* that week did a major feature on him under the headline 'The Name of the Game is Work', and noted: 'No one is saying anything for the record right now, but his Irish friends will be surprised indeed if O'Reilly spends more than the next two or three years at most as a full-time executive with the multi-national corporation.' Once again, it was wide of the mark.

In July, three months after the bid, the bank developed the second part of its plan: the enfranchisement of the B shares. Under this, O'Reilly would be offered shares which were convertible, depending on the level of profits, into ordinary shares. If profits rose, he would be a big winner, But if they fell, it was potential disaster. When O'Reilly's compensatory package for giving up control, were published, there was uproar. The *Hibernia* magazine produced one issue edged in black as a protest at what it termed the 'scandal' of O'Reilly running away with the company, and the Dublin stockbrokers Dudgeon & Sons reckoned the terms were 'much too generous to Mr O'Reilly'. Some of the big institutional shareholders indicated their intention to vote against it. O'Reilly, busier than ever at Heinz where that July he was made president, was forced to do the rounds of the shareholders, explaining carefully what he was doing and why he was doing it. It had been approved by all the merchant banks involved, acting for all sides, he insisted, and was perfectly fair. But the New Ireland Assurance Company, holder of 9.3 per cent, and of 16 per cent of Fitzwilton, refused to back him, and the best he could manage was to persuade it to abstain rather than vote against him. In September the terms were backed unanimously at a shareholders meeting, and he was through.

But the price, contrary to what *Hibernia* had said, initially at least, was high. Interest rates soared that year and he found himself paying 12 per cent on his borrowings—some £140,000 of interest compared to a measly dividend of £4000. That was actually more than his salary at Heinz, his only serious source of income. He had gambled on effecting an increase in profits at the *Independent*, forecasting them to rise in 1974 from £750,000 to £950,000, at which stage a proportion of his deferred shares would convert, and rank for dividend the following year. The oil crisis and the resulting world recession, which hit Ireland like a bombshell, scuppered that. Profits that year were not £950,000—they were £450,000. The following year, instead of hitting the forecast £1.2 million, they fell again, this time to £203,000. Not only was there no conversion, but the company could barely afford to pay the original £4000 dividend. Even more drastically, by that stage Fitzwilton was in deep, perhaps terminal, trouble. O'Reilly's smooth, perfect world was suddenly in turmoil.

13

Legalized at Last

BEFORE HE HIT HIS FINANCIAL CRISIS, O'REILLY HAD PUT DOWN STILL deeper roots in his native Ireland. When the family moved to Pittsburgh he had kept Columbia, his house in Delgany, with a commercial crop of tomatoes produced under his two acres of glass. Susan took the family back to Ireland each summer for six weeks, and he always joined them for a month of that. They spent most of it at Glandore in West Cork, which was their favourite place in all the world. Columbia, the name he had also given to his private company, was used less and less. That autumn a banking friend advised him to move. Now that Ireland was in the Common Market, he said, the bottom would fall out of the tomato market. 'The Dutch have big gas bubbles in the North Sea, and they can grow tomatoes the size of footballs twice as cheap as you can here,' he said. 'Go for the broad acres—there'll be a fearful amount of money made in the EEC in land. It's cheap now, but it soon won't be. I'll get you a good price. I have a place down in Kildare which is lovely. The land is in great heart.'

O'Reilly was rather proud of his tomatoes, which he reckoned he grew in the most automated agricultural business in the country. It had its own reservoir and generator, and Jim Kelly, his farm manager, was producing a double crop from his greenhouses. But he also knew that the market was about to change. Farmland in Ireland in the 1950s and 1960s had been absurdly cheap, tempting in many German and continental buyers, but with the Common Market—and O'Reilly's own efforts at Bord Bainne—dairy farming was booming, prompting a major spurt in land prices all over Ireland. His father may have hated farming, but O'Reilly had always wanted a farm, the ultimate dream of a boy brought up in the Dublin suburbs, and he could now afford it.

There was only one problem with the Kildare property, explained the banker. 'The house is a wipe-out. You'll have to put a bulldozer through it and build yourself a nice bungalow.'

O'Reilly had no interest in the idea of a bungalow, but he fancied the land and that weekend he and Susan drove down to have a look. The situation they encountered was very different from that portrayed by his banking friend. At Kilcullen, on the edge of the Curragh plain which is the heart of the Irish racing world, he found one of the gems of Irish Georgian architecture. Castlemartin House was shabby and neglected, its roof leaking, its gutters blocked, its plaster and floors rotting and infested. Small trees were growing out of the cracked chimneys. But, standing on the banks of the Liffey, it was still magnificent. It had been built in 1720 for an Anglo-Irish aristocracy which, all over Ireland, was either gone or could no longer afford the upkeep. Many of the finest houses had either been burnt by the IRA in the 1920s or had simply fallen down, and Castlemartin was in danger of going the same way. The last of the old Anglo-Irish family, Sheila Blacker, had lived in it for years and on her death it had passed to a distant British cousin, Lord Gowrie, later a minister in the Thatcher government and chairman of Sotheby's. A penniless young man at the time, Gowrie had let it to the pop singer Donovan and then to the Rolling Stones, whose musical instruments were scattered over one large room.

It was visibly on its last legs, but Tony and Susan loved it. Inside, a large front hall was dominated by carved Corinthian pillars, embellished with crumbling plaster cornices, which led into an inner hall and a great sweeping staircase. Many of the rooms had been sealed off and abandoned, and there was damp everywhere, but nothing that couldn't be restored. There were nine bedrooms, enough for the large family and a few guests, a large drawing room overlooking the Liffey, a library, a morning room, stables and outhouses. He was told it was 'the only undeveloped stud farm on the Curragh', and he was excited by that too: the stud paddocks were already there, beautifully sheltered by large trees planted at the turn of the century. He would own and breed horses, another visible symbol of the Irish establishment.

He bought it for £200,000, or £800 an acre, with the house effectively thrown in for nothing. Susan immediately began the major task of restoration, and was soon busy with architects and antique dealers. Most of the splendid fireplaces had gone and she set about replacing them, searching the little antique shops in Dublin. Tony owned some Irish paintings, but now, with the aid of the art dealer Willy Dillon, they became serious buyers: Jack Yeats and Orpen and Lavery. They would take their time and do it properly, fully restoring the house but making it a family home which the children could enjoy and where Tony could hold his increasingly large dinner parties.

The summer of 1973 was one of the happiest and most exciting of his life. The workmen were gutting and rebuilding Castlemartin, which had become a huge playground for the children. Susan allowed them to run riot, encouraging them to create huge pictures on the walls, which she then photographed before they were replastered. They were buying pictures, furniture and horses, landscaping the gardens, rebuilding the stable block, putting in a swimming pool and a tennis court, planting trees and making paths. By Irish standards, it was a fine summer and the sun seemed to shine all August. He was still battling with the Stock Exchange and the takeover authorities over his *Independent* enfranchisement scheme, and using every form of persuasion in his repertoire to get the big shareholders to support him, but that was a niggle. He now had not one but two major Irish companies under his belt, one of them the most effective power base in the country. In Pittsburgh he had just become president of Heinz and looked set to become chief executive when Burt Gookin retired in five years' time. He was thirty-seven, married to a woman with whom all his friends were in love, with six healthy children and a type of house which previous generations of Reillys had only seen from the servants' quarters.

These thoughts were flicking through his mind one fine summer's evening as he drove down from Dublin to Kildare. It was one of the few occasions when he preferred to drive himself, taking the wheel of an open-top E-type Jaguar he had bought for himself—another boyhood dream realized. He was just on the edge of Kilcullen, less than a mile from home, when he glided around a bend to find himself at the scene of a terrible accident. The police were already there, as were the fire brigade and ambulances, and someone came over to explain what had happened. A cement truck had hit a car, completely squashing it, only ten minutes before. 'They say there were three people in the car,' someone informed him. 'But they've found eight legs—so there must be four.'

When O'Reilly finally drove into his avenue, his high had evaporated. Since his own accident a dozen years before, he was all too aware of how easily it could happen to him. Suppose he had left Dublin ten minutes earlier, hadn't stopped for that final phone call? Consciously, he made himself reflect for a moment on his good fortune and luck and then, with the superstition that no Irishman ever sheds, tell himself it couldn't last. 'I remember it being a real jolt to me, and sort of saying, OK, life is pretty good now, but they'll always be tomorrow.'

There was another reason why he feared road accidents: his mother had been in one the previous autumn which, although not apparently serious at the time, had started a decline in her health which would eventually confine her to a wheelchair for the remaining sixteen years of her life. Since Jack had retired in 1968 the two of them had lived for their son and their grandchildren, eagerly seizing every opportunity to take the children on trips to the seaside, into the mountains, or to the parts of Ireland which Tony had so enjoyed as a boy. That autumn, while Susan was planning Castlemartin, they picked up little Susan and headed for the West of Ireland, with Jack driving a new Audi that Tony had bought for him. He drove on roads he knew well, choosing a picturesque route through Cavan, near the border with Northern Ireland. This had been his territory both as a young customs official and later, when he was head of the service. Aileen always contended later that he was driving too fast, given that there were leaves on the road, while Jack blamed the car for what happened. On a sharp bend he skidded and lost control; the car hit a wall and turned over before finally righting itself. Aileen held on to the ten-year-old Susan, but took the full brunt of the impact on her head. Jack climbed out shaken but intact, worried more about little Susan, who also had a bad bump on her head, than about Aileen, who was unconscious.

When Susan O'Reilly arrived at the hospital in Cavan, her daughter was bruised but recovering. Aileen, however, was not: she had 65 stitches in the face and would be scarred for life. But worse still, hours after the accident she suddenly had a stroke, probably caused by the bang on her head. Tony was in Pittsburgh when his wife got hold of him to tell him the news. His mother, he ordered, must be moved by ambulance as soon as possible to one of the leading hospitals in Dublin. He would drop everything and fly straight there.

The initial prognosis was not too pessimistic: Aileen was slightly paralyzed but had not lost her speech, and there seemed no reason why she shouldn't make a good recovery, according to the doctors. But she seemed slow to recover, and a few weeks later she had a fall in hospital and another stroke. It was the beginning of a long, slow decline in her health which nothing could arrest. Tony took her to one of the world's leading rehabilitation centres in Pittsburgh, but she hated it and insisted he take her out. He did his best to cheer her up—the only person in the world who could—but it became progressively harder. The accident seemed to bring out a smouldering resentment between her and Jack which was to affect the last years of their lives together. 'Papa was absolutely shattered that this had happened, and he spent the rest of his life just filled with remorse,' says Susan. 'I think he blamed himself inside, and there was a great sadness about Nana. He took great pride in Tony's achievements and that became his sole reason for being.'

Jack now spent more time in Pittsburgh, and Tony always included him in the dinner parties and other gatherings. 'He was a bit of a snob, and he loved all the glitz and the important people that were in Tony's life,' says an old family friend.

When the news of the car accident and Aileen's stroke reached Jack's wife Judith in Wicklow, her reaction was an astonishingly sympathetic one. Judith O'Reilly had never allowed bitterness or hatred to enter her life, and certainly never blamed Aileen for what had happened. Her daughter Eveleen was with her when she heard the news. 'I thought, as any young person would, now we'll get a great sense of revenge. But instead of that she was full of understanding and sympathy, and found a priest who would visit her and offer consolation.' Her children, knowing how lonely and frustrating her life had been, were amazed. 'I knew the humiliation my mother had had in those years, how she had had to cut herself off from society and prying eyes, and now was her chance to reign triumphant and say The hand of God has struck her down.' But not a bit of it appeared in her attitude, and nor would she allow any of us to gloat,' says her daughter.

Yet the accident was to hurry matters along on another front. As he grew older, and his son became more famous, Jack became obsessed with his marital status and the urgent need to do something to legitimize it, in the eyes of the law if not the Catholic Church. Judith was now sixty-six, two years younger than Jack, and in rather better health than him—she seemed set to outlive both him and Aileen. Divorce was still forbidden in Ireland, but for some reason Jack believed he could get an annulment and sought advice from the Church. One of the people he discussed it with was his nephew, Father John Geary, the son of his eldest sister Mary, an intelligent and sensitive priest, and one of the very few members of the Reilly family with whom he had any contact. Even that had only come late in life: when Jack had left his wife and children nearly forty years before, his sisters, including Mary, never spoke to him again, although he remained relatively close to his brothers. Geary, as the only priest in the family, saw himself as the bridge-builder. The story of how he came to talk to Jack illustrates the strength of feeling which Jack had to endure all his life, not just from the Clarke family, but from his own relatives—and which he hid completely from his son.

A few years before, when Jack's elder sister Cathleen, a nun in the Loreto Order in India, returned home after nearly forty-five years abroad, Father Geary tried to persuade her to see her brother. She refused, saying that she could think of nothing to say to him. For years the fact that her brother had another son by the woman he now lived with had been kept from her, and she only discovered Tony's existence when he became a star rugby player. But, back in Ireland for the first time since she was a novice nun, she found everyone talking about him and became intrigued. Father Geary, although he was Tony's first cousin and had grown up only a few miles away, had never met him, but he knew a lot about him. The night before his aunt was due to go back to India, she called Geary into her room and handed him a couple of gifts which she asked him to pass on to Tony and his wife. Geary could see her resolve was weakening, and later wished he had pressed her to let him take her round to see her brother for what both of them knew would be the last time—she would not be coming home again. The next morning she caught the plane back to India and Geary took her presents around to the house in Santry. 'Uncle John was very affected—he choked up when I told him where the gifts had come from,' says Geary. 'I told him his sister had gone back now, and she had definitely decided she didn't want to see him.'

From that visit came a family relationship which was to become as

close as any in Jack's lonely and isolated existence. He insisted that
Geary must meet Tony who, he said, had no other family than his
parents (in fact he had all Aileen's relations, whom he was close to),
and Geary was delighted to meet his famous cousin. They saw each
other only once in Ireland, but when Geary went to live in Toronto
to become president of the Holy Ghost Fathers in Canada he got
into the habit of spending every Christmas with them, making the
seven-hour drive from Toronto to Pittsburgh for a week which became important to him. Jack and Aileen were always there too, and
he found Susan 'one of the great women of my life'. His relationship
with his cousin ripened into a deep friendship, and he and Tony
stayed up into the night discussing everything from the family to
theology and philosophy.

On the question of Jack's marriage, which his uncle continually
brought up with him, Geary had no useful advice to give. At the end
of the day, however broad-minded he was and however fond of the
old man, he was a priest, with his duty to the Church and its laws,
and Jack was living outside them. He could see no way that the
marriage could be annulled: the fact that there were four children
was clear enough proof it had been consummated. Jack, however,
continued to pursue that line, even bringing it up with Judith. He
had developed a notion, based on goodness knows what basis, that
the fact that she had been pregnant when they were married was an
important factor which could lead to annulment. When he mentioned
this to Judith she was horrified, and produced some of his letters to
prove how much he had been in love with her. He backed off, but
he didn't give up.

The accident persuaded Jack to redouble his efforts. The pressure
probably came from Aileen, who must have contemplated her own
death in an unmarried state with grim foreboding. She also felt hu-
miliated every time she went through American customs because her
passport showed she was not married. Geary was with him at his
house in Dublin when, without warning, Jack raised the subject of
divorce with his eldest son Julian. There were just the three of them
in the room, a meeting ostensibly arranged by Jack for the two cousins
to meet for the first time but obviously with something else in mind
too. How did he think Judith would react? he asked Julian. Would
he raise it with his mother? Julian took the request calmly enough.
'It's a delicate matter, obviously,' he said, 'and I won't probe too

deeply.' But he agreed to ask her. Geary kept well out of it, reckoning that this was not an area in which he should be involved.

Julian duly raised the matter with his mother, who at first indicated she had no intention of divorcing her husband. Judith O'Reilly now lived on her own with only a housekeeper for company in the big family house outside Wicklow. She never complained, but her life had never been easy. Her second daughter Ria, academically the brightest of her four children, developed polio when she was seventeen and become paralyzed from the waist down. Ria had wanted to study medicine, but was forced to abandon it—in those days universities made no allowances for wheelchairs. Soon afterwards her eldest daughter Juliette, a domestic science teacher, had a serious car accident and was temporarily paralyzed down one side, and she and her six-month-old daughter moved in with Judith until she recovered. But these sadnesses had contained some moments of happiness too. From the family home, Ria developed a business selling small woollen toys—Aran ladies, donkeys and so forth—which her mother helped her turn into a useful money-earner. Then, despite her paralysis, Ria too got married and moved to New Zealand, where Judith visited her twice and where she lived happily until she died at the age of thirty-nine in 1968. She never met her famous half-brother.

Judith had demanded little from Jack, but did insist on keeping her married status, which was hugely important to her in the community where she lived. But by the winter of 1973, her resistance to Jack's pleas began to weaken. Jack urged her to go to London where she could live with her daughter Eveleen, gain residency after six months, and then they could divorce. She hated even having to discuss it. 'She was devastated,' says her daughter. 'She never recovered from that horrible sinking feeling that the idea of a divorce gave her.'

At Christmas 1973, Father Geary as usual drove down to Pittsburgh. Late one evening, as he, Susan and Tony were sitting around the dining room table drinking a bottle of Lynch Bages (O'Reilly's favourite, partly because of its Irish connection), O'Reilly said to him:

'Tell me, John, does my father ever talk to you about his rather unusual background?'

'He talks of little else,' replied Geary.

It was the first time Tony had ever talked to him about the subject, and Susan was only finding out about it now.

'Does he still think I don't know about it?' asked O'Reilly.

'Yes, he's absolutely convinced you don't,' replied Geary. 'He prays every night.' Jack, he added, feared Tony would cut him off once he found out.

O'Reilly was startled. For all these years he had believed they were aware that he had been told by the Jesuits—or had found out for himself. This was a burden he did not want his parents to bear for another day. 'I want you to get on the plane tomorrow night and fly to Dublin, and say to my father I've known for twenty-three years and it's not of the slightest significance to me,' he told Geary. 'I'll be there next weekend, and I'll come and see them on Saturday.'

There was one element of that evening's conversation which Geary, who came to know his cousin as well as anybody, would later ponder over. He remarked to Tony that Jack's situation didn't seem to have affected him over the years, and Tony nodded assent. Only later, as he saw the pace that O'Reilly set himself and the tremendous drive he had, did he begin to have second thoughts. 'I wondered whether there was some compensation mechanism at work here,' he said. He mentioned it to various other close friends of O'Reilly's, who indicated that they had had similar ideas. Geary and others became convinced over the years that, far from being of no importance, the marital position of his parents was in fact one of the primary driving forces of his whole life.

Geary went ahead to break the news to the shocked couple in Dublin, and O'Reilly followed a few days later, going straight to the house in Santry. He held his parents in a long, affectionate embrace, all three of them in tears. None of them ever mentioned it again.

Jack told Judith of these events with obvious delight and immense relief. 'My father was getting old by then,' says Eveleen, 'and he felt very proud and delighted that Tony knew, that he hadn't slammed the gates, and that he had coped so well with it. But he told my mother that Aileen had been very diminished by the situation.'

It is hard to imagine Jack's feelings at this time. All these years he had lived, needlessly, in fear that Tony would find out, although common sense would have told him that in Ireland a secret of that kind could not be kept, particularly when it related to one of the country's best-known people. But it further hardened his resolve to legalize his position. Two of his brothers, Paddy and Dermot, had died in their fifties, both from coronaries, and he too was suffering from the family disease of high blood pressure. Aileen could easily have another stroke and die. Jack now became desperate to formalize his common law marriage before it was too late.

Judith suddenly resigned herself to the situation. She had gone to London to stay with Eveleen, and one evening, after they had discussed it for hours, she suddenly announced that she would give him his divorce. 'If it's to be, it's to be,' she said. There was still no bitterness.

Julian flew in from the Bahamas to take her back to Dublin and negotiate the divorce, and Eveleen saw them to the airport. The legal process began but before it was complete, Judith's health gave out and, back in Wicklow, she took to her bed, and ten days later she looked up at her housekeeper and murmured: 'Isn't it strange how easy you could be taken?' They were her last words. She died a few hours later.

As is the custom, on the night before her funeral her coffin was taken to the church in the tiny village of Glenealy, just outside Wicklow, where she had lived all her life. Jack went down to pay his last respects, braving the hatred of the Clarke family which had gathered in the house. They treated Jack with a cold courtesy. Judith's brother, a priest, took him up to the room where she had lived all those years and where she had died, surprised by Jack's apparent lack of emotion. Eveleen and her husband flew in from London to find Jack in his late wife's house for the first and only time in his life. 'It was extraordinary to see him sitting there on these beautifully-made hand-stitched cushions made by my aunts who loathed him,' she recalls. 'He was lying back with a glass of whiskey, and it seemed so sad, so unfair.'

It was not the way either of them would have wanted it, but the way was now clear for Jack and Aileen to get married. A week later they were, in the same Jesuit chapel in Belvedere where O'Reilly had first learnt the news at the age of fifteen, and by the same priest who had told him. Jim McCarthy, best man to Tony and Susan, was their best man too. They did not invite their son, or any of the family, not even Father Geary. 'It was a minor course correction,' says O'Reilly now, 'not an event they wished to share.'

He happened to be in Dublin on the day and that evening rang the Stephen's Green Club to book a table for dinner. 'Oh, Mr O'Reilly,' said the manager, 'you must be coming to your father's party tonight. Oh, my God, they're having a party the likes of which you've never seen! We've got bottles of wine out of the cellar that haven't seen the light of day since the British were here. It's going to be fantastic . . .'

Politely, O'Reilly said they wouldn't be at that party. He took Susan around the corner to the Soup Bowl in Molesworth Street, and at midnight the two of them solemnly raised their glasses and toasted his parents.

Jack and Aileen O'Reilly did not have many years to enjoy their official marriage. Two years later, in April 1976 after an operation for a gallbladder problem, Jack too had a stroke, and Tony and Susan rushed back to Dublin to be with him at what they expected to be his deathbed. He lingered for another four weeks, but never recovered consciousness. Tony stayed with him until he died. He was seventy.

In England his daughter Eveleen heard the news from a relative in Wicklow. She and her brother and sister had known he was ill, but also knew that Tony and Aileen would be there, and they all stayed away. Now Eveleen went outside and systematically lopped the top off every flower, tears running down her face. 'All I could think about was, he never said he was sorry. If there had been just that one recognition of your rights as a child, that would have been enough. And now it was too late. He would now never say he was sorry.'

14

High-wire at Heinz

THE TAKEOVER OF GOULDING'S AND THE *INDEPENDENT* RAISED THE scale and profile of O'Reilly's interests in Ireland immeasurably. In the six months between the autumn of 1972 and the spring of 1973 they had moved from an almost experimental plaything into two very serious businesses. They were also largely unconnected—although Fitzwilton was a shareholder in the *Independent*, the only real common factor was him. High visibility, however, was a two-edged sword: the conflict between his Irish entrepreneurial career and his managerial role at Heinz was increasingly being commented on. 'Heinz shareholders might well ask how is it all done,' said the *Financial Times* in March 1973. O'Reilly's ready answer to that was the quip, partly at Gookin's expense: 'I don't play golf.' But he was aware that that wasn't enough. His contract with Heinz allowed him considerable freedom, but no one, not even O'Reilly, had quite expected his outside business interests to develop in the way they had. 'Put at its simplest, no one in, around or associated with Heinz can accuse the executive vice-president of not putting in the hours on their behalf,' added the *FT*. 'But they can—and indeed they do—say along the Heinz cocktail party circuit out in Pittsburgh that he does not neglect his own interests in the process.'

The Irish papers did not help his position at Heinz with their continual references to his 'Irish friends' forecasting that he would be home within a few years at the latest. O'Reilly himself had used the success of his Irish interests as a lever to push Gookin into making him president several years before he might otherwise have done, but that threat was now being turned back on him. For the most part, the criticism in Pittsburgh of his Irish interests was latent, buried under the success of Heinz's American operations and the sharp pick-up in earnings growth which O'Reilly, although not directly responsible for starting, visibly seemed to be accelerating. But it was present, and O'Reilly's sensitive antennae monitored and measured it, anticipating and trying to defuse trouble before it erupted. He could not always be successful.

'It wasn't just that Anthony O'Reilly was a foreigner that caused the raised eyebrows when he was made president and chief operating officer of Pittsburgh's venerable H.J. Heinz Co. last month,' remarked *Forbes* magazine in August 1973.

> After all, foreigners have headed other and larger US-based multinational corporations, such as Caterpillar Tractor. It wasn't even that O'Reilly was just 37, had been with the company only six years and was best known to the public as a famous Irish international rugby star.
>
> What seemed strange was that O'Reilly had, and will keep, extensive business interests outside Heinz.

The piece also quoted his well-rehearsed reply: 'In Ireland I am merely an investor strategically employing my capital. I am not at all involved in management, and investment decisions don't require as much time as management.' But could he be a first-rate manager and investor simultaneously, pressed the reporter, who had clearly picked up the Pittsburgh gossip. 'Perhaps I have a schizoid personality,' O'Reilly shot back. 'I love challenges and the one at Heinz is important to me. It means I have competed successfully against some of the best managerial talent in the world.'

For the moment that was an effective retort, because it was demonstrably true that O'Reilly had done just that. Yet the same question surfaced in newspapers and magazines all that summer, an indication of just how much it was talked about in the Pittsburgh country clubs at the weekends. Even the *New York Times* remarked on what a marvellous springboard Fitzwilton gave him to jump into the European Common Market with his 'American-style marketing skills without the onus of being an American company'. The *Times*, and others, predicted that he would soon be heading for home, probably to become Irish Prime Minister, using the *Independent* as his launch-pad.

In the autumn of 1973 a reporter on *Fortune* magazine called Tom O'Hanlon decided to go further and do an in-depth exposé of O'Reilly's dual life, which for a time caused a considerable flap in Pittsburgh. For weeks word kept coming back to Heinz headquarters of the aggressiveness of his questions, and the direction in which he was pointing. 'He says he's really going to get you, really knock the shit out of you,' Heinz's public relations people reported to him. O'Reilly wasn't too worried about the O'Hanlon's wilder talk but he was concerned with the assertion that he might not be devoting enough of his energies to Heinz. O'Reilly passed back to O'Hanlon the message that the Heinz board was fully aware of his Irish interests, that his contract allowed him to hold them, and that since he had joined Heinz the company's profits and earnings had improved sharply, a lot of it due directly to his efforts. He also prepared Gookin and other senior directors for what he warned might be a pretty antagonistic article on him. But he still waited with a considerable degree of trepidation for it to appear.

Towards the end of 1973, one of the Heinz staff in New York managed to get hold of an early proof copy of the article and read it down the telephone to O'Reilly. 'I was at the counter at Miami airport at six o'clock in the evening, surrounded by Spaniards and Cubans and the maelstrom of humanity, and I was trying to listen to him, and he was reading this article down the phone,' he recalls now, still with a slight shudder. 'And it turned out to be a pretty decent article. There was an interpretation that this was an unusual fellow, and he is after all working nights down at the local hostelry as well as keeping a job.' It was not entirely favourable, but, unless the reader knew the background, such criticisms as it contained were technical and relatively harmless. O'Hanlon was clearly suspicious of the way Fitzwilton was run in a city which he regarded as O'Reilly's back yard. 'An Irish businessman has never faced the restrictions that frustrate his US, or, for that matter, his European counterpart,' he wrote. 'Antitrust laws are nonexistent; there is no capital gains tax [there soon would be]; accounting systems are, to say the least, creative; and rules against stock trading are easily circumvented.' Given that climate, the *Fortune* reporter reckoned, an Irish conglomerator could 'set full sail on a direct course satisfied that no legal reefs bar his route'. O'Reilly, he implied, was very much on that course as he 'cooked up many a deal' in his penthouse office in Fitzwilton House, with its 'spectacular' view out over the whole south side of Dublin (O'Hanlon had visited it).

O'Hanlon also echoed a criticism of O'Reilly sometimes voiced among certain circles of Dublin society which could never come to terms with one of their own actually becoming an international success. He included quotes from left-wing Irish politicians and every O'Reilly enemy he could dredge up, to the effect that O'Reilly's career in Ireland had been opportunistic and self-serving. There was just enough truth in that to hurt, but it was more than matched by a quote from Gookin—'He is the most unusual, smartest young businessman I've seen any place'—and from Joe Bogdanovich—'Thank God they have a guy like O'Reilly' (to Joe B, the management of Heinz would always be 'they'). O'Hanlon even let some of the sting out of the Irish criticisms by using a Samuel Johnson one-liner he had heard from O'Reilly: 'The Irish are a fair people—they never speak well of one another.' The crisis had passed, and as the years rolled on and Heinz's growth accelerated, criticisms of his dual role would die, only resurfacing nearly twenty years later when Heinz hit a couple of tough times in the early 1990s.

At first O'Reilly didn't comment on the speculation that he would go into Irish politics, but as it continued to grow he was forced to deny it, insisting that he had no ambitions in that direction whatsoever—which was true, up to a point. His statements about Heinz, however, were more ambivalent. At the outset he had planned to stay five years; then it became eight, and then ten. He was certainly not leaving before he had succeeded Gookin to the number one job, but he left the door open beyond that.

Heinz by now was powering ahead, the years of work achieved by Gookin and continued on by the young president paying heavy dividends. The $25 million Mexican hit knocked profits back to $21.5 million in 1973, but the following year they trebled, then grew only a modest 3 per cent in the economic downturn which followed the oil crisis, but bounced up another 12 per cent the following year. By 1975 the split between US and overseas profits had reversed from 35/65 in 1967 to 71/29, and Wall Street was taking note. In 1976 Jack Heinz was pointing out that it had taken the group more than a century to reach sales of $1 billion, adding proudly: 'Now, only four years later, we are well on our way to our second billion.' Two years later, sales did indeed break the $2 billion level, having doubled in six years. By that stage profits were touching the $100 million mark, an increase of 135 per cent since O'Reilly had joined.

If Gookin had done much of the hard, pioneering work, the era from the mid-1970s on increasingly belonged to O'Reilly. The doubts about his commitment to Heinz when he became president dissipated against the background of the effort he put in and the visible success he was achieving. Increasingly it was his personality and his drive which set the direction and the philosophy of the company, he who dominated the strategy discussions, his the approval the younger executives sought. Each year the shareholders' report at the front of the annual report, previously only signed by Jack Heinz and Burt Gookin, was now signed by all three of the top people: Jack, Gookin and O'Reilly, with a new picture of them each year—a clear message of the importance of O'Reilly in the group. He tightened inventory controls, stepped up marketing efforts across the board, cut out low-volume, low-margin products, and energetically sought out new products and lines.

What might have been a mundane and tedious business to many was exciting to O'Reilly, basically because he enjoyed the exercise of learning how it all worked and then of considering how to make it work better. The tomato ketchup business alone required his full-time attention, and he focused on it. Heinz had first introduced ketchup in 1876 and by the time O'Reilly arrived on the scene the company was the biggest buyer of tomatoes in the world—2 million tonnes a year. Heinz had become expert in every conceivable tomato product, marketing it in sauces, pastas, condiments, juices, purees, paste, beans in tomato sauce and lots of others. In their never-ending search for new, cheaper and more reliable sources of supply, the company's agronomists had developed methods of growing tomatoes in areas which before the war could barely grow anything: the Mississippi Delta, the wet fields of Venezuela and the Australian desert. But when the California desert was irrigated, that became the main source of growing ketchup tomatoes (different from salad tomatoes), and today accounts for 90 per cent of Heinz's supplies. Through the 1960s, Heinz's tomato ketchup shared the market more or less equally with Hunt and Del Monte—and lost money. But a number of developments had begun to change all that before O'Reilly arrived in the US, giving Heinz an edge which the young president was quick to exploit. Instead of making ketchup from fresh tomatoes, which meant that a year's supply had to be produced in just a few months, the company's scientists developed a system of making tomato paste, which could then be transported in bulk, stored and turned into ketchup through the year. That considerably altered the economics, and, more importantly, meant that supply was no longer tied to the yearly harvest. The introduction of paste meant that Heinz's factories, which had a capacity of about 5 million tonnes in the mid-1960s, doubled that by 1969. Heinz also doubled the amount spent on advertising, and by 1971 the company had gained 34 per cent of the market—where it stayed until the mid-1970s.

When he took responsibility for Heinz USA in 1972, O'Reilly inherited a number of further technological improvements which were to make possible the next leap forward. The agronomists came up with a strain of tomato which was firmer, crack-resistant, disease-free, with a thick skin, higher pectin and better colour. The new generation of tomato was as hard as an orange, ideal for harvesting by California's highly automated growers. These were hybrid strains, impossible for competitors to steal because they did not reproduce themselves, and gave Heinz a key competitive advantage. By the mid-1970s huge tomato paste storage tanks had become regular features of the Heinz factories, which had also been heavily modernized and upgraded— the number sharply reduced and the production of ketchup concentrated in fewer and fewer plants (today there are three). O'Reilly discovered that it took an average of twenty-four tomatoes to fill a 14-ounce bottle, and the new production systems which he planned would eventually mean that from harvest to bottle could take between two and four hours when the plants were running flat out, twenty-four hours a day, during the season.

There were other developments too. Heinz found it was losing business in fast food restaurants which moved to bulk, non-branded ketchup. The company developed a large, flexible metallized bag to replace the clumsy cans it had previously supplied. The new Vol-Pak bag was placed in a rack and used to refill squirt bottles from a special valve, an innovation which was to prove crucial for Heinz's future business.

Gookin had appointed new men to run the ketchup business, by far Heinz's biggest business in terms of sales, before O'Reilly came, but despite the technology advances and greater emphasis on marketing nothing much seemed to change in terms of profits. O'Reilly's assessments to Ray Good, head of Heinz USA, which had been encouraging and supportive in the earlier years, began to show impatience. 'Your company is in a holding pattern,' he told Good in December 1975. Good's business plan, he added, 'gave an impression of coherence and unity which proved to be somewhat more apparent than real in certain instances. You had skilfully papered over the cracks of a measure of disagreement between your principal operating officers.' Coldly dissecting Good's proposals for the coming year, O'Reilly insisted he make a 'radical change in existing fixed costs'. He added: 'Tell us what you must do to get a 5 per cent NPAT [net profit after tax] in your business.'

When he said 'radical' O'Reilly meant it, and Good responded. By the spring of 1976 he had come up with his solution: he proposed restructuring the $500 million company into three businesses, each concentrating on its own product line. There would be tomato products and condiments as the main division; processed foods (soups, baby foods, entrees and frozen foods) as the second; and the third, one of Heinz's oldest and least profitable businesses, pickles.

O'Reilly accepted his plan for decentralization, but only as a starting point. He proposed going much further and shaking the whole organization apart, in effect almost starting again. In the past Heinz had gone for volume without seriously looking at the profit margins it made. That would now change. 'Heinz had made a god of volume, as a lot of American companies do,' says O'Reilly now. 'So we shot the god of volume, and we elevated a new god called mix.' The group produced 22 million cases of baby food and made nothing out of it in 1974 (there was serious debate in the mid-1970s about pulling out altogether). Now it produces 10 million cases and makes a large profit. Every aspect of the business, he ordered, must be put under a microscope, and waste and unprofitable lines everywhere eliminated. The whole company would be turned upside down, careers, lives and jobs changed for ever. In the coming years fourteen factories would be closed, warehouse space shrunk and some 8000 jobs eliminated. Each separate product was given responsibility for its own research, marketing and cost structure. Overheads were stripped down, inventories brought under control and tough criteria set for new products, investment and new hirings. O'Reilly even proposed taking a step which almost everyone else thought was heresy: he would dramatically reduce Heinz's involvement in pickles. Heinz had been founded on pickles, and was as closely associated with pickles as it was with tomato ketchup (indeed it was often referred to as 'The Old Pickle Company'); yet, as O'Reilly pointed out to Gookin and the board, Heinz never had more than 8 per cent of the American pickles market. 'It is a crop with one inventory production a year, and we have no recipe monopoly—any housewife can pickle onions or gherkins or anything she wants. And we have a hell of a lot of money tied up, and no margin on the product.' Heinz, he urged, should exit, and use the money to build big, new modern factories for ketchup and its strong products where margins could really be improved. The board, paling at the prospect, went along with it.

In effect it was to be the end of the old Heinz. 'A cradle-to-grave mentality and way of life was over,' wrote Eleanor Foa Dienstag in her history of Heinz. 'For some it was the beginning of the end. For others it was the day the sleeping giant, Heinz USA, at last awoke.'

It took six months to implement and by that stage Ray Good, its architect, had moved on to Pillsbury, to be replaced by the much tougher Dick Patton who, goaded by O'Reilly, added even greater momentum to the changes.

Each year Burt Gookin took his top management team to a meeting with the food analysts, usually a group of over a hundred people in investment houses and brokers' offices who followed the sector—and who for years had been disenchanted with Heinz. These meetings were really sales meetings, except that instead of selling products the company was selling its own shares—or at least the merits of its own stock. Gookin, O'Reilly and the others all had large share options in Heinz, designed to motivate them to make the company perform even better. But there was little real point for them in getting profits and earnings up if that was not reflected in their share price, which was not happening.

O'Reilly had been a popular figure at these meetings since he first appeared in 1971 and Gookin had tossed him a question on the growth prospects for baby food. O'Reilly had considered a moment, then said that the birth rate in Britain had been declining by 7 per cent a year but had now turned upwards. 'During that period I did my best to keep the fall as small as possible,' he added to general laughter, 'having six children under four at one stage. When I said I had six under four it was assumed I had a golf handicap rather than a family.' It broke the tension on an otherwise formal, stylized occasion, and the analysts loved it—even if the overall message was not so cheerful at the time.

By January 1977 Gookin had much more to boast about as he

faced the New York Society of Security Analysts. Heinz's problems were now behind it, and he flashed up charts to show that earnings per share had averaged 10.7 per cent growth for the past ten years, and net income had risen even faster: by 13.3 per cent. That, he went on, made it the fourth best performing company in the food sector, ahead of groups such as General Mills, Kraftco, Pillsbury, Campbell's and Gerber, and behind only Carnation, Ralston Purina and Kellogg. Since 1973, Heinz had substantially reduced debt (up went another chart); but, most importantly of all, said Gookin, putting to his *pièce de résistance*, Heinz shares had outperformed every other major food stock over the decade except for Carnation. Between 1966 and 1977 they had risen 180 per cent in a stock market which had barely moved. 'While this is gratifying,' said Gookin, looking around at the assembled analysts whose views could send the stock up or down 10 per cent the next day, depending on what they heard, 'we do not believe that our ability to increase earnings per share has been adequately recognized.'

He had a point, as his next chart showed: most of the food stocks sold on a rating of around fifteen times their annual earnings. Heinz, despite its good performance in the last few years, sold at only ten, an indication to Gookin and O'Reilly, sitting beside him on the podium, that the markets had still not understood the changes they had effected in the company. Heinz was now, Gookin emphasized, a strong *American* company, with domestic business accounting for 75 per cent of total profits, an important factor given the fact that half the world outside the USA was in recession.

At this session, although he was still only president and chief operating officer, most of the questions that followed Gookin's formal presentation were addressed to O'Reilly, clearly the heir apparent and the man from whom the analysts all wanted to hear. As a performer O'Reilly was head and shoulders above Gookin, and probably as good as anyone in America on a public platform. There were no jokes this time, but the detail of his answers showed him to be, as he intended it to, right on top of his subject. At these sessions O'Reilly's extraordinary recall could effortlessly produce the figures he wanted, and he got straight to their significance in exactly the way the better analysts were looking for. Afterwards he moved easily among them, remembering their names, reminding them of points they had raised the year before, mentioning bits of research they had produced during the year which he had read and could now comment on. There were not many senior executives who could have done it better. Gookin, acknowledging he was outclassed, appeared happy to leave him to it.

O'Reilly and Gookin had got on well up to the middle of 1976, but disagreed when Gookin proposed merging Heinz with Standard Brands. Standard Brands, later part of Nabisco, was almost the same size in sales, dollar for dollar, as Heinz, and run by an energetic manager who had shot up almost as rapidly as O'Reilly: Ross Johnston. O'Reilly couldn't see what Standard Brands brought to the Heinz party, reckoning that its brands were weak and its growth potential much poorer. But Gookin's plan, capping his career at Heinz, was to put the two businesses together, become joint chairman with the Standard Brands chief executive, Henry Weigl, and, as he remarked, let 'Ross and Tony fight it out for the position of chief operating officer between them'. In fact it was generally conceded that O'Reilly would get the role, but he would have two people, rather than one, above him.

O'Reilly attended a meeting at the bankers Morgan Stanley to discuss the merger terms and emerged even more strongly opposed. He and Gookin were completely at odds over this one. In the end the deal, opposed by both Jack Heinz, who still voted 25 per cent of the company, and by O'Reilly, was dropped, but for some time afterwards there was a coolness in their relationship. Gookin was still three years away from retirement, due in July 1979.

O'Reilly at this point received two approaches to leave Heinz: one was from Edgar Bronfman of Seagram's, who wanted him to join him (he did not specify in what capacity), and he had also been interviewed by Bill Paley of CBS who was looking for a new president. He knew his worth in the US market now, which he hadn't four years before, and was fully prepared to fight if he had to.

It was enough to persuade the Heinz board who, faced with losing him, decided to tie him more tightly to the company. At the next board meeting, in March 1977, the directors agreed a resolution that O'Reilly would take over as chief executive in July 1979. He would also retain the title of president. Burt Gookin would retire at that stage and leave the company, full of honours (and deservedly so). The succession was now set in stone, more than two years before it was due to happen.

Until this brief disagreement Gookin had always treated O'Reilly as his protégé and his own discovery; with the succession settled they returned to their old, courteous relationship, Gookin giving O'Reilly more and more rein as the time came for him to take over completely. When it was his turn, O'Reilly repaid his old mentor by persuading the board and Jack Heinz to keep Gookin as a director for another five years—an unusual request from a new CEO, who wouldn't normally want a predecessor around to look over his shoulder.

O'Reilly had now proved himself in the fiercest, most competitive and professional managerial market in the world. He was only the fifth chief executive of Heinz in its history. One of his main objectives in life had been accomplished. The other, to create a large enterprise and fortune in his native Ireland, was taking longer—and proving a great deal harder.

15

Adversity in Ireland

FOR A TIME FITZWILTON SEEMED TO BE EVERYTHING O'REILLY HOPED
for: a large, fast-growing, widely based industrial conglomerate with
a high profile and a fashionable stock market rating. In the tiny Irish
business pool it was a giant frog, its every flicker followed with intense
interest and speculation, and as it moved into Britain the City of
London investment community began to take note too. Fitzwilton
represented both glamour and solid businesses, an ideal combination
for the investor at the time. There were a few warning voices, but
on the whole they were drowned out by the enthusiastic cries of its
large band of followers. Dr Ken Whitaker, now the widely respected
governor of the Irish Central Bank, was worried not so much about
Fitzwilton but about the whole trend it represented. 'Within the past
two years we have witnessed an astonishing wave of mergers and
takeovers in these islands,' he said as early as 1972. They had, he
pointed out, thrown up huge capital profits in a remarkably short
period, all of them on paper. Asset values were being bid up at an
unhealthy rate, in turn sparking inflationary dangers which were
latent in the economy. 'If sections of the community come to have a
vested interest in continued inflation,' said Whitaker, 'will this not
tend to feed inflation further? It surely cannot be desirable socially
or economically that financial transactions should yield more gains
than production.'

O'Reilly argued in the many interviews and presentations he gave
at the time Fitzwilton was no paper-shuffling exercise, but the cre-

ation of a solidly based industrial conglomerate which would be good for Ireland, creating wealth and jobs; and for several years all went well for both the economy and Fitzwilton. For O'Reilly's Irish conglomerate the year to June 1973 was a good one, and the prospects for the new financial year looked even better. But the bull markets in London and Wall Street were over by then and, regardless of profits and prospects, share prices everywhere were falling. Fitzwilton shares peaked at 185p early in 1973 and by September, when Sir Basil Goulding announced that the company had beaten its forecast by 17 per cent, they had halved to 91p, wiping over £1.5 million off O'Reilly's net worth. There was nothing particularly sinister about it at this stage: merely the fact that in London the conglomerates were abruptly out of fashion, with Slater and his followers running towards problems which were not yet fully apparent but which few of them would survive. Fitzwilton would get caught in the backwash.

In Ireland there was a change of government in 1973: O'Reilly's friend Jack Lynch lost power and in came a national coalition government led by Liam Cosgrave. Ignoring the advice of Ken Whitaker, the new administration embarked on a period of borrowing which was to push foreign debt up from £126 million in 1973 to over £1 billion by 1976, with disastrous consequences for the economy in later years. Interest rates rose sharply, the Irish economy slowed, and the Fitzwilton trio concentrated on diversification abroad. Nick Leonard moved to London to look for more acquisitions, and O'Reilly kept his eye out in the USA. Early in 1974 Fitzwilton took a 20 per cent stake in an American coal mining equipment group, National Mine Service. O'Reilly arranged the £2 million financing from the Mellon Bank in Pittsburgh.

Nemesis, however, was not far off. The implications of the Yom Kippur war in October 1973 and the five-fold increase in oil prices that followed it were slow to dawn in Ireland, but as 1974 opened they arrived with a vengeance. In Britain the old year ended with the country deep in a miners' strike and a three-day working week, caused by power shortages, which would bring down the Conservative government of Edward Heath at the end of February. Under the new Labour government inflation hit 25 per cent by mid-year, and as interest rates rose property prices collapsed, sparking a wave of bankruptcies among the secondary banks and plunging the British financial system into its biggest crisis since the 1930s. Share prices everywhere fell through the floor (the London stock market fell, in real terms, by 90 per cent in two years), as did asset values. Ireland's fledgling industrial economy caught the full force of the blast and dived faster than almost anywhere else. The building industry came to a stop, and the Dockrell's business with it. Even sales of Coca-Cola, one of Fitzwilton's more recession-proof operations, suffered.

Fitzwilton, however well managed, was ill prepared for the tempest that now struck it broadside on. It had borrowed heavily to pay for its acquisitions and new investment, and was faced with penal rates of interest. The company staggered through to June 1974 to declare respectable enough profits before interest and tax of £5.4 million. But the danger signs were all too visible: interest on its debt took nearly £2 million of that profit, and the main business, Goulding's, was now in deep trouble.

In the past, fertilizers had withstood recessions better than most cyclical industries, but nothing had prepared the industry for its problems this time. By the autumn of 1974, O'Reilly began to realize that the charming Sir Basil Goulding had led him deep into a bog from which he might never extricate himself. Before the merger Goulding's had invested heavily in a new plant on Dublin's East Wall, a brilliant and sophisticated piece of engineering but obsolete before it was even finished. It was far too complex a process for what, the scientists now discovered, could be done equally well by a cruder and cheaper process which anyone could use. Worse still, Goulding's was entirely dependent on a ready supply of phosphate rock, and Europe had only one source of that raw material: Morocco.

The Moroccans had watched with keen interest the success of OPEC in pushing up the price of oil, and decided they would do the same for phosphate rock. They raised the price twice in 1974 and again in January 1975—a sixfold increase in twelve months. Goulding's was now hit not only by that savage increase in its raw material but by higher oil costs and interest charges. Desperately the company tried to pass some of the cost on, doubling the selling prices, but the Irish farmers, whose income had fallen 25 per cent in the past year on the back of lower cattle prices, just stopped buying. The overall fertilizer market fell 20 per cent, and for some Goulding products dropped by 40 per cent.

The combined effect was disastrous for Fitzwilton. Unsold fertilizer piled up outside the Goulding's plants in Dublin and Cork and the division plunged into hefty losses, taking the whole of Fitzwilton with it. The shares dropped all the way to 36p, threatening O'Reilly with a crisis of a different and entirely unexpected nature. He was now paying out £130,000 a year on his *Independent* borrowings, with no immediate prospect of his deferred shares converting. And his once substantial capital gain on Fitzwilton—at the peak, his original investment of £37,500 was recording a profit of 3400 per cent—had all but evaporated.

Yet no one close to him in these years ever remembers him showing the least sign of panic, or even strain. In Heinz his friend Joe Bogdanovitch, knowing where he had been over the weekends, would watch him closely on Monday mornings: not by the flicker of an eyelid, he says, did he indicate the pressure he was under. O'Reilly himself does not recall being seriously worried, to some extent seeing it as a test of his own abilities to handle adversity, and almost clinically watching and monitoring his reactions. 'I was full of piss and vinegar,' he says now. 'You didn't know till afterwards how near the edge you'd gone.'

Although the crisis had been caused largely by events outside his control, from the beginning O'Reilly reckoned that there were certain actions he could take to improve his chances of survival—and he took them. His own private borrowings were too high and he must get them down, because even his hefty salary from Heinz, now some $350,000, was going only part of the way towards covering the interest. Early in 1974 he turned what might have been a killer blow into the stroke of luck he needed to keep him going: he unscrambled his shareholding in Tara Exploration and Mining.

Tara is an extraordinary Irish story in its own right which O'Reilly entered in the spring of 1972, six months after he had moved the family to America. An old rugby friend, Oliver Waldron, approached him with a proposition: he could, he told him, make a fortune investing in Tara, a Canadian-backed mining company which was developing a huge lead and zinc mine at Navan in County Meath, not too far from his home in Castlemartin. 'This is a wonderful discovery,' enthused Waldron, who had been made general manager of the Irish project. 'The government is going to issue the mining licences, the shares are at $16 and they'll be at $60 before you can say—well before you can say Tara Exploration and Mining.'

It was potentially a world-class mine, there was no question of that, but that was the only part of Waldron's statement that was not to prove over-optimistic. O'Reilly was intrigued by the idea of Ireland developing its own minerals, and he was fond of Waldron, the source of one of his favourite little vignettes which he often told at dinners.

Some years before, Waldron, playing in the scrum for Oxford University against Australia, emerged from a loose maul with part of his ear bitten off. 'Since then, Ollie has been referred to by everyone as "O.J.W. Waldron, eaten at Oxford".'

O'Reilly set up a new company called Fitzwilliam Resources to invest in Tara, and raised $7.2 million from a group of friends, including Jim McCarthy, Des Traynor and the architect Sam Stephenson, taking half the capital himself. It was all borrowed money, and the bankers insisted that the investors take out life policies which would last long enough to see the mine into production. They all laughed at the time, but they still took their ECGs, little dreaming of the traumas ahead.

From the start the project was a nightmare, running into every kind of problem, political, environmental and financial, imaginable. The new Irish coalition government, lobbied on every side, never did issue the licences, and the mine became bogged down in a ferocious environmental battle. The shares, instead of rocketing to $60, sank to $12. O'Reilly joined the board, and was soon at loggerheads with a management which seemed to him to take a casual approach to the whole situation. He went to his first Tara board meeting straight that morning from a similar occasion at Heinz, under the formal chairmanship of Jack Heinz and the tight control of Burt Gookin. In Toronto O'Reilly walked into an elegant board room in the Royal Trust Building—and looked around him astonished. At one end was a man wearing a Hawaiian shirt open to his waist, and beside him was another man with a cap on. The newcomer sat down beside Paddy Boland, the company secretary, and whispered: 'Who's the fellow with the cap?'

'That's Pat's uncle,' quipped Boland, referring to the chief executive, Pat Hughes. 'He's going to sing in the coffee break.'

O'Reilly subsided into his chair, muttering: 'Jesus, we've got $7 million in this company!'

Then in early January 1974 he and Jim McCarthy were in San Juan, Puerto Rico, when the ancient telex machine started to record the details of the emergency budget announced that day by the Irish Finance Minister, Richie Ryan. Measure after measure seemed specifically aimed at him. Ryan confirmed the abolition of export tax relief for all mining products, one of the features which had persuaded O'Reilly to invest in Tara in the first place; he was also introducing capital gains tax for the first time as from 1 April, raising interest rates to a crisis 18 per cent, and making interest no longer tax-deductible. Between them these four measures added up to a package which potentially spelled disaster for O'Reilly.

'Macker, we're getting off the island now,' he snapped to McCarthy. Back home he immediately rang some of his old South Africa rugby friends who now worked for Anglo-American and put a proposition to them. Through two of Anglo's associated companies, Hudson Bay and Cominco, he said, Anglo could obtain control of the best lead-zinc deposit in the world—if it was prepared to take on Noranda, the backers of the Irish group which was behind Tara mines. Anglo was more than willing, and after taking a look at the prospects for Tara, agreed to buy the O'Reilly share stake at $25 a share, a notional—and optimistic—value placed on Tara by a firm of Canadian analysts.

Within a month, the biggest takeover battle Ireland had ever known was raging as Cominco and Noranda slugged it out for Tara. Noranda won (much to its chagrin—it later sold at a loss to the Finnish company Outokumpu), and the O'Reilly consortium got $11.25 million for its stake, a profit of $4 million. It was to be his life-saver through the next three years, enabling O'Reilly to keep paying the interest on his *Independent* borrowings.

In July that year, even while Fitzwilton and the *Independent* were turning sharply down, he received a boost to his fast-growing international management reputation: *Time* magazine named him as one of 150 people under the age of forty-five who 'have, or seem capable of having in the future, significant civic or social impact'. It missed the mark with most of its choices, which included Prince Charles, Peter Jay, then economics editor of *The Times*, the British Labour MPs Roy Hattersley, Shirley Williams and Eric Varley, and the Tory MP Nicholas Scott. With hindsight it was, typically of such lists, a remarkably poor guide to the future leadership of the world, but at the time it did O'Reilly no harm at all to appear on it.

If his own personal position was more solidly based, the situation at Fitzwilton was not. The year 1975 opened ominously and gloomily, with the banks making increasingly threatening noises about the size of the debt, which was now running towards £40 million. The banks were not impressed when they learned that Nick Leonard had sold half his shareholding at a price of 38p, realizing some £175,000, and Ferguson also sold shares—a fact which, although fully revealed and perfectly legal, would later cause the company some embarrassment, and leave both men with some explaining to do (in fact, as events turned out, they sold near the bottom). Fitzwilton ended the financial year to June 1975 still in the black, despite interest payments of £3.4 million, but prospects for the following year looked disastrous. In twelve months, short-term bank advances had risen from £1.4 million to £21.7 million, and Fitzwilton, once the star of the Dublin stock market and Ireland's representative of the new order of capitalism, was rapidly becoming a basket case.

In July 1975 the banks moved in to take effective control of the company. Sir Basil Goulding was rudely shouldered aside—'the last of the Gouldings, in thin parentheses, after 121 years,' he remarked sadly—never again to provide the world with his familiar homilies in the annual report. A new chairman-elect, Michael Dargan, the former chief executive of Aer Lingus, came in as the representative of the banks. With him came two other bank appointees, Lord Killanin, an old Etonian Irishman and a member of every committee in Ireland, and Tom Hardiman, later director-general of RTE, the Irish radio and television corporation. O'Reilly resisted the move fiercely, but with the losses continuing and the debts mounting he had to give way. He did manage to insist on one key appointment, however: he must have Jim McCarthy as the chief executive, otherwise he too would quit.

From the beginning O'Reilly resented Dargan, seeing in him the representative of what he regarded as the gross betrayal of the banks. Dargan was the man widely credited with the success of Aer Lingus in the 1950s and 1960s, and it was scarcely his fault that he now found himself with a different agenda from O'Reilly at Fitzwilton. He had been appointed to get back as much of the banks' money as he could, which in his view meant dismantling everything that O'Reilly had built, whatever effect that had on the O'Reilly reputation. The decision to put him in had been taken in London by Alex Dibbs, chief executive of National Westminster Bank, the parent company of Ulster Bank. O'Reilly knew Dibbs from his days at Heinz in London, and had gone to him when he needed a bank to get his original shell company off the ground. What he didn't fully understand was that Dibbs was now under a cloud himself, with NatWest badly exposed to the property and fringe banking crisis which had forced the Bank of England to step in with a lifeboat operation. Dibbs' job was on the line for taking Britain's biggest bank to the edge of bankruptcy, and he too would be pushed aside a few years later. It was Fitzwilton's misfortune to hit trouble when the British and Irish banks were stretched to their limits, and by appointing Dargan they were at least giving themselves some assurance that the company would be run for them rather than for its shareholders—who would have to take their place behind the banks and secured creditors.

Dargan and the new directors were suspicious of Vincent Ferguson and Nick Leonard; their offices were removed from the main building and transferred across the canal into a house which was soon referred to by the newcomers as the Cuckoo's Nest. 'They said, "Look, you guys got us into this, and you can help get us out, but not in this executive headquarters", and it was very cruel really,' says a Fitzwilton director. Jim McCarthy, suddenly elevated to the position of chief executive, found himself torn between the demands of the new board and his friendship with O'Reilly. He was uncomfortable in the role, and somewhat bewildered by the bankers who demanded urgent asset sales. 'It was not Jim's finest hour,' says one of the Fitzwilton directors.

In some ways, however, it was O'Reilly's. His golden boy image had taken a savage beating in these few months, and it might have been tempting to pull out altogether and concentrate his efforts on Heinz where his career was leaping ahead. Dublin dentists and doctors, who a year ago had viewed him as their greatest hero as they saw their shares soar, now turned on him with equal venom. Fitzwilton, which had been such fun in the early days, was a place of black inspissated gloom as the accountants lined up everything ready for sale. The creative sessions that O'Reilly used to hold with Leonard and Ferguson, when they all felt they could take over the world, had now been replaced by the calculation of whether they could come through with anything at all. Could Fitzwilton survive? If it had any chance, it could only be by asset sales as smart and courageous as some of the takeovers, and O'Reilly was determined he was not going to trust that to Dargan. If assets were to be sold, he and his friends would sell them where they possibly could. Even at the worst of the market they were convinced they could work their way out of the problems, repay the debt and get the banks off their backs. Leonard in particular now became an energetic seller, seeking out buyers with all the energy he had once devoted to finding sellers. It was Dargan and the banks, however, who dictated the first and most obvious sale: Fitzwilton House, their prestige headquarters building on the canal, was sold to the National Coal Board Pension Fund for what seemed

to them the absurdly low price of £3 million. 'If we'd been given a bit
more time we could have done much better,' says a former director.
'Everyone knew it was a knock-down price.'

After that, sale followed sale: two fertilizer companies in Ulster
went, followed by Fitzwilton's 20 per cent shareholding in New Ireland Assurance, an investment which had promised big things. The
Victoria Hotel in Cork was sold, as was a property site in Burlington
Road, across the canal from the Fitzwilton headquarters. Leonard,
operating out of London, got £4 million cash for the chemist's chain
in Britain, more than double what they had paid for it. But none of
these sales, welcome as they were for the banks, touched the real
problem: the fertilizer side was still leaking money at a terrifying
rate.

At Thanksgiving in 1975 O'Reilly took Susan and the children
down to Ocean Reef in Florida for a brief holiday, and while the
family played by the pool he sat in his room and began dialling.
For two days he rang every superphosphate manager in America,
offering a deal with Goulding's. At the end of it he had made nearly
two hundred calls and persuaded nine people to see him. Of the
nine, only one, the Williams Companies of Tulsa, Oklahoma, was
seriously interested, but one was enough. His idea was to get Williams
to ship its own rock phosphate from its American mines into Ireland,
replacing the Moroccan raw material. It would be the first time an
American supplier had cut across the Moroccan monopoly in Europe,
but Williams was prepared to do it. The Americans might not make
any money out of selling fertilizer in Ireland, but they would make
a great deal of money at their mines shipping the extra material.
Williams agreed the deal and on 14 June it was signed: Williams
would pay Fitzwilton $10 million for a half-share in Goulding's, and
supply it from America at world prices. They would also guarantee
a loan of a further £2 million to the fertilizer group. The fertilizer
crisis had been solved.

'I can tell you, that was a hell of a deal,' says O'Reilly now. 'Of all
the deals I've ever done, that was perhaps the most critical.' No one
else in the company could have done it, and certainly none of the
bankers could match O'Reilly as super-salesman, cold-calling potential customers, using his Heinz reputation and all his charm and
persuasiveness to the utmost—and pulling off a life-saving deal for
Fitzwilton and its backers.

There was a cost, of course: the Fitzwilton dream would now fade for a time, the company's profitable bits disappearing into other companies, the unprofitable ones closed. Within days of the Williams deal it announced that it was closing Sir Basil's expensive plant on Dublin's East Wall, where the workers, offered full redundancy, went on strike. For years afterwards O'Reilly would have Goulding's thrown at him in annual general meetings, and no matter how he explained it away, it rankled. He could, as he did, make the point— which was true—that without Fitzwilton Goulding's would have gone into liquidation over this period, with all its jobs lost. But as far as one section of the Irish community was concerned, he had taken over one of Ireland's largest and most profitable companies and four years later he had effectively closed it down again. There was no point in explaining that the deal saved Fitzwilton and the loss of other jobs. This was something more fundamental, something older than trade unions or even socialism—it was that curious and very Irish resentment against 'one of ours' who had done well.

But the Williams deal broke the back of the Fitzwilton debt, and further sales of assets would soon finish the job. Most of the textile division went, Jefferson Smurfit bought the plastics division for another £1.1 million, the soft drinks business was sold for £3.1 million (much to O'Reilly's regret—bought by a Nigerian company, it is today probably worth £100 million), and then finally came another major stroke of good fortune. The share stake in the American group National Mine Service, bought for $9 million in early 1974, had risen sharply on the recovering stock markets. It was a successful, profitable organization, and in September 1976 O'Reilly persuaded Chessie Systems Inc. to buy Fitzwilton's stake for $18.7 million. For the Irish group it was a double coup, because it had invested when the pound was at $2.40 and sold when it was $1.40, thus enjoying a handsome currency gain. The net profit to Fitzwilton after all costs was nearly £3 million. That finally put them in the clear.

In total over this period Fitzwilton sold assets with a book value of £43 million for £42 million, totally wiping out its debts and leaving cash in the balance sheet. In addition the *Independent* was now doing well, and by the end of its 1975–76 year Fitzwilton was able to disclose that its share of the profits was £448,000, which had risen to £547,000 a year later. Its capital gain on its investment was well over £1 million, silencing any criticism that O'Reilly had used Fitzwilton to bail him out of his problems on that front.

By February 1977, even as O'Reilly was preparing for the board meeting at which Jack Heinz would confirm him as the next chief executive, the banks' role in Fitzwilton was over. O'Reilly's initial resentment at Michael Dargan had dissipated as the crisis had been resolved, but even so he felt Dargan's job was now finished, and there was no point in him staying on. Before the board meeting in Dublin that month, he sent a message to Dargan saying that he should offer his resignation that day. At the meeting itself Dargan made a speech to the effect that the company had reached a sound position, had good relations with the banks, and should now effectively become an investment company. O'Reilly was furious. Dargan and the bank directors, he charged, had done nothing to help the company in the past two years—'we did it, we sweated through it, with our good names involved in it, we told you there was value in the company, and now you're telling us that we should go back in and borrow again to become an investment company—well, not with you as shareholders.'

Dargan, with some justification, saw it differently. He had been appointed to Fitzwilton by the banks when it was in serious trouble. The company was now solvent again, and from his point of view it was irrelevant who, inside the company, had done most of the selling— what mattered was the fact that it had been done. He wasn't to blame for the problems the company had got itself in to, but did reckon he deserved some credit for getting it out. As tempers rose, he suggested that he and the vice-chairman, O'Reilly, should step outside for a discussion. They went into Sir Basil's old room next door.

'It seems quite clear there's no future for me at this company,' said Dargan.

'That's an understatement, Michael,' said O'Reilly, who had nothing against Dargan personally but could not help associating him with all that he hated about the way the banks had behaved. 'It was our company, we started it, we've got it back. We started with £100,000 and now we've got £12 million of shareholders' funds and cash in the bank—that's pretty decent by anyone's standards.' There was, he went on, no place for Dargan or the other bank-appointed directors. 'There's no point in us saying we welcome you when we don't, and have fought for two years to get the banks off our backs.'

Dargan didn't argue and resigned with good enough grace that day, although Killanin stayed on. For several years Fitzwilton would have no formal chairman—O'Reilly ran it as deputy chairman—and it barely needed one. In December 1976 the magazine *Irish Business* published an article entitled: 'Fitzwilton—carry on stripping', which reflected the thinking in the financial community at the time. Written by the editor, John O'Neill, it concluded that, given the company's reduced status, 'the future for Fitzwilton makes little sense'. It should be liquidated and the money passed back to shareholders. That same thought was running through O'Reilly's mind. His own 1,323,000 shares, which had cost him £30,000, were still worth £400,000 with the shares at 30p, and the company had become essentially an investment entity, its sole remaining businesses being 50 per cent of Goulding's, which was barely breaking even, the Dockrell's business, which was still losing money, a 24 per cent stake in the *Independent*, which was highly profitable—and where his full conversion had now come through, two years behind schedule—and some minor textile interests. But he was against liquidation for various reasons: he had put a great deal of pain and effort into creating Fitzwilton and at the end of the day had a profitable and cash-rich company, a base from which he could start again. Secondly, his reputation for infallibility had taken a savage beating and he intended to restore it. He had no plans yet, but Ireland was expanding again and Fitzwilton could play a profitable part in it.

There was one bit of unfinished Fitzwilton business which would end sadly and controversially, and leave a festering sore through much of the 1980s. Jim McCarthy's role as managing director had now essentially come down to running the Dockrell's building business, which included his own century-old family decorating business. He had changed the name to McCarthy Dockrell, and although it was one of the biggest timber merchants and builder's providers in Ireland it was still losing money. It too was now for sale, and McCarthy himself wanted to buy it. He reckoned he could put the money together with the help of the management, the Irish institutions and some British investors.

O'Reilly thought it was a bad idea, not from Fitzwilton's viewpoint but from that of his oldest friend. He relied heavily on McCarthy, for his ability to weigh up a person's character in his shrewd, visceral Cork manner, which O'Reilly had come to trust greatly over the years. McCarthy had a deeply engrained work ethic, but with the economy in trouble, the timing for a leveraged management buy-out (the term was not used then) did not seem propitious.

But McCarthy was determined to go ahead, and the price agreed was £5.7 million, including some debts. The announcement, however, was widely misinterpreted in Ireland where every event at Fitzwilton was examined under a microscope. Why was O'Reilly agreeing to sell Dockrell's to his best friend? 'Eyebrows have quite naturally been raised at the prospect of the chief executive of a major public company bidding for a major division of the same company,' said *Business and Finance*. 'And some shareholders . . . are bound to feel that Jim McCarthy should have resigned from Fitzwilton before making the offer.'

On 30 June 1977, O'Reilly was in Dublin to chair one of the least comfortable public meetings of his life. Its purpose was to agree the sale of Dockrell's to McCarthy, but it soon turned into an occasion for shareholders to let loose their ire over the events of the past two years, when they had seen the brightest story of Irish capitalism turn into a litany of forced asset sales, factory closures, huge redundancies and near-financial ruin. O'Reilly needed every bit of his quick-wittedness and his mastery of facts and figures to cope, but spent most of the meeting in retreat. 'Despite Mr O'Reilly's best efforts,' reported the *Irish Times* the next day, 'shareholders were not happy and Mr O'Reilly had to face many arguments.' One woman demanded to know, rather presciently, how Jim McCarthy's new company was going to make Dockrell's work when Fitzwilton had failed. Momentarily nonplussed O'Reilly finally responded that 'a small independent operator' stood a much better chance than a conglomerate. But he was worried for the state of the building industry and therefore for his old friend.

Dockrell's was to cost Jim McCarthy dear. He had invested most of his family money in it, and borrowed the rest. If the Irish building industry had come out of its doldrums, as he expected, he would have made it, but his luck was rotten. He was hit by two fires in his premises, and although he was insured the disruption was expensive. By 1981, with receivership threatened, Dockrell's was unable to service its borrowing and defaulted on various loans due to Fitzwilton, which in the end had to step back in with a loan of £500,000, prompting further accusations and acrimony at the annual meetings.

McCarthy, although he lost Dockrell's and most of his money, came through it all with his optimism intact and his spirits, after an initial low point, irrepressibly high. Now nearing seventy, he remains as close to O'Reilly as any man in the world, and O'Reilly still relies, as he always has, on his wisdom and insight. He is still on the Fitzwilton board, still playing golf off a minuscule handicap—and still wishing he had his family business back.

16

Weight Watchers

IN 1978, A YEAR BEFORE HE FORMALLY TOOK OVER FROM BURT GOOKIN, O'Reilly made the biggest takeover yet in the history of Heinz, an acquisition which was to change the shape and direction of the company over the next decade. It began ordinarily enough when he met Joe Flannery, the head of a group called Foodways National, which was at the time offering itself for sale. It was a medium-sized public company, specializing in low-calorie frozen dinners and 'portion-controlled' entrees. 'Flannery told me what a great guy he was, and would I like to visit him at his place in New Jersey,' O'Reilly recalled later. He flew in and met Flannery in his own very Irish restaurant, staffed with waiters from Dublin who greeted O'Reilly as the legend he was to them. Over dinner, Flannery disclosed that he had received an offer from Beatrice Foods for his company, and wondered if Heinz would be interested in topping it. After O'Reilly had heard what the price was, he was very interested. It seemed a good fit with the frozen food business of Ore-Ida, which O'Reilly was keen to expand, and also a possible entry into a market that Heinz had identified as one of the best growth areas of the food business: nutritional, low-calorie foods for a nation which was demographically ageing and therefore becoming increasingly diet-conscious.

They agreed to meet again, and over the next few months the Heinz people carried out their usual detailed investigation and assessment, reckoning it was indeed a good fit. Then they encountered a problem: Foodways manufactured under licence a range of foods under the Weight Watchers brand label, and closer inspection suggested that Weight Watchers would have to approve any transfer of the licence. Foodways argued that they were entirely free agents and could transfer the licence at will, but Weight Watchers had other thoughts, insisting that they had the right to veto anyone they didn't like from marketing foods under their name.

It was a routine, technical hitch, the type of problem that inevitably arises in any takeover and which is usually sorted out by the lawyers in the end. Flannery suggested they should talk directly to the head of Weight Watchers and O'Reilly instantly agreed, partly to short-circuit weeks of legal wrangling, but also because he was increasingly intrigued by the Weight Watchers business and wanted to have a closer look at it and the man who ran it. 'His name is Al Lippert and you gotta meet him and his wife,' said Flannery, who went on to indicate his personal dislike—but respect—for both of them. A meeting was duly arranged in Palm Beach between O'Reilly, Flannery of Foodways, and Lippert of Weight Watchers International.

O'Reilly and Flannery arrived early in the restaurant, and were sitting over a drink when Lippert walked in. A slight, nervous man, he noticed that they were both in open-neck shirts, so he dodged behind a pillar and whipped his tie off before joining them. It was to be a seminal dinner, one of the most important in the career of all three men. Lippert, half the size of O'Reilly, was instantly entranced by him. 'It was, I would say, love at first sight, or fascination at first sight,' he would say later. 'I was so impressed with his vitality and his knowledge and his personality that basically we spent two hours just swopping stories, telling each other jokes and talking about incidents which had occurred in our lives.'

The reaction was mutual. 'By the end of the meal I am very fond of Al and suddenly I form a dislike of Flannery who has planted all this stuff in my mind,' said O'Reilly later. They talked about the Weight Watchers programme and its future, until Flannery, who had taken almost no part in this conversation, finally butted in.

'Well, do I have your approval to sell or don't I?' Flannery demanded of Lippert.

'Joe, you had my approval a long time ago because I am happy to be rid of you,' Lippert replied. Flannery was not one of his favourites either.

O'Reilly had gone to the meeting armed with every fact and analysis on Weight Watchers that his staff could muster, but in the past two hours he had learnt a great deal more. Lippert, he knew, had been to see almost every food company in America trying to find the right buyer for an enterprise he obviously firmly believed in, but needed to sell. Weight Watchers, however, was not a food company as such: its core business was a classroom system, aimed mostly at women between twenty-five and fifty-five who wanted to lose weight. As such it didn't fit naturally into any of the big food companies, and O'Reilly had only become interested because he wanted to manufacture the food it encouraged its millions of followers to eat in its classroom sessions. Weight Watchers' revenues were now $50 million, but in taking it that far Lippert had had two heart attacks and knew if he continued he would have another. In 1976 he had almost signed a deal with Pillsbury, but it had fallen through at the last moment, and there had been on and off discussions with various others since then. He was increasingly desperate to sell, and although there were willing buyers none of them entirely suited him. 'They're interested in us as just another profit centre, but they don't really understand what we're about,' he told O'Reilly. 'They cannot conceive and understand that we are an educational, ethical, highly honest company. We are out to re-educate people's eating habits and teach them to eat properly. There are no gimmicks, no secrets, no pills—it's just an honest effort to teach people what we ourselves have learnt.' His wife, he added, had lost 50 lb, and he had lost 53, and they knew their system worked. 'And none of these companies understand that.'

O'Reilly was intrigued. As the evening wore on, he became convinced that Weight Watchers could be just the growth business he was looking for—an operation which was connected to food, yet was something more, a retailing business with a largely untapped growth potential not just in the USA but worldwide. He knew enough about its history and position in the market to understand something of what Lippert was trying to tell him. Its philosophy and style of operation were very far removed from those of most food companies—Heinz included—but it could be made to work. And if it did, it could change the shape of the company.

Its origins were anything but secret: its creator, a forty-year-old housewife from Queens, New York, had written a book about it eight years earlier, and it had become a best-seller. Jean Nidetch was the wife of a bus driver, an apparently ordinary, suburban woman who considered herself, like many women of her age and background, too fat. She had tried dieting, but like many before and after her, she found it hard to stick to it. Finally she came upon the diet designed and recommended by the New York City Department of Health Obesity Clinic. This diet, although she did not know it at the time, was an inspired one, working on the basis that deprivation never worked and crash diets were hopeless. You had to eat to lose weight, but it was what you ate that mattered—a commonplace theory today but quite startling in the early 1960s. It would not have helped Nidetch, however, if she had not accidentally added the key element which within a decade would make it one of the most popular diets in the world. When she found she couldn't make it work on her own she roped in her friends and they dieted together, encouraging and supporting each other at their weekly meetings. Nidetch lost 72 lb, and as word went around the neighbourhood, people poured in to join her group. They found Nidetch almost evangelical in her enthusiasm for the diet and her self-help support sessions, and soon she had to set up other groups, holding her weekly meetings in people's houses.

By the end of 1962 her circle had widened to include the Long Island neighbourhood in which Al Lippert and his wife Felice lived. They too were an ordinary suburban couple, Lippert the merchandise manager for a chain of ladies' ready-to-wear stores, Felice an overweight former nutrition teacher who now went to too many coffee mornings. They were both keen participators in whatever the latest fad was: Friday night bridge parties, dance lessons and so on. When one of the neighbours said she had a friend who helped people lose weight, they invited her along as 'just another activity'.

The friend turned out to be a highly charismatic and pencil-thin Jean Nidetch who told the Lipperts and their friends the secret of losing weight. By now she was charging a modest fee for her classes, but spending more than she earned on travel and on the gold pins she insisted on giving everyone who lost 10 lb. The Lipperts were convinced enough to try it, without any great expectations, and at the end of the week found they had each lost 7 lb. They invited her back again—and again, for four months, by the end of which Al had lost 40 lb and Felice 50.

It was Lippert who suggested to her that she make a proper business out of it. 'I told her what to do—simple things like finding a place to meet and getting a table and chairs and getting it set up and getting some materials printed—and she would come back week after week saying she could not accomplish any of them,' says Lippert.

Finally Nidetch asked Lippert to run it for her, saying she would work for him if he would do all the organization. Instead he proposed setting up a partnership between four people: Nidetch and her husband Marty, and Al and Felice Lippert. Al would keep his job but would direct the business, Jean would do exactly what she had always done, Marty was to handle all the mechanical end of setting up the meetings and getting his wife to and from them, and Felice would handle the nutritional aspects—working out the diets, the foods and so on. Al then set out to find premises in the neighbourhood where Nidetch had started. He recalls:

> I found an empty place on the first floor above a movie house, and I rented it with funds from my own pocket, which was $75. I then got a man to paint and refurbish the place for another $10. So basically at a cost of $85 Weight Watchers was born. Now the name was a name we selected because I believe that names should tell their purpose, and we kicked around a lot of names. Weight Watchers was euphonious and it also told who we were.

In May 1963, they had a formal opening, at which Lippert told his own neighbourhood group that, instead of going to his house, they must go to the new centre, close to where Jean and Marty lived. 'And they came and we conducted the same procedure in this rented space. Jean brought a scale and we weighed everybody, and proceeded to lecture them on how to select foods and so on.' Lippert charged them $2 a head, basically because that was what the movie theatre below charged, 'and I decided our meeting was far more entertaining and far more beneficial'. He added a registration charge of another $2 to cover the cost of the forms and paperwork, and at the end of the first meeting he asked everyone to bring a friend the next week. There were twenty-two people at that first meeting and at the second there were sixty-six, so Lippert broke the group into two. 'But each week as we met it kept growing, as my friends told their friends who told other friends.' Lippert rented a second building near his own home on Long Island, and soon was opening up others. He picked out some of the successful slimmers from Jean's classes and had her train them up as new instructors. Soon fat people were pouring in from New Jersey and Connecticut to attend the classes,

persuading Lippert to think about selling franchises. This required
further training.

> I selected people who had all the qualifications, and we taught
> them what to do based on the premise that they first lose weight
> and arrive at what we had established as a 'goal weight', which
> was set by the Obesity Clinic and by many insurance companies.
> When they reached the weight and could communicate, I gave
> them the right to buy a territory which later became a franchise,
> and with the sale of the first franchise, which I gave away for
> nothing to one of my sisters-in-law, we established in Rhode
> Island.

In New York, Weight Watchers soon had a cadre of a hundred
leaders running meetings in every borough every day of the week.
Most of them were women, volunteers who did it for nothing. 'There
was a very evangelical spirit,' one of the leaders recalled. 'We didn't
get paid, we didn't get mileage. Leaders would get offended thinking
it was a business. Over the next four years Lippert sold 102 franchises
over the whole of the USA, an incredibly rapid expansion which was
only made possible through franchises. His system was a clever one:
he charged a nominal amount for each territory, but took a 10 per
cent royalty on the gross—the equivalent, as the Wall Street analysts
would later remark, of 'giving away the razor and charging for the
blades'. The franchisees became a breed of their own, as fanatical
and emotional about the system as Lippert was. Many of them were
to become millionaires in their own right.

He also did something which he would later classify as his greatest
'stroke of genius': he registered the Weight Watchers trademark
around the world. 'I actually took the first $50,000 that we earned
and spent it on legal fees to register it in over twenty countries.'

By 1967, four years after the launch, Lippert finally quit his regular
job. He was exhausted. 'Every two weeks I collapsed, because we used
to meet in the evenings after I left my regular work. First the meetings
lasted until nine or ten, but by the second or third year they were
running until 4 a.m.' He was getting home in time to sleep for an
hour before setting off again. Yet he didn't want to give up his regular
job. 'I felt I had the potential to advance to the presidency of this
firm, so I was reluctant to give it up.'

Eventually he had to, and as he concentrated full-time on Weight

Watchers the business really took off. They went into the food business, licensing companies such as Foodways to make slimming foods under their trademark to strict licensing conditions. They went into the publishing business: 'The first cookbook we ever published I made a deal with the publisher to give me $1 per book sold, and we sold 1.5 million copies.' They went into the appliance business, the restaurant business, the spa business and many others. The classroom system, however, remained the core of the company from which everything else emanated.

In 1968 Lippert took the company public and the stock, issued in the morning at $11.25, closed that night at $32, capitalizing the group at $20m (it was to go as high as $60 before being split). By the 1970s Weight Watchers had its own highly qualified nutritionists, dieticians, physicians, psychologists, chefs and home economists, all the time improving on the original diet and classroom system and adding new foods: its own wine, peanut butter, sugar and chocolate, for instance. The company was now ordering thousands of weighing scales a year.

The real star of the business, however, remained Jean Nidetch, still the best advertisement the company had, as well as the epitome of its soul. In 1973 the company celebrated its tenth anniversary with a party at Madison Square Garden, with Bob Hope and Sammy Davis Jr, both Nidetch fans. Nidetch presented gold pins to members who had lost 100 lb, and when she began to speak they wouldn't let her off the stage.

The Lipperts remained out of sight in Long Island but they were far from inactive, developing sophisticated control systems for the franchisees, keeping tight quality control on the food companies licensed to produce their food, opening up new markets overseas and much else. In 1973, Al hired from General Mills Kent Kreh, a professional marketing man, to beef up the ancillary food businesses, including the licensees. Lippert wanted to develop even more businesses around the classroom system, offering foods, magazines, cookbooks, camps for overweight children, a spa, restaurants and everything else his fertile mind could think of. They didn't all work, but if one failed there were always others coming up behind.

And yet it was going far too slowly for Lippert, by now seriously worried about his health.

> I was doing it at a snail's pace. I could not help it—I did it as
> fast as I could. I was in all these new areas but in a small way,

and I needed the dynamic marketing ability, and tremendous research ability and organization, of a big company, the ability to accomplish in one fell swoop what was going to take me a long time. But after three heart attacks I was having to take it a little easier. Although I had built an organization, like most entrepreneurs the burden of progress and growth fell on my shoulders. I was working very many hours, and Felice was working many hours developing her recipes and her cookbooks. And I'd taken the business about as far as I could.

Most of this story he told to O'Reilly that evening in Palm Beach, and the Irishman, already interested, was having trouble containing his excitement. 'It struck me suddenly the right way to do this was to buy Al first and Flannery second,' he said later,

even though I didn't want to manipulate the price, because I could see there were certain tax advantages. I could change the relationship and redefine some of the terms and conditions between Weight Watchers International and its franchisees— in this case Flannery's company—so that what would be a non-deductible expense became a deductible expense.

That, however, meant that the Weight Watchers deal would have to be done first, and he already had a deal with Flannery. He would have to move fast.

As they were leaving the restaurant, he turned to Lippert and told him he would like to continue their discussions. 'Al, I think I would like to buy the Weight Watchers company as well as Foodways,' he said. Lippert for his part was more than pleased. 'Tony, if you're really serious, call me and we'll take it a step further.'

He was very serious. He called Lippert early the next day. 'Al, I would like to do a deal but I don't want any lawyers, any bankers, any accountants involved. I'll meet you for lunch at a private room in the Plaza in New York, and at the end of it we will either do a deal or we won't.'

A few days later he and Lippert met, and with just the waiters around agreed they could do a deal. Back in Pittsburgh, O'Reilly now had a team preparing him a detailed report on the whole business, but when he met Lippert again, this time at Lippert's home, there were again just the two of them. The more he got to know Lippert, the more he realized he wanted him too, not just to run Weight Watchers but on the main board of Heinz where his innovative flair would be invaluable. He had also become fond of Felice, who he decided was as important as her husband. In the early summer of 1978 the Lipperts flew to Ireland and stayed at Castlemartin, where the O'Reillys had laid on one of their more entertaining weekends. O'Reilly had also brought along Paul Corrdry, then running Ore-Ida, and Ned Churchill, head of corporate planning, and their wives, to put the finishing touches to the deal. 'Paul and I were the picadors and Tony was the matador,' says Churchill.

> Paul and I were intended to soften Al up. It was not actually assigned as such but we kind of sensed that was why we were there, to soften up Al with humour and with comments about appropriate estate planning and just stuff that would be motivating him to sell his company, and then Tony would do his role of clicking Al on the whole thing. And I don't know who captured who on the whole thing frankly. I think Al did a lot of capturing of Tony.

That, he adds, was often the way deals at Heinz got done. 'Anyway, we had a delightful time,' says Churchill,

> with parties until the dawn and all that stuff. And of course Al and Felice, representatives of Weight Watchers, didn't drink anything but they did not eat like weight-watchers that weekend. And after that every time I saw Al he would mention that trip as being one of the keystones of our lives. We had a great time and the deal happened, and it was a very important one for Heinz.

Their fourth meeting was back in Pittsburgh, again just the two of them—no lawyers, accountants or even assistants. Lippert had a clear idea of the price he wanted, and O'Reilly, after a certain amount of haggling, agreed on $24 a share, valuing Weight Watchers at $72 million (it had $12 million of cash in it, so the net cost was $60 million). He wanted Lippert to sign a five-year contract as CEO of Weight Watchers, and Lippert was happy to do it. He would also join the main Heinz board, a recognition of how important Weight Watchers was going to be in the group. In the first week of August, after just four meetings between the two of them, Al Lippert and Tony O'Reilly shook hands. Then they called in the lawyers and accountants.

'We took care of all the details with that handshake,' says Lippert. 'And we made provision for everything, and it was all done smoothly and properly. And Tony's memory is such that we were able to cover everything when the lawyers came in: how to effect the changeover, how to expand, and provision for the territories and the franchises, and the foods and all the other businesses. And I thought he was brilliant.'

In fact it did not go as smoothly as Lippert remembers. Well before the deal was done O'Reilly had fallen out with Flannery, whom he had been forced to stall while the Weight Watchers deal was signed and sealed. Then Heinz bought Foodways for the originally agreed price of $50 million (less $11 million of cash in the company) and within a year had added Camargo Foods, bought from Bristol Myers, which held the Weight Watchers licence to manufacture and sell dry grocery products, for another $30 million. O'Reilly rationalized and concentrated the Weight Watchers business, pulling out of many of the peripheral projects that Lippert had added with such gusto. Diet drinks went, on the basis that Coca-Cola and Pepsi were moving into the same market and would slaughter Heinz. The restaurants, spa and summer camps went too, perceived as distractions from the main areas of expansion which were the foods. The Foodways business was merged into Ore-Ida, creating one of the biggest frozen food businesses in America, while the dry snacks, condiments and other products acquired with Camargo went into Heinz USA.

Then the US economy went into the recession of the late Carter years and O'Reilly and Heinz discovered an important point about Weight Watchers which they had missed: it was highly susceptible to bad times in the economy. In his rush for growth Lippert had never noticed it because he had never experienced it, but in 1979 and 1980 O'Reilly was bitterly disappointed with the slow progress. He had no doubts about the medium and longer-term potential, but he could have done with the growth he had projected in these years. What he had failed to notice, however, was a more serious problem which would take another few years to resolve. Heinz had never worked with a franchise system before, and had only half understood how the Weight Watcher class system worked. 'We were used to working with the authoritarian structures of business that we own and control directly ourselves,' said O'Reilly later. 'And we were not used to the retailing business, because selling classroom attendances is retailing. So we had to learn those skills.' Over the 1980s Heinz would become openly a retailer, recruiting people from retail businesses such as Burger King or Pizza Hut or the chain stores to run its Weight Watcher classes. Weight Watchers had 27 million class attendances the year they bought the company, and 24 million three years later. Yet he had seen enough to become even more convinced that he had the big winner he needed to power Heinz through the 1980s. What Ore-Ida, Star-Kist and the revival of Heinz USA had done for the 1970s, so Weight Watchers would do for the next decade.

O'Reilly had other problems to deal with in that first year of Weight Watchers which intruded abruptly into what otherwise should have been the celebratory event of taking over formally as chief executive—which he was due to do in July 1979. In April, shortly before the close of the 1979 fiscal year, Heinz was suddenly embroiled in an accounting scandal which raged for months, caused a deep division inside the company, cast a dark cloud over the final months of Burt Gookin's stewardship, and even caused the annual shareholders' meeting to be cancelled. Its origins went back some way, to a seven-year legal battle over what Heinz alleged were predatory pricing tactics adopted by Campbell's to kill the launch of its Great American Soups in 1972. Gookin and Don Wiley, the general counsel, decided to sue Campbell's for $300 million, and in the course of the ensuing action the Campbell's lawyers trawled back over the records of everything Heinz had ever done. Word kept coming back of former wives of Heinz executives being interviewed as potential witnesses, employees who had been fired being questioned, and tax and bonus schemes being investigated. Gookin and O'Reilly gawked at some of the material they read on the sex lives of their own staff as documents came in during the legal discovery process.

Then, in the spring of 1979, a former Heinz executive told the Campbell's lawyers that Heinz companies 'smoothed' their profits from year to year, hiding some of the bumper profits in a good year, bringing them back in a bad year—without, he said, ever telling the 'people at the top'. It was, he said, a widespread process among the main operating arms of the group, and had been going on for years. This piece of information landed like a bombshell at Heinz World Headquarters, where Gookin had no choice but to order an investigation by the Audit Committee. Heinz had always prided itself on its tight financial controls and ethical accounting standards, and the result of the initial investigation seemed to support the information given to the Campbell's lawyers. It caused pandemonium inside the group. 'There was a dramatic rift within the company, with the audit committee, mostly outside directors, insisting the matter should be taken to the SEC, and the internal directors who were totally opposed to that,' recalls a Heinz director. The audit committee won, and so the matter was referred formally to the Securities and Exchange Commission, guardian of American financial integrity, in Washington—which was singularly unimpressed by it all. But the matter was now public, with a considerable amount of highly damaging publicity for Heinz. The SEC did pose one probing question: did Heinz have an incentive compensation scheme for the main subsidiary companies, based on hitting profit targets? Heinz did—which was where the problem lay. 'These guys are sticking it to you,' remarked one of the SEC men laconically—he had clearly seen it all before.

He proved to be right. What the Heinz accountants now unearthed was this: several of the operating companies had for years been running systems whereby if, for instance, they were set a goal of $10 million and were going to make $12 million, they would conceal the extra $2 million from the accounts they sent up to head office. They would still get their bonus on the $10 million, and would also find it considerably easier to hit the following year's target—exactly the reverse of the intended effect of the scheme. Not only would the following year's goal be lower than it might otherwise have been, but they could write back the extra $2 million. It was simple to do—sales could be brought forward or postponed between fiscal years, as could payments to suppliers, depending on how they wanted to manipulate the profit figures.

As panic spread through the organization, a full-scale investigation was set up under a tough lawyer at Cravath, Swaine & Moore, which in turn brought in the independent accountants, Arthur Young & Co. The board urgently wanted answers to some key questions: did Gookin, an expert accountant, know about it? Was Frank Bretholle, the chief financial officer who was renowned for knowing where every dollar in the business was kept, involved? By a fortunate coincidence of reporting lines O'Reilly was clean of any suspicion: the financial officers of the various companies reported direct to Bretholle, and just the operating officers to O'Reilly; O'Reilly was outside the direct relevant loop on the organization chart.

By the time Gookin left in July, the group was in a mess. Says a director:

> 'You had the internal directors who were totally opposed to what the outside directors on the audit committee had done, which was go to the SEC, and you had senior officers in all the affiliated companies who had been doing this debit and credit caper over a number of years, who suddenly found they were faced with fraud charges, criminal charges and the possibility that they might go to jail.'

In July, once he had moved into Gookin's office, O'Reilly took over full control of the situation—a task which would not rank high in the official history of Heinz achievements, but which O'Reilly regards with some satisfaction. 'I think if ever I did anything with the Heinz Company that was remarkable in terms of leadership, it was over the next three months,' he said later.

The first action he took was to go for the man regarded as the best in the country for dealing with SEC problems: Arthur Liman of the big New York firm of Paul, Weiss, Rifkind, Wharton & Garrison. Late in September he took Wiley to New York and they checked in to the Pierre Hotel, where Liman came to see them. Wiley talked uninterrupted for an hour, starting with the predatory pricing, the discovery by Campbell's, the resulting investigation by Heinz, the calling in of the SEC, the behaviour of the audit committee which O'Reilly was still fuming over, the splitting of the board and the more detailed investigation by Cravath Swaine.

Liman's expression registered nothing during this long discourse and he never spoke a word, not even to ask a question. When Wiley finally came to a stop, O'Reilly turned to the lawyer.

'Well, there you are, Mr Liman. What do you think?'

'Absolute bullshit,' said Liman abruptly. 'You haven't got a problem. Who do you want me to talk to?'

O'Reilly, taken aback, remarked that he was reassured by this show of confidence 'but we have been led to believe that half our executives are going to be led away in chains. Indeed, in June and July the debate we were having internally was whether we would pay any bonuses at all to 240 executives around the world. And now you tell me it's bullshit.'

'They must be laughing their heads off at you at the SEC,' said Liman.

'Why?'

'Because this is a common-or-garden example of mild petty juggling, in which guys are trying to protect themselves year to year so they're not asked to perform extreme profit contortions in order to achieve their goals, and can pay for their mortgages,' replied Liman. 'I work for a lot of other guys who have very nearly been in chains, and I tell you, compared to what they faced this is not a problem. This is nothing.'

O'Reilly asked him if he would be prepared to say all this to the board, and Liman readily agreed: 'I'd be delighted.'

A few days later the whole Heinz board assembled in Pittsburgh for a meeting before flying up *en masse* to Boise in Idaho for the opening of a new Ore-Ida facility. Liman came in from New York as arranged and O'Reilly asked the internal directors to excuse themselves from the meeting while Liman addressed the rest of the board. Liman would become something of a legend later in the 1980s as he acted for most of the big players in the takeover boom, but even at this stage his reputation was known to most of the Heinz board. Before the meeting, even the outside directors were split between those who felt that the company had been betrayed by taking the issue to the SEC and therefore public, and those who felt that the audit committee had behaved properly, but now Liman, in his best trial lawyer manner, told them to relax. 'Liman gave them such assurances they were like schoolboys when the rest of us came back in to the room,' says one director.

The entire board flew out to Boise in a celebratory mood, a reunited family trying to heal the wounds of the past six months. All along O'Reilly had insisted that nothing had been done wrong, and he had shown that a month before by promoting Dick Patton, one of the people with a cloud hanging over him, to the board against strong opposition. 'How dare you do that!' one of the audit committee challenged him. 'Isn't he under suspicion?'

'I can tell you now he's innocent,' O'Reilly heatedly replied. 'And here's the reason. Dick Patton is a good leader but not a finance man. There's no way he has dreamed any of this up.' Now he was vindicated

Annual general meetings in two countries: Pittsburgh, top, with Jack Heinz II, grandson of the founder, Burt Gookin, chief executive, and, on O'Reilly's left, Don Wiley, the corporate lawyer, and below, Dublin, with J R McCluskey (company secretary), Nick Leonard, Jim McCarthy and (extreme right) Lord Killanin.

In 1979, O'Reilly, after six years as president, succeeded Gookin to become the youngest chief executive of a major American company. Ten years later when Jack Heinz (above) died, he became the first non-Heinz chairman.

Key men in O'Reilly's life in Ireland: Nicholas Leonard (left) and Vincent Ferguson (centre) were his partners at the start of Fitzwilton. The takeover of Sir Basil (right) Goulding's family company almost wiped them out.

Below, Jack Lynch, the Irish Minister of Finance who became Taoiseach wanted O'Reilly to join his government. Kevin McGoran (centre), was a schoolboy friend of O'Reilly and now runs Fitzwilton. Liam Healy (right), chief executive of the Independent Newspaper Group, now heads a group rapidly developing into an international media empire.

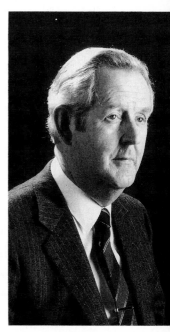

Castlemartin, on the banks of the Liffey, O'Reilly's classic Georgian house in County Kildare. The Rolling Stones occupied it before him.

Below, the entrance hall has seen many parties that run on past dawn. The piano was often played by Susan.

The O'Reilly children play their own brand of football in the garden at Castlemartin, and below, the whole family at Castlemartin where they went every August.

Different places, different faces. O'Reilly averages several dozen speeches a year in all parts of the world. Far right, relaxing in the Kildare countryside.

Henry Kissinger calls him a "renaissance man". Here they take the evening air at Castlemartin.

The Ireland Fund, begun in Pittsburgh with the Rooney family, is now international. O'Reilly at an Ireland Fund of Great Britain with the Irish novelist Josephine Hart (Mrs Maurice Saatchi), Lord Longford and the television personality, Terry Wogan.

Family business in Australia: the takeover of Queensland Provincial Newspapers made O'Reilly a profit of over A$120 million, owned by a family trust. From the left, Tony Junior, Cameron, Tony, Justine and Gavin.

At O'Reilly's 50th birthday party: Tony, Cameron and Gavin. Below, oldest friend: Jim McCarthy, captain of the Irish rugby team in 1955 when O'Reilly had his first game. They talk most days of their lives.

Marriage to Chryss Goulandris in 1991 changed O'Reilly's life. Above, on her wedding day in the Bahamas with her brother Peter. Below at Leopardstown Racecourse in Ireland in July, 1991 after their horse won.

Top right, watching the local rugby talent in County Cork and below, in Sydney on the day O'Reilly gave his London team instructions to dawn-raid Newspaper Publishing.

Founders of Weightwatchers, Al and Felice Lippert and below, Olive Deasy, who became O'Reilly's secretary in Cork in 1961, moved with him to Dublin, London and finally Pittsburgh.

Key men at Heinz: Top left, Joe Bogdanovich, simply known as Joe B, has been one of O'Reilly's biggest supporters of Heinz since he arrived. Three contenders to take over from him: David W Sculley, William R Johnson and William C Springer.

O'Reilly as seen by the artist Derek Hill.

and the whole board responded. After the opening ceremony in Boise there was a big party with O'Reilly the hero of the hour. 'The company was pulled together in that October board meeting of 1979, and it was an absolutely decisive moment in leadership within the corporation,' says one director.

> And in a way it was because O'Reilly didn't blink, because he said, 'It will be all right', without being sure himself that it was going to be all right, and because when the vital moment came he got the right man. And the company sort of said, this guy O'Reilly has good judgement, he didn't panic, he got the right man for us, the right man assured the board, the board is now assured, and they were 200 per cent behind O'Reilly. There were no scapegoats. There was a beating up of the audit committee, there were very modest penalties imposed on certain officers, certain guys took early retirement in a dignified way, and a new number two finance man was brought in.

The investigation had revealed a number of gaps in the system which theoretically could have been exploited, had that been the intention (it never was). By juggling the credits for glass returns, vendor payments and credits, the treatment of sales and the transferral of income between separate years there was, O'Reilly noted with a shudder, the capacity for someone to have siphoned off $10 million a year into a Swiss bank account without it being immediately noticed. Now the gaps were closed as firmly as they ever could be.

Despite the turmoil and accounting problems, the company actually had a good story to tell that year: sales for 1979 reached $2.5 billion, an increase of 14.4 per cent on the year—the sixteenth consecutive year of sales growth, which had now doubled since O'Reilly became president in 1973. Profits had also doubled over the same period, growing at an average 14.6 per cent for the past ten years and 13.4 per cent for the past five.

Burt Gookin was able to retire fully vindicated and given full honours. Frank Bretholle, the chief financial officer, remained under a cloud, not because he had participated in the account juggling exercise, but because this was his domain. But O'Reilly defused that problem too. The new finance man was the German-born Karl von der Heyden, and although O'Reilly was responsible for selecting him, it was the board which had insisted on bringing him in with the tacit understanding that he would replace Bretholle after a year when the existing chief financial officer reached retirement age in July 1980.

Von der Heyden arrived in November 1979 just at the right time in terms of the price at which his share options were issued, and immediately began to make his presence felt. O'Reilly had huge respect for Bretholle, whom he trusted completely, and hadn't yet got the measure of the new man. 'Karl was a very intelligent, very classy guy,' says a Heinz director. 'He was very gentlemanly, but he was slightly superior in the way he treated Frank Bretholle.

He went to Boise with O'Reilly, who took him aside to break the news that he wanted him to wait another year before taking over from Bretholle. Von der Heyden was shocked, but could see O'Reilly's plan. The board of Heinz had to accept his decision and join in the public exculpation of Frank Bretholle, who had served the company so well for so many years. 'It was a real test for Karl, who had taken the job in anticipation of becoming, pretty shortly, the chief financial officer. But to his eternal credit, he accepted it with grace and dignity,' says O'Reilly. 'And he performed as a real team man.' Von der Heyden got the job the following year, and when he left Heinz at the end of the 1980s to join RJR Nabisco (where he later became joint CEO) his shares were worth $20 million. O'Reilly by then had come to regard Von der Heyden as one of the finest financial officers he had ever come across.

On 10 September, 1980, at Heinz World Headquarters in Pittsburgh, Henry J. Heinz II rose to his feet, as he had done for nearly forty years, to address the company's annual meeting. He wanted, he said, to introduce the new chief executive officer, Tony O'Reilly. The introduction, he added, was a year later than it should have been, but 'alas, something occurred that caused cancellation of our annual meeting'. The 'something' of course was the SEC inquiry, now happily cleared up, though Jack had not been free to mention it directly.

'Five men—and five men only—have headed this company since its founding in 1869,' said Heinz. The first three were all called Heinz. 'For thirteen years following 1966, until 1979, the company was presided over superbly by Burt Gookin. Now, fellow shareholders, we enter the O'Reilly era.'

17

Family Reunion

SOMETHING HAD TO GIVE IN O'REILLY'S FRENETIC LIFE, AND THAT something was his family. He was keenly aware that he was neglecting them with his constant shuttling around the world, and the month he laid aside each summer to spend with them in Ireland was frequently interrupted by business calls, meetings and crises to be resolved. His son Gavin would later do a party piece of his father visiting the nursery in Fox Chapel. 'Mother would come in and say: "Now, attention everyone. I want everyone to brush their hair, wash their faces and put on your best clothes. This is a special evening: your father is coming to visit you tonight. You older ones will remember your father—he's the tall man with the red hair who you sometimes see about the house . . ." It was never as bad as that, and when O'Reilly was with them the children greatly enjoyed his company and he theirs; but all too soon he would be off again, answering the telephone, dictating letters, reading his papers and arranging meetings which increasingly crept into his own house. 'He was sweet with them, but he was hardly ever there,' recalls Susan. 'And he would rough and tumble with them for a little while, but he was not terribly involved.'

As early as 1973, when little Susan was ten and the triplets seven, he was acknowledging how heavily his neglect of them weighed on his conscience. 'It's the kids that pay for my peripatetic existence,' he told one interviewer, 'and I'm really wondering if the price isn't too high.' Then in a rare moment of reflection: 'Is anything worth

an absentee father? What is it I'm after now? Ego satisfaction? More
money? More success?'

He didn't attempt to answer his own question, but nor did he alter
his lifestyle, which, as the problems with Fitzwilton deepened, and
criticisms of his dual existence in Pittsburgh and Dublin increased,
became busier still. He loved his children and his wife and, had he
paused to enjoy it, he would have had the family life he had missed
out on by being brought up as an only child. The house in Fox
Chapel was very much a family home, a fifteen-room mock-Tudor
mansion overlooking the golf course, a short distance from the exclusive Fox Chapel Club where the family swam, played tennis and
mixed with the other better-off families of Pittsburgh. The children
could run wild in the manicured 8-acre grounds of the house, or
play hide-and-seek in the large greenhouse, the Scottish rose garden,
the Japanese garden with its arched wooden footbridge, or around
the tennis court and swimming pool. The house was always full, not
just with the family but with the eclectic bunch that O'Reilly gathered
around him wherever he was. The ubiquitous Olive was there, of
course; she had her own room and the run of the house, and over
the years came to know more than anyone else about how this family
worked and played an important role in making sure it did work.
There were also young Irish boys and girls, the children of friends
who needed help or a leg up the ladder, for whom O'Reilly was
always a soft touch. Some would stay for a few days and pass on,
others for months and several for years. O'Reilly could never resist
a plea to help someone find a job, a green card, a new career or
simply a bed for the night.

He loved to have the house filled, but it was hard on Susan, making
it impossible for them ever to have any time to themselves. Although
neither of them was aware of it at the time, he was already drifting
away from his wife in these years—their lives were starting to diverge
simply because they did not spend enough time together. By nature
Susan was an intensely private and gentle person, who found the
continual round of public dinners and speeches exhausting and tedious. She did her best, and Tony's friends and colleagues would all
agree that she did it remarkably well. But she never had Tony's
limitless energy, or his gregarious nature. In her mid-forties Susan
had developed into a mature but still very pretty woman, whose
charm, and her popularity with Tony's ever-widening circle of friends
and colleagues, had if anything grown over the years. She is a person

who tends to attract superlatives in attempts to describe her: she is variously 'remarkable', a 'class act', an 'exceptional person', 'one of the most lovely people I've ever known', and it is hard to find a discordant note. Tony adored her and in turn she worshipped him, but she felt her place was with the children rather than in an aeroplane or a foreign hotel. His need to shuttle back and forth from Dublin had imposed the first real strain on the relationship, particularly as, away from her influence in Dublin, O'Reilly would party all night.

Even in Castlemartin, where they went every summer, there were always people about. Every year, they held a party for two hundred guests, most of them people whom O'Reilly had known since childhood, or played rugby with, and at any mealtime there could be anything from twenty to sixty people, depending on who O'Reilly had bumped into that day. At weekends the house overflowed.

It wasn't all hard work. Susan loved Castlemartin, particularly the gardens which she had had landscaped so that there was now a perfect view of the Liffey from their bedroom and the front of the house. In summer the views were superb, with the long rows of old oaks and ashes, and the thousands of shrubs and ornamental trees she had planted. Susan's great joy was to fill the house every morning with her own flower arrangements, and she would be up and out early, cutting her flowers for the day in the greenhouse where she grew white lilies, sweet peas, snapdragons, blue and white irises and many others. She had her own favourite St Bernard dog, Dara, and would stroll through the grounds with her, checking the foals, the donkeys and the growing collection of horses on her way to the gardens. A poem that Susan wrote at the time talking about the 'special part of my heart in the garden of Castlemartin' gives an idea of her pleasure in the place. One stanza reads:

> *The chatter of children as they play in the hay*
> *And the fragile foals breathlessly trying to neigh,*
> *What joy to see the horses when I'm on the way*
> *What a blessing it is to begin every day*
> *In the garden.*

They had spent a small fortune restoring the house, and another fortune on the grounds. Jim Kelly, who had run O'Reilly's tomato-growing venture at Columbia, came into his own at Castlemartin to put new life into what had become tired farmland. Some of the great avenues of trees had been cut down for firewood in the war, and now the old stumps were pulled out, new trees planted, and acres of bad scrubland drained and developed. Fences which had long disappeared were replaced, crumbling walls and buildings repaired and roadways put in. One field was even marked out as a rugby field, with its own goalposts, and O'Reilly continued trying to play. 'We're running as fast as we can, lads, but it looks as if we're playing in slow motion,' he joked to his equally decrepit fellow players. Some of the outbuildings were totally derelict, and, as the house overflowed with people, they converted what had once been stables into an elegant poolhouse with guest rooms. 'The water from the farmyard at the back was literally flowing right through the rooms,' says Ronnie Dawson, by then a Dublin architect, who was brought down by O'Reilly to offer some advice. 'And it had to be diverted around the swimming pool and down to the river—a big task.' On the back of the house, near the tennis court, they added a long conservatory which would serve as a breakfast room and general living area; its windows looked south on to the river, transforming that whole end of the house (although it did not please the conservationists).

Both O'Reillys soon lost count of the money it was costing, but even through Tony's financial crisis at Fitzwilton and the *Independent* they kept going. Susan and her London architect David Laws oversaw the work on the house, but all of it was done under the watchful eye of Kelly who had personal command of the farm, and was in overall charge when they were not there.

At first the children had groaned at the prospect of going back to Ireland for the summer, but after the purchase of Castlemartin they changed their minds. 'In those first years, before business came more and more into Castlemartin, it was lovely for the children,' says Susan.

> Caroline, my littlest one, had a pony and I used to take her to pony camp. At first the elder children wanted to be in summer camps in America, which was what all their friends were doing, but then it became wonderful for them. And then there was a big touch rugby game every summer, and a big picnic and it was very happy. The summers were very happy.

Pleasant as Castlemartin was, their favourite family place remained Glandore, in West Cork. Literally the 'Harbour of the Oaks',

Glandore is one of the most beautiful little bays in Ireland, described by the guide books as an 'Irish Venice'. The view from their guest house, which they block-booked every year, was of the hills across the harbour covered with dusky grey woods, and of the fishing boats passing just below on their way in and out of Unionhall. Outside the harbour were two small islands called Adam and Eve, where the children sailed and landed, learning the age-old sailing directions for this area: 'avoid Adam and hug Eve'. Dean Swift, author of *Gulliver's Travels*, had written his Latin poem 'Carberiae Rupes' in these waters, but there were also grimmer reminders of Ireland's bloody past: the 1642 Munster rebellion had started in Glandore, when the Irish gagged several English to death and seized a Scottish minister, broiled a piece of his flesh and made him eat it.

The local residents became used to the annual invasion as the family arrived in a cavalcade of cars led by Arthur Whelan in the Bentley of which both he and O'Reilly were inordinately proud. For years they had come to this same guest house and when Estrid Good, the extraordinary Faeroe Islander who owned it and who had become their friend, indicated that she was getting too old to continue, O'Reilly bought it off her. He left her in residence but added various extensions and flats to house the drivers, the children (each of whom was allowed to invite one friend from Pittsburgh for the summer) and the guests who inevitably turned up. It would later develop into a serious complex, with its own saltwater swimming pool (it now has two—one for O'Reilly and one for his guests) and tennis court, but in these years it was fairly simple, and they loved it that way. The boys joined in the regattas at Unionhall, and swam, fished and played outside in the long summer evenings (in West Cork it is still bright at eleven in midsummer).

As they had become wealthier—by 1980 O'Reilly's income from Heinz had topped $1 million a year including bonuses, making him one of the highest-paid men in America, and he now had substantial dividends from the *Independent*—they took the children to more exotic places. The most notable of them was Lyford Cay in the Bahamas, an exclusive, mostly white private estate on Nassau with endless pink beaches, tennis courts and a golf course. Susan came to hate it, reckoning the children ran riot there, mixing with other rich kids and becoming, as she put it, 'brattish'. But it was a handy place for O'Reilly to hold some of his conferences, inviting Heinz executives or getting the Fitzwilton or *Independent* teams down for a break and a serious discussion on where the businesses went from there.

O'Reilly had created the perfect framework to give his children an idyllic childhood, yet there was something missing—and that something was him. He was there for them in the summer and at Christmas, but other than that they saw little of him. And they almost never saw him alone, never had much chance to talk to him properly. He was a tolerant, indulgent father when he was around but he left their education, their homework and their moral guidance to Susan, which to some extent reflected his own Irish upbringing—Aileen had done it all for him. If he hoped they would grow up as trouble-free and respectful to their parents as he had, he was soon to be disillusioned—and given the way they lived, and the loose control he imposed on them, it would have been astonishing if they had. For one thing, they were confused over their nationality, never quite identifying with America and never—at least until later—with Ireland. 'The children are now built into the American system,' O'Reilly told an interviewer in the summer of 1979. 'First they were Irish, then they were English, now they're American.' Later he would vehemently insist his children were always going to be Irish, but they had not always got that message. At home in Pittsburgh, O'Reilly jokingly spoke of them to visitors as 'the Vietcong', and six growing children, plus all the friends they were encouraged to invite, could indeed be a slightly overpowering sight. O'Reilly seldom went to school concerts, or parents' days at school, or even had time to watch them play sports. 'He was simply not around,' says Susan. 'It was something I didn't mind because I understood he was involved with so many other things.'

In some ways, O'Reilly was simply repeating the pattern of his own childhood. Jack had never gone to his school concerts, seldom watched him play rugby as a boy—not because he had no interest but simply because that was the tradition of the day in Ireland. Mothers went to those events, but fathers rarely did—and, as with most Irishmen of his generation, it was not important to O'Reilly. In England that had not mattered because the children were younger, but in America they were old enough to notice—and to complain, at least to Susan. In Pittsburgh there was much more of a tradition of fathers turning up for speech days and sports days, and the eldest boy in particular, Cameron, was hurt when O'Reilly was one of the few absent parents, leading to some friction between them.

As they hit their mid-teens, O'Reilly could no longer turn a blind eye to the growing problems within his own family. Susan, the eldest, was a bright girl who was also the natural leader, but increasingly Cameron (there was only thirteen months between them, and less than three years between all six) was vying for that position. In her early years, young Susan—or Susie—had been very much the favourite of Jack and Aileen who, the others would always allege, had spoilt her dreadfully, setting her apart from the younger ones. She, like all the others, had attended Fox Chapel Country Day School, where her mother was on the board of directors, and had left in the fifth grade to go to Ellis School and then to the exclusive Hotchkiss School in Lakeville, Connecticut.

The problem child was Cameron, who was always willing to try or dare anything. He went to the highly respected Shadyside Academy Middle School, where Jack Heinz and so many other rich Pennsylvanians went, but got into such trouble that O'Reilly was forced to remove him. When he was about fifteen, Cameron was sent to St Paul's in New Hampshire where he could make a fresh start, but that didn't last long either. Cameron became involved with a syndicate of boys who were bringing liquor into the school, and was once again expelled. O'Reilly's gentle tolerance wilted momentarily.

'Get him back to Europe and find a school for him,' he told Susan. When Cameron arrived home in Pittsburgh, it was one of the few occasions in his life O'Reilly was seriously angry with him. 'You're going to school in London,' he told him. Equally quickly, however, his anger cooled, and a few hours later he told Cameron he would take him to Twickenham to watch England play Ireland the following Saturday. They flew to London together, father and son, on Concorde, chatting amiably as if nothing had happened. 'He was so unpredictable in the way he handled the children,' says Susan. 'He was pretty soft on them all, and I suppose there was quite a bit of guilt inside him about not being able to give them more time. So perhaps with Cameron there was a little bit of self-blame. He was sometimes firm with them, but he was also sweet, and he loved to turn their adventures, however bad, into family stories.'

Getting Cameron into a suitable English school was not at all easy. No one wanted a rebellious fifteen-year-old and Susan criss-crossed England and finally met a priest who suggested Clongowes in Ireland, the Jesuit college where James Joyce had been. 'I had not wanted him to go to school in Ireland because he might embarrass his father,' says his mother now. But there was not much choice, and O'Reilly, although he had similar reservations, was not against it. He personally took Cameron to his new school where, after introducing him to the president, he left him with some misgivings on both their parts. Cameron had visibly flinched as he drove through the gates of what he felt was going to be a forbidding school. 'You're not really going to leave me here?' he asked plaintively. It was one thing to be thrown out of a school in New Hampshire where no one knew you, but if Cameron misbehaved in Ireland the whole community would soon know this was the great Tony O'Reilly's son. It also imposed considerable pressure on Cameron, from whom big things were expected, and his first response to the Jesuit college was entirely negative; but it was the turning point for him. Like the others he was academically bright, and once he decided to study he had little trouble passing exams. In his final year at Clongowes he was confident enough to try for Oxford. His mother had moved over to an apartment in Cadogan Gardens in London to be near her children, most of whom, including Caroline, were now in England or Ireland, and he joined her there, going to a crammer before taking his entrance exams. He was accepted by Worcester College and never looked back.

Young Susie meanwhile had gone to Yale, but she too had her problems. Her college friends remember periods when she was too upset to return to the family home, and she was forced to take a year out. She lived in London with Susan, who had just been through a major operation and wanted her near, and O'Reilly arranged for her to get a job at the advertising agency Doyle Dane Bernbach. Her mother found her 'very clinging', but she recovered, graduated from Yale and then she too went to Oxford. She went on to qualify as a pilot.

The third child, Justine, was in many ways the easiest of the six. From an early age she had quietly done her own thing, neither part of the Susan/Cameron battle for leadership of the pack, nor one of the triplets, Tony, Gavin and Caroline, who were a year younger and who hunted together. It was she who decided of her own volition that she wanted to go to boarding school in England at thirteen, and she was to end up as head girl at Cobham Hall. By the age of fifteen she was going to places such as Haiti, again of her own volition, to work for a summer with Mother Teresa's nuns among the terminally ill. Later she took a year off from Brown University to live in Tanzania where she went to the university in Dar-es-Salaam. Over the years, of all the children she would remain perhaps the closest to her mother.

Increasingly, the younger ones came to think of themselves as more Irish than American (their mother's passport gave them citizenship in

Australia too), a fact which posed some problems for young Tony and Gavin when it came to going to school. They, like Cameron, went to Shadyside to start with, but for their secondary education Tony Beresford persuaded Tony and Susan that the best school for them was Harrow, just outside London, and O'Reilly, who had been brought up to regard Eton and Harrow as the two most snobbish schools in the world, went along with it. It could scarcely have been a worse choice. 'From the first night when I took the boys there I knew it was going to be a disaster,' says Susan, 'and it was awful. One of the worst years of my life. They were just heartbroken and so unhappy.'

It was at Harrow that Ireland's turbulent history intruded for the first time most forcibly into the consciousness of the two boys. O'Reilly had brought them up to think of themselves as Irish, but because they had been to school first in England and then in America, they had only a fraction of his immersion in Irish culture. They were aware, as everyone was, of the bombs and the killings in Northern Ireland, but to those who lived in its Republic the North was another country, part of the United Kingdom, and the problems which had erupted there in 1969 were for the British to deal with. The younger boys were only three when the British government sent in ten thousand troops, initially with the principal object of protecting the Catholic minority from the militant Protestants, and they were not yet six when, on 30 January 1972, British paratroops shot thirteen unarmed civilians on an anti-internment march in Derry—the never-to-be-forgotten 'Bloody Sunday', the reverberations of which still echo today. Their father's background meant that they automatically sympathized with the Catholics in the North, but were totally opposed to the IRA violence. The revival of the IRA in December 1969 was largely a reaction to Protestant violence. 'The beleaguered Catholic ghettos were so short of arms that in the Protestant-encircled area of the Ardoyne there were only two shotguns,' wrote Tim Pat Coogan in his history *Disillusioned Decades*. That was when the letters IRA were written large on Belfast gable walls, as 'Irish Ran Away'. The first deaths and explosions would all be the work of the loyalists, but by the time the boys came to go to school that was no longer so. By then the Provisional IRA, or the 'Provos', had long emerged as a deadly, dedicated and well-armed organization which had carried its terrors to mainland Britain as well as the province of Ulster. The O'Reillys were in Ireland in the summer of 1979 when Earl Mountbat-

ten his family and young grandchild were brutally murdered by the
IRA in County Sligo, a day that would sear itself into the memory
of everyone in the country. But even that was one of the rare incidents
of terrorist activity in the South, which the IRA regarded as its training grounds, its supply routes and safe haven when the British forces
in the North made it too hot for them.

The younger boys were still at school in America at the time of
the Mountbatten murder, but their year at Harrow coincided with
another highly public event: the hunger strike and the death of Bobby
Sands. Sands, a hardened veteran of the IRA, was a prisoner in the
much-hated H-block of the Maze prison when on 1 March 1981, he
started a protest against prison conditions by refusing food. The IRA
and its political wing, Sinn Fein, made the most of it. Senator Edward
Kennedy, a friend of O'Reilly's in America, called on Britain to make
'new and urgent' efforts to halt the hunger strike, the Pope sent his
personal secretary, who visited Sands twice, and Prince Charles, on
an official visit to Venezuela, was handed a petition by eleven US
congressmen asking him to use his 'good offices as heir apparent to
the throne to intercede'. To add further to the British embarrassment, Sands, even as he lay dying, was selected to stand as candidate for the Westminster Parliament and was duly elected an MP.
He died on 5 May, and Northern Ireland erupted.

In Harrow the two O'Reilly boys, innocently protesting their
Irishness and the rights of the Catholic minority which they barely
understood, came in for some unmerciful teasing. Once they ran
away, ringing up on one of O'Reilly's accounts to hire a car and then
telling Susan where to fetch them. Justine and Caroline were by now
at school in Kent, and Cameron, less than four years older than the
triplets, was at Clongowes, so for much of this period their mother
lived either in London or in Castlemartin. O'Reilly, fighting his final
battles to succeed Gookin, then moving into the chief executive's
office and dealing with the profit juggling crisis, saw even less of
them all. He promised young Tony and Gavin that if they stuck it
out at Harrow for the rest of the year he would send them to school
in Ireland, and after a year they joined Cameron at Clongowes. That
was the making of them too and, like their brother, they coped well
after that. At Clongowes all three O'Reilly boys were expected to be
superb sportsman, but in fact, although both the younger boys had
much the same build as their father, they were no better than average

at rugby or tennis (with the exception of Cameron, the best tennis player in the family).

The burden of the family problems was borne almost entirely by Susan, who over these years spent long periods living away from Tony. She had moved into a little hotel near Castlemartin at the start of the restoration work and had spent months there without him, seeing him only at weekends when he flew into Dublin. Then there was almost a year when she was in London. They were still in love, but growing apart without either of them pausing to realize what was happening to them. They would both regret it later.

In the grounds of Castlemartin, a few hundred yards downriver from the house itself, was the ruined fifteenth-century church of St Mary, built by the FitzEustace family who had owned the original castle on the site two centuries before the present house was built. The church was reached along a curving path through the oak and ash trees that ran along the river, one of the favourite walks of O'Reilly and Susan in the evening. As the house neared completion, O'Reilly pondered about restoring and reconsecrating the ruin, turning it back into what it had once been—a family church, where all future O'Reilly weddings, funerals and other events would take place. It was an elaborate procedure, but the work was complete by 1981, in time for its first ceremony for centuries: the reinterment of his father.

O'Reilly still missed his father, and hated the infrequent visits to his grave in the inhospitable Glasnevin cemetery. The church at Castlemartin, he felt, would be a perfect last resting place for him, the start of a new family burial plot. It was also to be a dramatic occasion for another reason: he proposed to invite Jack O'Reilly's first family. When he told Aileen, by now confined to a wheelchair, she was stunned. 'She just cried her heart out, and said "I don't want to see them",' recalls Susan, who pleaded with O'Reilly not to do it. 'You will hurt her so much,' she said. But O'Reilly was insistent. Jack, he reminded her, had been their father just as much as his, and they also had rights which had been trampled on all too many times. 'Nana was stony-faced, and she said, "I won't come to Castlemartin," ' says Susan, 'but it was Christmas time and she wanted to see the children, so in the end she did come.'

It was a strange day. Jack's eldest daughter, Juliette, had attended the first funeral, but there had been so many people there that she was lost in the crowd and O'Reilly barely noticed her. Neither Eveleen nor her brother Julian had gone. O'Reilly had sought out his half-brother Julian in the Bahamas several years before, but he barely knew his half-sisters. He had specifically invited all of them to Castlemartin for a union of the family over their father's grave. In the event Julian stayed in the Bahamas, but the two women went, approaching their meeting with Aileen with as much trepidation as she did. 'I'd never even seen this woman in my life, and when I saw her I felt almost as if my mother had taken over,' says Eveleen, 'and there was a moment of contact between my mother and her that I couldn't control. And she began to cry. She was very paralysed, very face was very twisted. While she was at rest it wasn't noticeable, but if she strained to speak or say anything she became agitated.'

Eveleen desperately wanted to mention one incident in particular, something she had felt guilty about for forty years. 'Over the years I had often thought about Aileen,' she said later. 'On my sixteenth birthday at school, she sent me a cake and the nuns made such a commotion about this because of who it had come from. And I wrote a letter of thanks and they brought it back to me, and they said they didn't think it was wise to send that letter. Suppose it got back to my mother?'

When she had got over the shock of meeting her in Castlemartin, Eveleen began trying to explain all this with a puzzled but attentive Susan and Jim McCarthy trying to aid understanding. 'You sent me a birthday cake, and I didn't get the opportunity to thank you for it, and I want to thank you for it now,' Eveleen said, trying desperately to explain.

'Oh, she's thanking you for the birthday cake,' interpreted Jim McCarthy, attempting to lighten the atmosphere and make some sense of what was rapidly turning into a pantomime, 'that you sent her when she was sixteen . . .' he trailed away, looking at Eveleen helplessly.

'And I'm now fifty-six,' said Eveleen, causing them all to laugh.

Jack's body was duly interred in a new plot on the south side of the church, facing the Liffey. In due course, everyone including Aileen knew, Tony's mother would join him there. One day, too, it will be O'Reilly's own final resting place.

18

Oil in the Atlantic

We shall not cease from exploration
And the end of all our exploring
Will be to arrive where we started
And know the place for the first time.

T. S. Eliot, *Four Quartets*

IN 1980 THE OIL FEVER WHICH HAD SWEPT THE WORLD IN THE WAKE of the second OPEC crisis came to Ireland. For a time, as government ministers dreamed of the country becoming the Kuwait of Europe, serious geologists talked about rock formations off the coast capable of supporting 'major' commercial fields producing up to a billion barrels of oil. Some of the biggest international oil companies set up offices in Dublin or Cork, and moved their drill ships and rigs from the North Sea, Indonesia and the Gulf of Mexico to spud in in the even more hostile waters of the Atlantic. Ordinary Irish citizens, whose previous closest contact with the oil industry had been a visit to the local petrol pump, became instant experts, talking knowledgeably about Jurassic and Cretaceous structures, 'farm-outs', and the virtues of the Porcupine Basin versus the Celtic Sea. The Dublin stock market was soon caught up in the frenzy, floating off little companies that offered nothing more than hope at absurd prices to people who had never bought a share in their lives but who saw this as at least as good a gamble as the horses.

O'Reilly caught the mood as passionately, and in the end, as disastrously, as anyone in the country. The search for Ireland's oil was to prove the most costly and disappointing venture of his corporate career, a black hole into which he poured millions of pounds of his private wealth, never to produce a single barrel of oil. Almost as bad as the damage to his wealth was the harm to his reputation: his enthusiasm for the search, which went on through most of the 1980s, tempted thousands of small investors to speculate in his shares, making him a hero when they soared but a villain, innocent though he was, when they crashed again.

It began with hope. Neighbouring Britain and Norway had found oil in huge, rich quantities off their shores in the 1970s; the Forties and Brent Fields in the North Sea were as profitable as anything in the world. 'Surely God couldn't have been so unfair as to give it all to the Brits,' said someone, and it was a view that echoed around the Dublin bars that year. There were snags, of course, but in the euphoria that reigned they were dismissed as no more than technical: the water off the Irish coast was deeper and wilder than anything yet successfully developed anywhere in the world, and a certain amount of drilling and seismic work had already been done, though with indifferent results. Forty-two wells had been drilled in the Celtic Sea, off the south coast, without yielding a drop of commercial oil. Yet Marathon and Exxon had found gas off Kinsale Head, almost within sight of O'Reilly's house in Glandore, and where there was gas there was often oil. It was the sole commercial find, but it was enough to keep hope throbbing. Phillips Petroleum began drilling in the Porcupine Basin in the Atlantic off the coast of Clare, its rig crews subjected to unmerciful grilling by the locals in the pubs when they came ashore. The pundits in the public bars were forecasting big things. BP had moved a drilling rig into the Celtic Sea and there were others off Fastnet, in the neighbouring blocks to Kinsale Head. All of Britain's oil had so far been found off the east coast, but there was no geological reason why there shouldn't be oil off the west coast too, between Britain and Ireland, or further out, on the edge of the Atlantic shelf—still in Irish waters.

For O'Reilly, and for many like him, there was something wonderfully romantic about exploring for this black gold, which might have lain hidden all these years under the wild waters of the Atlantic which hitherto had never yielded anything more valuable than fish. Even a medium-sized field, such as were being found in the North Sea every other month, would have a major impact on the tiny Irish economy. A major discovery of the size of Forties, capable of producing oil at 500,000 barrels a day, would cost several billion dollars to develop but would make Ireland self-suffient overnight at a time when the high price of oil was crippling the economy. For the individual entrepreneur, oil seemed the miracle short cut to making an instant fortune such as no man in Ireland had ever owned, and there were plenty who dreamed about it that year.

Everywhere O'Reilly went in the world, there was talk of oil. He had now joined the board of Mobil, one of the Seven Sisters oil companies, and listened intently to the discussions of demand/supply equations, forecasts of continually spiralling prices (even though oil had now risen fourteen-fold from its pre-1973 levels, all the oil companies expected it, wrongly, to go on up), and assessments of new exploration areas. In Pittsburgh, where Gulf Oil had its headquarters before it was taken over by Chevron, the talk at cocktail parties, in the Heinz office or at the Fox Chapel Club was all of companies and individuals investing in oil plays in Texas or Oklahoma or the Gulf. In London, tiny exploration companies which had yet to drill their first wells were commanding incredible valuations. In Australia, the Far East or South America the picture was the same—everybody was into oil.

Nowhere did the fever burn more fiercely than in Ireland. In September 1980 a Fianna Fail senator called Professor Richard Conroy floated a little company on the strength of nothing more than a tiny stake in two interesting blocks in the North Sea. The shares more than doubled overnight. An even smaller company, Gaelic Oil, acquired a 20 per cent stake in a wildcat well to be drilled in the Fastnet Basin off the coast of West Cork, and its shares, issued at 20p, soared to 140p. Aran Energy, a more substantial company which had stakes in actual producing fields, saw its market value soar to £50 million—four times the value of Fitzwilton.

The catalyst for O'Reilly's entry into the potential oil bonanza was provided by Jim Stafford, an aloof and distant figure on the Irish scene, an intensely private tax exile who lived in Monte Carlo and kept his distance from the circles in which O'Reilly moved.

He and O'Reilly had never met but were brought together by an odd chain of events. Nearly three years earlier Independent Newspapers, observing the growth of tabloids in Ireland, had realized it must get in to this market if it was to protect its own position. In January 1978 O'Reilly agreed to pay £1.1 million in cash and shares for a 58 per cent stake held in the *Sunday World*, a lively Irish derivative of Rupert Murdoch's *News of the World* (often banned in Ireland), which had been started only in 1973, but within five years had outstripped sales of the *Sunday Independent* with a circulation of over 300,000. It

was even threatening to start a Dublin evening paper in rivalry to
O'Reilly's *Evening Herald*. Hugh McLaughlin and Tom Butler, two
of the founders, were willing sellers, but the real driving force was
Gerry McGuinness, who O'Reilly wanted almost as much as he wanted
his paper. McGuinness joined the Independent board, where O'Reilly
encouraged him to expand his operation (he eventually teamed up
with the British United Newspapers group to launch the jointly
owned *Star* daily tabloid). McGuinness and the *Sunday World* were to
prove a significant addition to the growth of Independent Newspapers in the 1980s.

Fitzwilton by this stage was little more than an investment company,
with stakes in the *Independent*, the residual half-share in Goulding's
(which it was trying to dispose of), a continuing involvement in the
ubiquitous Dockrell's which it been forced to step back into after
McCarthy's problems, and cash. What better home for some of the
cash than an Irish oil exploration company?

They would have to move fast if they were to participate in the
well the Phillips consortium planned to drill when the Atlantic season
opened in the spring of 1981. It had drilled one well in these deep
waters in 1978, and had found sufficient oil traces to believe there
might be a commercial field at the higher prices. Getty Oil, which
owned 37.5 per cent of the consortium, wanted to spread its risk and
to 'farm out' some of its holding. Stafford had already had talks with
them about buying some of it.

O'Reilly took little persuading, and by the end of 1980 they had
their little group together. O'Reilly would be chairman of a new
company which they would call Atlantic Resources and which would
raise £1.25 million by issuing an initial 2.5 million shares at 50p each
to its founders. Half of that would come from Fitzwilton, the rest
from a group of investors who would include O'Reilly (15 per cent),
Stafford (15 per cent), and lesser amounts from McGuinness, Vincent
Ferguson, Nick Leonard, Jim McCarthy and even Sir Basil Goulding.
They would later raise another £2.5 million at £1 a share from banks
and financial institutions, making an initial capital of £3.75 million—
not much in the oil game, where big fields could cost billions to
develop, but it would get them started, allowing them to buy from
Getty a 10 per cent stake in the Phillips Maroon Group and cover
their share of the new £16 million well. All of them were perfectly
aware of the costs and the risks: the well, they were warned, would

take five months to complete and go to a depth of 14,500 feet, where the seismic tests suggested they might find oil.

At a meeting just before Christmas O'Reilly got the agreement of the Fitzwilton board for that company to participate, and early in the new year they set out to hire a managing director to run Atlantic. Don Sheridan was a veteran oil man, a Yorkshire-born geologist who had taken his degree at Trinity College, Dublin thirty years before and had worked in the Middle East for years before being sent to Ireland, where for the past thirteen years he had overseen Marathon Petroleum's interests. He had been responsible for Marathon's extensive drilling programme off the south coast, and it was Sheridan who had brought in the commercial gas field off Kinsale, still Ireland's only producing field. When Stafford, who had made it his business to get to know most of the operators on the Irish scene, put his name forward, both O'Reilly and Vincent Ferguson, who knew his family, were enthusiastic. Stafford took Ferguson, now chief executive of Fitzwilton and in overall charge of O'Reilly's business interests in Ireland, to meet him. Sheridan took some persuading, and it was O'Reilly who did the final negotiation. He was only interested, Sheridan said, if Atlantic agreed to apply for licences in the Celtic Sea which Marathon had abandoned and where he was convinced there were fields to be found. O'Reilly in turn mentioned the possibility of expanding into metals and minerals onshore, something he had always thought about since his brief involvement with Tara Exploration. On those terms, Sheridan accepted.

And so Atlantic Resources, a name that for the next half dozen years would be on the lips of every Irish investor and gambler, was born. In March they issued the second tranche of shares to the Irish institutions, who were only too willing to join this interesting little party at £1 a share. It meant that O'Reilly and Fitwilton had already doubled their money without even a drill bit going down, and they had enough in reserve, after farming in to the Porcupine, to think about the Celtic Sea. Drilling off Clare began in mid-March, and by April 1981 excitement was beginning to build. No one wanted to sell at this early stage, but when a small number of shares was made available on the Dublin Stock Exchange it resulted in one of the most frenetic trading sessions that staid institution had ever seen. When the market opened, shares in Atlantic Resources, which O'Reilly, Stafford and the other founders had paid 50p for, started their turbulent public life at 290p, but were soon 335p, then 375p and 395p by the lunchtime break. An RTE television crew which had filmed the shrill braying of twenty or so brokers in the morning discovered it had forgotten to put film in the camera, and the whole proceedings had to be re-enacted in the afternoon. The shares closed the day at 340p after some profit-taking, and the events made the national news that night. Fitzwilton was showing a paper profit on the day of over £3 million and O'Reilly and Stafford £1 million each. It was only a foretaste of the feverish swings which were to come for this extraordinary stock.

By now there were three wells being drilled off the Irish coast, and by the end of 1981 there would be eleven (only one involving Atlantic). Surely, the punters reasoned, something must be found. But who would find it? The newspapers soberly pointed to the enormous cost of drilling in the deep waters of the Atlantic—$115,000 a day—and also the low chances of finding a commercial field, but for the moment hope reigned over reality.

With the Atlantic share price in the stratosphere and fever mounting daily, O'Reilly wanted to take advantage of the investor enthusiasm to create something which would be more than a single-well speculation. Sheridan probably knew the waters in the Celtic Sea better than anyone in the world and was keen to begin drilling as soon as possible. 'A deposit, to be commercial there, need not be as large as in the deeper waters off the west coast,' he told the others. Companies of the size of Marathon had little interest in small, marginally profitable fields, but for a company the size of Atlantic they could be a godsend. The technology to develop small fields already existed, and there had also been a significant leap forward in seismic technology since Marathon had first surveyed the area in 1965. By May, two months after Sheridan joined, Atlantic had applied to the Irish Department of Energy and been allocated six exploration licences in the Celtic Sea off the Waterford and Cork coasts.

By now O'Reilly had the bit between his teeth, and was already negotiating with Gulf in Pittsburgh to be his operating partner in this new area. Just as Atlantic had 'farmed in' to the Porcupine field, so now he offered Gulf a 'farm out' in his blocks in the Celtic Sea. Gulf, which had huge storage terminals on the Kerry coast, agreed, bringing in Union Oil to share the risks. Between them the two US companies agreed to pay $7.5 million for two-thirds of the blocks, which meant that Atlantic had acquired the other third for nothing and also had a $7.5 million contribution towards the cost of its first well, which was soon underway on Block 49/9, off the Waterford coast. O'Reilly was also investigating the possibility of buying in to some gas prospects in Oklahoma and West Virginia, where the chances of bringing in a commercial find were greater and which would give the group some actual income.

The shares remained as wild as ever, rising or falling every time a fishing boat went past the rig and saw signs of activity. The pattern of dealing, which was to cause a great deal of controversy over the years, was by now established. There were groups on the fringes of the company who saw the stock as a perfect dealing chip, buying in when it was down and selling on the next rumour. It was an unattractive element of the oil boom, which particularly attached itself to Atlantic, and which coloured the views of many legitimate investors not only about the company but, however unfairly, about O'Reilly too (who never dealt in a single share).

The shares were back at 245p when O'Reilly went for another placing to finance the American interests and drilling in the Celtic Sea, raising £5 million at a price of 210p, a 17 per cent discount on the market. Fitzwilton and O'Reilly both took up their full placing, but some of Stafford's friends, given shares in the early placings, had already sold. Even loyal O'Reilly associates chose not to subscribe. By midsummer the shares were down to 175p, but then began to rise again as the Phillips Maroon consortium approached its target depth. By August the *Sunday Times* in London was speculating that the consortium had 'struck it rich' and the shares surged back to 300p, and by October, when the results of the well finally came through, they were 375p.

It was to be a short-lived recovery: although Irish ministers talked of the results being 'encouraging', Phillips was less sanguine. It had indeed found oil on block 35/8 in the Porcupine, but the flow rates were poor, and this well by itself was far from being a commercial find. Despite pressure from the Irish government, Phillips, which had found oil twice in the area, did not even want to drill there again. The price of oil was now dropping as the world recession deepened and a glut developed, and wells in the Atlantic were expensive and risky (the last well had gone well over budget). Although they did not spell it out at the time, it was clear to the Phillips management that unless the price of oil went through the roof, and the Irish government offered them a far more inviting tax regime (a constant theme of O'Reilly's in speech after speech over the 1980s), this field was not worth spending another dollar on. The Porcupine field to this day is still undeveloped, the wells capped, and what oil exists is still sitting there.

Atlantic's first prospect had not paid off, but hope did not flicker out. In the meantime there was natural gas to be explored for in West Virginia and in the Anadarko Basis in Oklahoma, plus the more exciting oil prospects of the Celtic Sea. True, there were quibbles, notably from Fitzwilton shareholders who by mid-1982 were complaining that the £2 million the company had invested in Atlantic had been earning 16 per cent in the bank at a time of record high interest rates, but was now earning nothing. Fitzwilton's investment had doubled on paper (Atlantic were now back to 200p again), but there was no way the company could sell if the drilling proved unsuccessful, they pointed out. On the other hand the Dublin stockbrokers J. & E. Davy estimated that Atlantic shares were worth anywhere between 229p and £18.90 (on the basis of no data whatsoever), so the criticism, such as there was, was muted.

At Atlantic the tensions which had been simmering from the start between Stafford and the rest began to surface. Stafford had opposed the US investments, insisting that Atlantic was being regarded by the Americans as 'the ultimate out-of-towners', to be ripped off at will. He had gone with the other directors to Pittsburgh where O'Reilly gave them dinner at the Fox Chapel Club, prior to flying them all down to the Anadarko field the next day.

Over the following months the rift steadily widened, as Stafford continued to criticize the American ventures (with, in the event, some justification).

O'Reilly in the early days was tolerant enough, leaving it to Ferguson and Sheridan to deal with this disaffected partner, but he became increasingly irritated and angry with Stafford as the months went on. He was also dismayed at the speed at which some of the investors whom Stafford had brought to the table had scrambled out of their stock. Stafford accused the others of not properly monitoring the American investment, of placing themselves in the hands of the locals who would take advantage of them, and of poor management of the company. 'He was becoming a maverick completely,' says Ferguson. Stafford suggested bringing in a new firm of London stockbrokers, Greig Middleton, to replace Laing & Cruickshank; the others were opposed to this. He also suggested bringing in several outside directors to balance the preponderant O'Reilly appointees. When that failed, the relationship became impossible.

The final showdown with him came in May 1983. The dizzy ride of Atlantic had continued through the winter, but by the spring, with Phillips confirming it would not drill again in the Porcupine, the shares had fallen back to 120p. Stafford by now was at loggerheads with the board over almost every issue, and clearly could not stay on. O'Reilly and Ferguson accused him of picking a fight over his expenses and making that the issue on which he finally resigned. Stafford told a different story to Harry Walsh, the author of a book called *Oh Really O'Reilly* which relied heavily on Stafford's version of events. This has him resigning over his opposition to an executive share option scheme which the board had agreed at a meeting that he had not attended. Whatever the truth, he left the board, threatening to sue the company, but made no public statement (nor did the company, and the Irish press barely even noticed the departure of one of the key founders).

The first well on Block 49/9 was completed and plugged. There had been traces of oil and the geologists reckoned they had learned a great deal about the structure, but they would have to move the rig and drill again. It was costly for Atlantic and the company was running out of money once more, but O'Reilly, his enthusiasm whetted by the first few wells, decided on yet another money-raising operation. This time they would raise £4.7 million at 80p, a hefty discount on the share price. By this stage, including $14 million borrowed to pay for the American investments, the company had raised £26 million in twenty-six months, more than half of it through equity placings, and for the first—and only—time, the markets baulked. Fitzwilton indicated it would not be taking up most of its rights but agreed to pass them to an outside investor, the Saudi Arabian millionaire Suliman Olayan, who was on the Mobil board with O'Reilly. Nick Leonard declined to take up his shares too, as did several other directors. But O'Reilly paid up for his full quota, as he, alone of all the original founders, would continue to do through the many fund-raising operations of this volatile company.

In the event, the rights issue was a flop. In London the oil frenzy was ending even more abruptly than it had started and oil shares were suddenly out of fashion. Atlantic had so far drilled two wells which had effectively been 'dry'. Apart from O'Reilly and a few of the big institutional backers, no one was prepared to take the shares—

not even the government, which had been given a 5 per cent stake free and which now allowed itself to be diluted down to 2.8 per cent, half O'Reilly's personal holding of 5.6 per cent. The company still got its money because the issue had been underwritten by its merchant bank, the Industrial Credit Corporation, but 66 per cent of it was left with the underwriters. Amid some despondency and recrimination, the shares slid on down to 42p. The Atlantic Resources dream seemed to be over.

But it wasn't—not even nearly. Three weeks later the shares were again on the move as rumours began to leak of exciting developments out on the rig on Block 49/9, where Gulf was drilling Atlantic's second well in the area. By now there were small boats circling the rig hoping for the slightest indication of what was happening three miles down under the ocean; every nuance was interpreted—usually misinterpreted—ashore and rig workers were unmercifully pumped for information in the pubs when they came ashore. On 9 July the *Independent* was reporting 'No oil yet but the Celtic Sea hunt is on', while the *Irish Times* on the same day announced 'Oil fever grips stock market as Atlantic Resources price soars to 105p'. The famous one, however, which Jim McCarthy spotted and which became a catch-phrase between him and O'Reilly, was the *Cork Examiner*'s 'Workers Dance on Rig'. By early July oil fever was again at fever pitch, this time with some apparently better reasons for it. 'Ireland's long search for offshore oil may have paid off at last,' said the *Sunday Times* that weekend, reporting rumours from the rig of a find which could contain 400 million barrels of oil—a hefty find in such shallow waters close to shore.

O'Reilly was back in Ireland in July when the news, as opposed to the rumours, began to come ashore. He had invited Henry and Nancy Kissinger to Castlemartin, the first time they had ever been to Ireland, and he played host all weekend, walking Kissinger around the grounds of the house, inspecting the horses and Susan's flowers. In the evening they strolled along the Liffey walk to his father's grave, chatting amiably. He had organized a serious programme for the former American Secretary of State, including a luncheon at Iveagh House in Dublin with the Taoiseach, Garrett FitzGerald. Heinz was now targeting China and O'Reilly wanted to hire Kissinger to advise on the best way of getting in. At the end of a two-day trip he waved the Kissingers off on the Heinz plane, and the next morning was lying late in bed, as was his wont sometimes on a Sunday morning, when the phone rang. It was Don Sheridan with some amazing news. For weeks he had been getting daily reports from Gulf of the gas shows in the Celtic Sea, plus the depth and the quality of the oil-producing sands found by the drill, and the geologists' assessment of the formation. That morning Gulf had finally decided to make the big test and had blown the charges in the hole. To everyone's delight, oil started to come up the pipe with gathering momentum. 'It's running at three hundred barrels a day now, and it's still build-ing,' Sheridan reported, his voice cracking with the excitement.

By the end of the day the rate was running at nearly ten thousand barrels a day, which, even on the most pessimistic projection, seemed to suggest that the field contained a minimum of 100 million barrels of oil. They had done it. Oil had been found. The shares continued to rocket and by the middle of August 1983, when Gulf finally con-firmed that oil had been tested at 9901 barrels a day from the well, they were 335p. The announcement sent them into orbit. The same shares which investors had spurned two months before at 80p and which had sunk as low as 42p now went to 610p, with Ireland's first serious oil find now taken as a fact by everyone in the country, including the government (and O'Reilly). Already that weekend there was feverish adding up of what it meant for the Irish economy—even if the field was 'only' 250 million barrels, said the *Irish Independent*, it would supply half of Ireland's needs and add £50 million a year in petroleum taxes to the Irish revenue.

For Atlantic, which owned a third of the field, the implications were enormous. The London stockbrokers Hoare Govett reported that the find could be worth anything between £2 and £12 a share, and others thought it might be more, depending on what they discov-ered with the next appraisal well. 'There is no doubt that the excite-ment surrounding Atlantic Resources has enticed people to invest through the Irish Stock Exchange for the first time,' reported the *Irish Times*. 'Some investors did not even know what to ask for and even raised a second mortgage on their home.' The well, known as 49/9–2, was temporarily closed down for further evaluation and the shares began to yo-yo again, dropping to 300p, then bounding back to 600p again, with the usual group of professional operators taking full advantage of the volatility, but there was no indication from the operators that anything was wrong, despite what the rumours said.

At the Fitzwilton annual federal meeting at the end of October O'Reilly was in top form, his oil punt at last justified. 'It is no exaggeration to say that the oil find is a major event in the economic history of this country,' he told shareholders. The previous year there had been queries about Fitzwilton's heavy commitment to this gambler's chip, but now the tone of the meeting had reversed—and O'Reilly rubbed the point home. The company's £2 million invested in Atlantic was worth £13.7 million (the price was then 685p), he pointed out. 'With hindsight it may be said that we should have taken up our rights in [Atlantic],' he added, knowing full well that there were many there who had flatly opposed subscribing for the rights. Atlantic by this stage was capitalized at £140 million, the fourth largest company in Ireland, bigger than Smurfit or Waterford Glass, and five times the size of the Irish Independent group.

There was some argument about where to drill next, with Gulf, basically only interested in a large field, arguing they should go to what the geologists suggested was the outer perimeter of the field and drill at a slant—a 'deviated' well—to delineate the field. It would be an expensive and time-consuming way of doing it, only justified if there really was a large field there, and Sheridan was against it, suggesting they drilled a simpler and cheaper 'appraisal' well designed to prove what they had already found. Gulf, as the operator, prevailed, moved the rig and began drilling the fateful well 49/9–3, which to a large extent was to determine the future, not only of Atlantic resources, but of Ireland as an oil-producing country. A great deal hung on this well, and as the work began hopes had never been higher. In November Atlantic shares broke through the £8 barrier, and a few weeks later crossed £9. They would reach almost £10 in a final burst before beginning the long retreat.

Off the coast of Waterford, all was not well. This well was not only expensive ($21 million) but complex, its deviation from the rig involving a series of articulated joints which kept jamming or getting lost. O'Reilly flew out to the rig in a helicopter, taking a party of interested investors, and listened to the problems the drill crew were encountering. 'Every time we have to put more extensions on the tube or put a new drill head on, we have to take the entire thing out,' explained a foreman, gesturing at the deck where hard-hatted men in boiler suits were unwinding section after section of pipe. 'All these thousands of feet come up, and the rods have to be unscrewed, and the new bit put on, and then it all has to go down again, and these articulated joints make it a nightmare.' O'Reilly came back to relate in awe—and some exaggeration—the stories he had heard on the rig. 'Amazing things are happening out there: guys are falling down the hole, bottles are falling down the hole, things are coming up the hole . . .' To the oilmen they were the normal problems encountered with any well, exacerbated by the deviation technique (which is now pretty standard practice but was in its infancy then), but to O'Reilly they were novel—and sobering.

The well, however exciting its prospects, was rapidly eating up Atlantic's resources, and by the end of the year O'Reilly was again forced to raise money, some £15 million, this time through a placing of shares with institutions at £6 a share, a discount of £2.90 on the then market price of £8.90. Even that would be rapidly devoured.

By December the rumours, intense enough before, had become wild as the entire country watched and awaited the result of well 49/9–3. Over Christmas it became known that the bit had been 'lost' in the hole and drilling had to be suspended while they searched for it. Then a 5000-foot cable became stuck. It was finally retrieved, but an electric logging tool was still stuck in the hole, and Gulf was forced to fill it with cement and drill another deviated hole to the side. The days stretched into weeks, still with no news—but plenty of rumour. In January an article in the *Irish Press* by a man called Lloyd Smythe quoted 'oil industry sources' as saying that the appraisal well was dry. 'As soon as the news leaked out to workers on board the rig, panic orders to sell Atlantic shares were placed immediately.' It was largely fantasy—there was no news to leak because no one, even on the rig, knew what the drill would discover once it got to the target area, which was still some way off, but in retrospect Smythe would claim a scoop. The story was contradicted within hours by another classic headline in the *Cork Evening Echo* on 10 January: 'Rig workers elated: Another major oil find'. O'Reilly would later fiercely deny that anyone, either in Atlantic or Gulf, had any prior knowledge of the results of the well:

> Nobody knew until the very end, and even then there was a debate as to whether it was dry or not. If there had been any knowledge earlier, two things would have happened: the government would have been forced to announce it on the spot, and secondly, there was no way Gulf, at $100,000 a day, would have gone on drilling for another thirty days.

By the end of February 1984 the shares had halved and Atlantic was
running out of money yet again. A small firm of Cork stockbrokers,
dealing heavily in the stock, was hammered with debts of £2 million,
adding further to the bearish sentiment that was beginning to build.

The result of the crucial appraisal well, when it was finally announced in April 1984, was shattering. Gulf had found only flows
of salt water in the first two zones, and although testing was still going
on in the third, that would later prove dry too. The shares collapsed
back to 350p and kept heading south, despite a plan for a five-to-
one split—each 25p unit to become a 5p unit.

Although it would be another four years (and not entirely then)
before hopes of a significant find in the Celtic Sea finally died, the
great days of Atlantic Resources were now over. O'Reilly put a brave
face on it, trying to convince his shareholders that such setbacks were
to be expected in the oil exploration business. He also blamed Gulf,
who Sheridan claimed had drilled in the wrong place. But public
opinion, which would have raised him sky-high if oil had been
pumped ashore, had turned against Atlantic, and so had the press.
'What is Atlantic Resources?' mused the magazine *Business and Finance*
in May 1984. 'Is it a vehicle which makes a lot of money for a select
group of people, or is it a means whereby the amateur investor can
end up losing his home and wrecking his family?' Was it just a media
invention, a wild animal over which the Irish authorities had no
control, the author, warming to his theme, went on to wonder. 'Or
is it just one of the more remarkable episodes in the multi-coloured,
larger than life story of A. J. F. O'Reilly, Ireland's most famous ex-
footballing, expatriate businessman?' The answer was a bit of each,
he concluded. There was a serious point buried in this homily, which
would strike home with O'Reilly. 'The O'Reilly spell has made its way
into the marketplace and that is where it counts. If the man's magical
powers cannot be turned into money then a lot of people have been
wasting their time.'

This was an issue which O'Reilly had never properly addressed,
and which caught him at a disadvantage when it was raised. It had
never occurred to him, when he launched Atlantic Resources, that
he would be taking a risk not just with his own and Fitzwilton's money
but with his reputation as well. He was now being forced to accept
that his following in Ireland was such that if he believed in its prospects—which patently he did, subscribing for every rights issue—
then it had to be a good bet. The Irish punters flocked to it in droves,

some 18,500 of them on the register, a huge number for an Irish company, partly at least on the back of his commitment and public enthusiasm. Atlantic had come to represent far more than Fitzwilton ever did to the Irish financial community, offering hope, untold riches and an instant solution to the country's economic ills. O'Reilly had never considered any of that at the outset, and it is doubtful if he would have behaved any differently if he had. As far as he was concerned oil prospecting was like horse racing. There was a good chance of finding oil off Ireland, and he wanted to be in the lead in the process, but, too late, he began to realize Atlantic symbolized rather more than that.

A seasoned oil veteran might have given up at this point—as Gulf wanted to do—but O'Reilly would have none of it. He had found a good oil flow in the Celtic Sea with his second well, he argued, so obviously it was there. The third well had been drilled in the wrong place, that was all, because Gulf had been too ambitious and had gone too far out. Gulf's Sedco rig, battered after fifteen months in the sea off Ireland, went off to Scotland for repairs, but by the autumn a new rig was in place and another well planned, this one on the neighbouring Block 50/6. By now the company had raised £30 million in equity and £10 million in loans, and had spent some £35 million in expenditure on the search for oil and gas—with only that find in Block 49/9 to show for it.

Gulf was increasingly convinced that, despite the flow on the second well, the field on 49/9 contained no more than 8 to 12 million recoverable barrels—too small for a multi-national to bother with, particularly in what was becoming an increasingly hostile tax regime for oil operators in Ireland. But the find could still be of interest to Atlantic, and O'Reilly was so determined to get his oil out that he sought and obtained government permission for Atlantic to drill yet another well on its own. 'We have discovered with well 49/9–2 a flow of oil which by any standards is exciting,' he said in an interview with the *Sunday Press* in August 1985, 'and we drilled in 49/9–3 a well which is now conceded as not having been an appraisal well. Therefore, the appraisal well to the original discovery has to be drilled and we as a company want to make sure it is drilled, and as soon as possible.' He leaned on the government for permission, and he leaned on Gulf, and on 19 October 1985 Gulf began drilling its fourth well on the block. To pay for it, Atlantic raised £10.5 million with yet another share placing (O'Reilly himself invested another £1 million of his own money). Again the pattern was repeated, with the shares soaring as hopes rose, only to crash as fresh rumours came in of further drilling problems. In November 1985, O'Reilly announced that the results so far were 'both positive and encouraging' and that the Atlantic board awaited 'the outcome of future exploration and appraisal wells with enthusiasm'. He was admitting to no despondency. 'It is the belief of your company that the drilling results obtained during 1983 and 1984 confirm that the Celtic Sea is a new hydrocarbon province, fulfilling every hope and expectation held by the company at its foundation.' In the meantime BP was partnering Atlantic in still another well on a neighbouring block and drilling soon hit gas shows, although not enough to make it commercial.

The new Gulf well, 49/9–4, also hit signs of gas and oil, but had to be plugged and abandoned. Early in 1987 they began drilling 49/9–5, and this one, all agreed, had to be make or break. Gulf, Atlantic believed, was still being too ambitious, and the new well would be even nearer to their pool of oil found with 49/9–2, where they would be absolutely certain of finding oil and developing their existing field.

That at least was the theory. The practice was to prove very different. They had now been drilling in the area for six years, during which time Atlantic had sunk over £40 million into wells and seismic work. They had found oil, but that tantalizing flow of 9901 barrels a day had not been repeated anywhere else. Sophisticated seismic surveys and the results of the other wells sunk had now given the geologists a pretty clear picture of what was down there, and this last well would complete the task. 'Psychologically and financially, failure now would be disastrous for Atlantic,' a London analyst was quoted as saying in April 1987. 'The downside is massive, and the chances of success are, at best, reasonable.' A Dublin analyst agreed. 'If it comes up empty, Atlantic will probably call it a day,' he said. 'It would be very hard for it to maintain any credibility whatsoever if this one fails.'

In truth, even if O'Reilly and his friends had high hopes, the stock market expected little, with the shares now all the way back to 11p (55p in the old form). The American investments, misconceived from the start, had proved disastrous, running into the glut of natural gas which followed the end of the oil boom. By the mid-1980s Atlantic's American interests could not even cover interest charges on the considerable bank debt, and as the situation worsened O'Reilly finally did a deal with the banks, repaying the debt in full. He sold or closed down what remained. Atlantic had lost the best part of $10 million in its US operations, giving Stafford and his friends the satisfaction of being proved right, albeit for the wrong reasons. The company now had no other drilling prospects other than the Celtic Sea, so everything hung on this final well on Block 49.

Once again they found oil, and initially it looked promising. Gulf, however, was disappointed at the rate of flow—less than two thousand barrels a day, whereas the operators reckoned it should have been closer to the ten thousand barrels a day rate of 49/9–2 which it had found in 1983. The signs began to look ominous, and a few days later the operators realized they were in sand. 'That was the real disappointment of the whole Atlantic operation,' says Ferguson. 'That was the beginning of the end, and after that we were just trying to keep the whole thing alive, finish the programme of drilling we had to honour but which this field was supposed to finance.' What it clearly showed was that the original find, far from being extensive and putting Ireland 'one step away from self-sufficiency', as O'Reilly had rashly promised at the time, was no more than a tiny pool of oil, not even commercial at falling world oil prices.

At Atlantic's annual meeting a few days later, however, O'Reilly refused to accept any pessimism. The well, he said, was of 'no mean importance' to Atlantic. 'We have established a record second to none on our exploration activities,' he blazed when someone dared to criticize him. 'The record along the Jurassic oil fairway of blocks 49/8, 49/9, 49/10 and 50/6, an area some 400 square miles for a so-called non-proven oil province is a staggering 50 per cent success rate. There can be no question but that our exploratory effort to date in these blocks has been highly successful.'

Although technically this was correct, it was stretching the facts towards their breaking point. Atlantic had found oil all right, but the difference between a well which produces a sustainable and potentially commercial find and a well which produces gas or oil traces is vast. Only one of his five costly wells in the Celtic Sea had produced anything bordering on the commercial, and even that was increasingly looking as if it was an anomaly. 'We may have hit the only puddle of oil ever found,' O'Reilly would admit ruefully later. But he would not admit it at the time, not even to himself.

By early June 1987 BP had begun a new well on the neighbouring 50/6 block and two weeks later O'Reilly announced yet another fund-raising operation to pay for it, this time for £4.3 million. The follow-

ing day Sheridan rang with disastrous news. With three weeks still
to go before it reached the target levels, the drill, biting its way
through the Upper Jurassic and on into the Middle Jurassic before
hitting the Cretaceous, suddenly came on a time-zone that shouldn't
have been there. Many millions of years before there had been an
uptilt, which meant there could be no oil. Bitterly disappointed,
O'Reilly had no option but to call off the financing and abandon the
well. When the news was revealed on Monday to a shocked stock
market, the shares crashed from 32p to 21p. Soon they were 10p,
the equivalent of where they had started all those years ago, and they
would eventually drift back to 3p.

Although drilling would go on for another few years, that was
effectively the end of Atlantic's hopes in the Celtic Sea. O'Reilly would
not give up, arguing that the geologists had at least proved there was
a 'baby' field down there, containing some 10 million barrels of oil,
but attempts to persuade a bigger group to develop it failed. The
economics of the field, now grandly called the Helvick Head field,
were at best marginal: even assuming there were 10 million barrels
down there, the geologists warned that only between 5 per cent and
40 per cent was recoverable, depending on the pressure regime of
the structure. The bottom figure would mean only 500,000 barrels
of oil coming ashore, worth some $7.5 million compared to the cost
of $20 million of getting it out. The 40 per cent figure could yield
a profit, depending of course on the world oil price; at current world
oil prices it would be marginal. As yet no major oil company has
agreed to take the risk, and to this day, other than a few investments
in North Sea fields, it is all that O'Reilly has to show for the £6 million
he personally invested in Atlantic, and the £50 million that he helped
raise in the search for Irish oil.

'I'll guarantee you this,' he says with determination, 'it'll be the
first Irish oil ashore, and one day we'll bring that oil ashore. It's
Ireland's only puddle of oil, and we own it 100 per cent now, and
we'll still do a deal with someone on the basis of they can have 50
per cent in return for doing the drilling.' That may be some years
away yet, since the oil price in the course of 1994 was only a third
of what it was when Atlantic embarked on the North Sea with such
hopes.

But in the meantime there is the Galmoy lead and zinc mine in
County Kilkenny, on which O'Reilly's hopes of being Ireland's only
minerals king rest. The shares in Atlantic were down to 2p at the

end of 1991 when he arranged a merger with the much smaller Conroy to give him, eventually, effective control of the enlarged company. Conroy was being threatened by its two major shareholders, the Finnish group Outokumpu, which had originally bought him out of Tara Exploration, and International Corona of Canada. Conroy owned some interests in small producing oil wells in the USA, but what caught O'Reilly's imagination was Galmoy, which he was not going to leave to the Finns to develop, and another lead-zinc deposit at Lisheen in County Tipperary. They were—are—two of western Europe's major deposits, and if O'Reilly had missed out on oil he was determined not to miss out on minerals entirely.

It was not to come easily, however. Conroy's merger with Atlantic sparked a major board room battle which resulted in the Finns and Canadian shareholders ousting Professor Conroy from the board. But O'Reilly was ahead of the game, buying out the Canadian stake of 16 per cent to take his own personal stake in the enlarged group— which would be called Arcon, the 'AR' for Atlantic Resources—to over 20 per cent. By March 1992 O'Reilly had levered his own men on to the board and the Outukumpu people off. By the autumn he owned 23 per cent, making him the biggest shareholder, and put his younger son Tony O'Reilly Junior, then twenty-five, into the business to continue, with some skill and assurance, the delicate process of getting planning permission. In 1993, as the shares continued to drop, he bought the Finns out and replaced Conroy as chairman.

It will be 1995 at the earliest before the Galmoy mine, after fighting its way through the most tortuous of environmental complaints and government and local regulations, comes into production, the first Irish mine to come on stream since Tara twenty years ago. It will cost $100 million, and already represents an investment on O'Reilly's part of some $25 million, including the money he pumped into Atlantic.

The story of Atlantic Resources, now Arcon, while never central to O'Reilly's fortunes, nevertheless reflects as well as anything his relationship with Ireland and the strange, self-inhibiting contradictions of Irish life. He went into it for a mixture of motives; part avarice, part patriotic and he was to learn, as he had done a decade before with Tara, some hard lessons about the politics of envy that surround investment in Ireland. Later he would dwell angrily on the political mishandling of Ireland's natural resource policy, which he reckons is the real story of Atlantic Resources. In the early 1970s, he would argue, there was a simplistic public notion that Irish oil and minerals belonged to the Irish people at large—what O'Reilly called a sort of Sinn Fein mining policy—which was to prove utterly destructive. In the mid-1970s, the coalition government introduced a series of measures, including the abandonment of export tax relief and a combination of royalties, state ownership rights and corporation tax which added up to an effective tax rate of 85% on profits, killing exploration for the rest of the decade.

The oil crisis and the boom in North Sea oil gave the country a second chance but again the ball was dropped, with the Labour leader Dick Spring and Justin Keating showing a complete lack of commercial awareness. O'Reilly, who liked Spring personally, argued vehemently that the find on 49/9-2 was the moment to proclaim to the world that potentially Ireland was the next oil province, and to change the terms to make it so. 'This is a ratio game,' he argued again and again to anyone who would listen. 'If 100 oil companies want to develop 150 exploration theories in Irish waters with international capital, what has Ireland to lose?' Oil companies, he pointed out, understood well enough that terms were often toughened after major discoveries had been made. But to do so before exploration even began was a huge mistake. 'The world of oil exploration is a poker game, and we simply didn't know how to play it. 1983 was the year to show we understood the business and the politicians failed the test.' A later Fianna Fail government, recognising Spring's folly, made the terms much more favourable, but it was too late: a unique opportunity to make Ireland self-sufficient in oil and gas had gone.

19

Double-kicker at Heinz

HEINZ WORLD HEADQUARTERS, PITTSBURGH, 11 SEPTEMBER 1985. Precisely as he had done every year since H.J. Heinz went public thirty-nine years before, Henry John Heinz II rose to address the shareholders who regularly turned up for the company's annual meeting. Most of those present, representing the big insurance companies, banks, trusts and investment funds who held Heinz stock, were familiar faces, long-time followers of the group, greeted as old friends by the seventy-seven-year-old Heinz chairman, but there was a smattering of new ones who had recently bought into a share that was becoming one of the hottest blue chips on Wall Street. Although O'Reilly's address would be the highlight of the day, Jack too was an attraction, personifying as he did the spirit and the culture of Heinz, the man who represented a living link with the company's founder over a hundred years before. Now that Henry Ford II was dead, not many of America's grand old companies were still chaired by a member of the founding family.

As always, Jack played his role immaculately, the personification of the grandee proprietor smiling beneficently on the custodians of what, he seemed to suggest, was still his family business. His elegant opening address made the ritual references to his ancestry, gently reminding everyone whose company this really was. 'There was a time,' said Jack to an appreciative little chuckle, 'when the year-end results were summarized in a few vital statistics on a single piece of notepaper and delivered for the personal scrutiny of my grandfather and father.' That was not possible today (more laughter). 'Nor, for that matter'—and here a note of regret crept in—'can this or any other company today escape the close examination of many publics.'

'But I'm sure Grandfather Heinz would have coped with this new accountability. I do know he was a remarkable man, an entrepreneur in the literal meaning of that term.' Old HJ had seen it all coming. 'He foresaw, with clarity unknown to his day and age, that there would be a market for processed pure food products in the America that was emerging from the Civil War.' He had seen that Heinz would expand abroad, that the entire world would one day be 'our field', and it was exactly a hundred years ago that he had sold his first products to Fortnum & Mason. 'The process continues today in places like China and Zimbabwe, as Heinz and Heinz-affiliated brand goods reach out for new markets.' Jack held court in this vein for just the requisite length, and then, with perfect timing, made his connection.

> I shall now perform the duty of introducing our president, Tony O'Reilly, for his state-of-the-company summary. In so doing, I can think of nothing more complimentary to say of him than to compare his energy, vitality and genius for worldwide salesmanship and statesmanship most favourably with the man who founded this company 116 years ago.

O'Reilly could scarcely have asked for better. With his keen sense of history and apostolic succession, he was, he understood, receiving not only the benediction of Jack Heinz but of all the past generations of Heinzes too. Jack was now anointing him publicly as his heir, the mantle of the founder passing down the generations to rest on the shoulders of this Irishman. O'Reilly had been chief executive for six years, and he and Jack had rubbed along perfectly amicably if distantly: O'Reilly consulted the old man from time to time, but never let him think he had any more power than he did in Gookin's day. The company, deemed by the markets and the rest of the food industry to be a failure in the 1960s and early 1970s, was now rated a spectacular success, each year outperforming all but a couple of America's big food companies. That year Merrill Lynch said that Heinz showed 'the best unit volume and gross margin gains in the currently strong industry', while Morgan Stanley noted 'the quality of consistency in its earnings and the corporate focus on shareholder value'. Its performance had strengthened and consolidated O'Reilly's commanding position inside the group, stilling the criticism that he was spreading himself too thinly, and caused Jack, one of the richest men in America, to glow appreciatively as he gave yet another $10 million cheque to the city of Pittsburgh (to which he donated some $300 million in his lifetime). The share price, going nowhere through most of the 1970s, was now a glittering performer, rising from $10 in 1980 to $55 by the autumn of 1985 as food shares generally, but Heinz particularly, became fashionable.

In many ways, luck was with O'Reilly in these early years as chief executive, although as the decade wore on he would make his own luck. For a start, despite Gookin's efforts the Heinz O'Reilly took over had plenty of fat, with too many employees working in too many out-of-date factories, layers of excess middle management, and an abundance of non-productive salesmen. There was always a nostalgic or paternalistic reason for Jack Heinz not to have closed a particular factory or brand line and, although Gookin had broken the old feudal system, the task of streamlining Heinz had barely begun when O'Reilly replaced him. Without qualm or hesitation, he closed factories and entire product lines, took the capital realized and put it back into the most profitable and fastest-growing areas of the business.

Inflation was the great friend of food companies with their narrow margins and tough competition through the 1970s. 'We passed on our increases and then some,' O'Reilly recalled later. 'I love the euphemism "rounding up". I've never heard of any price decision taken on the basis of "rounding down".' Inflation in America had peaked at over 10 per cent in 1981, but it was 1984 before it had dropped back below 4 per cent and the inflation mentality took still longer to disappear—long enough to swell the nominal value of Heinz's sales and to expand its margins far faster than costs. In addition, the heavy expenditure on modern plants, begun under Gookin and accelerated under O'Reilly, was now kicking in, swelling margins and return on capital.

But there was a fourth factor, another one-off effect, which had in these years added greatly to O'Reilly's now fast-growing fortune in Heinz stock and that of all other Heinz shareholders (and senior executives, most of whom were now wealthy men). The share price was responding to the higher earnings, which had averaged 15.1 per cent growth for the past five years (more than twice the rise in sales), and dividends, which had risen at a compound 16.6 per cent. But it was also reacting to something else: Heinz shares were being re-rated, not exactly to the glamour status of the fast-growing electronic stocks of Silicon Valley, which often sold at 30–40 times annual earnings per share, but to the top of the food manufacturing sector. Where once its shares had sold at seven times earnings now they sold at fourteen times much higher earnings. Heinz was becoming something of a cult stock among pension funds and other institutions who liked their money invested in solid, well-managed companies growing at better-than-average but sustainable rates, with low borrowings and good dividend prospects. Sales had passed the $1 billion mark for the first time in 1972, the year after O'Reilly moved to Pittsburgh. Now, thirteen years later, sales, helped considerably by inflation, were over $4 billion and the stock market value of the company, $600 million then, had grown to $4.3 billion with the same number of shares in issue.

This was the background against which Jack Heinz felt able to endorse O'Reilly so fulsomely, and O'Reilly for his part didn't miss a beat as he accepted the baton. Sitting beside Don Wiley, the company's general counsel, he rose, squeezed Jack Heinz's hand warmly, and moved over to the rostrum to accept his applause. 'Whenever you and I get together,' he began, looking over at Jack, 'I am smitten by the fact that this company has had only five chief executive officers in its 116-year history. I am the latest, you are precisely in the middle, and you have personal memories of the first, who was your grandfather, and of the second, who was your father. You are to be profoundly envied.' After that it scarcely mattered what he said: the audience was on his side. 'He had them eating out of his hand,' said one former director. 'He has an extraordinary ability to communicate, particularly when he's on his feet in front of an audience, and in the euphoria of that day he was good.'

His address was a mixture of hard financial detail and market analysis, with lists of new products, acquisitions, a homily on the demographics of America—it was getting older—and his usual smattering of carefully woven quotations, including one from Alvin Toffler, author of *Future Shock*, which had impressed O'Reilly when it first came out. Toffler, he told the meeting, said that 'future shock is the dizzying disorientation brought on by the premature arrival of the future—it may well be, he says, "the most important disease of tomorrow" '. Heinz, O'Reilly implied, was in good shape to meet whatever shock tomorrow brought. He flashed up slides to show the shareholders how every financial ratio that seriously mattered to them was good and getting better: pre-tax return on average invested capital was at a record 30.5 per cent, and return on shareholders' equity had risen from 15.4 per cent ten years before to an all-time high of 22.6 per cent, well above the average of other food companies. Since the end of 1980, he said triumphantly, a Heinz shareholder who reinvested his dividends (which some of the pension funds would have done) had realized a 433 per cent increase in their investment, compared to 76 per cent for the average of American shares in general.

His most triumphant statistic, however, was the success of Heinz's takeover policy which Gookin had begun with the Star-Kist tuna company and Hubinger, a wet corn miller which made high-fructose sweetener used as a replacement for sugar in Heinz's tomato ketchup (and which was to prove a huge success for Heinz, which paid $46 million for it in 1976, invested another $35 million and sold it in 1992 for $326 million). In ten years Heinz, he said, had spent $370 million on acquisitions, including Weight Watchers International and its associated companies, Foodways and Camargo. The buying spree had included a Burger King chain in Puerto Rico, Nadler salads in Germany, the Country Kitchen mushroom company in Britain, Jerky Treats dog food in Texas, a couple of tuna companies (one in France, another in Canada) to expand Star-Kist, the Sperlari candy maker in Italy, the Olivine edible oil business in Zimbabwe ... nineteen companies in all, none of them spectacular, but adding up to an imposing range of new businesses between them. 'From that list of small, well-focused acquisitions,' said O'Reilly, 'we produced $60 million after-tax contributions to fiscal 1985 earnings', which was 22 per cent of the total. On most criteria, he added, these acquisitions were now worth $1 billion, which meant, he elaborated for those who had not quite got the point, that every $1 of extra value had cost it 37 cents.

There were new products, too, which he reeled off: instant vegetarian meals for infants, concentrated spaghetti sauce, an 'exciting line' of Weight Watchers frozen entrees, cat foods, dog foods, barbecue sauces, desserts—Heinz, he said, was spending $50 million a year on new product lines. What he did not mention was that some of the acquisitions, notably Nadler, were proving troublesome, and some of the new products, such as the barbecue sauce, had bombed.

The previous year, he went on, Heinz had launched what he grandly called 'The Year of the Operator', by which he meant that

Heinz had embarked on the most radical examination yet of its cost structure with the aim of becoming, in the jargon used around Heinz, 'the LCO', or 'low cost operator' in every one of its activities, the only way to stay in low margin businesses now that inflation was slowing down again. One of Heinz's new non-executive directors, Dr Richard Cyert, president of Carnegie-Mellon University in Pittsburgh, had articulated the principle which was rapidly sweeping through corporate America. 'It is incumbent on business to automate, emigrate or evaporate,' said Cyert, and Heinz was rapidly automating. In the longer term, O'Reilly preached at his management meetings, the food industry was going to grow at an overall rate of 1 per cent a year, and to do better than that Heinz had to grab market share, to produce new products in 'niche' markets, or to cut costs. O'Reilly was intent on doing all three. From 1983 onwards he had preached the dangers of relying on inflation continuing to bail out inefficient companies. 'The inflation party's over,' he kept saying. 'If we can't get our profit out of volume and out of price, we've got to get it out of cost.' In the UK alone, where the Heinz business was being seriously threatened by the growth of supermarket own-label, the modernization programme was costing £100 million and resulting in a drop in the British workforce from the 10,000 when O'Reilly was there to 3600. 'We are succeeding in this pretty brutal battleground by becoming more capital-intensive,' O'Reilly told a group of analysts later that year.

At the end of his address, Heinz shareholders crowded round to ask a few more detailed questions of O'Reilly and his team, but there were no real complaints. Heinz was on a roll, and O'Reilly's corporate status in America with it. America was now entering a new business phase, one which *Fortune* magazine, which put O'Reilly on the cover of its June 1986 issue as being the most visible symbol of it, dubbed 'The New Economy'. It was, the magazine said, an exhilarating time:

> Rarely have so many gratifying things happened so suddenly to the economy. Interest rates have plunged, the dollar has weakened, and inflation is advancing at its lowest rate since 1967. The stock and bond markets have been booming, and the economy, 42 months into an expansion, is still growing in the steady, moderate fashion that many economists consider ideal.

But among the paradoxes of the new economy, it added, was that more would be demanded of corporate managers than ever before. 'The competition between companies and between nations has grown fiercer, and the margin for error has shrunk.' O'Reilly, it said, 'a leading apostle of cost-cutting', was a marketing visionary who was 'managing for the new economy before there was a new economy'. Interviewed twice by the magazine, O'Reilly was quoted as saying, 'We're a nickel-and-dime business, an industry that takes no prisoners.' His latest strategy for cost-cutting, noted *Fortune*, was 'about as radical as an industrial company can pursue: he threatens to quit manufacturing'. This was something of an exaggeration. What O'Reilly had said was that he was enquiring of his executives whether the company should buy or make. Heinz should look at whether it was cheaper to get someone else to make its products for it—small manufacturing companies which could manage factories better than it could. The mere suggestion had, he said, galvanized the people at Heinz whose jobs were at stake—which was what he intended. 'We discuss this with our factory managers, and it creates a new level of constructive tension.'

Although Weight Watchers would soon take over as the new engine of growth, the early 1980s belonged to Heinz USA, the laggard of the 1960s and early 1970s, where there was ample room to cut costs. Dick Patton, as O'Reilly would later write to him in a retirement note, had 'taken the company by the ears' in 1976, but it was from 1980 onwards that profits began to surge in earnest. Inside the company these would later be known as 'the J. Connolly years', the time when the company's biggest subsidiary was run by J. Wray Connolly, a tough lawyer who had become treasurer of the company in 1973. Connolly was a native of Pittsburgh, one of the few senior managers who had not been imported. When Gookin bought Hubinger in 1976, he and O'Reilly sent Connolly in to sort it out, and he did so with considerable success, earning promotion to the top job at Heinz USA when Dick Patton was promoted to area vice-president. Patton had reduced the workforce by two thousand and done much of the hard work by the time Connolly arrived, but there was a lot more to be achieved, particularly in realizing the profit potential from the product with which Heinz was still most closely associated: tomato ketchup. There had been some major innovations in ketchup in the 1970s, most notably the Vol-Pak containers for the food services industry,

but by the early 1980s Heinz was experimenting with a squeezable
plastic ketchup container which was to revolutionize the way ketchup
was sold. 'Somebody had done some packaging research that focused
on leading packages which consumers were the most dissatisfied with,'
recalls Connolly.

> And one of the packages was our ketchup bottle, and the reason
> they were dissatisfied was because they couldn't get the product
> out of the bottle. And that research was done by American Can
> or one of the big packaging companies, and they brought it to
> us, but the problem was they didn't have the material that would
> provide an adequate moisture barrier. Shelf life on ketchup is
> at least two years, but in fact it's often much longer than that—
> it's a very high acid product and it really can't spoil.

A Heinz team went to work with American Can, and three years
later they had produced the squeezable plastic ketchup container a
full eighteen months before their competitors. It was an instant success. Until then, the mature ketchup market had seemed to have
gone ex-growth, but the new packaging proved otherwise, and later
innovations, such as a salsa-style ketchup, would prove the same point
again and again since. When they launched the 28-ounce bottle,
Heinz's market share surged a full five points. Soon there was a
smaller 20-ounce bottle, a 44-ounce, and even a 64-ounce bottle which
O'Reilly dubbed the 'hernia-size'.

From his early years in Pittsburgh, and right up to the time he
became chief executive, O'Reilly had taken direct responsibility for
Heinz USA and would continue to keep more than a close eye on it
after that. But it was Connolly and his team, many of whom were to
go on to the most senior positions within the group, who now drove
forward his strategy far better than he could have hoped. The growth
of the fast food chains, with their huge demand for ketchup, faced
Heinz's strong brand with a potential problem which it turned into
an asset. Heavy advertising and clever promotion made the Heinz
bottle one of the few branded products acceptable—indeed necessary—on the tables of a good American restaurant. 'It is part of the
secret of our profitability,' confides a Heinz man. 'Curiously, you
define the quality of a restaurant in America by whether it has got
a bottle of Heinz ketchup on the tables. In a restaurant in Britain,
if you found a bottle of ketchup you'd say, "Jesus Christ this is Nick's

Diner we're at!"' At the other end of the spectrum, through the 1970s Heinz had built up an 'institutional food services' business, or IFS, which essentially means selling in bulk to the big retail chains and restaurants which are more interested in cost than brand. By the 1980s it was offering its restaurant customers ketchup in every form from single-serve sachets to 450-ounce Vol-Pak bags hanging in wall racks in the kitchen, refilling in an instant the bowls on the tables or the reusable squeezable bottles. Heinz was synonymous with ketchup when it had only 36 per cent of the market in the early 1970s. Now the market share was pushed over 50 per cent (today it is 52.5 per cent in volume and 57 per cent in dollar terms) for the first time. They had already taken out rafts of costs by closing factories and combining the production into modern units, particularly at Fremont (which today can produce 130,000 cases of 14-ounce ketchup bottles a day), so the effect on profits was dramatic. From break-even in the 1970s and a small profit in 1980, Heinz USA grew to the point where it made $375 million on the same volume.

By the 1986 annual meeting O'Reilly was able to tell shareholders that, although sales growth had slowed, profits were bounding ahead even faster. Heinz, he said, now had $405 million of cash in its balance sheet, roughly the equivalent of its borrowings, so its advance had been achieved without borrowing money and without issuing new shares. 'The steady and consistent improvement in the value of your investment is, in my view, not an accident. It is, I stress to you, our primary goal.' The market value by then was $6 billion, and O'Reilly and his senior colleagues were becoming seriously rich from the share option scheme put in place by Burt Gookin and extended since. Weight Watchers that year made $60 million and was now growing faster than any other part of the group, its sales rapidly approaching $1 billion—a level only achieved by Heinz after 100 years in business.

The apparently inexorable rise in profits over these years hid a number of problems, and O'Reilly soon had to accept that for every success there would always be a setback—sometimes more than one. In 1983 Star-Kist suddenly slowed down as the western Pacific opened up as a fishing area and cheaper tuna, mostly from Thailand, flooded the American market. Joe Bogdanovitch, now past seventy, found he could not compete against labour costs a fraction of what they were at Terminal Island. Something radical had to be done and O'Reilly quickly accepted that his old friend, whom he still regarded as one of the more invaluable members of senior management, was not the man to do it. Bogdanovitch was in the same paternal position as Jack Heinz had been—too emotionally wedded to his business, and particularly the operation at Terminal Island, which was now hopelessly uncompetitive.

O'Reilly called up Dick Beattie, whom he had used to sort out problems in Heinz USA, Hubinger and Heinz UK, each time with clinical success. If ever there was a 'numbers man' it was Beattie, a dedicated, relentless executive who, set a task, ploughed straight ahead, intent only on delivering the result that first Gookin and now O'Reilly asked of him. Beattie quickly decided that if Star-Kist was going to compete it could do so only by achieving what O'Reilly was trying to do in every part of the group: become the low-cost operator. There was no way it could do that at Californian wage rates, so he invested heavily in new equipment and systems for processing and canning in Puerto Rico, where Heinz already had a canning factory, and in Western Samoa, where wage rates were a third of the American operation. In 1985, with O'Reilly's support, he closed Terminal Island—thus killing the age-old tuna industry in San Pedro, to loud protests from the local community. It cut costs by $5 a case, and probably saved Star-Kist. 'We did it just in time,' says Beattie. 'The low-cost exporters from the Philippines and Thailand were taking over the American own-label market.' He also cut back the fishing fleet, and decided that the big growth area for Star-Kist was pet food, which he reckoned could become a much bigger player in the Heinz family. Bogdanovitch had taken the company into pet foods in the 1940s as a by-product of tuna, and by the mid-1970s 9-Lives, its main cat food brand (represented in its advertising by Morris the cat, which was to become one of the best-known characters in American advertising lore) had sales of $81 million and a 21.5 per cent market share. By the time Beattie arrived it was in trouble in a market which was fiercely competitive, but again by cutting costs, spending heavily on promotion and with the help of a number of acquisitions, pet food would become an important contributor to Heinz by the late 1980s.

Star-Kist is an interesting example of O'Reilly at work at Heinz: logical, decisive and commercially cold-blooded, doing what his head rather than his heart told him, prepared to face up to the consequences, even at the risk of deeply offending one of his oldest friends and supporters (Bogdanovitch remained a friend, and, now past eighty, is still on the Heinz board). If he had ducked the tough decisions and not acted in a manner which to outsiders might be seen as ruthlessness, O'Reilly would never have got anywhere near the top of Heinz—and even if he had, he would not have stayed there long. O'Reilly was probably no tougher than most CEOs in large American companies, but on the other hand he was no less so either. His senior executives all talk about his ability to analyze a problem quickly, and decide on a course of action, and he himself confesses to a liking for problems and the intellectual satisfaction of cutting to the heart of them and deciding what action to take.

In O'Reilly's time at Heinz—or at any of his other companies—there was never a period without a problem, ranging in intensity from the fight over the profit-juggling to an over-supply of tomato paste which threatened to smash prices, a new entrant into the cat food market, or the dominant position of Campbell's in branded soups. There was, for instance, the Star-Kist problem in Canada in 1985, when some of its tuna was condemned by public health officials. Rather than withdraw all its product instantly from the market— 23,000 cases of it—the Star-Kist management under Beattie protested, arguing that the tests were wrong. The news leaked and blew up into a major media issue in Canada before O'Reilly was even aware of it. When he did find out, he was furious. It broke every rule in his management book, notably his frequent warning to all his executives that World Headquarters in Pittsburgh should never be presented with surprises—the instant a potential problem was brewing he wanted to know about it. 'One broad principle emerges from this,' he wrote to Joe Bogdanovitch in October 1985 in his annual end-of-term report sent to each of his senior vice-presidents, 'and that is that there is *no margin whatsoever* in H.J. Heinz Company or any of its subsidiaries taking on public health officials in the area of sanitation claims. Broadly speaking, we are on a hiding to nothing.' From now on, he ordered all his senior managers, they were to take the view that 'in *all* situations, the public officials are right, whatever the cost of product write-off (we have examples as in Italy where the product write-off cost us over $12 million).' He was not going to allow any risk with the Heinz brand, and it must never happen again. 'The durability and quality image of our brands remains the distinctive reason why we have such strong image and share price and I, as I am sure you also, intend to keep it that way,' he told Bogdanovitch. The thought of a similar event happening in the USA, he ended darkly, was 'too chilling for words'.

Each problem deserved and got his full attention at the time, some successfully, others less so. Under his jokey, good-humoured and collegial manner there was an icy, analytical nature which all the Heinz executives, without exception, encountered at some point, and which all dreaded for fear it was turned on them. Beattie says his relationship with O'Reilly was never the same after the Canadian affair, and his last years at Heinz were unhappy and frustrated ones. His old opponent John Connell never felt comfortable around O'Reilly either, and ran foul of him in the early 1980s.

O'Reilly's annual assessments, even of his most successful and senior managers, were merciless and unsentimental. In this period he had seven area vice-presidents immediately beneath him, the key four being Dick Patton, J. Connolly, Joe Bogdanovitch and Paul Corddry, all of them experienced, hardened and hard-working executives. O'Reilly, however, never let them slacken off or allowed them a mistake. He thought of himself as an unambiguous leader, providing a clear sense of direction, and spent a lot of time and thought communicating precisely what he wanted and expected from his key people. 'I write to each of the [area vice-presidents] every year categorising their virtues and what I perceive to be their shortcomings,' he told *Business* magazine in June 1986,

> saying things like 'You'll never be president of Heinz' or 'Your style is professorial: I want you more action oriented'. The notion of collegiality has triumphed and, with it, the need for me to behave like a shit has substantially diminished, though the process is not so emollient as it sounds. There are some very acerbic exchanges. What comes out of them though is absolute clarity of objective.

These remarks were based on his most recent assessments of his senior managers, which were obviously still running through his mind. Dick Patton was told that two of the four companies under his control, O'Reilly told him, the Canadian and Australian subsidiaries, were having difficulties which he had not done enough to rectify. Patton, O'Reilly acknowledged, had considerable strengths; but he had weaknesses too and O'Reilly did not draw back from pointing them out.

Patton, Connolly and Corddry were probably among the best in the food industry, with track records to prove it, while Bogdanovitch was a one-off, but the O'Reilly assessments make it clear just how demanding he was of his managers, and how hard it was to please him. If there was a good reason for something going wrong, and he was told about it in good time and in the proper way, he was generally understanding and supportive, helping to find ways of dealing with it. But if he thought the reason had to do with poor management, or an over-optimistic budget, he could be unforgiving. Either way, the individual executive was made clearly aware of O'Reilly's feelings, which would be spelt out in some detail in his annual assessment. 'One of the characteristics of Tony, which I noticed early on,' says Dr Richard Cyert, a Heinz non-executive director,

> which is one of the most difficult characteristics to cultivate, is his ability to get rid of people who are doing a marginally satisfactory job. In other words, an executive you might give a 'C' to, who's not failing but you can see a better job could be done with another person. Those are very difficult people to fire. And Tony has the guts to get rid of very good people, and he does it in a very humane way—people go away pretty rich from Heinz—but they are still 'C' executives. And that's real leadership, the things to me that make him an outstanding CEO.

Despite the atmosphere of creative tension, O'Reilly liked to describe his management style as 'collegial'. And for the most part it was—just so long as you were allowed inside the college. Dick Beattie, for all his dedication and hard work, never quite understood that atmosphere and after the Canadian debacle he saw a different side of the Heinz boss. Beattie recalls the tremendous pressure that O'Reilly imposed on him to make his numbers, and his cold anger when things were going wrong, or when he thought a local management was hiding behind orders coming down from Pittsburgh. 'Once he misunderstood what I was trying to say to the executives in Star-Kist, and I heard he thought I was pandering to them at his expense, saying they couldn't have this perk because world headquarters had decided against it,' says Beattie.

> And he gave me a real pasting down the telephone. I was dumbfounded, and he really chewed my ass off, and I couldn't believe it. I felt so bad afterwards because my intentions were

totally honourable and I never intended to undermine Tony's decision, and I saw myself as a dedicated servant doing his best. Unfortunately my command of English wasn't good enough or something.

Beattie says he for one found it hard to get close to O'Reilly. 'I often envied some of his Irish friends, who had this brotherly, very friendly relationship, as opposed to ours which was cool. I suspect that part of his style is to keep people always on their toes, never cock-sure of their position.'

O'Reilly often said that playing rugby for Ireland had taught him how to be a loser, and, although naturally competitive, he knew when to retreat in business too. 'If I were to depict one simple underlying philosophy of Tony O'Reilly, it would be commercial cowardice,' says one of his senior-vice presidents. He does not, he quickly adds, mean it unkindly—O'Reilly himself would agree. 'Picking a fight or joining in a Star Wars–type battle with a Goliath in general might be quite interesting but generally would be profitless,' the executive goes on.

> To be in the Coca-Cola wars or the orange juice wars, or to be attacking Proctor & Gamble who traditionally have limitless pockets, is the type of battle Tony has been trying to avoid all his life. He likes to be in markets where Heinz has either a proprietary brand, or a dominant position, so that we are in control, as opposed to being the number three, picking the battle with the monolithic giant. Or being in a less competitive market, so the profit margins are more reliable. That's one reason why in the United States we have not attacked Campbell's by introducing a major brand of soup, even though we're the brand leader in many countries around the world. Campbell's has 80 per cent of the American soup market, and although it's a battle we'd dearly love to win, it's a battle which would be too bloody to fight. So that's commercial cowardice, but it's also good commercial sense.

One executive, hearing O'Reilly talk in this vein for the first time, says he muttered to himself: 'My God, this man has no stomach for business', but he soon changed his mind. 'If you dig a little deeper, you understand the debris of the bones of CEOs along the route, of people who took on 70 per cent market shares and lost everything.'

O'Reilly probably had a more fundamental philosophy, however, which was to arm himself with as much information and facts, good and bad, as he could before making a decision. 'I have a view facts are friendly,' he said in a 1986 interview. 'I keep saying to my people, "Tell me what the situation is. Don't tell me the good news, tell me *all* the news." You cannot have too much information coming into your desk about your business.'

He was also, he added, devoted to 'the principle of rapid response', and his counter-attacks could be savage. 'If you are fighting Heinz in the market place and you gain one point of market share,' he said in that interview, 'you can be sure that will be followed swiftly by retaliation from us and we are generally able to deliver because we have a lot of reserves.'

Every Friday night, no matter where he was, he got the sales figures from every Heinz affiliate in the world, together with commentaries and comparisons with budget and with the previous year. Where other CEOs might look at more sophisticated figures (and O'Reilly got others as well), these raw sales data acted as his antennae, an early warning system from which he could sense a business starting to turn sour. 'It all starts with sales,' he would insist as he stood over the telex machine (now fax) reading the figures as they came through. From these he could get a feel for how the highly successful Plasmon operation in Italy was doing in its efforts to promote Weight Watchers or its new range of baby foods which dominated the Italian market. What was wrong with the new Stanley Wine acquisition in Australia which was not paying off? What about sales of ketchup in the tricky Belgian market, or imported British meat products in Canada? 'If you're making the sales, then with our tight budgetary systems everything else falls into place,' he continually told his executives at their regular management meetings to review performance and budgets. 'If sales waver, you're going to have to do something pretty quickly.'

If O'Reilly was tough on his Heinz executives, he was equally tough and demanding of himself. Now in his late forties, and with his share options in Heinz worth more than $50 million, he was working harder than ever, and as his success at Heinz demanded even greater effort to replicate and improve on it. Observing him closely, the new president of Heinz USA, David Sculley, was astonished by the amount he could get through. O'Reilly had identified Sculley, younger brother of John Sculley, the former chairman of Apple Computers (the third brother, Arthur, is managing director of Morgan Guaranty Trust), as one of the company's stars, a possible O'Reilly successor when he steps down as CEO.

Sculley, ten years O'Reilly's junior, is a lean, elegant man with a relaxed, attractive style which appealed to O'Reilly from the first time they met in 1973. Brought up on Long Island, the son of a lawyer, Sculley graduated from Harvard with an economics degree in 1968 and joined Lever Brothers, where by the age of twenty-five he had already become group product manager for All detergent, one of America's biggest-selling lines. Two years later he was head-hunted for a job at Heinz. When he turned up for his interview at the Pierre Hotel in Manhattan to meet the company's president he had no intention of taking the job, but then he fell under the spell of Tony O'Reilly. To the high-flying Sculley at that point, both Heinz, one of the dullest companies in the unexciting food sector, and Pittsburgh, which he regarded as a provincial backwater (he had never been there), held little interest, and he wasn't even sure why he had gone to the interview. 'Pittsburgh didn't even have a field hockey team,' he complained (Sculley had played for the US men's field hockey team). But as O'Reilly told him of the changes taking place at Heinz, and his plans for rejuvenating Heinz USA with its enormous un-tapped potential, a flicker of interest began to stir in Sculley. This might just be fun. But what about Pittsburgh? Come and see it, O'Reilly urged him, it was actually a great place to live, work and raise kids in. In the middle of the interview the telephone rang and Sculley watched as O'Reilly broke off to handle a crisis. There was a fire in a Heinz factory somewhere which was blazing out of control. O'Reilly, says Sculley, reacted with impressive coolness, identifying clearly what was going on, who had been hurt, what the damage was, and then giving precise and clear instructions on moving supplies in from other plants. By the time he had put down the phone Sculley was mentally halfway to Pittsburgh—he could enjoy working with this man.

He moved to Pittsburgh a few months later to join the grocery division of Heinz USA and O'Reilly, identifying in him a disguised toughness and fierce ambition as well as a willingness to take risks, soon promoted him and kept doing so. He made him a vice-president in 1982 and, after a spell in London under John Connell, president of Heinz USA in 1985, where he succeeded the newly promoted J. Connolly. (Sculley today is senior vice-president of the parent group, one of the top four executives at Heinz.)

Sculley came to travel a great deal with O'Reilly as they toured the plants, talked to the suppliers and customers, gave sales talks and so on. Far from these being a chore to his chief executive, Sculley quickly realized that O'Reilly was having fun on these trips. 'Tony is on the road continuously,' says Sculley, 'because he likes to be where the action is.' As a former sports star himself, he also—as others had done many times over the years—made the analogy between O'Reilly's character-building tours with the Lions rugby team and his abilities as an executive. 'He is an incredibly competitive person, with a passion for life and a passion for business,' he says.

> I think in many ways business for Tony is very much like a continuous rugby match, with its ferocious competitive environment, where market share and profit and return on equity are the points on the board, the ultimate measure of success. I view him very much as a player coach, a person who not only brings extraordinary leadership skills but is also on the field with you—he's not the sort of person who sits on the sidelines.

Although used to hard work, Sculley soon found travelling with O'Reilly taxed even him. A day in the life of O'Reilly when they are on the road, he says, often begins at six—maybe seven if it has been a particularly late night. O'Reilly would order every newspaper available, the more the better, from as many parts of the world as possible. 'So obviously he will read the *New York Times*, the *Wall Street Journal*, the *Financial Times*, some of the London and Irish papers—these are standard for him, and he'll go through them in detail,' says Sculley. 'That's for immediate information, not only what's going on in the business world, but the world in general. He sees the political world as not only very interesting, but also as having an impact on the way he sees Heinz and the way he sees business.'

O'Reilly's other early morning intake is a stack of faxes that can run to a hundred pages, possibly 70 per cent of them relating to articles that have been sent from various parts of the world, such as Australia and Ireland, but mostly from his control centre in Pittsburgh. Ted Smyth, a former Irish foreign affairs official who is now head of corporate affairs at Heinz and who usually travels with him, supplies him with the results of his office's detailed trawl of business magazines and reports—anything which might have even the most peripheral interest for Heinz. Through the day there is more: battle-

field reports by fax from Heinz affiliates around the world, weekly
flash reports from every single company, detailed information on
events which might affect fish prices, tomato prices and much else.
'So Tony is as well informed as any leader I know,' says Sculley
and he uses an informal network of communications which must be
unique. If you are in a country such as Australia or New Zealand,
South Africa or Zimbabwe, he knows the Prime Minister or the President and we get invited to dinner or a drink, and he always has ways
of getting hold of people who can help him.' Sculley would find
O'Reilly on the phone early in the morning, faxes and newspapers
spread around him, checking in with key lieutenants throughout the
world in their different time zones. 'He relies very much on the
continuity and the information of those people,' says Sculley,

> and he has absolutely no hesitation whatsoever in breaking the
> traditional chain of command and going right down in the
> organisation to talk to whomsoever he feels an issue may be
> more relevant to—if he's not able to get a particular managing
> director, or a senior vice-president, he will simply call the gen-
> eral manager in charge of sales just to talk to them, and no
> one minds, because that person usually brings his superior up-
> to-date with the conversation.

Much of that, says Sculley, is done by 7.30 when they start the day
proper with a breakfast meeting in O'Reilly's room where the other
Heinz staff update him on the schedule for the day. O'Reilly doesn't
travel with a secretary or assistant, and is actually remarkably self-
sufficient, packing and unpacking from a single suitcase with a skill
born of much travel over many years. He is never without his diary,
the one piece of information he has with him twenty-four hours a
day. 'His time is a fixed commodity,' says Sculley, 'and he has to
constantly reallocate that time in order to fit the needs of the world.'
It is a simple Heinz diary, such as everyone else in the company uses,
two pages facing each other representing the seven days of the week,
and within each day an hour-by-hour list tells him where he is going
to be, who he's having lunch with and so forth. Sitting beside him in
the plane or at meetings, Sculley noticed how he worked his diary
constantly through the day. 'Like we've got to cancel a trip to London
because we've got a problem in California,' he says,

so we'll be going to California tonight and he'll be having lunch with the head of the Fishermen's Association, and we'll be visiting two factories in the afternoon, then he'll be giving a speech and flying back the next evening. So London has to be rescheduled, which impacts something else—it's a constantly dynamic world which he's able to adjust. He doesn't rely on anyone else to do it, he keeps control of his own time and he basically reorders the priorities on a constant basis. We'll have a meeting and throughout it he'll probably receive three or four telephone calls and usually he'll call those people back. But if something is critically important he'll talk for a few minutes. He's able then to pick up the conversation precisely where we left off. You only have to brief Tony once, then it's off to wherever the schedule is for the day, visit two or three factories, meeting the factory workers, getting a feel for what's going on. Say it's the Bloomsburg pet food factory, the biggest in the world, so we get a briefing, look at the statistics, the productivity improvements and so on, and he loves these details—if you give him a document to read, whereas most people read the executive summary, he will read the whole thing and the exhibits and appendices as well.

Then maybe for lunch we've flown up to another city and he'll have a number of action meetings which are stacked one on top of the other which will probably take us up to seven, and if there have been any problems he will pick the phone up straightaway. There is a phone in the car and a phone in the plane and he's constantly using it, and he always wants to have the most up-to-date information.

Then it's more faxes, and then the highlight of the day which is always dinner, and a typical dinner would be ten people, but sometimes there may be a hundred people there, with ten people each at ten tables, and they all want to be on Tony's table. Tony is always the head of his table and the conversation usually revolves around a current event, which is maybe half the topic, and everybody at the table participates, so at his table the conversation seldom breaks off into conversations of two people each—it's the entire table and it's intellectually interesting and a lot of fun. If you were a fly on the wall and looking down, you would see the table with the most laughter surrounding it is Tony O'Reilly's, and not only is he dealing with issues and getting everyone's point of view—which he will remember—but it will remind him of a story or a joke and he's able to add a lot of interest, spice and fun to the topic. The last table to break up in the evening is always Tony's table, and there's a wonderful sense of fun and insight.

It'll probably be well past midnight, then it's back to the hotel, where there's another hundred pages of faxes waiting for him. What's interesting to me is that if I'm meeting him at seven the next morning, somehow in between that and his next hundred pages of faxes and his morning newspapers he's read a couple of hundred pages of a book that has nothing to do with business, but is the latest biography or history or book on Greek art.

Others were less impressed with his wide-ranging reading habits. Dick Beattie was amazed at how relaxed O'Reilly was as they set off on a factory visit. 'There was Tony and I on the company plane, and Tony would be carrying a book he was reading or an armful of newspapers, and I'm over here working my tail off out of my briefcase. It used to depress the hell out of me.'

Sculley describes a recent week with O'Reilly.

On Monday morning he was in Florida with the Heinz Canadian sales group—they're having their national convention, and he sat through the presentations and delivered the keynote speech at lunch. Then he hopped on the plane and met me in Dallas that afternoon where we were having the national sales meeting for another of our companies, and we had a briefing for an hour in his suite. Then he came to the cocktail party at 6.30 and met a number of brokers and sales people, and then we all spoke at the dinner that night and took questions and answers right up to eleven. Since we had an executive meeting the next day at Pittsburgh we hopped on the plane and arrived in Pittsburgh local time at three in the morning and started the next day at eight. And so on for the rest of the week.

O'Reilly keeps it up day after day, often using the weekends for longer plane flights—to Tokyo, Sydney, New Zealand, South Africa or Zimbabwe where, from the mid-1980s onwards, Heinz had become a major employer. He uses the Heinz plane as a travelling office containing carefully selected files and records of all that he might need. From his early executive days he developed the habit of keeping separate briefcases for different issues, and as his interests grew so the number of briefcases he travels with grew too. Today there may be as many as seven or eight, allowing him in an instant to pull out a briefcase containing all the information he needs on the different divisions of Heinz or one of his Irish investments.

No one other than himself really knows what he keeps in the briefcases. 'A lot of them are sort of permanently packed,' says one of his staff. Sculley has often seen him sort out his faxes and papers into different piles to go into the different briefcases, but several are general files to which he seldom refers. In the office in Pittsburgh he would call up his driver Mike from the basement, and say, 'I want to take all that stuff with me', and Mike would carefully pack it away into a briefcase, but usually it was O'Reilly himself who carefully put it away, and it was he who sorted through it later. Olive in the Pittsburgh office played little part in the process, unless he asked her at a later stage to unpack a briefcase (which he would already have sorted, probably on the plane) and file it. Essentially, however, they were filled with material that the eclectic O'Reilly had gathered at his various management presentations, and which he would keep until it was out-of-date or he had no further use for it. 'He is a man that, when he sits through presentations, keeps pulling out pages,' says one executive.

> And you can often tell when you're presenting to Tony whether you provided him with insight into something that's worth him keeping. It usually has numbers on it rather than words, and Tony will simply take that out of the three-ring binder. He'll pull the page out, circle some numbers and put it on the side. So at the end of a two-hour presentation, let's say the presentation was a hundred pages long, if it was unsuccessful he wouldn't have pulled anything out and the presenter's face is pretty bleak. He hasn't learnt anything, he hasn't decided to keep anything. An extraordinary presentation is where he has pulled all the pages out, and he'll keep those, refer back to them when he's on the plane. He occasionally goes back through just to look at them one more time, and he has quite a photographic memory. He'll keep them in file folders, in his briefcases. He

gets so much paper it's amazing how he can deal with it. Yet
he's always able to put his fingers on it. He travels with an
entire library, that's why having his own plane is so important
to him. It gives him terrific accessibility in different parts of
the world. The other reason is security, given his high profile
international image.

It is not necessarily the best-organized system, and for a person
with a less retentive memory than O'Reilly it could be disastrous. He
stuffs into his pockets odd bits of paper on which he has written
some information, but from whatever source he seems to be able to
call up what he needs when he needs it—and not even Olive can
understand how. O'Reilly keeps two secretaries in Pittsburgh, including Olive, but he is essentially in charge of his own arrangements,
designing and revising his own timetable. He usually writes his long
reports in his own hand and sends them back to Olive to be typed
up, but seldom spends long dictating replies to letters, preferring to
make a phone call. 'He's very disciplined about replying quickly,
particularly to an individual,' says an executive. 'A person he knows,
he will write a personal letter to and sign it back in Pittsburgh. Otherwise, he will have someone phone them.'

'He's not a meticulous man, but he's an extremely well-organized
man,' says Sculley. 'He's not necessarily the neatest of men. He doesn't
have to tie his shoes absolutely perfectly, but he's extremely disciplined and organized, and that's a quality that's very important for
anyone who is successful.'

Sculley always noted how O'Reilly began the day with a list, written
out on little five-by-three-inch correspondence cards with a blue border and the legend 'A. J. F. O'Reilly' embossed on one side. In his
neat script he would write the date (the British way—the day of the
month first) and then the names of the people he wanted to talk to
during the day. The list lengthened as the day went on and phone
calls came in, but at the same time he was ticking many of them
off as he worked through his calls. 'He's constantly updating and
changing,' says Sculley.

I can see his diary during presentations, and he's working on
it if there's a lull because he's so fast he's usually well beyond
the presenter. So he's constantly reviewing two things in his

mind: first, the list of priorities that he's working on that day or that week—people to call, follow-ups, business plans to be discussed, and so on, and secondly, he's working his diary.

O'Reilly would sometimes boast he could tell a person where he would be, to the hour, two years ahead, and to an extent it was true. To make his life work, he had to have certain fixed points in his schedule around which he worked the rest of his key dates. He and Olive started his diary every year by putting in the Heinz board meetings, which O'Reilly treated as sacrosanct—he has never yet missed one. There are ten a year, one of which may be held abroad, the others all in Pittsburgh. But there are other immovable Heinz meetings too. Once a year in October/November the senior executives fly in from all over the world to present their business plans at long sessions, originally held in the Rolling Rock Club, an idyllic former Mellon shooting lodge in the woods of Pennsylvania, or overseas in the Bahamas, Acapulco or even Ireland. At these sessions O'Reilly goes through every aspect of each one of the businesses, devoting at least half a day and often a whole day to presentations and group discussions on each one. He analyzes Weight Watchers with Les Parducci (actually a Scot, despite his name), Australia with Terence Ward, Italy with Luigi Ribolla (one of Heinz's most successful managers for the past twenty years) and Lino Ghirardato, Ore-Ida with Dick Wamhoff and so on. In this week he and his senior executives, including Sculley, J. Connolly (before he retired), Bill Springer, Bill Johnson, the Englishman Derek Finlay, a former McKinsey consultant who is now in charge of corporate development, Dave Williams, and the chief financial officer George Greer, who was at Heinz UK when O'Reilly first arrived there, look at where the company is going, examine and challenge the plans put forward and work out where best to spend the company's capital.

Says Sculley:

> We're saying, here's where we are going the next three to five years, here are the numbers and the issues, here are the products, here is the advertising, here's the way we're going to spend our capital, here's how we're going to deliver to you, Tony, the earnings you expect, and here's how we can do even better if you are prepared to take this risk with us.

Each senior executive presents a tier-chart of his own management and assessments of people that work under them, identifying high-fliers or second-raters. Executives whose names are in red are going nowhere, in yellow they have a chance to be promoted, and in green they're ready to be promoted. 'Tony is always fascinated to get the biographies of the young Turks—those who are going to be the new leaders of Heinz tomorrow,' says Sculley.

The five-year plan is put together in Pittsburgh, the numbers added up, the strategies consolidated by November. In January there is another fixed point, a mid-year budget review which takes two weeks and can be held anywhere in the world (in 1994 it was in Lyford Cay). The business plan is reviewed in another intensive session in May, often in places such as Acapulco or Florida, but in a bad year in Pittsburgh. It consists of another seven full days of presentations and discussions, with O'Reilly reading the riot act to anyone falling behind budget. In between there are presidents' meetings, when everybody flies into Pittsburgh for an afternoon for which O'Reilly has to be there. And of course there is the annual meeting, always in Pittsburgh in September, which is combined with a board meeting and executive reviews.

In addition to his daily meetings with the Heinz World Headquarters senior management, O'Reilly on average reckoned to meet his twenty-five top line managers between once a month and every six weeks, working through a formal agenda and alerting him quickly to things going wrong: 'The art of concealment is difficult to practise at Heinz,' says a Heinz executive. At least one Heinz meeting a year is held in Ireland, coinciding with the Heinz-sponsored 57 Stakes at Leopardstown racecourse outside Dublin, around which O'Reilly fits a major dinner for over two hundred people and a crowded weekend of entertaining at Castlemartin. O'Reilly had always spent August in Ireland, and he fitted in meetings around that time. His peripatetic wanderings would often take him to Dublin for Ireland's two annual rugby matches at Lansdowne Road, or Paris or London if they were playing away. Again dinners, speaking engagements and business meetings were slotted in around them, so the matches were used for corporate entertainment. It was a frenetic, energy-sapping schedule which only someone buoyed up by the adrenaline of the challenge and success could have sustained. By the middle of the 1980s it was proving too much for Susan O'Reilly, who as the years wore on decided she didn't want to live that kind of life any more.

*   *   *

On 25 February 1987, Jack Heinz died at the age of seventy-eight. He had been chairman since 1941, and had worked at the company for some fifty-six years. The whole of Pennsylvania, and half of America's great and good, turned out for the funeral of the last of three generations to run this most visible of Pittsburgh companies.

O'Reilly succeeded him as chairman, the first non-Heinz in the history of the company to take on that role. He kept his other titles of chief executive officer and of president as well—all three rolled into one. There were no further heights to be scaled at Heinz.

20
Life at Fifty

IN THE FIRST WEEK OF MAY 1986 O'REILLY WAS BACK IN IRELAND, feigning innocence of the frantic activity which had secretly taken over his entire household in Castlemartin, as well as his own offices in Dublin and Pittsburgh. Everyone was involved in the grand conspiracy. All his children were home, talking in whispers in the corridors, and his wife wore a harried and uncharacteristic frown. Friends he had not seen since rugby days kept phoning from all over to the world to say they just happened to be heading towards Dublin. Andy Mulligan, now living in Washington, casually mentioned he might drop by. The great Irish out-half, Dr Jackie Kyle, let it be known he was flying in from Zambia. Senior Heinz executives, including Joe Bogdanovitch, J. Connolly and Dick Patton, suddenly discovered they had urgent meetings in Ireland. Even Burt Gookin expressed a desire to pay another visit to the Irish golf courses and was on his way.

It would be O'Reilly's fiftieth birthday on 7 May, and for a year Susan, aided by Olive and Jim Milton, his public relations man in Dublin, had been working on what they planned would be the party of the decade. Over five hundred guests had been invited from every part of his life: school and childhood friends such as the McAleeses, McGorans, Peadar O'Donnell, Sean McKone and Frank O'Rourke; his family, mostly O'Connors from his mother's side, would be there, though the only relation from his father's side was his cousin, Father John Geary; half the Lions teams he had played with, including Niall Brophy, Ronnie Dawson, Phil Horrocks-Taylor, Clem Thomas and

Cliff Morgan; Mrs Pat Casey, widow of his old bank manager, was on her way up from Cork; there were his old Bord Bainne and Sugar Company colleagues, his senior staff from his Irish companies, his old university lecturers, his horse trainers, and even his former fiancée, Dorothy Connolly. His mother, now aged seventy-four and totally wheelchair-bound, would have pride of place. Unlike many O'Reilly parties, this was not a gathering of the great and the powerful, but of all the people who his wife, his mother and his secretary could think of who had been personally important in his life.

The party was the worst-kept secret in Ireland, and the news leaked in the Irish papers weeks before the event. The items had been filtered from O'Reilly's usually efficient cuttings system, but on 6 May, the day before the great event, the *Irish Times* unsportingly ran a headline 'Tony O'Reilly's birthday secret'. If he saw it—and he missed little—he pretended not to, but he could have been forgiven for some slight puzzlement. The story in the *Irish Times* indicated that the party was to be at Castlemartin where a huge marquee, it said, had been erected. Looking furtively out of his window that morning, O'Reilly could see nothing. If there was to be a party— and he would have been a very disappointed man if there wasn't— he could not work out where it was going to be.

In fact it was at the local community hall in Kilcullen, where for weeks the party planners had been secretly at work, bedecking the entrance with flags and bunting, and covering the walls inside with giant, garish murals depicting the life of O'Reilly (according to one press report, they were 'awful, truly awful'). The invitation said 7.30 sharp, and O'Reilly, as arranged, arrived in the teeming rain well after everyone else, his appearance elaborately orchestrated by his son Cameron. He went through the motions of expressing astonishment, and in truth he was genuinely taken aback by the range of old friends there. 'I have a very convincing family when it comes to deception,' he remarked to the assembled press. Cliff Morgan, as he had done on the 1955 Lions tour, led the singing of 'Happy Birthday', and as O'Reilly appeared on the balcony the band played 'Land of Hope and Glory', a choice which, although suitably rousing, was not without a certain irony in republican Ireland ('God who made us mighty, make us mightier yet' was precisely what generations of Irishmen had fought to reverse). 'Darling, I'm sorry about the song,' apologized Susan. 'I wanted "Hail to the Chief".' The band at Kilcullen clearly hadn't got the music for that one.

'You may be surprised that Valéry Giscard d'Estaing, Henry Kissinger and Ronald Reagan are not here,' said Cameron who, as the eldest son—and a former auditor of the Oxford Union—was the master of ceremonies for the evening. 'There's a very simple reason for that—they weren't asked.'

Fifty for O'Reilly, as with most people, was a time for taking stock. Physically he was as strong as an ox, but the years, the constant travel and the pressure had all taken their toll of his once superbly tuned physique. There was not a trace of auburn left in his hair, which was still thick but grey. His struggle to keep his weight down had become tougher, and all the dinners and hours sitting on an aeroplane had resulted in a mid-life paunch which he sporadically diminished through intensive bursts of dieting—only for it to appear again when he stopped. He was still a handsome man, but the once finely angular jawline had become fleshier, the jowls more pronounced, the second chin more obtrusive. When Heinz took over the Cardio-Vascular Fitness Corporation, a company dedicated to the prevention of heart attacks among overworked executives, O'Reilly dropped into its New York gym for a stress test. The result seriously rattled him. 'Obviously aggressive, takes no prisoners,' it said. 'Driven, but leads a sedentary life except for wild games of weekend tennis. Conclusion: a classic profile of the man most likely to get a coronary.' His father, grandfather and uncles had all suffered from heart complaints without the stress and the overeating which O'Reilly put himself through—had died early (his uncle Patrick of a coronary in 1958, aged fifty-five, and his uncle Dermot, also of a coronary, in 1967 aged fifty-nine and his father, the healthiest of them, of a stroke aged seventy). Suddenly at fifty he had intimations, almost for the first time, of his own mortality. He knew what he should do and for months at a time he would do it, giving up wine altogether in January and in Lent (he later added November and December), increasing his exercise, trying to play tennis at least twice a week and every day on holiday. But as he entered his fifties he became only too conscious that any slackening off caused his weight to move rapidly up again. The glasses which he wore increasingly, his sober double-breasted pinstripe suits and the extra pounds he was carrying gave him a more solemn, ponderous air, although that was quickly dispelled by his flashing smile when he began to talk. The gaze was as level as ever, the teeth, capped after his rugby exploits, were as even and the handshake as firm. But Tony O'Reilly was showing his age.

His analysis of his priorities at this time, although a thoughtful one, was not a novel event for him. He had always been introspective, every so often making space in his frenetic life to be alone and think about what he wanted to do, working it out as he would any business proposition. 'I like to take out great sheets of paper and to make some order out of the chaos of life,' he said in an interview he gave to the Irish journalist Ivor Kenny that year,

> because I get such little time to ask myself the question, What am I doing? I'm making ketchup in the United States. What *should* I be doing? Now that I have a certain degree of financial independence, where should I be allocating my time and energies? What time have I left? I now have reached that part of my life where two major phases are gone and there's only one phase left. The real question is, should I be doing anything different and, if so, what?

As he grew older, his options narrowed, the time available to achieve his still considerable ambitions becoming shorter. Heinz and America had absorbed most of his energies between the ages of thirty-three and fifty, but did he want that to be so for the next decade? Heinz was still very important to him both financially and psychologically—it was the central leg of his commercial life on which his reputation largely hung. He had done a lot with the company, but there was much more to be done in the constantly changing kaleidoscope of one of the most competitive industries in the world. He didn't want to give it up, or even pull back.

But Ireland featured very large in his priorities too, and again there were commercial as well as psychological reasons. The value of his shares in Independent Newspapers, which was beginning to grow rapidly, was almost equal to the value of his Heinz stake. He had not abandoned hope that Atlantic Resources would strike it rich in the Celtic Sea, and he was utterly determined that Fitzwilton, the perennial dog of his portfolio, should get its head off the ground and start to regain some of the goodwill it had cost him.

He had abandoned any serious interest in an Irish political career, but ironically it was the prospect of going into American politics which crystallized his thoughts about Ireland. In the 1980s O'Reilly had moved as effortlessly among senior American politicians as twenty years before he had mixed with Irish civil servants and ministers. Henry Kissinger, who did some work for Heinz in Washington, and whose description of O'Reilly as a 'modern renaissance man' was widely repeated in most profiles written about him afterwards, had introduced him to Republican party circles, and O'Reilly, his easy social skills honed and perfected after years of practice, was soon a significant presence in the party. His continual round of dinners, conventions, conferences and lunches (often as the guest speaker) allowed him to widen his influence, as did his election to the board of the *Washington Post* and later the New York Stock Exchange. By the mid-1980s he had become friendly with Vice-President George Bush, the man tipped as the most likely Republican candidate for the 1988 election. Bush invited him to play tennis at the White House, and O'Reilly got into the habit of calling on him when he was in Washington and of inviting him to big Heinz events.

O'Reilly's political thoughts were no more complicated than those of the heads of many other large American companies, but he was interested, and because so many decisions with profound implications for the food industry were taken in Washington, it was a place he often had to be. Despite his inclination to the GOP he had never wholeheartedly espoused Ronald Reagan's supply side economics, nor had he much time for Thatcherism in Britain, although what he was doing for Heinz was in practice classic Thatcherism. He was roughly on the right in economic terms, but drew back politically from what he regarded as the harsher aspects of free market capital-ism—while practising it at Heinz. The highly visible and much-com-mented-on share option scheme at Heinz, under which the twenty-one top executives benefited generously if the company met its target of 12 per cent annual compound profits growth, was to many eyes an over-generous incentive scheme and an extreme of capitalism; but O'Reilly would defend it to the hilt, suggesting a degree of self-interest in his political philosophy. On the other hand, when Rupert Murdoch moved his British newspapers to a new green-field site at Wapping in East London, O'Reilly was disapproving of the way thousands of old-style and unproductive print jobs were wiped out—something that O'Reilly would not do in the equally over-manned, high-cost print plants of the *Independent* in Ireland. Like most Irishmen of his generation O'Reilly was very pro-European unity, advocating monetary union and other federal institutions such as a Europe-wide Securities and Exchange Commission modelled on the American version; but he was far from passionate about any of it, conserving that part of his energy for his business interests. Where he *was* politically passionate was on the Irish situation, and he had some radical and persuasive proposals for solving it, including a new Marshall Plan to which Britain, the EC and the USA would contribute. In Irish politics there was no traditional right or left division in the sense that there is in Britain or France, and O'Reilly, although a fully committed capitalist in his business life, was a political pragmatist, almost an agnostic.

When Bush suggested that he might think about joining a future Republican administration, possibly as Secretary of Commerce, if he won the 1988 presidential race, O'Reilly had to think hard. Initially it sounded intriguing, a public recognition of how far he had come from that house in Griffith Avenue in Dublin. Over the years his name had been linked in the gossip columns with all sorts of jobs— he was to run for the presidency of Ireland, he was to succeed Roy Jenkins as President of the European Commission, he was to be head of CBS Broadcasting, he was to be the new chairman of Guinness (he had been approached before Ernest Saunders) and so on. Should he now make a move, not into Irish politics, on which the rumours had always centred, but into government in America? The Kennedys had moved from famine-hit Wexford to the White House in three generations, and although O'Reilly, being Irish-born, could not aim that high, he could at least become part of the policy-making machine of the most powerful nation on earth. It was a heady thought, but was it what he really wanted? America was so huge, and members of the administration so anonymous, that it would not greatly enhance his standing in that country. Who would it impress? More to the point, who did he want to impress? No one in America particularly, he concluded gloomily. He was never going to leave a great mark on American life, no matter how he tried—the country was simply too big, too anonymous for that. Whatever impact he could have on Heinz, his reputation there would be ephemeral, largely forgotten by the next generation—he had seen that with Gookin. In Ireland, however, it could be different. His question about whether he should be doing something other than making ketchup in America was essentially a rhetorical one, because the answer was still no, and he knew it. The longer he stayed at Heinz, the more he hated the thought of leaving it, loving the challenge and the feel of the well-oiled corporate machine with its almost unlimited resources of capital and people. In Ireland, by comparison, business was a desperate struggle, a place of limited horizons and petty jealousies. Yet that was where, he now accepted, he wanted to leave his mark—an O'Reilly dynasty which he would bequeath to his children and which would survive even them.

He said no to George Bush's half-offer, and thought again about what he could do in Ireland. He had already made a considerable contribution, more than even the most successful Irishmen make in a lifetime. O'Reilly had promoted Ireland all his adult life, either through sport or through business, with an intensity that few British people, for example, would devote to Britain. He was prepared to go to considerable trouble to help attract investment into Ireland, acting as an unpaid consultant and supporter whenever he was asked—as he often was. For instance in 1980, when the Industrial Development Authority in Dublin asked him to help lure the American car-maker John DeLorean to Ireland, O'Reilly hosted a dinner party for him at Fox Chapel and expounded on the virtues of investment in Ireland as opposed to Puerto Rico which was also trying to land the DeLorean car plant (it eventually went to Belfast and cost the British taxpayer some £84 million).

One of O'Reilly's biggest contributions to his native country was the Ireland Fund which he and an Irish American from Pittsburgh, Dan Rooney, founded in 1976. The Rooneys were a Pittsburgh institution, at the other end of the social scale from the Heinz family, but probably held in higher regard in this football-mad city. Dan was the son of the legendary Arthur Joseph Rooney, father of five and grandfather of thirty-four and owner of the Pittsburgh Steelers which had just won the Super Bowl for the second year running. From the time he arrived in Pittsburgh, O'Reilly had loved the Rooneys, and they had equally appreciated this new addition to their Irish mafia. In 1933 Art Rooney, then a professional footballer at the end of his career, won £2500 on the racetrack and, instead of blowing it again, used it to buy the local run-down, third-rate football team. He soon changed that, but for four decades, and under sixteen different coaches, the Steelers failed to win a major title. Then in the mid-1970s they became by far the best team in America, getting to the play-offs in eight successive years and winning the Super Bowl four times in six years.

It was at a dinner in New York in 1976, which O'Reilly and a group of Irish-American friends organized to honour Art Rooney, then seventy-five, that the idea of the Ireland Fund evolved. All of them were continually besieged by requests for help from every charity in Ireland and every Irish Catholic nun or priest in America. O'Reilly and Art's son Dan suggested setting up a fund to which all requests could be channelled and which would counterbalance Noraid, which was raising American money for the IRA. O'Reilly had been at a number of Jewish fund-raising dinners and been greatly impressed by the efficiency of the group which organized them, the American United Jewish Appeal, which raised over $400 million for Israel every year. It had also lobbied Congress into giving Israel another $2 billion in aid. There were, somebody told O'Reilly, 44 million Americans of Irish extraction, far more than there were Jews; many of them were wealthy and had some feeling for Ireland which it must be possible to harness. Even the Mellons were Irish—Presbyterian Irish from the North, but Irish none the less; they would not be excluded under O'Reilly's plan.

He and Rooney conceived the fund as strictly non-sectarian, embracing the interests of the whole of Ireland, North and South. Its members would represent both the Orange and the Green: the Westons, Eatons and Mellons sitting alongside the Rooneys, the Keoughs and the Dunfeys. It would hold dinners, balls and other fund-raising events all over America, creating committees in some of the biggest cities and drawing on the goodwill of the better-off Irish American community. All the money raised would go to Ireland, concentrating on community-level, self-help projects which promoted cross-community contact and understanding. There was already an Irish American fund-raising organization in existence, the American Irish Foundation, founded in 1963 when President John F. Kennedy visited Ireland, but it was not very active, and O'Reilly's new organization soon eclipsed it and eventually absorbed it.

He began by getting together a group of leading Irish American figures, personally ringing them or writing to them to invite them to a dinner which he hosted. He outlined his ideas for the fund, saying it would be committed to the principles of reconciliation and integration—'a peaceful and fruitful co-existence in which both nationalist and unionist identities are mutually respected'. In contrast to Noraid, which was receiving a worrying amount of support even from middle-class Americans, it would be devoted to peace, encouraging economic and cultural development on both sides of the border. O'Reilly had another object, almost as important as the money: he wanted to make American business and the public better informed about the complexities of the Irish situation.

From among those who turned up, he and Rooney put together a committee. Then they hired a full-time secretary to run it, and they were away—the beginning of a fund that has since held countless dinners, lunches and other functions, and has raised over $50 million for Ireland. The Ireland Fund would owe a great deal to its first director, Judith Hayes, whose perception and network of contacts in Northern Ireland in academic and everyday vocational life was to give the organisation its dynamic. It was Judith who recruited Dr Maurice Hayes (no relation), Paul Arthur, Roy Bradford, Hugh Frazer, Colm Cavanagh, Paddy Doherty, Martin McCullough, Denis Whelan, and Derek Wilson, the key players in the organisation in the early days.

Apart from the money which began to flow into Irish projects from 1977 onwards (now some $5 million a year), the fund has chipped away at the great block of dangerously romantic views held on the subject of Ireland. Irish American Catholics—and, despite the pan-Irish nature of the fund, it was mostly Catholics who supported it—held ill-informed and anti-British notions which more accurately reflected the times of the guerrilla war of 1918–20 than they did the modern-day reality. Part of O'Reilly's mission—and the Ireland Fund soon became a mission for him—was to teach a little history, and introduce his audiences to a little of what was really going on. When O'Reilly heard normally intelligent Americans talking about Ireland, he found their views, were 'simplistic, antiquated, and with a medieval directness to them' which deeply disquieted him. 'It behoves those of us who know the reality of modern Ireland, who know the aspirations of young people, both North and South, Catholic and Protestant, to try to urgently communicate to them there is a new Ireland, and not the one their grandfathers talked about,' he said.

In 1976 the Ireland Fund held its first dinner in New York, a lavish affair which ran so much over budget that it took the second dinner a year later to pay for the first. But soon there were other annual dinners, in Chicago, Boston, Los Angeles, San Francisco, Miami and, of course, Pittsburgh. In these early years—and even later—O'Reilly tried to get to all of them, his speeches sprinkled with Irish jokes, wittily told in his range of perfect Irish accents, but with a more serious message too. O'Reilly was already one of the most sought-after speakers in America, basically because he was so good at it. He gave his audiences, which could range from the National Association of Independent Schools to the Congress of the International Center of the Food Trade and Industry, his thoughts on everything from 'Managing for Quality' to 'Heinz's Goals for Global Excellence'—with some good laughs in the mixture. Although he prepared the big ones—or had Ted Smyth do it for him—very often his speeches were made from a few notes he had scribbled on his place card a few minutes before. He had become so adept and so practised over the years that he could take his cue from the speaker in front of him. 'You often see him, his head down as the chairman is up there introducing him, and he thinks of the jokes he wants to start with, a few quotations that are apt, the main points he wants to make and then who he has to thank. That's often all he needs. He then thinks on his feet,' says Ted Smyth, veteran of thousands of O'Reilly speeches.

His routine was as polished as any professional performer, even down to the props. O'Reilly likes to speak from a podium, not because he needs it to hold his notes, but because it is often part of his warm-up routine. He developed a little trick of walking up to the microphone holding a brimming glass of wine in one hand, his notes in the other, and pretending to search for a convenient shelf on which to place his glass. 'I can see this podium was not designed for an Irishman,' he would say, drawing an appreciative roar of laughter before he even began. He had other favourites, that were equally professionally crafted. Sometimes after a good dinner he would tell his Brendan Behan story, using a perfect Dublin working-class accent. Behan, he would say, was on a trip to America at which he received wonderful hospitality from the American Irish. 'Well, I'm going home now to Dublin,' he said on his last evening, 'and I'm going to tell them how well yiz are all doing over here, and how far up the social ladder yiz have all climbed. That'll put them in right bad form for Christmas!' Or it was the Irish company chairman who at his annual general meeting stood up and began—and here O'Reilly would switch from his normal clearly articulated slight Irish accent into a broad Cork brogue—'Ladies and gentlemen, when I addressed you all last year, I said things were bad and we stood on the edge of a precipice. Well, I'm pleased to report that since then we've taken a great leap forward.'

He always stopped short of stage Irish and, unusually for a humorous after dinner speaker, carefully avoided off-colour stories. At the

Ireland dinners, once he had his listeners where he wanted them—
and his props and tricks were simply insurance—he would expound
the serious message. Sometimes that would be a history lesson which
started with the Norman invasion in 1170 when Ireland was 'a cul-
de-sac, a sanctuary island, an island behind an island . . . which had
generated the most civilized society in all of Europe in the fifth, sixth
and seventh centuries'. He would take them up to the battle of Kinsale
in 1601 and pause on Cromwell, a name he had first heard from his
father whose stories of the sacking of his native Drogheda had left
an indelible mark on O'Reilly's mind. 'The savage character and
subsequent plantation of Cromwell poisoned irreversibly the relationship between the old Catholic Irish and the new ascendant Protestant
Anglo-Irish,' he said in one lecture at Boston College.

> Simply put, in the period from 1601 to 1700, the Catholic Irish
> were dispossessed of all their possessions—their land, their
> citizenship, their capacity to worship publicly, their ability to
> secure education and their participative role in politics and the
> professions. No Catholic could own a horse, seek an education
> or practise his religion. By 1714 land ownership by the Catholic
> was reduced to a paltry 7 per cent. The die was cast. Catholic
> Ireland was vanquished.

O'Reilly was not intending, as he was sometimes accused, to fan
the flames of Irish nationalism—quite the opposite. His history lessons were usually objective and he was faultlessly accurate in his facts,
his research checked by professors of history. Even in Britain O'Reilly
had been astonished at the ignorance of Irish history among even
well-educated people, and argued strenuously that there could be no
solution until people understood what it was they were trying to deal
with. 'I want you to know the complexity of Irish history,' he would
explain after taking his listeners all the way up to the present troubles
in the North. 'I want you to understand why there is such a durable
struggle punctuated by a firm sense of righteousness on both sides
of the tribal divide. I want you to know there are no simple answers
to the Irish question.'

By the late 1980s O'Reilly had added the Ireland Fund of Great
Britain, co-chaired by the author Josephine Hart, with a committee
which included many of the London Irish mafia. It included Sam

Stephenson, his old chum from Belvedere; the merchant banker George Magan; Terry Wogan, the broadcaster; the publisher Kevin Kelly; David Davies, a Welsh-born industrialist who lived in Ireland; and the Earl of Gowrie, former owner of Castlemartin. The Australian Ireland Fund was already in existence by then, as was the Ireland Fund of Canada, and there soon followed the Ireland Fund of France and the Ireland Fund of Germany—seven funds in all, with more on the way in Japan and South Africa. For all of them O'Reilly had the same message: 'This brings together the Orange and the Green traditions,' he said. 'Ireland is a country in a development phase. It needs jobs, investment, tourism, cash and encouragement. What it used to get was generous words of goodwill once a year on St Patrick's Day. I am trying to encourage, if you like, people to repay a national debt.'

It meant more dates to be slotted into his diary, trips to Australia where he could combine business for Heinz, for Independent Newspapers and for the Ireland Fund into one busy week before flying on for more of the same somewhere else. As the fund grew, it took on more staff, and in these early days much of its momentum was provided by his friend Judith Hayes, who took on the task of organizing the dinners and speeches and according to one of the key people in the Ireland Fund, she 'provided an intellectual insight into what it was to be a Northern Protestant in modern Ireland.' Without her, adds O'Reilly, 'there would not have been an Ireland Fund.' The dinners, particularly in America, became glittering $5000-a-table events, with many non-Irish turning up simply for the occasion. In Washington, on St Patrick's Day in 1993, Bill Clinton, wearing a green handkerchief which O'Reilly had hastily tucked into his breast pocket, spoke to a packed dinner which included twenty senators and eighty congressmen, as well as the Irish Taoiseach, Albert Reynolds. The actor Paul Newman, a frequent visitor to Castlemartin (O'Reilly helped him launch his Hole-in-the Wall Gang camp in Ireland in 1993), usually attends at least one dinner a year, as do other actors such as Lloyd Bridges, Gregory Peck, John Forsythe, Leslie Nielson, and Robert Wagner. The fund has become a significant forum for the Irish to get their views across, as well as to raise funds (Clinton and Reynolds, for instance, had a long discussion on the Irish situation at the dinner). In one interview O'Reilly claimed that by the end of the 1980s it was absorbing some thirty days a year of his schedule. That was a message for Irish consumption, an exaggeration of the real facts. But it did take time and it took intellectual energy—and it took his money.

He was also intent on leaving other more lasting marks on Ireland. When the Provost of Trinity College, Dublin, Bill Watts (a former rugby player), asked him for a contribution towards TCD's 400th anniversary fund, O'Reilly readily agreed, offering £1.5 million from his own pocket towards a new O'Reilly Centre to be built at the back of the college. He had not been to TCD but his father had, and he would dedicate this building to his parents. Later he would agree to pay for an even more prominent building at the campus for his own university, UCD, when the President, Paddy Masterson (a friend from Belvedere days), asked him.

Yet for all his success at Heinz and the work of the Ireland Funds, views about O'Reilly in Ireland remained mixed. He sometimes made fun of the Irish resentment of success, but in fact it was not entirely a joke. In America, O'Reilly's achievements were a matter for congratulation in most places he went. Not so in Ireland, where respect for O'Reilly's success—and he was now among the top half dozen richest Irishmen, as well as its most visible businessman—was always grudging, tinged with that peculiar element of envy and suspicion that the Irish reserved for their own. In the Dublin bars the talk now reflected in a book written by Harry Walsh was that, while O'Reilly was obviously a great star when he was working in a big company like Heinz, as an entrepreneur he was much less sure-footed.

This type of carping, which would become even more unfair as he rescued Waterford Wedgwood from near-certain bankruptcy to become Ireland's biggest employer, niggled him, even though he understood it for the small-minded tavern banter that it was. Even his lavish entertaining when he was in Ireland was turned against him.

Yet it was from Irish society that O'Reilly most wanted the respect so easily available to him in America—and which he felt he had earned back home. His expressed optimism over the prospects for Atlantic Resources was a source of simmering resentment, despite the fact that it was he who had lost more money than anyone else. In much the same way as thirty years earlier he had been unable to show his rugby skills at their best in an Irish shirt at Lansdowne Road, so through the seventies and eighties his business operations in Ireland met with mixed success. Independent Newspapers was doing very well, his shareholding in it accounting for half his total wealth which had passed the £100 million mark by 1986. But Fitzwilton would only become a serious business again in the 1990s.

'The scale of my priorities was always Heinz, number one—and I never missed a board meeting or an executive meeting in all my time there—then Independent Newspapers, number two, and very much number three, Fitzwilton,' says O'Reilly now. 'I was interested in Fitzwilton, excited by it, sheet-anchored by it, but never really gave it any detailed attention other than in that extraordinary period 1975 to 1977 when I felt that my own career might be imperilled by the collapse of Fitzwilton,' he said later. 'Then I went at it in a big way.'

He had rescued it, certainly, yet Fitzwilton's progress continued to be extraordinarily erratic, its problems of the 1970s dragging on well into the 1980s even though by that stage it was no more than a cash shell. Profits hit £3.5 million in 1974, slumped to a net loss of £5 million in 1976, rallied again to a profit of £2 million, but then trailed away again to £561,000 in 1983, setting the pattern for the rest of the decade and beyond (in 1990 it made over £10 million, the following year only £200,000). In 1982 a group of fifty disgruntled shareholders, particularly concerned by Fitzwilton's investment in Atlantic Resources, commissioned a report on the group from a firm of management consultants. Afterwards their leader said that the result 'has set my mind at rest', but from that time Fitzwilton put no further money into Atlantic. By the mid-1980s the dividend had been halved, and the auditors were raising questions about the way in which losses on the remaining half of Goulding's were treated. The accounts were often heavily qualified by the auditors, and the analysts and investment community regarded the declared profit figures with some scepticism. By 1985 earnings per share, which had hit a peak 7.34p in 1979, were less than half that, and that year O'Reilly and the board were accused by an angry shareholder of 'indulging' themselves at shareholders' expense. Neither the financial press nor the Irish public were inclined to be charitable towards them. 'Fitzwilton is one of the great mysteries of Irish finance,' wrote the magazine *Irish Business* in January 1986. 'The faithful are not required to understand it; they are expected only to believe. In spite of this, the sceptical scholastics of the Irish financial press have pointed out for many years that faith without good works does not suffice for salvation.'

In mid-1986 O'Reilly finally unloaded the last half of the Goulding's millstone. The buyer was a Dublin-based co-op, the Irish

Agricultural Wholesale Society, which rescued not just Fitzwilton but Jim McCarthy's ill-fated vehicle Capstan, which had bought the Americans out of their 50 per cent stake. Fitzwilton also sold what remained of Crowe Wilson, its original drapery business, to Capstan, and wrote off its investment and loans to the McCarthy group. The effect was to plunge Fitzwilton once more into hefty losses, although with over £10 million cash in the bank there was no crisis this time. O'Reilly, partly blaming the company's misfortunes on the miserable state of the Irish economy, announced that he now intended to invest in Britain and the USA, whose economies were 'stronger than our own'.

The dream of creating an Irish-based financial conglomerate, a rival to Hanson or BTR, which was to have taken over, modernized and internationalized chunks of Irish industry for the greater good of the country, had to be postponed. It also represented yet another change of course in what so far had been a bewildering ride for shareholders. Fitzwilton had begun life as an industrial holding company, but by the mid-1980s O'Reilly was telling his shareholders, 'We view ourselves for the long-term as an investment and not an operating company, and our medium-term strategy orientation will direct itself to this end.' Two years later he told them that Fitzwilton 'has decided to remain a trading company and has forsaken the option of becoming a purely investment company'. Although the changes of course had to some extent been forced upon the company by outside factors, O'Reilly was also continually reacting to fairly elementary mistakes and poor timing (the move into Britain was to prove no exception). A Heinz manager producing a Fitzwilton-style record would not have lasted until the next executive meeting, yet O'Reilly bridled ferociously at any suggestion that Fitzwilton was a management failure. 'On the contrary,' he insisted, 'it represents one of the most remarkable defensive actions I have ever been through . . . We had massive retrenchment and losses—that's what separates the men from the boys—and it has survived and prospered.' For a person who was by nature and training so clear-sighted, O'Reilly's instincts at Fitzwilton were dulled, many believe, by his friendships.

This began to change in 1987 when he increased his shareholding from 5 per cent to 10 per cent, and he made a determined effort to kick it into life. For a start he brought in one of his lifelong friends as executive deputy chairman—effectively chief executive—to take over the running of it. Kevin McGoran had been his tennis-playing partner since their early days at Belvedere, and, like O'Reilly, had gone on to UCD, later to qualify as an accountant. He had stayed in Dublin, rising steadily until he became the financial director of Jefferson Smurfit. He became a consultant and then O'Reilly moved him in to replace Vincent Ferguson, who stayed on the board. It could have led to more 'jobs for the boys' allegations, but McGoran had a high reputation in Dublin and O'Reilly insisted they were lucky to get him. He was ready for a new phase in Fitzwilton's up-and-down history.

The first deal of any significance was the purchase for £13.3 million of a 30 per cent stake in Keep Trust, a British motor dealer and general engineering group. This, O'Reilly announced, was to be a new beginning, the launch of Fitzwilton Mark II. Motor dealing was a growth sector of the British economy, he said, and Keep Trust, where he became chairman, was to be his vehicle for expanding into it. 'This is my opportunity to establish a presence in a vibrant economy,' said O'Reilly cheerfully. Fitzwilton would, he forecast, become a 'major player' on the British motor distribution scene.

The stakes at Fitzwilton were by now getting higher. The 1980s in America had brought the biggest takeover wave of all time—huge leveraged bids paid for by the issue of billions of dollars' worth of junk bonds. The crash of October 1987 had changed the direction of the wave, and the day of the LBO, or the leveraged buy-out, had come with a vengeance, culminating in the biggest takeover of all time, that of RJR Nabisco, a key player on many of Heinz's markets. Just as O'Reilly had fretted about missing out in the Slater boom which had inspired Fitzwilton all those years ago, now he saw opportunity in the new era, not so much for Heinz, which he kept on a tight rein avoiding the excesses (and opportunities) of the period, but for Fitzwilton. There were billions of dollars pouring into LBO funds, one of them being put together by John Kluge, the seventy-five-year-old media mogul whom he had come to know, which were just looking for homes in which to invest. Fitzwilton could be plugged into this rich source of cash. 'We've got a lot of people lined up on Wall Street who are ready to go,' he hinted to the *Irish Times* in February 1989. 'An enormous amount of preparatory work has been undertaken in 1988. Resourcefulness and judgement are the impediments—not resources.'

Some of those Wall Street sources—or their equivalents—had already appeared on the Fitzwilton scene. Kluge, one of the richest men in America (Rupert Murdoch paid him $2.5 billion for his Metromedia companies in 1985), had been so impressed with O'Reilly's concept of buying some of the major luxury goods names of Europe, starting with Ireland's own Waterford Wedgwood, that he readily put up his money, becoming a 10 per cent shareholder in Fitzwilton at a cost of £3 million. The French Canadian Paul Demarais, who controlled the Power Corporation, also agreed to O'Reilly's suggestion that he back Fitzwilton as a new vehicle for leveraged buy-outs. Ann Getty, wife of the billionaire Gordon Getty and an American publisher in her own right, also joined the party, as did the Swiss-based Leebart Bylock, linked to O'Reilly's old backer Suleiman Olayan, which took a 10 per cent stake (and whose Mark Thomson would join the Fitzwilton board). 'We will be the front office for the guys who will revolutionize Europe,' O'Reilly told *Business Week*, concentrating on unearthing buying opportunities in Europe and then bringing in some of America's largest leveraged buy-out companies as co-investors. 'You cut through three years of business-building with Fitzwilton's contacts,' he added.

With this hefty firepower behind him, the rumours quickly spread that O'Reilly was looking at a billion-dollar, highly leveraged deal for Fitzwilton, with everyone talking (correctly) about Waterford-Wedgwood as the first target. It was a considerable let-down, therefore, when the first deal was a £6.8 million bid for a majority stake in a Manchester-based cash-and-carry business. 'For those investors who like to ride on the coat tails of the "smart money", this was not the sort of mega-deal they had been hoping for,' commented the Lex column in the *Financial Times* disdainfully. A £774,000 investment in a manufacturer of reflective road signs was not what the market hoped for either.

In April 1989 Fitzwilton bought out the other 70 per cent of Keep, and in all was to invest £60 million in the British motor business—at precisely the wrong point in the economic cycle. What it had failed to read was the growing signs of overheating in the British economy which was already causing the Chancellor, Nigel Lawson, to slap on the brakes and to raise interest rates, and go on raising them until at 15 per cent they did the trick, plunging Britain into the longest recession since the war. Sales of cars went through the floor and in 1993 Fitzwilton finally sold Keep, taking a write-off of £29 million on its accounts.

The big one, however, was to be Ireland's premier manufacturing company, Waterford Glass, which in 1987 had swallowed the British-based Wedgwood China business to become Waterford Wedgwood. After years of what could only be described as indifferent management its wage costs had become absurdly high, sales had fallen sharply, debt had risen to £150 million, and by 1990, with the crystal side having lost over £60 million in three years, it was on the edge of bankruptcy. O'Reilly's interest went back to 1983 when, at a meeting at Coolmore Stud with the great Irish trainer Vincent O'Brien and his disciple John Magnier, he suggested putting together a consortium to bid for it. He even went so far as to commission a market research report, done for him by John Meagher, later to become his chief executive at Independent Newspapers. It was a sobering report, showing that only 30 per cent of Americans who bought Waterford Glass knew that it had been made in Ireland, and even they didn't much care. O'Reilly, who had paid £44,000 for the report, gave it as a present to his old friend Paddy Hayes from Cork, when he became Waterford's chief executive in 1985.

In 1988, when the Waterford share price was 120p, he looked again, this time entering into talks with the management led by Howard Kilroy, who replaced Hayes. Amid some acrimony with Kilroy, also chief executive of Jefferson Smurfit, the talks came to nothing. But by the spring of 1990 Waterford's position was so parlous that it had no choice but to do a deal. It required a mighty equity injection, far too big for Fitzwilton to support on its own, so O'Reilly brought in the New York investment house Morgan Stanley which he had worked with for years at Heinz and which was prepared to invest some of its leveraged equity money as well as that of Mrs Getty, Kluge and company. The deal, negotiated over many months, involved an injection from the joint Morgan Stanley/Fitzwilton/O'Reilly consortium of some £80 million at a price of 37.5p, with Waterford raising another £23 million through a rights issue. Morgan's investors would have 15 per cent, Fitzwilton 9.4 per cent and O'Reilly 5 per cent. It valued the whole of Waterford Wedgwood at not much more than the £230 million that Waterford had paid for Wedgwood three years before.

For a time O'Reilly was ecstatic, talking about building a Great Brands of the World Corporation which might include those of his South African friends, Anton and Johann Rupert, who owned Cartier, Dunhill and Rothman's. There were, he reckoned, only 250 global brands in the world, and Waterford and Wedgwood were two of them. He could build a company modelled on the French group Louis Vuitton-Moët Hennessy, which had linked with Guinness.

He had drastically underestimated the problems. Waterford's crystal business was in serious, possibly terminal trouble, its designs outdated, its factories in need of investment and its industrial problems seemingly insurmountable. Howard Kilroy departed after a year to be replaced by the tough Irish American banker Don Brennan of Morgan Stanley. To bring the unions to their senses, the company threatened its workers with closing down factories in Waterford and making its glass in eastern Europe. Its new Marquis brand was already largely made in Slovenia, without the brand seeming to suffer. Everybody, other than the unions agreed that the crystal side had to shed thousands of jobs, but for two years there were strikes, disruption, short-time working and confrontation in Waterford, where the glass company used to employ half the town. For a time Waterford stopped producing glass altogether and the group's existence depended on the acceptance of the Marquis brand—which turned out to be a major success. In 1992 the share price sank to 14p, delivering a hefty loss to O'Reilly and his backers, who were rapidly losing heart, and it was the autumn of 1993 before the labour problems were finally sorted out.

Fitzwilton meanwhile had been transformed and reshaped by its biggest deal yet: in October 1992 it agreed to pay £122 million for a chain of Northern Ireland supermarkets owned by the debt-laden Gateway group Isosceles. This time there was no sign of Morgan Stanley, or of the other rich investors. The deal was far too big for Fitzwilton, then capitalized at only £45 million and barely profitable, to finance on its own; O'Reilly agreed to put in £14 million of his own money, the rest coming from a mixture of institutions. It represented yet another change of direction, the group now becoming largely a food retailer. It was a profitable, steady business, free of the cut-throat competition of mainland British supermarket groups which refused to venture into Northern Ireland.

By early 1994, when O'Reilly took over as chairman, Waterford was back on its feet, its share price back to 48p—at which level Brennan confessed that the Morgan Stanley investors were just about breaking even after financing costs and inflation. Fitzwilton has an option to buy the Morgan investors out which, if it is exercised, will take it to 24 per cent of the equity.

The big consolation was that Independent Newspapers, after that anxious wait between 1973 and 1977, was a much happier story. The Independent mattered far more to him financially because, while his holding in Fitzwilton had been diluted to less than 10 per cent (it is now back to 15 per cent) he owned 30 per cent of Independent Newspapers and had no intention of giving any of the equity away. Nothing he could ever do at Fitzwilton could make it as profitable for him personally as the newspaper company. By O'Reilly's fiftieth birthday, Independent's profits had risen to £3 million and the share price had trebled in the past two years. O'Reilly had come to respect the Murphy management led by Bartle Pitcher and Liam Healy, and just as he left the running of Atlantic to Don Sheridan and that of Fitzwilton to Vincent Ferguson, so he left the day-to-day running of the Independent to Pitcher. But as he watched the development of the world's media giants, notably Rupert Murdoch, from the mid-1970s O'Reilly was already dreaming of a global empire. The Independent dominated the Irish market, but if the group was to grow it must be overseas. In 1977 Nick Leonard, who had moved to England several years before, persuaded O'Reilly as his first venture to buy some local papers in London's East End. It was a bad start, and they sold them again at a loss to a group called Greater London and Essex Newspapers (which Independent Newspapers bought in 1986). A year later a friend of O'Reilly's, Jeremy Arnott, who was involved in the outdoor advertising business in Britain, persuaded O'Reilly to invest in outdoor advertising in Germany, mostly three-sided—or 'trilateral'—poster sites in car parks where planning permission was not needed. That lasted a couple of years, by which time Arnott had taken O'Reilly into a magazine business, *Moving House and Home*, in Canada. 'It didn't do too well, that one,' says Healy, then the finance director, ruefully. They moved it into America and closed that one down too eventually, writing off £225,000 on the North American magazines.

The acquisition of the *Sunday World*, moving the group into the profitable tabloid market, made up for some of the mistakes. And then, in the 1980s, Independent Newspapers had two strokes of luck which were to lift it on to a different plane.

The first, rather surprisingly, was in the field of Mexican radio. In California one day O'Reilly ran in to a man called Edward J. Noble, a US citizen who ran the largest advertising company in Mexico. He and a group of friends had recently started a radio station in Tijuana, 10 miles south of the American border, which beamed music and advertisements on the medium wave into a large part of southern California, including Los Angeles. Mexican law forbade a non-Mexican owning a Mexican radio station, and there were tough laws on non-Americans owning American stations, but O'Reilly was able to get round this by buying for Independent Newspapers a 30 per cent stake in the companies which had the exclusive licences to sell advertising time. It sounded like a great deal to everyone in Dublin, and Liam Healy flew out to join the board of the company which would operate the radio licence. Unfortunately it made no money, and by the mid-1980s O'Reilly was beginning to think about selling again.

Then he heard that Beatrice Foods, which had somehow got into the radio business, wanted to sell its station K-JOI, the number three FM station in Los Angeles, actually beamed from across the Mexican border. There was a problem about ownership, but Liam Healy, whose rounded, genial exterior hid a keen financial brain, structured a deal which got round that, with variable interest rate bonds which would effectively drain all the cash out by way of dividend. Independent ended up with 100 per cent of the economic interest in the station but only 25 per cent of the equity. It cost it $18 million, which it financed off balance sheet, the loan secured on the station. There was a third radio station beaming out on long wave which could be picked up all the way to Vancouver. They put the three stations together, and suddenly they had an economic proposition.

It was Healy's first big deal and the enterprise paid off.

The stroke of luck came in 1985, a year after the acquisition of K-JOI, when the rules on ownership were changed and suddenly radio stations were in demand. O'Reilly and his new deputy chairman, John Meagher, decided it was time to take their profit and sold, right at the top of the market, for $45 million, netting a profit of $12 million after repaying all the loans and costs. It had been a bit of a scramble, nerve-racking at times, but in the end it had been worth it.

The other bit of luck was Reuter's, which until the early 1980s was seen by all the newspaper groups in Britain and the old British Commonwealth which subscribed to it as a news service to which they paid their subscription each year, and which every so often had to be recapitalized to stop it going bust. The electronic information revolution changed all that, and by the mid-1980s Reuter's was preparing for a stock market flotation where it would be valued at well over £1 billion (today it is valued at £8.2 billion). All the British and Irish newspaper groups ended up getting a slice of it. The Independent's stake, valued at £1000 when O'Reilly bought the paper, realized some £10 million.

These two windfalls transformed the Independent's balance sheet, allowing it to modernize its plant and to get well ahead of the rival *Irish Press*, bedevilled by strikes and financial problems. Meagher, who had built up a successful marketing business and who was also a funny mimic and raconteur, replaced Bartle Pitcher when he retired and accelerated the expansion overseas: they bought Buspak in Australia, a business selling advertisements on buses; outdoor advertising in France; two giveaway magazines in London, *Ms London* and *Midweek*; and a weekly newspaper published in London's Docklands. O'Reilly, of course, was all the time thinking far bigger than that: there were plans to launch a new national paper in Britain at the time when Eddie Shah launched *Today* and Andreas Whittam Smith started the *Independent*; he discussed a satellite channel with NBC and American Express to beam financial news into Europe's twenty-five thousand hotels (O'Reilly's old chum Andy Mulligan, who had previously been a journalist with the *Observer* and with ITN and the BBC before becoming information officer for the EC in Washington, was to have 10 per cent); and he looked at buying the Martin's newsagents chain when Guinness sold it. By 1985 O'Reilly's reputation for buying almost anything that moved was epitomized by an episode that took place one day in the office of John Meagher. A man came to see him at his office in Hatch Street in Dublin, where Fitzwilton, Atlantic Resources and the solicitors Cawley Sheerin Wynne, where O'Reilly was a partner, were all housed. Would the Independent like to buy a meat plant? the man enquired. Meagher said no, that wasn't the type of diversification he had in mind. Well, would Fitzwilton like to buy it? He had nothing to do with Fitzwilton, said Meagher firmly. Well, what about Atlantic Resources? persisted the man. 'No? Well, how about yourself and Tony?'

The company's profits were now rising rapidly and between 1982 and 1987 the share price rose eightfold, taking the value of O'Reilly's own shareholding to £55 million. The group was still building up its cash resources, and by 1988 O'Reilly was confidently talking about having £50 million ready for a major bid. He was to find it, not in Britain or in America, but in Australia.

21

Down But Not Out in Australia

AUSTRALIA HAD ALWAYS BEEN LUCKY FOR O'REILLY. HE WAS TWENTY-three when he first went there with the 1959 Lions rugby tour, struggling to recover his form after chipping a bone in his leg the previous season. He missed the first few games, but met Susan Cameron, one of the most important events of his life. He was fit for the first Test match, and six minutes into the game he scored, smashing his way through the Australian defence to touch down in the corner, leaving a trail of players on the ground behind him. In the second test a fortnight later he scored another try, one of the most memorable of his career, lining up the full-back Jimmy Lenehan at the end of a 20 yard run, then crashing both of them over the line. The grainy black and white film of it is one of his prouder possessions.

At Heinz, too, Australia continued to be good for him. Burt Gookin included it in his responsibilities in 1972, and he went down to find a business that was a mirror image of Heinz in the UK, even down to the union problems. Jack Heinz, for political reasons, had built a plant in Melbourne in 1935 when logically it should have gone into Sydney or Brisbane. Although the structural problems would only be resolved when Heinz took over Walties in New Zealand twenty years later, it was not hard to cut costs and Australia became a good profit-maker for Heinz. As president and then as CEO, O'Reilly went there every year to review the business plans, getting to love the country more and more. His children held Australian passports, and Susan was always keen to go back.

Then one day in the early 1980s, on his weekend shuttle between Pittsburgh and Dublin, he found himself sitting next to an Irish woman he knew, Tina O'Flaherty, then married to one of Ireland's richer businessmen, Stephen O'Flaherty, who owned the Volkswagen franchise in Ireland. Tina mentioned her son, Peter Cosgrove, by her first marriage to an Irish vet; he was, she said, now working in Australia in outdoor advertising. 'That's a business the Independent should be in,' said O'Reilly thoughtfully. 'What's the name of the company?' It was called Buspak, she explained. They agreed that the next time he was in Ireland, young Peter Cosgrove would see the Independent's chief executive, Bartle Pitcher, and possibly talk about doing business together. Cosgrove turned out to be a very bright young entrepreneur, and Pitcher went down to Australia to take a look at Buspak. He eventually bought 49 per cent of it for A$600,000, and by the time it came to buying the other 51 per cent, the business was so profitable, that the Independent had to pay $16.8 million.

In 1988, on a Heinz visit, O'Reilly gave an interview in which he talked about wanting to extend his media interests in Australia. The story was carried in the *Melbourne Herald* along the lines: Heinz chief says it's time for buying in Australia—which of course it was not. Within two years the country was to be hit by its biggest recession for fifty years.

But luck was again on O'Reilly's side. Rupert Murdoch's News Corporation had just paid A$2.5 billion for the Melbourne Herald and Weekly Times group, a company which his father had run for years, giving him over 60 per cent of all the newspaper circulation of Australia. As a result Murdoch had to divest himself of some of his interests, among them a 46 per cent stake in the Provincial Newspapers of Queensland group, which published a series of papers in Queensland and northern New South Wales. They were mostly small papers, with titles such as the *Chinchilla News* (circulation 4,400), the Coffs Harbour *Examiner* (7,932), the *Gold Coaster* (25,000) and the *Bush Telegraph* (4974). The biggest paper, the *Northern Farmer*, sold 63,000 copies every week. But they were profitable, accounting for a third of all the provincial newspaper sales in Australia, with a combined circulation of 200,000 newspapers daily, and a weekly press run of 1.6 million newspapers. When Chris Innes of Hambros Bank asked him if he would be interested in buying, O'Reilly immediately indicated that he would.

'What do you think we could get it for?' he asked Innes.

'I think you could get it for $6.25, maybe $6.50 a share,' Innes told him. 'It would be just about financeable at that.'

A few days later, O'Reilly rang Murdoch at his office in New York. 'Can I see you?' he asked.

Murdoch was immediately agreeable. 'When are you next in New York?' he asked. O'Reilly knew the answer to that without even having to consult his diary. 'Wednesday, the fifteenth', he said instantly, the date Katherine Graham had set for the next board meeting of the *Washington Post.* 'Terrific,' said Murdoch, 'come and have dinner.'

At the end of the *Post* meeting, Graham suddenly announced, in her regal way, that she expected everyone to stay on to dinner at the Newsweek building. It was a command rather than a request, difficult even for the most august board member to refuse. At the pre-dinner drinks, an embarrassed O'Reilly told her he had to slip away to another meeting. 'Oh, you're so devoted to the Heinz company,' Graham chided him. 'Very well, you can take the night off.'

A few minutes later, O'Reilly was in Murdoch's apartment on Fifth Avenue. At the end of dinner with Murdoch's wife Anna and son Laughland, O'Reilly broached his business. 'Well, you know why I'm here, Rupert. I would like to buy the property. But I'm very poor and can only afford A$6.25.'

'That's ridiculous,' said Murdoch instantly. 'I've got an offer of eight.'

'Couldn't you shade that a bit?' asked O'Reilly. 'That sounds unfinanceable.'

Murdoch explained that he couldn't. 'I've got shareholders too, and if this guy offers me eight, I'll have to take eight.' But, he added, the deal was not yet done. 'The fellow's going to call me next Thursday, and I'll let you know what his offer is. You'll have to match it if you want it.'

O'Reilly called him again the following Thursday. 'You'll never believe this,' said Murdoch. 'The most the fellow will pay is A$7.75.'

'I'll match it,' said O'Reilly.

'Can you finance it?' asked Murdoch doubtfully, knowing the sums on the paper did not make an easily bankable proposition at that level.

'How good is gold?' replied O'Reilly.

Murdoch laughed. 'That's great—good as gold. You've got a deal.'

O'Reilly's problems, however, had just begun. For a start, under Australian law, Murdoch could only transfer 19.9 per cent directly to him, although if O'Reilly made a public offer, he could accept for the rest. O'Reilly's plan was to have the Independent buy 50 per cent and three major Australian institutions buy the rest. But the Australian authorities, increasingly concerned by the concentration of press ownership and the threat of the big international media companies, had different ideas. The Foreign Investment Review Board insisted that the Irish group, as a foreign company, could only own 15 per cent. It was a bombshell, completely wrecking his careful plans. O'Reilly had to do some hasty rethinking.

Eventually he agreed to buy the company on the basis that the Independent would take its maximum 15 per cent and he would personally buy the other 85 per cent through an Australian trust he set up in the names of his children who had Australian citizenship. The total sum involved was A$150 million, a hefty sum to pay for a company making A$11.5 million in an economy heading into recession. It was also a large sum for him to find from his personal wealth, but he had given his word to Murdoch and to go back on it would have been humiliating. The financing was a tricky affair: the only actual cash involved was $10m, of which the Independent put up A$1.5 million and O'Reilly personally put up the other A$8.5m. Then on the back of that the Independent issued a junk bond for another A$20m, and Murdoch agreed, reluctantly, to leave A$23.4 million in the company as a subordinated five-year loan at 14 per cent. That made A$53.4m. O'Reilly had no choice but to guarantee personally a $25 million loan to the company. With that as collateral, he went to the banks and raised the rest. It was a close thing, but he just made it.

His position now was potentially perilous and exposed. Counting Murdoch's debt, there was $140 million of interest bearing debt in the company, $120 million of it at rates up to 14 per cent requiring servicing (the interest on the junk bond rolled up). Interest alone was A$16.8 million a year, some A$5 million more than the company was earning in profits. But O'Reilly and Liam Healy (as well as O'Reilly's eldest son Cameron who would play a significant role in the recovery of the company) had done their homework, and were relying on several factors swinging their way. First of all, the company had become what one director described as a 'mosaic of retirement plans' for the three founding families (most of them originally Irish). There was a head office of fifty people, which could go. Healy also worked out that cover prices could be increased, with a considerable impact on the bottom line; but more importantly, the paper's advertising rates were low, particularly in towns where the group had a monopoly. New technology and simple improvements to the existing presses could produce significant savings. Within weeks Healy and Chris Tipler, a management consultant from the Melbourne firm Collins Hill, and Cameron O'Reilly, who, after a spell at Goldman Sachs, the New York investment bank, would serve his apprenticeship in the business before eventually emerging as deputy managing director (with considerable success), were proposing sweeping changes. Only a couple of people were left in what had been the head office; the whole board went, as did thirty-five executives, with decision-making passed down to the individual newspapers. Local managers were incentivized through profit sharing and share option schemes. The number of print centres was eventually reduced from eleven to eight, and O'Reilly invested in new plant and equipment which produced both greater revenues and substantial cost savings.

The result was that profits went from A$11.5 million to A$21 million, to A$28 million and in 1993, to A$30.5 million. By that stage, interest rates which had risen in 1989 and again in 1990, had fallen dramatically, and the debt was being paid down. In May 1992 they took the company public, selling 45 per cent on the market for A$80 million less expenses, which took out most of the debt.

It was probably O'Reilly's best ever deal. The shares, issued at A$1, rose quickly to A$1.50 and by May 1994 were at A$1.75. The public sale caused the Independent's stake to drop to 8.5 per cent and O'Reilly sold it another 12.5 per cent from his trust in return for A$20 million. Today the trust has 35 per cent of the group, 54 million shares worth well over A$100 million. So O'Reilly, in return for his $8.5 million, received shares and cash worth $120 million—a clear profit of over $110 million in five years. As for the Independent, its investment was A$1.5 million in return for a holding which is today worth A$65 million (O'Reilly of course owns another 29 per cent of that).

The flotation was largely Cameron O'Reilly's work. He had started at the lowest rung in the group, which they renamed Australian Provincial Newspapers (APN), selling advertising for Presspak, the national marketing arm they formed, became a director, worked right through the reorganisation phase, earned his spurs in the year-long battle for Fairfax which he oversaw, and spent five months preparing the prospectus. 'The flotation was Cameron's Kerrygold,' O'Reilly kept telling everyone proudly.

The APN deal by itself was big enough to make O'Reilly a rich man, but well before the flotation he and his team from the *Independent* had embarked on an even more ambitious Australian adventure, the attempted takeover of the publishing house of John Fairfax. This was a fight for control of one of the world's greatest newspaper groups, which would have transformed the whole of the Irish Independent Newspaper group but was to turn into the longest-running and most public takeover battle Australia has ever seen, and which is still not over: in September 1994 it is set to move to the courts for what seems likely to be a commercial case of epic proportions.

The fight for Fairfax, which ran right through 1991, pitted O'Reilly against some of the most powerful media men not just in Australia but in the world. For twelve months the financial pages—and even the news and features pages—were full of little else. The man who unexpectedly emerged as his principal rival, Conrad Black, a battle-hardened veteran of many a hard-fought dispute in his native Canada, later described it as 'the roughest takeover battle I had seen'.

In October 1991, O'Reilly's group delivered a bid for Fairfax with a face value of A$1.429 billion, which was ahead of a rival bid from the Melbourne-based group, Australian Independent Newspapers (AIN), which offered A$1.365 billion, and considerably more than an offer of A$1 billion from the Tourang consortium led by Kerry Packer and Conrad Black. It was not accepted, however, and nor was his bid in a second round in December. The merchant banker, Mark Burrows, acting for the banks which had lent over A$1.25 billion to Fairfax (now in receivership), chose Tourang, again the lowest of the three bidders. O'Reilly took legal action to try to block the bid, but when the court would not hear his application at a final hearing before completion of the sale, he decided instead to pursue a claim for damages against Burrows and others. AIN joined him in the action, which Burrows and other parties named are strongly defending. The action is expected to run well into 1995, and is likely to make Australian legal history.

The details of the year-long battle for Fairfax, some of the more dramatic moments of O'Reilly's non-Heinz career, are, because of the pending court action, *sub judice* at the time of writing, and will have to await a later edition of this book. They, and the court action itself, will make interesting reading.

22

Divorce—and Remarriage

BY THE TIME O'REILLY HAD DECIDED TO GET INVOLVED IN THE BID FOR
Fairfax he had lost the two women who, up to that point, had been
the most important people in his life. His marriage to Susan was
over, and his mother Aileen was dead, two events within a few years
which had been more painful for him than any others in his life.
Aileen's death had been no great surprise, the inevitable end to the
long decline which had begun with her car accident and stroke sixteen
years before. The break-up of his marriage, however, although it
had happened over a period of years, had come as a great shock to
him. Fortunately, after an unaccustomed period as a bachelor, he
had, to his own astonishment, found a new focus for his affections
by the time the Fairfax bid reached its conclusion.

He had looked after Aileen as best he could in her final years: he
bought her a house in Anglesea Road on the south side of Dublin,
paid for a car and driver to be permanently available to her, tele-
phoned her all the time, called on her when he could and had her
driven down to Castlemartin to see the children whenever they were
home. She was given the place of honour at the formal opening of
the O'Reilly Institute for Communications and Technology at Trinity
College, dedicated to her and to Jack. And he sat her close to him at
the many big functions at Castlemartin, including his fiftieth birthday
party. Yet her last years were not easy: her voice grew more and
more indistinct and she became almost completely wheelchair-bound.
She lived now only for her son, scanning the papers for every mention

of him in the same way she had since he was a boy, waiting on every scrap of news. If she heard he had been through Dublin without seeing her—and his visits were usually fairly public—the blast of anger could be felt all the way to Castlemartin. Several times her bemused driver Gay turned up at the Kildare house with the car laden with photographs of Tony—all removed from Aileen's walls and sent back to her son for daring to neglect her. It became a signal of her mood towards him. 'Are the pictures up or down?' he would ask his driver Arthur as he arrived at the airport, intending to drop by on his way to the Fitzwilton office or to Castlemartin.

O'Reilly was with his mother when she died in a clinic in Blackrock just before Christmas 1989 at the age of seventy-five. Almost his last words to her were their little private joke, which went all the way back to his first rugby match when he was six: 'The little red fellow's the best'. Two former Taoiseachs, Jack Lynch and Garret FitzGerald, turned up at the packed funeral mass in Donnybrook, and Charles Haughey the then Taoiseach, sent his aide de camp. She was buried at the little church at Castlemartin beside Jack.

All six of the children were at the funeral, as was his wife Susan, but by the time Aileen died, the O'Reilly marriage was well over. For twenty-two years they had seemed, particularly to their children, a golden and glamorous couple, deeply in love, seldom quarrelling, always presenting a united front even on potentially divisive family issues. 'I always thought my parents were like those television characters Hart to Hart,' says one of the boys. 'You know, Mum and Dad off in their G2 going round the world, and although they weren't solving crimes they were doing something else that was great. There was such togetherness, and even when we were scattered around the world, there was an incredible family bond.'

The reasons for any marriage breakdown are inevitably complex and intensely personal, and both Susan and Tony have tried to keep it so. Outsiders could speculate, but they knew only a fraction of the overall picture, and the family closed ranks around their parents. All that can usefully be said is that the breakdown was due to a combination of factors, not least of which was the pace and pressure of O'Reilly's multi-faceted business career which had taken a severe toll on his life with Susan. 'The contradictions between family life and business life raise the question as to whether, in this modern world, particularly in that period of establishment, it is possible to have an orderly married life and a successful business career,' he would say later. In his case, working so many hours at Heinz and commuting all over the world at the weekends, the contradiction and conflict had been all the greater. In his rare moments at home, Susan seldom saw Tony alone. There were always so many people staying in the house that if they wanted to be alone for a meal, they had to go out. Susan complained it was unfair on the children who never saw their father alone, but in effect it was her on whom the situation was most unfair.

There would be other reasons, too, of course but whatever the verities that underlie the particular case of the O'Reillys, the outcome was that two people who inherently loved each other—and continued to love each other—divorced. There was no bitterness, and today there is no indignation on anyone's part either—but there *was* immense sadness. Susan moved to London where O'Reilly bought her a house, and by the time Aileen died their separation was a formal one. For several years he nurtured hopes they could get back together again, but when Susan finally asked for a full divorce, O'Reilly gave it to her. No divorce is ever agreeable, but this one seems to have been as civilised as any can be. Over the years they would grow back together again, meeting for special family occasions, such as Justine's degree ceremony at Brown University, Rhode Island, in June 1988, or the opening of the Trinity building, or for the weddings of their children. Meanwhile they talked all the time, discussing, as they always had, the progress of their six children, their sons-in-law, daughters-in-law, and their growing number of grandchildren which provided the continuing focus of their joint affection. Both have been intent on their children appreciating and picking up the qualities of the other—*his* work ethic, and *her* value systems, which O'Reilly insisted the children should aspire to. 'It is fair to say that all the girls want to be like their mother in terms of their disposition, and all the men in the family wish to marry women who mirror the characteristics of their mother,' says O'Reilly. 'You can't ask for a greater compliment to a woman than that.'

The break-up of his marriage was happening slowly through the latter half of the 1980s, and for much of that time O'Reilly was, for the first time he could remember, companionless. He had lived at home with his parents until his marriage to Susan (and even for six months afterwards) and had then gone straight into a married home, with six young children arriving within four years. Without Susan, the heart had gone from Castlemartin and Pittsburgh, and he felt lost. There were plenty of women happy to console him, and for a time he was a much sought-after dinner or weekend guest in every city his peripatetic life took him to. None of it filled the void.

Yet O'Reilly might well have remained a bachelor the rest of his days, still pining for Susan, had he not met, several years after his divorce, Chryss Goulandris, an event which was to change the latter part of his life as effectively as Susan had changed the middle years. Now in his mid-fifties, he had not expected to encounter another woman who would engage his affections as deeply as Susan had, and certainly never expected to have anyone in his life to whom he would so willingly make the concessions and commitment he would do for Chryss. He still considered himself blessed to have met Susan Cameron. He did not expect it to happen twice.

Chryss Goulandris was a striking, attractive, sophisticated and multi-lingual woman, a dozen years his junior, who instantly intrigued him. She was, he quickly discovered, single, with an independent social and business life of her own, which set her apart from most of the women he had become close to. The more he probed, the more interesting she became. She had delicate, fine manners which hid a wit as quick and appreciative as his own, and underneath her well-bred Greek reserve was a personality as warm as any he had encountered. She had the elegantly slim figure of a teenager, a low, soft American accent, and large brown eyes which looked directly back into his.

Her background, when he found out more about her, could scarcely have been more different to O'Reilly's. Chryss Goulandris was born in New York of Greek parents, and brought up in a close-knit family, originally from the Greek island of Andros where for at least four generations the Goulandrises had operated their own ships. Her grandfather, along with his five brothers, shipped wheat from the Black Sea to the southern European markets, and Chryss's father, the eldest son, was born into what was already one of the most prominent Greek shipping families of the pre-war years. When the Germans invaded Greece in 1941, the family, along with most of the Greek shipowners, moved their operations to London. By the early 1940s, Chryss's father had moved on to New York where he lived in the Savoy Plaza Hotel, and married Maria Lemos, a member of an even more prominent shipowning family whom he had known since childhood. The family took full advantage of the shipping boom that followed the war, at one stage either owning or managing more than two hundred ships, many of them Liberty vessels, and they were among the first to move into the highly profitable oil tanker boom of the early 1950s.

But when Chryss was only three and her brother Peter just a baby, their father, aged forty-two, died of a heart attack while on a holiday in Paris. Maria, although an attractive young widow, never remarried, remaining close to her husband's family who carried on the business. Although the family was now scattered, Maria instilled in her two children the value of family unity, and the responsibilities she expected them to assume as adults. Every year the extended Goulandris family of cousins, uncles and aunts, gathered in Andros at the family house or on the large family yacht where, although English was their first language, they talked in Greek (Chryss, like the others, spoke French as a third language). They spent weekends in Connecticut and Christmas in the Bahamas or in Switzerland, where they also had houses. Their friends were the international Greek shipping families, and Chryss's brother Peter, when he was still at Harvard, had a much-publicized relationship with Christina Onassis, one of Chryss's best friends. Maria believed in education and after the best schools in America, Chryss went to the Sorbonne in Paris to study French civilisation and then came back to join the family business, working in the offices for several years. By now the family fortune was spread across a wide range of assets: it was in property, in stocks and commodities, and Chryss played her full part in helping to manage it. As a sideline, she became fascinated by the commodities markets, and as an exercise to amuse herself took $5000 and began investing it in the futures markets, taking small positions at first but gradually increasing them. She studied the price charts every morning, read the papers and tapes avidly, and within eighteen months her $5000 had grown to $1.5 million. Unfortunately, she then discovered silver just as the Hunt family of Texas tried to corner the market. When the Hunts pushed the price to $50 an ounce, Chryss decided it had to be the biggest sell of all time, and went short, selling silver she didn't have at $50 in the hope of being able to buy it back lower down. In fact the price went all the way up to $80, and Chryss's $1.5 million was turned into a large minus $400,000 in three weeks. She retired from the commodities market, wiser but poorer.

Chryss spent every summer in Normandy with an uncle who had created a fine stud farm, and when he died in 1978 she took it over, carrying it on as a working business. It was not something that could be done successfully part-time, and Chryss devoted herself to it, learning by heart the pedigree lines and developing her naturally good eye for horses. By the time O'Reilly met her, she had bred three Group One winners and several Group Two, getting into the list of the top five breeders in France every year since 1980. She was fortunate in inheriting a close working relationship with two of France's greatest trainers, the retired Etienne Pollet, once known as the Vincent O'Brien of France, who kept a watchful eye on her horses, and his protégé François Boutin, today one of the world's best trainers, who was to become a good friend. But she worked hard at the business herself, taking huge pleasure in the success of her horses.

She happened to be in New York when Alekko Papamarkou, one of the great international fixers of the business world whose acquaintances and clients include everyone from Rupert Murdoch to Lord Weidenfeld, prime ministers, Chinese billionaires and members of the European royal families, contacted her brother Peter. Papamarkou, it turned out, was helping his old friend Tony O'Reilly find potential investors willing to invest in an interesting and potentially very profitable operation in Ireland, the refinancing and regeneration of the Waterford Wedgwood company. Would Peter and his family be interested in meeting O'Reilly to talk about it? Peter had heard of O'Reilly, and was indeed interested. They agreed they would meet the next time O'Reilly was in New York, and Peter suggested he should also bring along his sister Chryss who was an art historian and had some interest in the background of Wedgwood in particular. A few weeks later, brother and sister went to the Pierre Hotel, where O'Reilly habitually took a suite when he was in town, and sat down to wait. O'Reilly, as ever, was late, and brother and sister stared in some amusement at the piles of papers and half-dozen open briefcases spread around the room. Chryss, who had barely heard of Tony O'Reilly before, was flicking through some of the papers in the hope of finding some stock tips when O'Reilly breezed in. The Goulandris family, impressed by O'Reilly's presentation, was indeed interested in investing in Waterford Wedgwood, but at this first meeting, although Chryss found him charming, she had no thought of a romance.

A year passed before they met again, this time in Ireland where he invited her and Peter to attend the Heinz 57 race meeting he sponsored every summer at Phoenix Park. A horsebreeder herself, Chryss knew Ireland well and was seriously considering buying a stud in Tipperary. From this meeting, the relationship began to blossom, but it wasn't until the following Easter that it became serious. O'Reilly took some of his children to Lyford Cay, where the Goulandris family had owned a house for years, and where he liked to spend a few weeks every year. Maria Goulandris, Chryss's mother, invited the O'Reillys over for dinner, and soon he and Chryss were a couple. Chryss went to Castlemartin to visit him, and by the spring of 1991 the stories of their relationship began to appear in the gossip columns. 'Friends of the couple assure me that Chris [sic] and O'Reilly will shortly be plighting their troth,' said the *Daily Express* with remarkable prescience. The couple themselves had not got that far yet.

Marriage to Tony O'Reilly would mean colossal change for Chryss. She had enjoyed her independence, yet the thought of moving to Pittsburgh, living in O'Reilly's established homes and as the chairman's wife in an essentially alien corporate culture, never daunted her. She was prepared to become the mistress of Castlemartin, and take on Tony's six children, his friends, his rugby, his Heinz business, the Ireland Fund dinners and all the rest of it with no misgivings.

When he asked her to marry him, she accepted without hesitation, fully aware of the upheaval it would mean for her. Ever since she had finished school in New York and gone to the Sorbonne, she had met new people, made new friends, in new countries essentially on her own, and was quite accustomed to new places and new faces. But up to this point her background had made her an intensely private individual with an almost genetic dislike of personal publicity. 'Being in the public eye imposes constraints which I had no need or urge to subject myself to, prior to my marriage,' she would say later. Up to that point she had valued her freedom and considered herself fortunate not to be accountable as a public figure.

That would now change abruptly, but she willingly changed with it. Given O'Reilly's schedule, they both concluded there was no point in being married unless they could share their lives, which meant that wherever he went in the world, she would go too, travelling all over the world, attending, where possible, the same meetings. She would not, as Susan had done, live apart half the year. She insisted he make time just for the two of them and that they fixed weeks and weekends in his diary which would be sacrosanct, time spent in Lyford or in Glandore where she had plans to build them their own private quarters away from the old guesthouse.

He readily agreed, and they were married in Lyford Cay in September 1991. Jim McCarthy was the best man, the third time he had performed that role for the O'Reilly family—twice to Tony, once to his father. Chryss continued to manage her breeding and racing operation in Normandy, as well as her own part of the family business, but she would also take on a number of Tony's interests, including the Ireland Fund dinner in Pittsburgh which with Dan Rooney and Dr George McGovern she turned into the second most successful event (after Boston) for the fund, raising over $1.5 million in three years. She would also become more and more involved in her husband's business interests, becoming a director of the Wedgwood Trust, and taking at least as keen an interest as he did in the revival of the Wedgwood business. Tony was delighted when she decided she would turn Castlemartin Stud into a world-class stud farm, and also supervised the restoration of the old house's roof and upper floor. When their friend Paul Newman agreed to create a branch of his Hole in the Wall Gang camp for children with life-threatening diseases in Ireland in Barretstown Castle, Chryss became its chairman. She also became a director of the Irish National Stud, actively involved in returning it to a profit.

In the past three years, they have seldom been apart, even for a single night.

23

Ireland's Richest Man

MARRIAGE TO CHRYSS GOULANDRIS CHANGED O'REILLY'S LIFE more than any other single event since his move to America twenty years before. To the outside world he was much the same: he still ran Heinz, dominating the company in his capacity as chairman, chief executive and president, roles occupied at one point in Burt Gookin's time by three people. He was still chairman of Independent Newspapers and Fitzwilton, and Waterford Wedgwood was beginning to turn around. He lived in the same houses in Pittsburgh, Kildare and County Cork as he had always done; made the same number of speeches at Ireland Fund dinners; took large parties of business contacts and friends to the Ireland rugby matches; travelled the world on Heinz business to develop his close contacts with Robert Mugabe in Zimbabwe, Nelson Mandela in South Africa, Paul Keating in Australia, Jim Bolger in New Zealand and many others; and generally seemed to keep the same schedule he had done for years. Around him, too, were the same group of people there had always been: Olive Deasy, his indispensable secretary in Pittsburgh; Arthur Whelan, his driver in Ireland; his friends Jim McCarthy, Andy Mulligan, Kevin McGoran, and his now adult children whom he also treated as friends, and who he probably now saw more of than he had when they were young. Ostensibly life was the same, but in fact it had changed.

O'Reilly was trying to pace himself. Most of his ambitions and dreams, which had expanded with the years, were still there, but Chryss had forced him to reconsider the pace at which he drove himself towards them. No constitution, however strong, could go on indefinitely taking the punishment which O'Reilly meted out to his system, and once past his mid-fifties he had begun to feel the cumulative effects of years of over-use. He could still live and work at a pace which left most people gasping in his wake, but there were enough warnings for him to be keenly aware that he was demanding too much of his body. He thought more about his uncles and father who had suffered high blood pressure and heart problems from their mid-fifties. If he was to improve his chances of a reasonable quality of life in his later years, O'Reilly accepted that he had to start looking after himself now. For the first time in his life he deliberately blocked time off to be together with Chryss—something he had never done with Susan until it was too late. Every January he would be in the Bahamas for one (relatively) work-free week, there would be long weekends at Glandore, he would spend days with Chryss at her stud farm in Normandy, and the weekends at Pittsburgh would be much more private than they had ever been. That at least was the intention, and to an extent it became the reality.

Chryss had eased herself into the homes organized by Susan, but she also wanted to create something of her own. At Glandore she refurbished an old cottage next door to his sprawling Shorecliffe complex as a house just for the two of them. But she wanted to add something more. Each year they stayed in Lyford Cay on the island of Nassau with Chryss's mother, Maria Goulandris, but they had been searching for two years for a house of their own. By the winter of 1993 they had seen most of the houses on Nassau but had never found anything suitable, until one day an estate agent took them to a house no more than half a mile from Lyford Cay clubhouse which a German woman was offering for sale. They loved it instantly, but the price was steep: some 50 per cent more than any house had ever sold for in the area. 'That's my price and it's not negotiable,' said the woman.

The house was exactly what they wanted, built to a standard and finish probably unique in the Bahamas, where good workmanship is rare. This house had been designed and constructed with loving care complete with a beautiful guest house right on the beach. O'Reilly's earnings the previous year from Heinz had been $75 million, including share options which had grown through the 1980s, making him the highest-paid man in America, and his dividend from the Independent was £4 million a year. He had heavy outgoings with his various houses, the jet when he wasn't using it on Heinz business, a large family, a former wife and dozens of staff, drivers, grooms and farm managers, but even so he could afford it—as could Chryss.

'We'll take it,' he said finally. 'But on one condition. You leave everything—every bit of furniture, every picture on the wall, down to the last teaspoon and bottle of wine in the cellar. You take your clothes and your personal things—but leave everything else.' The owner readily agreed, and within a fortnight she had gone and the O'Reillys were in. There was shock in recession-struck Lyford Cay when the word spread of the price they had paid for their new home, but within months it looked clever as three or four lesser properties went for even more; it looked a rare bargain.

Heinz had for years used the Lyford Cay club as one of the regular venues for its annual management planning sessions, and that now became one of the fixed points in the year. O'Reilly felt fitter and better in the Bahamas, adopting a routine which was far less punishing physically and mentally than the old one. Here he could start the weekend with a swim, have breakfast with Chryss while reading his papers and his faxes, handle the early calls in his dressing gown. Lunch was always taken at the club house around the pool where the other guests could include everyone from Lady Thatcher, busily working on her memoirs in a rented house in Lyford Cay, to Nelson Mandela, to whom the O'Reillys lent their home twice in 1993. During the day he would work, and at six every day for an hour he played tennis with the coach, an intense, competitive game of singles which he treated as one of the most sacred times in the day. Dinner was always late—as it is in every O'Reilly household—and invariably there would be guests, maybe up to twenty. All his adult life he had dieted sporadically, but now in his late fifties he was punctilious about it, carefully controlling his wine intake and shedding 25 lb to bring himself back to his rugby-playing weight and shape. After dinner there would be more telephone calls into the early morning.

By this stage in his life O'Reilly had accomplished many of the goals he had set himself. He was the richest man in Ireland, his shares in Heinz, Independent Newspapers and Fitzwilton worth some $450 million between them. He had reached the top of one of America's largest corporations, whose market value since he took charge had increased tenfold—which meant that 10 per cent of the company's value had been created in its first hundred years, the other 90 per cent in the decade and a half he had been chief executive. He was on first-name terms with half the world's leaders, and his chain of contacts was as great as anyone's. His interests in Ireland, after the lean years of the 1980s, were starting to come right, with the potential of Waterford Wedgwood coming through. The Ireland Fund was growing larger and more influential by the year.

Yet for all Chryss's influence, and for all the different tempo of his life, O'Reilly's ambitions were probably greater than ever. There was still much unfinished business at Heinz, whose double-digit growth through the 1980s had come to an abrupt stop in 1992 as price wars raged through the industry. Heinz shares slipped back from $48 to $30, and Weight Watchers, which had been O'Reilly's single most profitable acquisition through the last decade, ran into losses. O'Reilly was now even more determined to leave on a high note, with Heinz back where he insisted it should be: at the top of the growth tree and he was prepared to stay on as long as necessary to make this happen. His Heinz record, he had long accepted, would be the one on which history would judge him as a manager, and as he approached the point at which he would retire he was aware how much that mattered. 'I want to be remembered as the man who changed Heinz,' he would say in one of his rare reflective moods. But there were lots of other things he wanted to be remembered for as well. For most of his younger years in Ireland Waterford Glass had been the country's single most successful manufacturing and export business, an icon of excellence and commercial success in a country where manufacturing industry had traditionally only survived through subsidy and tariff protection. Now, after years of longing, O'Reilly controlled it, and he had ambitious plans for it. He talked to Johann Rupert, the South African whose family interests included not only Rothman's but Cartier and Dunhill, about a merger of their brand interests; but Rupert was not interested, and O'Reilly continued to pursue his theme elsewhere. The Wedgwood side of the business, more troubled than the Irish glass crystal division, caught the imagination of Chryss. 'It would be a very pleasant responsibility, which I could share with my wife, eventually to run such a prestige company as that, with its British-Irish connotations and its two great brands,' says O'Reilly. 'I'm intrigued by that business, which is a very elegant business, in terms of design, and the provenance of it.' Josiah Wedgwood, founder of the company, became a great hero of both O'Reillys. For years the two companies had just been surviving, but now they were steering into different waters. Profits in 1993 climbed back to £10 million and the analysts were projecting £20 million for 1994, with much more on the way as the new team got the marketing geared up. The shares, which had been as low as 12p since he bought them, rebounded to 60p.

By the autumn of 1993 he was moving to the point where he reckoned the 'investment' side of his life was coming much more into focus than it had ever been. The newspaper side was now a serious international business, and would become more so with several major deals in 1994. Two of his three sons, Cameron in Australia and Gavin in Dublin, were now working in the business, being groomed to take over at some future date—but only, he warned them both, 'if you're good enough'. With the acquisition of the supermarket group Well-worth in Northern Ireland, and the turn-round in its investment in Waterford Wedgwood, Fitzwilton finally had a good cashflow business inside it and the prospect of a major capital gain if the hopes for Waterford Wedgwood were realized. O'Reilly, with his habit of positive thinking, put Fitzwilton's troubled years completely from his mind, looking only at his hopes for the years ahead. 'Through various ways I have created these great investments and they are now nearing port, with wonderful opportunities,' he said. This time he believed finally he had got it right, and the initial signs are that he probably has. Waterford and Wedgwood are both strong, under-marketed brands with considerable potential in the USA and Far Eastern markets, and with the cost structure of both companies now under tight control and new management installed, there is no reason why they should not return to their former glory.

His professional associates would occasionally—very occasionally—accuse him to his face of relying too heavily on his old friends, pushing them into senior management positions in some of his Irish companies when he would never have dreamt of doing so at Heinz. O'Reilly challenges the criticism, pointing out that Independent, Fitz-wilton, Wellworth and Waterford Wedgwood are all run by professional managers who he would back against anyone.

> I stick with my pals when maybe I shouldn't, but I've built a very great fortune on a much more acute set of roots than others. I never give up. I am trying to build companies which will exist long after I've gone. Waterford Wedgwood, I hope, will be a real monument. We were savagely attacked by everyone when we went in, but look at it now—and it will be there

for generations to come. If we hadn't put in that $100 million injection, it was gone, and that would have been the end of Ireland's greatest exporter.

He had other interests to pursue, too—many pieces of unfinished business. In the middle of November 1993 he arrived in London for another intense week when he would combine twelve-hour days of Heinz presentations, analyses and decisions with breakfast meetings and dinners with senior politicians, bankers and journalists. There would be telephone calls and meetings of Waterford Wedgwood staff too, and of Independent Newspapers—and much else crammed into the hours when other executives might have slept.

On this occasion, as on many other such visits, there would also be an Ireland Fund of Great Britain lunch, a typically grand affair held in the Banqueting House in Whitehall under the ceiling which Rubens painted and which was, as O'Reilly remarked, the last scene on which Charles I rested his eyes before being taken outside to be executed. This was networking on an impressive scale. Organized by the Anglo-Irish banker George Magan, the lunch included heads of half the biggest City banks, including Sir David Scholey of S.G. Warburg, as well as a gathering of senior industrialists: John Cahill, chairman of British Aerospace, Liam Strong of Sears, Gerry Robinson of Granada Television, Maurice Saatchi of Saatchi & Saatchi (whose wife, the novelist Josephine Hart, ran the Ireland Fund in Britain), leading politicians such as Lord Wakeham and Nicholas Soames, and many others, either with or without an Irish connection. O'Reilly sat in the centre of the room flanked by the former British Foreign Secretary Denis Healey, the main speaker of the day, and the Marchioness of Dufferin and Ava, a member of the Guinness family. His own Independent Newspaper executives, including Liam Healy, had flown in for the occasion, and of Heinz executives including its British president, Andrew Barrett. In the room too was another Irishman from north of the border, who would soon feature prominently in O'Reilly's life: David Montgomery, a wiry, serious and intensely ambitious former journalist whose appointment as chief executive of Mirror Group Newspapers a year earlier had done much to deprive the Independent of the chance to take over the tabloid group.

O'Reilly's message that day was a familiar one to those who had attended Ireland Fund events before: the image of the Irish as disor-

ganized, feckless and fiery had never been accurate but today could
not be more wrong. Ireland was a serious place in which to invest,
he said: it had highly educated young people, energy and keenness
to play a leading role in Europe. He stood there, as he always did at
these events, as the epitome of Irish success: funny, charming, relaxed, immaculately groomed in his Savile Row suit, making serious
points amid the laughter which greeted his perfectly timed jokes,
moving easily on from the odd sporting joke to *bons mots*, tailored
for the audience, such as his fail-safe motto for succeeding in
America: 'Look Irish, think Yiddish, dress British.' The audience
laughed appreciatively.

There was other business to be done on this trip too. The Irish
Independent group was becoming a significant success, its share price
rising from 50p in 1986 to over 500p, making O'Reilly's personal
stake, which had cost him a net £1 million, worth £100 million. The
success of his takeover of Queensland Provincial Newspapers, where
his personal shareholding was worth another A$120 million, had
shown what could be done by way of bold takeover. One of the
obvious markets for an Irish newspaper group which controlled
nearly two-thirds of its own native industry was Britain, where the
market was nearly twenty times larger—and the rewards, if you could
get it right, were of the same order.

The previous year an opportunity arose which O'Reilly seized on
eagerly but, as events were to show, probably too cautiously. Mirror
Group Newspapers had been Britain's leading tabloid newspaper
group until Rupert Murdoch's *Sun* eclipsed it. Taken over by Robert
Maxwell, after his death and the collapse of his empire it had ended
up in the control of the banks. Initial indications suggested that the
banks might accept 100p a share for their 54 per cent stake, but at
that price the Mirror represented a hefty mouthful: it would cost
£400 million, bring with it another £400 million of debt and a liability
of some £250 million to the pension funds from which Maxwell had
pilfered. A commitment of over £1 billion was a tall order for the
Independent, even if O'Reilly backed it with his own personal fortune. But they began buying shares, getting into a position to take a
controlling stake. By August 1992 his Irish Independent had accumulated 5 million shares in the Mirror—1.3 per cent of the equity—at an
average price of 60p. They hired Roy Greenslade, one of Maxwell's
former editors, as consultant and editor-in-waiting, and continued

to buy, treading carefully into what might be a minefield which could destroy the Irish company.

In the event the Independent left it too long. In October 1992, the banks appointed David Montgomery and pledged to back him for at least a year. Montgomery, a former editor of two of Rupert Murdoch's tabloid newspapers, instantly set about an even tougher (and necessary) cost-cutting exercise at the Mirror than O'Reilly would have dared. As the shares passed 100p, O'Reilly accepted that the company had got away from him and sold, taking a profit of some £3.5 million, but kicking himself as the shares later went on to 200p. The banks eventually sold at 175p, valuing the company— without its debt—at £750 million.

A year later he took a look at an even bigger prize: United Newspapers owned the *Daily Express* and *Sunday Express* as well as a wide range of magazines and provincial papers. Headed by Lord Stevens, it was a perpetual takeover target which in the past had attracted the attentions of Conrad Black and Sir James Goldsmith among others; but it had always survived, largely because its stock market value was so high that the sums of breaking it up and selling off the assets did not add up. O'Reilly invited Stevens and his wife to stay with him in Castlemartin and they talked about a possible deal with Independent Newspapers. Nothing came of it, but O'Reilly continued to keep an eye on it.

In the autumn of 1993 another offer came up: would he be interested in taking a minority stake in Newspaper Publishing, a group only founded in 1986, but which coincidentally sold its two newspapers under the *Independent* title? O'Reilly, like everyone else in the publishing world, was familiar with the story of the group. It had begun as a fairytale come true, the bold creation of a small group of journalists who broke free of the *Daily Telegraph* (just before Conrad Black bought it) to start a serious newspaper free of any major proprietor, backing no political party, beholden to no one other than its own shareholders and its own independently minded journalists. It would take advantage of new technology, still not widely used among its competitors, employ no printers of its own and exploit the market gap which research had indicated existed among the readers who were fed up with the *Times* or the *Guardian*. It raised £18 million from City institutions and, under the clever Saatchi-created 'It is . . . are you?' advertising slogan, launched itself on to a receptive market.

The group's success stunned its rivals. The *Daily Telegraph*'s editor Max Hastings sent its founder Andreas Whittam Smith a good luck note—and a wreath. Within a year, as the *Independent* recorded a circulation of 350,000 and rising, Whittam Smith offered to return it. In Wapping, Rupert Murdoch solemnly warned his editors that within two years its circulation would pass that of both the *Times* and the *Guardian*—and when it almost did, he appointed a new editor at the *Times*.

Seven years on, when O'Reilly first looked at it, the story of the *Independent* looked very different. The creative buzz which had accompanied everything it did in the early days had given way to rancour, bitterness and disillusion. The photographers who had made their names on the paper with its adventurous and innovative use of pictures had drifted away, its best columnists had been hired by richer papers, and the early reverence for Whittam Smith among his staff had been replaced by acrimony. Circulation had fallen back sharply to the point where the gap with the *Times*, once only a few thousand, was nearly 200,000, and advertising revenues had slumped in the recession, plunging the group into losses. In 1990, in a move which was to be destructive for the group, Whittam Smith had insisted on launching the *Independent on Sunday*, which had drained it of both cash and editorial resources. When he ran short of money Whittam Smith had brought in two European groups, which had both, coincidentally, launched newspapers in 1976 on very similar philosophies to that of the *Independent*: the Rome-based Espresso International, part of the De Benedetti empire, which published *La Repubblica*, Italy's leading quality newspaper, and Prisa, one of Spain's largest private media groups which had launched *El Pais* in 1976 (daily circulation 400,000 and 1.1 million on Sundays). A year later Whittam Smith had been forced to ask them to put up still more money, so that by 1993 they had injected £32 million in return for 38 per cent of the equity, split evenly between them, in a company which was facing its most serious crisis yet.

The transformation from success to disaster was exacerbated by a series of ill-judged management decisions. In the spring of 1993 Whittam Smith attempted to buy the *Observer* from Tiny Rowland's Lonrho, prompting uproar among his own staff who saw it as a betrayal of the independent, non-aggressive, non-proprietorial principles on which the paper had been founded. But more to the point, it also failed: Lonrho accepted a better offer from the *Guardian* and

Whittam Smith was left with a disgruntled staff, a damaged reputation and a bill for £350,000. A redesign of the paper and an expensive advertising campaign just ate up money and failed to halt the slide in circulation, and a cover price increase, just as the *Times* cut its price by 10p to 30p, was the final straw in a crisis of a potentially terminal nature. The gap between the *Independent* and *Times*, down to 5,000 at one stage, widened to more than 200,000 and would go on rising.

On 20 December O'Reilly lunched at the Savoy Grill in London. On one side of him, as always, sat Chryss, elegant and poised; on the other was Susan O'Reilly, looking many years younger than her actual fifty-eight, with her daughter Justine. Former and current wives chatted amiably while O'Reilly beamed in the middle at this public show of unity between the women in his life, past and present. The two wives had met before, of course, on various family occasions such as the weddings of Cameron and of young Susan. Still beaming, O'Reilly left to drive back to his suite at the Berkeley Hotel for a meeting with Liam Healy and the merchant banker Victor Blank Charterhouse. He was planning to get involved in the bidding for Whittam Smith's company.

What he didn't know was how far advanced Whittam Smith was with his own plans for bailing out the company. A day later, on 21 December, Whittam Smith informed his board that he and his Italian and Spanish shareholders were going to mount a bid for the group. There would, he told them, be another partner, a 'trade investor' or, as Whittam Smith called it, 'Fleet Street Partner X'. This would be a large newspaper company which would take over the printing contract for the two *Independent* papers, handle the buying of newsprint and the distribution of the papers, sell the advertising and take on all the back office administration. The only area it would not be responsible for was editorial—that would remain strictly in the hands of Whittam Smith and his team. The relationship, he reckoned, could save the company at least £8 million a year and possibly more. He withdrew from further board meetings to pursue his bid, refusing to name the new partner.

'We thought it was Conrad Black,' said Ian Hay Davison, chairman of Newspaper Publishing. So did the rest of the press—and so did O'Reilly. In fact it was David Montgomery and his Mirror Group Newspapers, who for months had been holding secret talks with the Italian and Spanish shareholders, and with Whittam Smith. Black was certainly interested but, unknown to the outside world—and to him—he had been ruled out on the grounds that his involvement with the two *Independent* titles would inevitably have sparked a Monopolies Commission inquiry. Although by now most of the other big newspaper groups were expressing an interest, in reality there was only one serious player: Montgomery.

As O'Reilly went off to Castlemartin for Christmas, Whittam Smith and his partners quietly put together the deal which they reckoned would lock out any outsider: between the European shareholders and the founders, who held 10 per cent of the shares, they controlled 48 per cent of the equity of Newspaper Publishing even before Montgomery came in and the real bidding opened. Their plan was to make an offer for the rest, in partnership with the Mirror, with the Italians and Spanish holding a controlling 50 per cent of the new company, the Mirror 40 per cent and the founders the rest. Given their head start, they reckoned it would be a mighty brave, or foolish, outsider who tried to disturb their plan.

O'Reilly was still not aware how far down the road the consortium was when he flew back to London on 31 December, now determined to get involved in the British newspaper group. He was puzzled that his approaches before Christmas, which he had indicated were wholly co-operative and friendly, had been rejected. He would now force the pace a bit, and that morning went again into the City to the offices of Warburg where he and his Irish Independent colleagues made a presentation to Ian Hay Davison, chairman of the Newspaper Publishing board. O'Reilly was well aware by then that the board was not going to determine this issue: control rested in the hands of Whittam Smith and his European shareholders, and it was them he had to convince. He met Whittam Smith for the first time, and outlined his case. O'Reilly was at his most persuasive, insisting that his Irish Independent group was a natural fit with the similarly named *Independent* newspapers in Britain, a franchise they could expand into other markets. His company was a substantial one, he said, with a current market value of £400 million, and another £100 million in Australia. In Britain, where it was relatively unknown, it owned fourteen small newspapers, mostly in East London and Essex, with a combined circulation of a hundred thousand. It also had a 50 per cent stake in the Buspak transport advertising business, and a partnership with Associated Newspapers to publish the *Ms London* and

Midweek giveaway employment magazines, which had a circulation of 250,000.

Fluently and convincingly, he laid out the elements of his offer: he would put up, say, £15–20 million for a minority stake in the company. It would be new capital—he had no interest in buying out any of the existing shareholders—but it would tide the group over its financial crisis. He would then put in some of his own management from Irish Independent Newspapers who would put the print contract out to tender, reckoning to get the keenest price by dealing with more than one group. Lord Stevens of United Newspapers, he indicated, was interested in such an arrangement, and there were others. Finally, he said, he had enormous respect for the principles on which the *Independent* had been founded (which was true) and for Whittam Smith himself (which was not quite so true), and would like to keep him on in whatever role he chose for himself.

Whittam Smith courteously thanked him, said it was an interesting conversation, but it was too late—he and his partners were too far down the road with their 'Fleet Street partner', and they did not want to turn back now and cause further delay and damage to the titles. He could not, he added, see what O'Reilly was 'bringing to the table' other than cash—and their own plan provided that. What he needed to save the *Independent* titles was a large London-based newspaper publishing house which could take on the printing and distribution; O'Reilly did not have such a facility, so there could be no deal.

By the middle of January, with O'Reilly now in Lyford Cay chairing two weeks of Heinz meetings, Montgomery and the Mirror finally broke cover. It was, the partners indicated, a done deal, with the consortium already preparing to make an offer for the outstanding 52 per cent of the shares they didn't own. There was no room for O'Reilly or any other outsider.

It would have been easy for O'Reilly to have walked away at this stage, his only costs being some fees. No merchant banker would ever advise a group to launch a bid against such odds, but O'Reilly, as with Atlantic Resources, Fitzwilton or Fairfax, did not give up easily. He still held some cards and he reckoned it was worth playing them.

On 13 January he arrived in Paris with Chryss and checked into the Crillon, his base for the usual bout of meetings and entertainment at this time of year. Two days later Ireland would play France at

rugby and O'Reilly, as usual, would take a large party of Heinz contacts, clients and friends to the match. But his mind was now focused
on Newspaper Publishing and how to prise the consortium apart.
He had talked to Carlo de Benedetti on his yacht, but the Italian
tycoon had insisted he didn't want to be involved with the decisions
relating to the *Independent* which he left in the hands of Count Carlo
Caracciolo. O'Reilly then rang Caracciolo in Rome and suggested
they meet.

The day before the match Caracciolo and his Spanish partner,
Juan Luis Cebrian of *El Pais*, joined him for lunch in his suite. It
lasted nearly four hours, with O'Reilly deploying all his persuasive
powers to lever them out of their partnership with Montgomery
and Whittam Smith. He reckoned that Whittam Smith's *Independent*
needed an injection of £20–25 million, and he was prepared to provide it, he said, in return for a 25–30 per cent stake. The Europeans
could still have their 50 per cent between them, and Whittam Smith
could stay on. 'My view is very simple,' he said. 'There is over-capacity
in the printing and distribution industry in Britain, and some of
those facilities could be used to print the *Independent*. It doesn't have
to be the Mirror.'

'He was very eloquent and charming,' said one of the consortium
afterwards, 'and set out the benefits of having him aboard with us
instead of the Mirror. He offered money, but we didn't need money.
We explained what we planned to do, what the deal with the Mirror
was, and asked him what did he bring to the party other than money?
He came up with nothing.'

O'Reilly continued his bombardment the next day, and went off
to the rugby match convinced he had at least shaken the Europeans'
confidence in their deal with Montgomery. Back in London, however,
the consortium was holding tight, moving steadily towards completion of a deal which O'Reilly seemed unable to stop. If he really
wanted to control Newspaper Publishing, Hay Davison and the sympathetic board of the group (excluding Whittam Smith) advised him,
he would have to make a bid for the whole company at a price they
were unlikely to match. O'Reilly was tempted, but realized he could
easily end up putting some £100 million into two newspapers which
at that stage were losing £15 million a year and which could seriously
damage the profitability of his own Irish group.

There was a halfway house, and he went for it. Late in January
1994 the phoney war turned it into a real one as O'Reilly made his

first, sighting, offer of £32.5 million—£20 million as a loan, the rest to take a stake in the company at £2.50 a share. He knew the Italians and Spanish would reject it, but he reckoned it would win over the Newspaper Publishing board (which it partially did) and disorientate and disrupt the smooth running of the opposing bid. It also had another objective: it would bring the Monopolies Commission into play and would make it almost certain that the bid from the Whittam Smith/Mirror consortium, when it arrived, would be referred to the commission. But it was still not enough. By now in Tokyo on his way to Australia, O'Reilly was in contact with his men on the ground in London, Liam Healy and Brendan Hopkins. Over the first weekend in February, O'Reilly was growing impatient. His initial offer had not worked and he was about to be blown out of the water when the consortium finally put in its bid; it was time to raise the stakes dramatically.

The Mirror bid was 250p a share, and that night from his Sydney hotel O'Reilly ordered his brokers into the market at dawn the next day. In a single morning he spent £18 million and by the following weekend he owned 25 per cent of Newspaper Publishing, bought at 350p a share. 'It was not a subtle move,' wrote the *Sunday Times*,

> more a shoulder-charge than a side-step by the former British Lions winger. But it was devastatingly effective. At a stroke, O'Reilly had bought his place at the negotiating table, secured the support of Newspaper Publishing's board, thrown into confusion the consortium's detailed plan of attack and won the admiration of the *Independent* journalists.

Well before the Independent had been resolved, he was consummating a deal which he reckoned was many times more valuable to him. South Africa was approaching its first-ever democratic elections, and with the end of the white minority in sight, the Anglo-American group decided it was time to dispose of one of the two newspaper groups it had controlled for decades. The Argus newspapers represented most of the prestigious and powerful newspapers in a country of 40 million people, with a total output of 750,000 papers a day and a turnover of £140 million a year. They were controlled through the Anglo associate, Johannesburg Consolidated Investments (JCI) which, anxious not to upset Nelson Mandela and his African National Congress party, moved cautiously. The new and fashionable word in South African was 'unbundling', which is how the ANC policy-formers described the process by which they wanted the big corporations, notably Anglo-American, to sell off some of their interests, bring the black community into the heart of the business sector, and widen the business base of a country dominated by just half a dozen large enterprises. Unbundling the newspapers, however, was likely to be a tricky and political issue, and JCI had no intention of disturbing its relationship with the ANC. Any buyer, the directors decided, must be someone Mandela personally approved of, and there were not all that many on that list who also had the interest and ability to take over the newspapers. O'Reilly was one.

O'Reilly had originally been introduced to Mandela by his friend—and fellow Jesuit—Robert Mugabe of Zimbabwe, and O'Reilly invited him to give the Heinz Fellowship lecture at the University, the high point of Mandela's second visit to America. Previous speakers included Helmut Schmidt, Valery Giscard D'Estaing, and Prime Minister Nakasone of Japan. It was in Pittsburgh that Mandela first met Henry Kissinger, and the visit left a considerable impression on the South African leader. Later, O'Reilly invited him to Lyford Cay and twice Mandela had accepted, spending two weeks over Christmas and the New Year of 1993/94 at the new O'Reilly house. The relationship had blossomed into friendship as they talked about everything from rugby to American politics and the prospects for bringing big international corporations back in to South Africa.

In Johannesburg, the Argus chief executive, Doug Band, knew of the relationship and put O'Reilly at the top of his list, ahead of other interested parties including Conrad Black, whose relationship with Chief Buthelezi and the Inkatha Freedom Party would produce problems. He was also aware that O'Reilly's sporting connections had provided him with a unique level of contact in a country which still remembered that 1955 Lions tour, and O'Reilly's interest in South African rugby since. It was through rugby that O'Reilly had formed a relationship with the State President, F W De Klerk, and with Dawie De Villiers, a former captain of the Springboks who is now a key minister in the government. O'Reilly, he reckoned, had some powerful friends in South Africa.

In the event JCI decided to 'unbundle' in stages, first transferring control of the biggest selling newspaper in the group, the entirely black edited paper *The Sowetan*, to an African-controlled trust. The second stage would be to offer their 30% stake in Argus for sale— with O'Reilly the favoured bidder.

No deal ever goes smoothly, and this one hit an unexpected bump along the way. O'Reilly flew to South Africa in February 1994, en route from Australia back to Pittsburgh. Heinz was in discussions with two food companies, Tiger Oats and Premier, about joint ventures. South Africa was building towards its elections of April 1994, and the excitement in the country was palpable. Mandela and the ANC were clearly heading for a victory in the polls, but Buthelezi was still outside the election process and there was violence and bloodshed everywhere, a foretaste of what might happen after the elections if the Zulus were not brought in to the democratic process. JCI was anxious to get the deal signed and sealed before the election, but a nervous board was clearly anxious that its sale would be perceived by the new government as a genuine unbundling, and a positive step towards democratisation of the media in South Africa. In effect, what the JCI directors wanted was a definite signal that O'Reilly's investment would be welcomed. A great deal hung on Nelson Mandela's reaction.

'Is Mandela in town?' O'Reilly asked the JCI directors when he met them. They watched in some amazement as, one telephone call later, he was in Mandela's home drinking tea with him. It was clear to JCI that Mandela did indeed welcome O'Reilly as a prospective investor in the new South Africa, and would be an advocate of further overseas investment. Indeed, four months later, O'Reilly was a prominent speaker at a conference in Atlanta organized by Vice-President Gore to promote American investment in South Africa.

The deal was signed that afternoon in February, giving O'Reilly a 31% stake in a group which, if the political situation remained stable (as it shows every sign of doing), could become the Irish Independent's most important offshoot to date.

24

Putting Points on the Board

WEDNESDAY, 16 MARCH 1994, NEW YORK. THERE WERE 270 food analysts representing the big Wall Street and investment houses in the room as Tony O'Reilly rose to begin what was probably the most important Heinz presentation in his life. 'The atmosphere was electric,' remarked a Heinz executive afterwards. 'It was like a prize fight.' O'Reilly himself remarked that as he got up to speak 'I could feel the tension in the room, with all these people who had written bad reviews about us.' Heinz, high fashion with this same group of analysts in the 1980s, was out of favour, as were most food stocks. The battle for the *Independent* in London and his takeover of the South African newspapers had been widely covered everywhere, and only a fortnight earlier the *Wall Street Journal* had run a piece under the headline, 'Heinz Chief Has Job on the Side: Global Publisher'. It was one of several damaging articles at the time questioning his commitment to Heinz. The company, it said, was stuck with slow growing brands, while bad weather and the Los Angeles earthquake had hurt Weight Watchers badly. A number of analysts had downgraded their forecasts of profits, which had fallen in 1993 for the first time since O'Reilly joined and were set to be disappointing again for the year ended April 1994. More hurtful for O'Reilly were the comments attributed to a number of (named) analysts who took a close interest in the stock: 'Perhaps O'Reilly's efforts should be focused exclusively on the company,' said one. His newspaper interests 'must dilute his focus and efforts on Heinz,' said another.

This type of criticism, which had first appeared when O'Reilly became president in 1973, had quickly disappeared again as Heinz became the star of the food sector and O'Reilly's reputation grew as one of the most able and innovative managers in America. At the same analysts' meeting two years before, a Dublin journalist remarked to his neighbour that O'Reilly was spreading himself thinly. He was, he pointed out, just taking a controlling stake in Waterford Wedgwood, a far bigger company than anything he had tackled so far outside Heinz. 'Don't you guys worry about that?' he asked.

The analyst looked at him coldly: 'Look, no one gives a shit about what O'Reilly does in his private life or his free time. So long as the share price of Heinz goes up, no one will question him.'

But now Heinz's double-digit earnings growth, which had run all the way through the 1980s and into the first two years of the 1990s, had come to an abrupt stop—and suddenly the analysts did care. Nomi Ghez of Goldman Sachs, a long-term supporter of Heinz stock, had recently downgraded her rating and cut her estimate of earnings for the fourth time in a year. The Heinz expert at First Boston had dropped his estimates on the same day as Ghez, quoting higher-than-expected currency losses in Europe and 'cost-reduction efforts that haven't taken hold as quickly as anticipated'. There was much more in the same vein.

In fairness, both financial commentators and analysts were prepared to acknowledge O'Reilly's record too, which stood comparison with any. Since he had become president of Heinz in 1973, sales had risen sevenfold and earnings fifteen-fold. The $1 billion of sales which Jack Heinz was so pleased to achieve for the first time in 1972 was now $7 billion. During the 1980s Heinz shareholders had averaged an impressive 28 per cent annual return, and O'Reilly himself had earned $105 million in the fiscal years 1991 and 1992 on exercised stock options and salary geared to performance during the decade of the 1980s. It was a record that few mature corporations in America could equal, particularly in the slow-moving food industry where overall growth was 1–2 per cent.

O'Reilly was only too aware of the change of mood in the past year, and he had put a great deal of time and effort into pondering how to reverse it. The figures were against him for the first time in his career, but there were good reasons for that—reasons which were largely beyond his control or that of any other executive. In 1991 America and most of the other Heinz markets had finally reached the end of their long inflationary phases, which had been so good for the food companies, and plunged into general price deflation for the first time since the 1950s. Heinz had anticipated it better than most, with its drive towards lower costs and new and efficient factories, but even so it was caught in the gale. In a single year O'Reilly found himself fighting five separate price wars, all with savage effects on Heinz's profit margins. He hit back with still more cost-cutting, setting up a special task force under Dick Wamhoff, CEO at Ore-Ida, to negotiate agreements with suppliers on behalf of the whole group worldwide which would save Heinz $100 million a year. In two years he spent $275 million to restructure the company and make it still more efficient, reducing the workforce by another three thousand in the process. When his competitors cut the price of cat food to levels which seriously hurt Heinz, he dropped the price of 9-Lives even more and increased market share—but at a loss. He did the same in tuna, facing savage competition from Thailand and Indonesia, and hit back hard against Weight Watchers' competitors, several of whom were driven into bankruptcy. He sold companies which were not part of the core, including Hubinger and Sperlari in Italy, at handsome profits, and spent $1.35 billion on acquisitions, including JL Foods (for $500 million), to strengthen areas in which he wanted to expand such as fast growing food service and infant feeding. That year O'Reilly was unrelenting, driving his team harder than ever. In Pittsburgh the previous summer he had begun his address to his senior executives sombrely. 'Last year,' he began, 'the baton passed to a new generation of managers. In almost all cases—it has been dropped.' When some of them didn't meet the new tough numbers he set, he fired them or moved them to other jobs. He demanded more cost-cutting, more sales, higher margins. If the investment community felt he was easing up, no one in Pittsburgh did.

Now in New York in March 1994 he reckoned he had a good story to tell, and he would do it with confidence. The room hushed as he began. 'Your question must be: Is this an enduring problem or a temporary phenomenon?' That was precisely the question at the top of the minds of everyone in the room. 'My objective today is to show you that it is temporary,' he went on. 'I believe the H.J. Heinz Company has successfully weathered the storm of the past two years and is well poised for a break-out.'

The sentiment among many analysts, semi-hostile to begin with, shifted as he began to make his case. He ticked off the factors which had hit every company in the sector, including 'Marlboro Friday', the fateful day in April 1993 when Philip Morris had decided to cut its prices to counter the non-branded competition, knocking $40 billion off the value of branded companies in a single day. But now, said O'Reilly, it was Heinz's turn again, 'just as it was in 1979 when our stock was a lowly $3 a share'. Even now, Heinz was one of the world's most profitable food companies with an operating profit margin of 15.1 per cent, sharing third place with Campbell's Soup among its peers. Only Kellogg and Gerber, both essentially one-product companies, did better. Heinz ranked 91 among the US top 100 companies by market value and 65th by sales. The full benefits of restructuring were still to come through, but would, he indicated, add considerably to future profits. He had sold still more companies, and had bought Wattie's of New Zealand, a 'mini-Heinz' all by itself, which allowed him to cut Heinz's workforce in Australia by 30 per cent and create an $800 million-a-year business in the area. In three years the group had invested $1.1 billion in capital expenditure to upgrade its facilities, but that phase was over, and that year expenditure would be well down and cashflow well up.

On the other hand there had been some major disappointments which O'Reilly could not avoid that day. Weight Watchers, his star performer of the 1980s, had fallen out of bed. It was no consolation that the competition had done even worse, with Jenny Craig in trouble, Nutri-Systems filing for Chapter 11 protection from its creditors, and Diet Centers declining rapidly. He flashed up a chart to show that, for four years after he bought the company in 1979, classroom attendances had gone down until Heinz found the right formula in 1983; after that attendances grew rapidly, doubling to 32 million by 1991, which turned out to be the peak year. Then the whole industry ran into recession, and Americans cut back on dieting (this problem, oddly, was peculiar to America—in overseas countries people went on dieting regardless). Weight Watchers had had a bad year in 1993, and an even worse winter in 1994, as America suffered its worst weather in decades. Classroom attendances sank by 10 million, and since each attendance was worth $10 in profit to Heinz, the difference to the bottom line was $100 million. In 1994 the two Weight Watchers businesses, classroom and food, were budgeted to contribute $80 million to profits, but in fact lost $60 million—a difference of $140 million.

There were many experts in the room who reckoned that the

dieting business was finished, a fad of the 1970s and 1980s which was no longer applicable to the 1990s. But O'Reilly strongly disagreed and produced his figures to prove his point. America was becoming fatter, with obesity in the young particularly alarming. It was, he reckoned, nearing 'epidemic' proportions, which the American government now calculated could cost the country $140 billion a year. Some day it would be tackled, and Weight Watchers would be at the forefront. Fewer people were dieting, he agreed, but those who were had become keener than ever, and Heinz's job now was to persuade those who had tried it before to come back to it again. They had discovered that 80 per cent of those attending classes were people who had previously attended at some point in their lives. How to make them come more often? Television advertising was not reaching them in the way it had done in the past, and was costing $80 for every new customer, who spent an average of $110. But there were new systems of direct mail, followed up by a telephone call two days later, which were proving highly effective. O'Reilly's confidence in the business was already being reinforced by figures showing the corner had been turned and classroom attendances were turning up.

But if Weight Watchers was having a lean time, there were other parts of the business which were going well. Foodservice, 'the unsung hero in our portfolio', now had sales of $1.4 billion and profits of $200 million. And there was baby foods, where Heinz was now almost as big as Gerber. 'You get Gerber for free,' he quipped, a line validated three months later when Sandoz paid $3.5 billion—30 times earnings—for Gerber's. The company had never disclosed its figures for baby foods before, but now he did: sales worldwide of $631 million (90 per cent of Gerber's) and profits of $170 million. Heinz had only a 17 per cent share in the USA, so the analysts tended to ignore it, but even there it was a highly profitable business; and Heinz had 90 per cent of the market in Italy, Hungary, Canada and Australia, 97 per cent in New Zealand and 60% per cent in the UK and 50% in China. He had now moved one of the previous stars of the business, Brian Ruder, from Weight Watchers to baby foods, where he was planning $250 million worth of acquisitions including Farleys. These two businesses, food service and baby foods, overlooked in the past, were actually making nearly $400 million out of Heinz's $1 billion-a-year earnings.

O'Reilly was now building towards his finale. He produced three charts showing the performance of Heinz since it went public in

1947. He, of course, had not been in charge for the first thirty-two of those forty-seven years, but when he took over from Gookin in 1979 the value of the company was $865 million. It was now worth over $9 billion, which meant that 90 per cent of the value of the company had been created in the last fifteen years. What was more, he went on, most of the managers who had made that happen—and he reeled off their names: Dave Williams, Bill Springer, David Sculley, Larry McCabe, Luigi Ribolla, Bill Johnson, Andrew Barrett, Dick Wamhoff and others—were still around, and as committed as ever. Heinz had been through a rough two years, but the next five were going to be good ones.

The room erupted into applause as he sat down, and O'Reilly basked in the analysts' reaffirmed approval as he fielded questions for forty-five minutes. How would he get back to double-digit growth? Three to 4 per cent from volume, 2 per cent from cost, 2 per cent from price, 2 per cent share buy-back, and a couple of per cent from acquisitions, he replied instantly. Tuna? China? Private label? GATT? He dealt readily with them all. When someone asked why he didn't hedge against currency losses, he caused instant hilarity by replying 'Where is George Soros now? Hiding behind his hedge.' Soros, the legendary currency speculator and hedge fund manager, had just admitted he had lost $600 million in a single day in the turbulent currency markets.

The key question, which he had been waiting for, came at the end. How long did he expect to stay at Heinz? O'Reilly had thought about leaving on his sixtieth birthday in May 1996, but that was before the dip of the past two years. 'I'll address that question very squarely,' he said after a pause. 'I'm going to stay with the Heinz company until it again enjoys the premium rating that it had for thirteen of the last fifteen years. That certainly will take a two- or three-year period.' His 'total management commitment,' he added, was to Heinz. 'I hope I have been able to convey that to you today.'

The adrenaline was still running as he moved among them afterwards, thinking to himself: 'That was an important day in my life today.' It was also an important day for Heinz. He and his colleagues anxiously watched the tapes, desperate to see how the markets would react. Back in their offices the analysts were already hitting the phones, and the message was clear: buy Heinz. The shares started the day at $30 3/8, then moved to $31, and an hour later they were

$32. The number of stocks traded that afternoon was three times the normal volume, and three times the normal volume the next day. On Friday, as the message sunk in, it was four times, by which stage the shares were $33, putting $500 million on the value of the company in two and a half days. By then the analysts had sent out their written reports to support their earlier phone calls. 'We're upgrading Heinz to a buy,' said C. J. Lawrence/Deutsche Bank Securities. 'We're targeting a price of $40.' A. G. Edwards rerated the company as a 'buy for conservative investors'. Nomi Ghez of Goldman Sachs admitted that she had been 'positively impressed' by O'Reilly's annual presentation. 'He was ready to realistically assess the company's strengths and weaknesses, and guided investors to a credible level of earnings.' Another analyst, Beth Lowey of UBS Securities, noted that Heinz was now 'positioned to prepare for the future', and her target price for the shares was $45.

O'Reilly himself bought $1 million worth of shares that Friday, bringing to $3.5 million the amount he had bought in the last few weeks. It was intended to be an indicator of his own confidence. It brought to 3.25 million the number of shares he owned, worth $107 million. On top of that he had 4 million share options that vest on 1 January 1995 at $29, worth $80 million if the shares go to $50 million (he can exercise it at any time up to the year 2004, or three years after he leaves the company). If the analysts were to be proved right, and the shares hit $42—a modest enough target—O'Reilly's holding in Heinz will be worth $180 million.

That weekend he did a quick calculation of his global wealth: he had 22 million shares in Independent Newspapers at £5 each, which amounted to £110 million. There were another 53 million shares in Australian Provincial Newspapers at A$2.00 a share. Adding up his stakes in Fitzwilton, Waterford Wedgwood and Arcon, and his investments in the Irish castles-cum-hotels, Dromoland and Ashford, his total wealth was of the order of $450 million. A survey done by the Irish magazine *Business and Finance* in April 1994 estimated his wealth at £400 million, well ahead of any other Irishman. He took some satisfaction from that—before working out how to get the figure above £1 billion.

At the end of the day, O'Reilly would say later, 'Heinz is the story', the achievement for which he would most want to be remembered. 'I'd like people to be able to say "He's the man who made Heinz",' he says, and although no single man ever did that, his meaning is clear enough. He had put a great deal of money and effort into his other interests but it was true that Heinz had priority, and O'Reilly still managed to give it more time and more effort than most full-time CEOs did. He still liked to quip that his time spent on other interests was his 'substitute for golf', and, although that was stretching it a bit, there was still a lot of truth in the remark. If the analysts and journalists occasionally questioned his commitment, few of his senior executives in Heinz did. And after this meeting the analysts were prepared to back him again.

Reaching the age of sixty is the next watershed in his life, the time at which he will think about passing over the reins to a younger generation and move on. Although Gookin had chosen him seven years before he actually took over, O'Reilly would delay his choice of a successor until the last moment. But the race is on, essentially between four Heinz executives: David Sculley, Bill Johnson, Bill Springer and Dave Williams. Once he has restored Heinz to a dynamic growth phase again O'Reilly plans to sell up in Pittsburgh and go, leaving the corporate historians—and the next generation of analysts—to judge his contribution to the company's history.

That would leave him free to create the worldwide media empire he wants—and which he is well on the way to achieving—and to building up Waterford Wedgwood, over whose prospects he glows with excitement. 'Waterford is truly an epic story,' he insists.

> Here is a company which had lost £250 million, unparalleled in Ireland's history, not bailed out by the state but bailed out by capitalists who put up their own money, stood up to the unions, took a fourteen-week strike, found an outside source for its products, validated the notion of portable brands, and introduced in Marquis by Waterford the most successful new brand in crystal table top ever introduced in the history of America. It's a fantastic story.

The Ireland Fund would feature prominently in his future plans too. He plans to leave a chunk of his fortune to the organization, but long before that he reckons it will have an endowment of $50 million, and be in a position to put $10–20 million a year into Ireland for the many causes that are clamouring for help there. 'That would be the achievement of a lifetime,' he says. 'Because it's not just America, it's the Irish round the world standing up to be counted.

It's Seamus Heaney's notion of we being two people at once, both
Irish and international, proud of our Irish roots in a non-assertive,
non-nationalistic way.'

He has already created the largest fortune in Ireland since Arthur
Guinness, but curiously has little interest in leaving behind a Guin-
ness-style dynasty. 'I've got a core set of values which I think are
worth fighting for, and which I hope I have passed on to my children,'
he says. 'They're a blend of my education, of my parents, of my
Irishness and what I've learnt myself and I've tried to teach them to
my children. I hope they in turn will pass them on.'

In the final stage of his active life, Ireland will play the dominant
part.

> Who am I? Well, I feel I'm a representative of Ireland. I keep
> coming back to the fact that I come from that small island of
> Ireland and we are an estimable people, with great achieve-
> ments behind us and in front of us. I represent one of the new
> Elizabethans from Ireland. Every time I achieve something or
> fail to achieve something, although there is not much economic
> consequence to it these days, I feel the weight of being Irish
> and being a representative of the hopes and aspirations and
> dreams of the Irish around the globe. I hope I will have made
> the climb a lot easier for subsequent Irishmen and Irish women.

Bibliography

Alberts, Robert C, *The Good Provider, HJ Heinz and His 57 Varieties*, Weidenfeld, 1973

Bardon, Jonathan, *A History of Ulster*, Blackstaff, 1992

Beckett, J C, *The Making of Modern Ireland, 1603–1923*, London

Berisford Ellis, P, *History of the Irish Working Class*, Pluto, 1985

Black, Conrad, *A Life in Progress*, Key Porter, 1993

Brown, Terence, *Ireland, a Social and Cultural History, 1922–1985*, Fontana, 1985

The Belvederean, 1943–1953

Coogan, Tim Pat, *Disillusioned Decades*, Gill and Macmillan, 1987

Coogan, Tim Pat, *De Valera, Long Fellow, Long Shadow*, Random, 1993

Coogan, Tim Pat, *Ireland Since the Rising*, Pall Mall, 1966

Crozier, Michael, *The Making of the Independent*, Gordon Fraser Gallery, 1988

Foa Dienstag, Eleanor, *In Good Company: 125 Years at the Heinz Table*, Warner, 1944

Garland, Nicholas, *Not Many Dead*, Hutchinson, 1990

Glover, Stephen, *Paper Dreams*, Jonathan Cape, 1993

Griffiths, John, *British Lions*, Crowood, 1990

Hussey, Gemma, *Ireland Today, Anatomy of a Changing State*, Viking, 1994

Jenkins, Vivian, *Lions Rampant*, Cassell, 1956

Jenkins, Vivian, *Lions Down Under*, Cassell, 1960

Lee, J. J., *Ireland 1912–1985*, Cambridge University Press, 1989

Kee, Robert, *The Laurel and the Ivy*, Hamish Hamilton, 1993

Lorant, Stefan, *Pittsburgh—The Story of an American City*, Lorant, 1988

McCafferty, E D, *Henry J. Heinz, A Biography*, privately printed, 1923

Cruise O'Brien, Maire and Conor, *A Concise History of Ireland*

O'Connor, Anthony, *He's Somewhere Out There*, Foxgate, 1975

O'Connor, Anthony, *Clubland*, Martin Brian & O'Keefe, 1976

O'Donovan, Donal, *Dreamers of Dreams*, Kilbride, 1984

O'Reilly, A J F, *The Marketing of Agricultural Produce: Strategy, Structure and Performance*, PhD Thesis, 1980

Potter, Stephen, *The Magic Number: The Story of '57'*, Max Reinhardt, 1959

Ryan, Colleen, and Glenn Byrge, *Corporate Cannibals*, Mandarin, 1992

Walsh, C H, *Oh Really O'Reilly*, Bentos, 1992

Index